Presented to the Salvation Army
School for Officer Training
Central Territory, In Memory of

COMMISSIONER SAMUEL HEPBURN

THE
SPEAKER'S BIBLE

EDITED BY
REV. EDWARD HASTINGS, M.A.
JOINT EDITOR OF 'THE EXPOSITORY TIMES'

FOUNDED BY
JAMES HASTINGS, D.D.
EDITOR OF
'THE DICTIONARY OF THE BIBLE'
'THE ENCYCLOPÆDIA OF RELIGION AND ETHICS'
AND OTHER WORKS

THE BOOK OF JEREMIAH

"THE SPEAKER'S BIBLE" OFFICE
ABERDEEN, SCOTLAND
1944

The aim of THE SPEAKER'S BIBLE is to preserve all that is worth preserving of the modern interpretation of the Bible. It is the thought rather than the expression that is retained, though the expression has not been rejected when it seemed worthy. So much, however, has been done in the way of condensing, re-arranging, re-writing, adding to, and illustrating, that the sources have not as a rule been given. But so far as these are published sermons, they will be found in the Index to Modern Sermons which accompanies each volume. THE SPEAKER'S BIBLE contains also much that is new, written by the Editor and others.

BOOK
PRODUCTION
WAR ECONOMY
STANDARD

THIS BOOK IS PRODUCED IN COMPLETE CONFORMITY WITH THE AUTHORIZED ECONOMY STANDARDS

MADE AND PRINTED IN GREAT BRITAIN BY MORRISON AND GIBB LTD., EDINBURGH AND LONDON

THE SPEAKER'S BIBLE

THE BOOK OF JEREMIAH

INTRODUCTION

I

THE BOOK AND ITS STRUCTURE

1. JEREMIAH is known to us with greater intimacy and detail than any other character in the Old Testament. Misnamed the 'weeping prophet' by those who have never really been introduced to him, his character displays, on a nearer view, a sharpness of outline, and a combination of contrasts, that are at once bewildering and endearing. We admire the patriarchs through the mists of the half-legendary records of their wanderings that have reached us; and Moses for the codes of law, heterogeneous and at times contradictory, that are attributed to him. David makes his appeal to us, whether as the young champion of liberty, the Robin Hood of the Judean highlands, or as the father bent in misery over the death of his beloved and good-for-nothing son. But we can hardly say how many of the Psalms such glimpses and episodes will allow us to ascribe to him. We can come nearer to Isaiah and Ezekiel. We have writings by them as well as notices about them. But the Book of Isaiah (see Introduction, vol. XXV.) is really an anthology of prophecy; of Isaiah of Jerusalem but little is left to us. Ezekiel, at least until a generation ago, was allowed to have written most of the forty-eight chapters that bear his name; but, beyond the death of his wife, we gather nothing about the circumstances of his life with the exiles in Babylon; and his writings reveal such violent psychological transitions that the key to the riddle of his character still escapes us.

With Jeremiah the scene is widely different. The fifty-two chapters of his Book contain poems whose authenticity there can be no reason to doubt; addresses and sermons which, however different their style, can hardly be assigned to any other writer; a series of conversations or colloquies with Yahweh which constitute a fascinating and unique *journal intime;* a number of notices of events in his life whose vividness suggests the pen of a close and intimate friend; added to these, a historical appendix, a series of prophecies (like those of Isaiah, Amos, Ezekiel, and others) on foreign countries, and two isolated passages (x. 1–6 and xvii. 19–27) which seem to belong to some other period.

2. We have, indeed, what might be called the equivalent of 'the life and times of Jeremiah.' Like other members of the 'goodly fellowship of the prophets' he is not mentioned in the historical records of the time; but his Book is far richer in contemporary information than anything else we possess; and, in particular, he has made the last years of the Jerusalem kingdom better known than any period of Hebrew history; and, as he was bidden to distinguish the valuable in his own work from the worthless (xv. 19), so he has made it easy for us to separate his own work from the additions which forced their persistent way into every prophetic collection.

The Book, however, has puzzles of its own. Some of its sections, like some in Isaiah and more in Ezekiel, are carefully dated; others are not; and those which are appear in an order which is very far from chronological; so that if we rearrange these, we still have the problem of fitting in the undated sections. The nature of the problem will be clear from an analysis of the Book as it stands. Chapter i., after a

3

14896

brief preface, contains the account of the prophet's call (the commission and two visions) ; ii.–vi., a series of denunciations, emotional and passionate, but with no concrete references ; vii. is a long address in prose ; viii., ix., x., poetic fragments, in which the author passes from attack to description and from description to meditation ; xi. and xii., another address, and a colloquy with Yahweh on the plot against the prophet which he had discovered ; xiii., an autobiographical account of a journey to the Euphrates, followed by further laments ; xiv.–xvii. 18 contain more colloquies ; the remainder of xvii. is a prose fragment on the observance of the Sabbath. In xviii. and xix. are addresses and reflections suggested by a potter's shop ; xx., the prophet's outburst when placed in the stocks. In xxi.–xxiii., further addresses, prose and poetry, containing for the first time a message of hope (xvi. 5 ff. should probably be placed here) ; xxiv.–xxviii., incidents and sermons in the reigns of Jehoiakim and Zedekiah, mainly in prose, as from a diary ; xxix., a communication to the exiles ; xxx.–xxxi., a collection of consolatory pieces, including the great passage on the law written on the heart ; xxxii.–xxxiv., further notices, apparently autobiographical, of the siege ; xxxv.–xxxvi., the Rechabites and the roll read to Jehoiakim ; xxxvii.–xxxix., the last days of Jerusalem, with an autobiographical note ; xl.–xliv., the tragedy of Gedaliah and the migration to Egypt, with a note on Baruch. In xlvi.–li. we have the prophecies against the nations, rounded off with the account of a commission to Baruch's brother Seraiah. The whole composition is concluded with a historical summary of Zedekiah's reign, almost identical with that found in 2 Kings xxiv., xxv.

3. The poetic sections (save for the prophecies in xliv.–li. ; see below) are clearly the work of a powerful and emotional writer, whom we cannot but regard as Jeremiah himself. The sermons, which are generally prefaced by ' the word which came to Jeremiah from Yahweh,' were presumably written down either by Jeremiah or by an amanuensis or secretary such as was Baruch (chap. xxxvi.). The colloquies, too, must be attributed to Jeremiah. The narratives are sometimes in the first person (xxiv., xxvii. 12, xxviii. 1 ; contrast vv. 5, 12), sometimes in the third (xx. 2, xxvi. 12). Chaps.

xl.–xliv. seem to be the work of a very close companion, like Baruch again. Certain indications in the language suggest that chaps. xxvii.–xxix. had an independent existence or have been edited. Chap. xlv. reads like a private note by Baruch himself added to his memoirs. In addition to these, whether we have to thank Baruch or some later editor, there are a number of detached oracles and comments (v. 18 f., ix. 23 f., x. 11 in Aramaic, xxxi. 26, xxxii. 17–23 ; and a quotation from Micah occurs in xxvi. 18). The section on the Sabbath in chap. xvii. is almost certainly a much later addition ; it is as foreign to the outlook of Jeremiah as it is akin to the protests of Nehemiah a century and a half later.

4. How then and by whom did it all come to be written down as we have it now ? We are not left wholly to guess-work. Isaiah took care that his words should not be lost, like the oracles of the Cumæan sibyl (Is. viii. 16, xxviii. 10) ; and there are a number of references to writing in Jeremiah (xxix. the letter to the exiles ; xxx. 2 preceding the ' book of consolation ' ; li. 59 the ' doom-letter ' sent to Babylon to be sunk in the Euphrates, and xxxvi. the roll which Jehoiakim destroyed as it was read to him). The nucleus of our Book would seem to be the prophecies referred to in chap. xxxvi., re-written and enlarged after Jehoiakim's defiant action. This would include all the public prophecies hitherto delivered (verse 2), though probably not the private journals nor (if they were already in existence) the predictions of the return of the Northern Kingdom. Later, Baruch wrote down his own memoirs, dating each of them. Like the colloquies, these appear in our Book in no intelligible order. The Book was still later enriched by the collection of foreign predictions ; these may contain some Jeremianic material ; but parts of them point to a later time ; and the long and majestic prophecy on Babylon, reminding us of some of Ezekiel's most effective writing, could hardly have been written, when Jeremiah was looking to Babylon as Yahweh's instrument for his judgment on Judah, or receiving genuine kindness from the Babylonian authorities. The collection on the nations must, however, have existed as a whole comparatively early in the history of the book, as it is inserted in the Greek translation immediately after the reference to such prophecies

4

in xxv. 15. The first three verses of the Book, and the last chapter, were added later, while notes and additions could always be inscribed in the margin of a MS. owned by the reader, *en route* for a place in the text itself. The riddle of the disarrangements, specially of chaps. xxx.–xxxiii., seems insoluble. Did they originate in a MS. hastily patched together after some disaster ?

5. One word should be added as to the text. All our Hebrew MSS., as is well known, are of late date (none are much earlier than the end of the first millennium A.D.) and, save for minute details, identical with one another. The Greek translation known as the Septuagint (LXX), however, takes us back to a much earlier text existing at most some four hundred years after the time of Jeremiah. The character of the translation of the different books in the LXX varies considerably ; but it is noteworthy that the Greek text of Jeremiah is much shorter than the Hebrew text ; the same is true of the LXX of Ezekiel. The differences, which apply to the Book as a whole, and not to one or two of its component parts, show that the variations arose after the Book was completed. The obvious conclusion would be that the Greek represents the older and purer text ; this is not certain ; but that editors far later than Baruch regarded themselves as entitled to modify, amplify, or omit, cannot be denied.

II

The Man

1. Fascinating as is the problem of the construction of the Book, its real interest lies in the individual around whom every chapter turns. In dealing with the better known books of the Old Testament, we are contemplating for the most part the march of events, the fortune of a people ; and the poets and philosophers make much of their subject, little of themselves. But Jeremiah, though he was no more able than his prophetic colleagues to forget that he was concerned with a divine message to the people of Yahweh, concentrates attention, even if unconsciously, on himself ; and since God chose human beings—all too human, one is sometimes tempted to say—to blow His

trumpet-tones, it is but just to notice their strength and their weakness ; could one do otherwise with the Servant of Yahweh in Second Isaiah, or with St Paul ?

Jeremiah was born at Anathoth (i. 1), a little country town not more than four miles from Jerusalem, but looking towards Ephraim (now, politically, no more) rather than to Judah, and still more to the countryside. Every city dweller in Palestine was familiar with the country ; but few lived in it so whole-heartedly as Jeremiah. Each of his poems is full of rural sights and sounds, the life of the animal and the bird and the changing drama of the fields and the seasons ; the flight of the stork (viii. 7) the instinct of the partridge (xvii. 11), the distress of the wild creatures in drought (xiv.), the roar of the lion in the jungle (iv. 7), the she-camel in rut (ii. 23), the sheep-gathering at the trodden pool in the evening (xxxi. 24), the happy noise at the wine-press (xxxi., 4f.), the songs at some village merry-making (xxx. 19), and—how the phrase comes back to him !— the voice of the bridegroom and the bride (*e.g.*, xvi. 9). Not for him the hubbub of the narrow city streets, the garish self-assertiveness of the palaces of the rich or even the pompous beauty of the Temple. The only country scene for which he had no interest was the dark shadow of the grove where pagan rites were still celebrated with their dimly veiled obscenity. His ideal for the future was a country life purified and secure, a habitation of shepherds causing their flocks to lie down (xxxiii. 12), like that of the half Bedouin Rechabites, who would never pass within a city gate if they could help it. Isaiah and Ezekiel might have their visions of some miraculous transformation of nature and society. It was enough for Jeremiah that Yahweh should cause his people to dwell safely, free, as we might say, from want and from fear ; each under his own vine and fig-tree.

2. He was born into an old priestly family. Hilkiah, his father, was descended from Abiathar. Abiathar and Zadok had been the two consistent clerical supporters of David ; but Abiathar had made himself unpopular at court, and the aged monarch had decided that he should be dismissed from his office at the Temple (1 Kings i.). There would be little love at Anathoth for the courtly ritual of the building

that from the days of Solomon had always been something of a royal chapel. But the young Jeremiah went further. There was no place either for ritual or for ceremonial or even, it would seem, for the Temple or the altar itself, in his conception of the genuine worship of Yahweh (chaps. vii., xxvi.). Neither Amos (v. 25) nor the author of Ps. li. nor of the Epistle to the Hebrews was more convinced of the futility of the shedding of the blood of bulls and goats. Like Jesus, he would enter the Temple to preach; we do not read of either that they entered it to worship. Nor had he the least sympathy for the priests and the prophets; the order, as we might say, of the official clergy or the ranks of the official preachers (xiii. 13, xxxii. 32). Officialism in religion he abhorred. The reason for this was, doubtless, practical rather than theoretical. He had watched the conduct of the prophetic gangs. But it bit deeper. Yahweh was one who spoke to the individual; He was neither to be apprehended through the medium of a religious go-between or revealed in the hireling of a court preacher (v. 31, vi. 13). Jeremiah, like Ezekiel, is often said to have been an individualist, because of his protest against the doctrine of children suffering for their parents (xxxi. 29; cf. Ezek. xviii. 2, 3)—a doctrine unhappily ratified by experience. The importance of the individual in religion had a surer foundation. As Dr A. C. Welch has said of Hosea, his ' conception of religion implied a relation of such a quality as could not be posited of a nation. Only the individual soul could desire to fulfil the demands which Yahweh's love made or could rejoice in its austere loveliness.' It is useful to remember such words at a time when the possibility of forgiving a whole nation is being discussed. None the less, Jeremiah, like all the prophets, not excepting Isaiah with his idea of the ' remnant ' (x. 20, xi. 16) regards the nation as a unit before the judgment-seat of Yahweh. More important than his alleged step from the nation or society to the individual—an impossible one—is his insistence that Yahweh's worship does not consist in the performance of rites, which naturally necessitates a group, but in the allegiance of the reason, the convictions, the emotions; and this certainly is a matter for the individual, or rather for the whole person. Yahweh's covenant must be written ' on the heart ' (xxxi. 31).

3. All this suggests a combative or self-assertive attitude towards what was perhaps not wholly evil in the religious practice of the prophet's time. But the shyness and diffidence with which he met the conviction that he was destined for a prophet (i. 6) did not disappear. No doubt the older members of his family would have scant respect for a youth who would wander in the fields, ' rapt, twirling in his hands a wither'd spray.' But that was not all. The moment that revealed to him his insufficiency revealed also that his destiny was to destroy one order and construct another, not only in his own nation, but in the world. It was an international rôle (i. 10), like that of the Isaianic Servant (Is. xlix). There were other contrasts, equally striking, in his nature (viii. 18). No one could lament with more tender sympathy and distress for the invasion which he saw advancing relentlessly on his country (iv. 19); no one could pillory the guilty causes of it in more scathing and even brutal language (v. 1–8, vii. 16); no one could shrink, as a gentle lamb (xi. 19), more timidly from the personal violence which the words naturally roused (the word for ' lamb ' is different in Is. liii. 7); no one could set his face like a flint (Is. l. 7) more stubbornly (the words of Isaiah's Servant Songs recur again involuntarily to the memory) when that violence was to be denounced and defied.

Perhaps the contrast is not really a contrast at all. He at least does not feel it to be such. Like Hosea, he even projects the double emotion into the mind of Yahweh. ' No one shall turn me from destroying thee; yet how, Ephraim, can I give thee up?' (xxx. 23, xxxi. 18, Hos. xi. 8). If on the surface they are opposed, yet in the depths ' the sense of tears in mortal things ' is married to the awe at the unchanging holiness of God. Were there moments when cowardice or compromise got the better of his desperate courage? Once at least, it has been alleged, in a last interview with the trembling Zedekiah (xxxviii. 26). But it is easier to bring such a charge against men like Jeremiah than to substantiate it. Only the most heroic courage can approach the height of ' My father, if it be thy will, let this cup pass from me.' Only the most fearless eyes can bear to ' weep like a fountain of tears ' (ix. 1, xiv. 7) for the sins which the prophet's words condemn to the horrors they help to bring about.

4. It will not be surprising therefore to discover in Jeremiah's work some of the most affecting and lovely passages in Hebrew poetry. He had all the imagination, the passion, the creative power of the poet, whether he is describing the despair of a prolonged drought overwhelming man and beast (xiv. 1–6), the horror of darkness and desolation at the end of the world (iv. 23), or the lament of the ancient tribal mother over her lost children (xxxi. 15 ff.), a passage which was surely in the mind of the prophet of the actual return fifty years later (Is. xlix. 14 ff.).

He may well have been less successful, to judge from the fragments that have been preserved, as a preacher; his style has too much, now of the ecstatic (xxii. 24 ff.), now of sheer prose (xxxii. 36 ff.). But he had the rare power of making his contemporaries (whether we owe the lightning sketches of them to himself or to Baruch) reveal themselves for what they were; and no ancient portrait gallery is more vivid than that of the men among whom Jeremiah moved in Jerusalem, Pashhur (xx.), Irijah (xxxvii.), Gedaliah (xl.), Johanan (xlii.); and, as in a single flash, the otherwise self-effacing yet always prepared and competent Baruch (xlv.).

III

THE HISTORICAL BACKGROUND

1. So far, we have been content to take the documents in the Book of Jeremiah as we find them, and to draw our own conclusions as to the author. We must now look for the further light which we may expect from a study of contemporary history. Nor is there any set of men who lived closer to the living issues of their time than the Hebrew prophets. The two centuries which separate Amos from Second Isaiah, from 750–550 B.C., form a kind of tunnel. The scene into which we emerge at their end is entirely different from that which we leave behind as we enter that turbulent period. Jeremiah lived when the turbulence was at its wildest.

We can best imagine the situation if we think of Palestine as at the centre of two concentric circles; on the circumference of the smaller lie the smaller states of Edom, Moab, the Philistines, Tyre, and Syria; constant rivals, yet equally threatened by the great powers on the circumference of the larger circle, Assyria, Babylon, Egypt, and, later, Persia. The smaller states, indeed, play the part of a kind of Balkan peninsula to the ambitions of the great powers, who covet them, but dare not leave them alone.

At the opening of this period, 722 B.C., Samaria, the capital of the stronger and richer of the two Hebrew kingdoms, fell before the legions of Assyria; and Judah, in spite of her miraculous escape in 701, became, as she was long to remain under Manasseh, a vassal state (698–641). This involved religious assimilation as well as political submission; the worshippers of the 'one Yahweh' (Deut. vi. 4) were driven into opposition or hiding; and the ritual laxity of the nation had its reward in comparative prosperity and peace.

2. From 550 onwards, however, the star of Assyria was declining; and when after the brief reign of Amon (641–639) Josiah ascended the throne, hopes for both political freedom and religious purity flamed up. The two indeed naturally went together. At first the growing weakness of Assyria meant plots and invasions, which kept all the Near East in turmoil. But in 621 Josiah took action. He began by repairing the Temple, as a fitting prelude to national revival. In the course of these repairs, a document was discovered which purported to be a developed recension of the traditional laws of Yahweh given to Moses, and which included a command for all worship to be centralized at Jerusalem. This meant the forcible suppression of the local shrines, such as that at Anathoth, where paganism could linger and inspection was difficult if not impossible. It also meant a new importance, social, political, and economic, for the capital and the monarch.

The king at once accepted the code as authoritative. How far its provisions were actually carried out, we cannot tell. The court party, priests, prophets, and statesmen, would all naturally support it. But within nine years Assyria fell with a crash which resounded over all Western Asia, and whose echoes can still be heard in the glowing pæan of Nahum (chap. iii.). It now became clear that Babylon and Egypt would be rivals for Assyria's heritage. The 'Balkanized' states had to make up their minds for which kingdom they stood. Josiah chose Babylon; and when the Egyptian forces were passing through Palestine on an Eastern expedition, in 608, he met them at Megiddo, apparently to oppose their passage, and was killed (2 Kings xxiii. 29 ff., 2 Chron. xxxv. 20 ff.). Egyptian commissioners set Jehoiakim, Josiah's eldest son, on the throne, as a pledge that Judah would remain loyal to Egypt.

3. These hopes were not disappointed. Babylon was now the enemy. The trusted statesmen of Josiah's time, Ahikam, Shaphan, and others, were pushed into a virtual opposition; pagan worship (though of an Assyrian or Babylonian rather than of an Egyptian type) began to spread once more; and the geniality and *bonhomie* of Josiah (xxii. 15) was replaced by the ostentation and tyranny of his son. Egypt, true to her character a century before (Is. xxx. 7) gave little but promises; but in 601 Babylon, which was now rapidly gaining control of the territories in the West, was openly challenged by the little state, and Jerusalem was invested. In 597 Jehoiakim died; his son Coniah surrendered to the besiegers; the cream of the population was deported to the Euphrates valley; and Jehoiakim's younger brother, Zedekiah, a feebler version of himself, was left to hold the city for the conqueror. But the 'younger statesmen' of Jehoiakim's court soon re-established their ascendancy in spite of Nebuchadrezzar's brilliant victory over Egypt at Carchemish in 605. The attitude of defiance was maintained, with a striking mixture of patriotism and bravado. There could be only one end to such a policy. The Babylonians again laid siege to the city. It was defended, as it has so often been, with reckless courage and determination through two long and desperate years, and when at last it fell, it was laid in ruins.

Nebuchadrezzar was by no means the capricious and cruel tyrant who meets us in the Book of Daniel. He carried out a depopulation measure on a much larger scale than eleven years before, but he set himself to govern the province as an 'occupied territory' on the principle of what we now call 'indirect rule.' He seems in general to have exercised a statesmanship of which we have no example in Assyria or Egypt. He left the little territory of Judah, no larger than an average English county, to the charge of Gedaliah, a younger member of the house that had kept faithful to the policy of Josiah. Shortly after, Gedaliah was murdered. His second in command fled to Egypt. In fifty years Babylon collapsed before the advance of Cyrus.

IV

JEREMIAH THE PROPHET

1. We now return to Jeremiah. There is a sense in which every great writer is not for an age but for all time. Among the greatest writers the Hebrew prophets may claim their place. Yet if their own age was not taken as their starting point, they would be unintelligible. Every prophet is Yahweh's mouthpiece to his own generation. Recent theological writing has familiarized us with the term *kairos*, which, from the simple meaning of 'season' (its usual translation in our own New Testament), comes to suggest a season of special importance; a crisis; a herald of some decisive event; a precursor of Yahweh's definitive judgment on the nations. The world after it will be radically different from the world before it. To the prophet's burning eye, the time in which he lived was always a *kairos*. To no prophet was this conviction more exigent than to Jeremiah.

His prophetic activity begins with his call in the thirteenth year of Josiah (i. 2), *i.e.*, in 626. It was natural for a young prophet to regard himself as marked out—'a dedicated spirit '— by some psychic experience. Isaiah had his vision and the touch of the 'live coal' on his consecrated lips in the temple (Is. vi.). Ezekiel witnessed twice over a far more elaborate theophany in the home of the exiles in Mesopotamia (Ezek. i., x.). Amos describes four visions which are most naturally interpreted as his call (Amos vii.). Second Isaiah tells neither of a call nor of any other experiences that befell him; but the call of the Servant of Yahweh is impressively set forth in Is. xlii. 1 ff. The combination of vision and audition will at once occur as forming the starting points for the missions of Moses and St Paul (Exod. iii.; Acts ix., xxii., xxvi.). The prophet was always a ' seer '; and it was as natural to speak of his seeing the word or the message of Yahweh as of hearing it (Is. i. 1).

2. The account given by Jeremiah of his call (chap. i.) reminds us of that of Amos, if we may so understand Amos' visions. We have

no details of time or place; simply, 'Yahweh told me he had marked me out from my birth to control the destinies of nations. As a sign he touched my mouth, and he appointed me to an unending conflict with the whole kingdom of Judah.' In the course of this interview, the youth was bidden to look at an almond tree (the 'waker') and at a kettle, facing in the direction of the North; two common objects of the country-side; and to learn their inner significance, that Yahweh was 'waking' over his word, and that calamity would come, as so often in Palestine it did, from the North. We do not know whether this account was set down at the time, or, like Isaiah's and St Paul's, at some later date; but nothing could express more vividly the spirit of Jeremiah's life-long conflict; we often hear echoes of Yahweh's words then (e.g., xii. 11, xviii. 7, xxxiv. 2, xxxix. 8). The directness of his relation with Yahweh is seen with equal clearness, even more than with Isaiah or Ezekiel. God spoke with Moses, we read, as a friend; the account in Exod. iii. is striking as both a parallel and a contrast.

The first messages that resulted from this interview (the word can hardly be avoided) are contained in chapters ii.–vi. They are introduced by two words seldom heard from Jeremiah; the first familiar to Hosea and the second at home in Deuteronomy; kindness and love; the characteristics of Judah

> while yet she stood
> In first obedience and her state of good.

The former of the two, often translated 'mercy,' really means that sense of affection, coupled with the recognition of mutual rights and duties, which is seen in the relationship of husband and wife, patron and client, God and man. If the word, however, is rare in Jeremiah, the thought is constant; Israel has broken the bond, the covenant (xxxi. 31). Yahweh, for all the tragical consequences, will remake it (iii. 17, xxxi. 1–3). But this opening prophecy is one of unrelieved doom. There is indeed no such detailed attack on social evils as in Is. iv., v.; but moral and social sins have corrupted the heart of the nation (e.g., ii. 34, v. 7 ff., vi. 13, vii. 9).

3. These chapters also contain forebodings of a barbarian incursion (iv. 29, v. 15); perhaps the Scythians mentioned by Herodotus (i. 103,

5). This did not take place. It was not the only instance of an apparently falsified prediction. More important and pressing was the discovery of the law in 621. It was natural that Jeremiah should welcome the humanitarianism of its precepts, and the abolition of the disreputable country shrines, even if his own family at Anathoth was affected. He certainly admired Josiah, and he appears to have undertaken propaganda for the new régime, and to have been, consequently, regarded as a renegade by his own kinsfolk (xi. 6, 18). But he was speedily disillusioned. The new ritual was only the old superstition writ large. Yahweh was not to be worshipped by the rites of the altar but by a change in the heart. It may be that we should place in the later years of Josiah (621–608) three sets of writings for whose provenance no date is given: (a) the 'colloquies' with Yahweh (in chaps. xii., xvi., xvii., xx. 7 ff.); (b) the prediction of the return of the exiles, especially of the Northern kingdom (chaps. xxx., xxxi.); (c) the prophecy of the gift of the new heart and the new covenant (xxxi. 31 ff.). It is difficult to place any of them either in an earlier or a later period of Jeremiah's career; but we may at least guess that after his disappointment and apprehensions he was flung into a new wrestling, like Jacob or Job, with Yahweh; that he was fired with a burning conviction that if only a new heart would satisfy Yahweh, Yahweh would give it; and that when, from 615 onwards, it was clear that Assyria was doomed, he pictured the return of the children of Rachel to their ruined homes, as Second Isaiah, seventy-five years later beheld, in the irresistible advance of Cyrus on Babylon, the return of the Jews across the desert to re-people the waste and desolate places (e.g., Is. xlix. 14 ff., lv. 12).

4. Whether the brighter period of hope fell in these years or not, the death of Josiah at Megiddo caused an intensification of the struggle, announced at the prophet's call, which was to last for twenty-two years and more. For Jehoiakim he had neither sympathy nor respect. The gage was thrown down in an uncompromising speech in the Temple (chaps. vii., xxvi.); Necho's defeat at Carchemish (605) was enough to suggest the worst. After an interval he was imprisoned (xx. 1–6), and he then formed the plan of collecting his speeches (xxxvi. 4) with

the help of Baruch, a man of distinguished family in Jerusalem, who is hereafter constantly at the prophet's side. The existence of this collection came to the knowledge of the ' older statesmen '; and they sent Baruch with it to the king. The king listened and contemptuously destroyed the sheets as they were read to him. The result was another and larger collection; and from now on it would appear that Baruch took careful notes alike of the words and actions of Jeremiah. The prophet was no mere preacher or orator. His words and actions alike came from Yahweh; they had hands and feet, as it were; they were alive; and as such, they would accomplish Yahweh's commission to them (Is. lv. 10).

5. But how could Jeremiah establish the authenticity of his words? To this ' patriot king' and his entourage, courageously defying the whole might of Babylon, he was a defeatist. 'You will know,' he replied, ' by the event.' The event came; Jerusalem was taken, but not destroyed. ' You see,' retorted the survivors under Zedekiah, ' we are still here; like the choice meat in the caldron' (Ezek. xi. 3 ff.). Jeremiah's rôle was unchanged. Zedekiah, on whose shoulders the heavy mantle of his brother had fallen, could not shake off the fear that Jeremiah might be right; indeed, as the years passed, only fanaticism could expect anything else. But fanaticism was riding the unhappy king hard. Jeremiah did not waver. Imprisoned more than once, in circumstances which sorely tried the now ageing man, he repeated his warnings that Egyptian help would accomplish nothing; Babylon would never be driven back. His enemies never, as it would seem, tried to get him put to death, like Uriah (xxvi. 21 ff.); and he was in a position both to address the envoys who visited the capital from Moab, Ammon, and elsewhere (xxvii.) and to communicate with the heads of the exiled society by the Euphrates (li. 59). Though he and his younger contemporary Ezekiel, now with the exiles, never mention each other, there are signs that Ezekiel had been profoundly influenced in thought as in expression, by Jeremiah (e.g., Ezek. xviii. 2; Jer. xxxi. 29; Ezek. xxxiv., xxxvi.; Jer. xxxii., xxxiii.).

6. For the two years of the siege we have more information than for any other period in the life of the prophets or the history of the city. His daily contacts and clashes with higher and lower officials and with Zedekiah himself, as puzzled as was Pilate by a nobler and still more perplexing prisoner, are described with a vividness which St Paul's companion never quite attained. But, varied as were the incidents, the monotony of his denunciations was unbroken. ' If you would return to Yahweh's allegiance— ; but you will not ; you cannot. Your only hope is—to surrender at discretion.' The end came ; the long train of captives was dragged off. Nebuchadrezzar showed his exasperation by his treatment of the king. But along with the survivors of the pro-Babylonian party, Jeremiah himself was kindly treated. The story of the days that followed is told with still greater precision (chaps. xl.–xliv.) ; yet it is little more than a weary anti-climax. Jeremiah, as a person to be reckoned with in Jerusalem, even though feared and detested, was one thing ; Jeremiah, attached to a little band of harried fugitives, mocked by a request for advice that they were resolved not to take, and by an undisguised scorn for any word that he chose to utter, was another. Despised and rejected before, he was to become, in the Egypt that he loathed, still more closely acquainted with grief.

Did the author of the Servant Songs know of his tragedy? It is hard to imagine anything else. Whether he suffered martyrdom and ' made his grave with the wicked,' we do not know. Something has sealed Baruch's lips, as the lips of the companion of St Paul. Did the fellow-exiles understand, before the end came, that it was for their transgressions that he was wounded, for their iniquities that he was bruised (Is. liii. 5), or did they mock him to the last as men mocked beneath the Cross at Calvary? All we can say is that if the last of these songs reveals the spirit of the Atonement as no single passage in the New Testament, so Jeremiah reveals in his own dauntless life the spirit of Yahweh's servant as no other of all the characters that move through the pages of the Old.

V

THE PROPHET AND HIS GOD

1. ' Thus saith Yahweh '; or rather, ' thus hath Yahweh said.' This is the keynote, as it

is the preface, to every genuine prophetic utterance. With Jeremiah it introduces poems and sermons alike. Occasionally the message of Yahweh comes in sleep (xxxi. 26). He passes to it from his own reflexions (ix. 7), or he will give his own comment on the message (xiii. 15 ff.). When it came, he had no doubt about it. Can we share his certainty? How did it come to him, and how can we be sure about its source? With his generous self-revelation, Jeremiah gives us more material for an answer than any other. None the less, the answer is not always to hand. It is clear, however, that what we ourselves should call our impulses, the day-to-day suggestions that send us here or there, Jeremiah put down to Yahweh's guidance and inspiration; for example, his visit to the potter's shop and the sermon (very like his other sermons) for which it gave him the text (xviii., xix.); his mysterious journey with his new belt to the Euphrates—or was it the Wady Farah? (xiii.). When his cousin Hanamel comes to see him during the siege, to ask him to exercise the right of buying part of the family estate that was coming into the market, even though the land was at that very moment occupied by the besieger's camp, he guessed beforehand, as one might say, that Hanamel was on his way (xxxii.); he attributed to Yahweh both this conviction and the assurance of future deliverance that followed the transaction, for whose completion Hanamel could hardly have ventured to hope. Sometimes the 'word' tarried, as when, early in the reign of Zedekiah (xxvii.; not as in R.V.) the prophet appeared at Yahweh's command wearing a wooden yoke on his neck to signify the defeat of the coalition which was forming in Jerusalem against Babylon. Hananiah the official prophet ridicules the prediction and breaks the yoke. Jeremiah acquiesced; was the wish, like Balaam's, father for the moment to the belief? subsequently came a briefer but sterner message (xxviii. 13 ff.); and Hananiah, like Pelatiah (Ezek. xi. 13) died shortly afterwards. When the survivors after the fall of the city consulted him as to their projected flight to Egypt, it was ten days before the answer came, though everyone who knew Jeremiah might have predicted what it would be (xlii. 4, 7).

2. Were there then two levels in Jeremiah's insight? Here, the 'colloquies' are illuminating (xii. 1–6, xiv. 12–xv., xvii. 12–xviii., xx. 7–20). We are allowed to overhear a conversation with something like Tennyson's 'still small voice.' There is nothing in Jeremiah that he attempts to conceal from Yahweh; he utters no formal prayers; he expresses no conventional opinions. He is too conscious of one who tries the reins and the heart for that. He is vindictive enough towards the members of his family who 'do not believe in him' (cf. Jn. vii. 5); and his desires are accepted (xi. 20, xii. 14). He complains of the prophets, and Yahweh condemns them (xiv. 14 ff.). Yahweh bids him weep for his country, and then pronounces his sympathy fruitless (xiv. 13, 17, xv. 1 ff.). He laments the agony of his continuous defiance of his fellow-citizens, and Yahweh renews his promise of final deliverance (xv. 15–21; cf. Is. i. 4 ff.). To the complaint of xvii. 12 ff. no answer is recorded. Later, he roundly accuses Yahweh of having deceived him; here, the mood passes of itself; no further word of Yahweh is vouchsafed, nor even when, as it seems, the mood returns, and, in language repeated by Job on his dung-hill (Job iii. 2), the prophet curses the day of his birth (xx. 7–18).

Like Ezekiel (ix. 8) Jeremiah feels Yahweh opposing unflinching severity to his own tenderness. Yet at other times he finds in Yahweh the tenderness that Hosea knew (Hos. xi. 1 ff.). It is as if he saw now one part and now another, in the manifold purpose of Yahweh; sometimes He is the fierce avenging deity whom Marcion was later to denounce as a false god; sometimes He seems none other than the God and Father of our Lord Jesus Christ (iii. 14; cf. Rom. xi. 25 ff.). So, it would seem, with the unfulfilled predictions of the Scythian invasion and the fall of Jerusalem. Jeremiah knew the principles of Yahweh's action; he did not always know their detailed application.

3. This is in part a problem for the psychologist. All the prophets, earlier or later, 'collegiate' or solitary, were expected to predict. Dr. A. Guillaume (*Prophecy and Divination*) has discussed predictive powers as found both among the Hebrews and the Arabs. Did these powers rest on abnormal psychic illumination, or common sense, or both? Possibly, E. C. Jones' amusing *Road to Endor* is not to be taken

purely as a parody or a caricature. This is not the place for a discussion of the whole subject, or even of Hebrew foretelling. If, however, we return to Jeremiah, we find in his dealing with the future something altogether too massive for individual prediction. He is at the opposite extreme to the soothsayer or the miracle-worker; both Elijah and Elisha are left far behind. He is bidden not only to speak, but to act; to be, literally, Yahweh's vicegerent; to pluck down, to build up, and to be an impregnable wall against all the might of Judah. His nature underwent no sudden transformation. In fact, it does not seem to have been changed at all, until, perhaps, the bitterness of the later conflicts finally dried up the milk of human kindness in his veins. The shrinking, the shyness, the susceptibility, the longing for the soft human joys, the diffidence, are all there as his vision widened and his sense of Yahweh's dominance grew stronger. And from these were begotten, or hammered out, their opposites, the iron resolve, the fierce defiance, the desire for what the victim would call vengeance and the admirer justice.

All this, the psychologist can understand. It is an escape or a compensation. No man can be harsher than he who longs for a wife and has undertaken a vow of celibacy (xvi. 2). But whatever may be true of Ezekiel, there is no trace of schizophrenia in Jeremiah. It is not that he is at once tender and hard, calling his tenderness his own and his hardness Yahweh's. Yahweh is inexorably hard yet infinitely tender (*cf.* xiv. 19 and iii. 7). And the contrast which he finds in Yahweh, and which is borne out by the whole prophetic tradition, exists also in himself. The difference is that what is unstable, emotional, fleeting, he recognizes as his own; when he is dealing with what, at least at the time, he cannot doubt, with what lies at the heart of his universe, with the existential, as our modern philosophic jargon has it, he hears the word, the message (never, with Jeremiah, either the voice or the spirit) of Yahweh. Once more, his business is to separate the costly from the worthless (xv. 19).

4. But this also raises a problem for religion. Was our prophet right in identifying this inner certainty with the God of the whole earth, the eternal Father who sent His son for our redemption to the Cross? If we hold it enough to think of God as 'a loving father,' Jeremiah was guilty of no such sentimentalism. Nor was Jesus. 'The Father in heaven' is represented in the Gospels as capable of the sternest words and acts. Jesus, who revealed Him, holds out no hope for the unrepentant; while the most gracious of His words shine with a radiance they might have caught from Jeremiah. The truth is that the infinite God cannot impart His whole mind to any human receptacle. The vessel would burst asunder. Even with the teaching of Jesus, it is 'line upon line, precept upon precept; here a little; there a little' (Is. xxviii. 10; Matt. xiii. 11). Nor is there any outside and inside in the communications of God to men. 'Thy words,' said the prophet, 'were found and I did eat them' (xv. 16; cf. Ezek. iii. 1). The message becomes a part of himself; and it is conditioned by himself. But if the severest and soundest test of a prophet is measurement by the yard-stick of Jesus, then he who was like a lamb led to the slaughter-house, even though his words were but seldom quoted by Jesus, was indeed a prophet of the living God.

VI

JEREMIAH AND OURSELVES

1. Jeremiah, we said, is the best-known character in the Old Testament. Can we add 'in the whole Bible'? Comparison with the apostle to the nations (Jer. 1.; cf. Acts ix. 15, xiii. 46 f.) leaps to the mind. Both were called from their birth (Jer. i. 5; Gal. i. 15); both were rejected by their own people; both knew —and were agonized by the knowledge—that those who rejected them rejected God (Jer. xi. 18 ff.; Rom. ix.-xi.; cf. Matt. x. 19). Both were masters of the fierce retort (Acts xxiii. 3); and both went down into the dark by a way that no man knows.

But Jeremiah had no gospel of the resurrection to preach; he had never seen his God in the 'dear disfigured face' of Jesus. He had no little group of eager friends in city after city; he rejoiced in no growing churches. He knew solitude as St Paul never knew it; and what he has shown to us of himself, again and again, and not only in the colloquies, St Paul, with all his eager self-expression, unveiled but once (2 Cor. xii. 8 ff.).

2. No preacher will ever value Jeremiah above St Paul. Yet every preacher will recognize that St Paul's days were farther from our own than were Jeremiah's. In two world wars we have lived nearer than our fathers to the 'tunnel' period of the prophets, and specially to the supremely critical last days of Jerusalem. We know, as Jeremiah knew, the stern significance of the *kairos*. We have seen whole nations plucked up and broken down, destroyed and overthrown. We look to see them built and planted (i. 10). And if, as no one else, he has shown us the heroic submissiveness of the Lamb of God Himself, he has summed up in his long and much-battered life what is, perhaps, the noblest passion of the Hebrew race, whether we see it in Jacob at the ford, 'I will not let thee go,' or in Job, 'I know that my champion and rescuer is alive,' or in Daniel, 'he will deliver us; but if not . . .!' He will never appeal to the self-centred and the sheltered. But an age which has witnessed brutalities more atrocious than any imagined by the most ruthless tyrant of Nineveh or Babylon, and on a scale which in their wildest dreams they could not have conceived, calls for the great Hebrew doctrines of the restoration that follows repentance, the obedience that springs from the renewed will and not from the sacred rite, and of the covenant of God with men, written, where it can never be erased, on the heart; and it finds them at their clearest and most luminous in Jeremiah.

W. F. LOFTHOUSE

The Call of Jeremiah

Jer. i. 1, 2.—'The words of Jeremiah . . . to whom the word of the Lord came.'

1. JEREMIAH'S life begins for us with his call to the work and office of a prophet. His home was at Anathoth, a quarryman's village within easy walking distance north-east of Jerusalem. He was born towards the end of the long disastrous reign of Manasseh, one of the worst of Jewish kings. Though he reigned for fifty long years the Old Testament historians have little to tell us about this Manasseh. The less said, no doubt they felt, the better. They summed him up in this sentence, 'Manasseh did that which was evil in the sight of the Lord.' When these words recur, as they do, in the Old Testa-

ment, they always have the same significance. They mean that Manasseh had turned from the worship of the one true God to heathen deities. He had built altars to Baal. He had done the unforgivable thing. He had brought idolatrous worship into the very Temple itself. When true religion declines, private and social morality decline with it, and superstition grows. If the scholars are right in declaring that Micah portrays conditions in Manasseh's time, how abominable these were. The poor were ground down and elementary human rights were ignored. No one trusted his neighbour. No man's word was his bond. Judges took bribes, and the very idea of justice was in eclipse. Shopkeepers used false weights. Happy family life was unknown. The good man, says Micah, had perished out of the earth. And all this was happening not so very long after the work and ministry of Isaiah. All the sermons and influence of such prophets had apparently been forgotten. Nay, Manasseh was determined that they should be forgotten. No prophet, no priest, was safe who remained loyal to the true religion. Second Kings gives a grim account of the kind of thing with which the Gestapo has made Europe familiar: 'Manasseh shed innocent blood very much till he had filled Jerusalem from one end to the other.'

In our own day we have witnessed a swing-over from the worship of the one true God to paganism, and men are ready to sacrifice their very children to a new God, to the power and glory of the Totalitarian State. And are we not seeing the same moral consequences as in Manasseh's time? It is in those lands that are exalting the worship of the State above the worship of God, that openly or in practice are denying the validity of the Bible revelation, it is especially in those lands that elementary human rights are being disregarded, that the very idea of justice is in eclipse, and the solemn covenant made is not observed.

¶ In Guy Thorne's book, called *When it was Dark*, there is painted an imaginative picture of a world in which faith has died and the Bible is discredited. The writer's world is a place where cruelty, robbery, savage enmity, and aggression prevail. Thirty years ago, when Thorne wrote, that may have been an imaginative world, but is it so to-day? Is it not rather the world we know?[1]

[1] A. Gemmell.

But Micah was wrong in thinking that the good man had perished out of the earth, even as Elijah had been wrong in thinking that he only was left of the faithful to God. In Manasseh's time there was a devoted remnant who met in secret, like the Covenanters of old, and fed their hearts on the word of God given to the prophets, and looked to God in hope of a better time. It is a reasonable conjecture that Jeremiah's father was one of them, and that in little Anathoth the flame of the true faith was kept burning. The little circle there did not know that the baby born to Hilkiah was an answer to their prayers. But so it was. As a boy, Jeremiah would be told stories of the glorious past, would hear of men who had died under the persecution of Manasseh rather than be traitors to God; would be taught to pray for the time when true religion would come into its own again. He was a boy of genius, and as he listened to the talk around him, to the fears and doubts, the miseries and unconquerable hopes of the faithful few, and as he walked the country roads, he must often have asked himself what his part in the future should be, what was God's will for him. He had not long to wait for light. There came to him the experience recorded in this first chapter when the word of the Lord was laid on him.

2. The word of God came to him, he says, and he knew with an absolute conviction that he was called to be God's ambassador and prophet to the times. How did he know? It is always an incommunicable secret how a man is sure that God has spoken to him. There is no need to assume visions or supernatural voices in Jeremiah's ear. Suddenly his whole past lit up with significance and Divine meaning, and he felt in his bones, as we say, that God had been preparing him for a prophet's work from the beginning, aye, before he was born into the world. 'Before I formed thee in the belly I knew thee—before thou camest forth out of the womb I sanctified thee, and I ordained thee to be a prophet unto the nations.'
Not at once did Jeremiah accept the call. He felt that the impulse was Divine, but questioned his own ability to sustain the great part. He knew what it meant to be a prophet. He was of a timid, shrinking disposition, and thought himself not fit for the terrible responsibility. He fought against the impulse. 'Alas, O Lord

God, behold I cannot speak, for I am a child.' This was more than the natural diffidence of youth. It was not mock humility, nor was it a light refusal; it was the sense of weakness which comes from a feeling of the importance of the work. With Jeremiah it was a complaint of real pain. He was a man of peace, and to be a prophet unto the nations, to harden his brow like flint against his brethren, to tell of woe when he would fain speak peace, was an alarming prospect. He had no desire to enter the arena, to contend with priests and false prophets and princes and people. He would rather live his life of faith in quiet. This was the grief of his life; he was a tender-hearted man who craved love and had to drive it from him. 'Woe is me, my mother, that thou hast borne me a man of strife and a man of contention to the whole earth. Every one doth curse me.'

I was not born
Informed and fearless from the first, but shrank
From aught which marked me out apart from
    men;
I would have lived their life, and died their
    death,
Lost in their ranks, eluding destiny.

Does not this bring us near to Jeremiah? Sometimes, perhaps, we have sought the will and guidance of God for us, and had a way pointed out from which we shrank. That is far from being unusual. Sometimes the word of the Lord comes to us without our seeking, in some duty or sacrifice to which conscience and honour point, but which we feel to be beyond us. We have known too, perhaps, the urge and dominance of some word of the Lord that we shrank from accepting. It was touch and go, it may be, at this time with Jeremiah. Do not think of him as a young man whose will was irresistibly borne down by the will of God. God never forces anyone. Jeremiah and his fellow prophets had our struggles, fought our doubts, knew our depressions, like us had to make up their own minds one way or another, and having chosen God's way, had to walk out into an unknown future in faith.

3. But encouragement to obey the call of God came to Jeremiah. It came to him through the spring-time blossom on an almond tree. 'Moreover, the word of the Lord came unto me

saying, Jeremiah, what seest thou ? And I said, I see a rod of an almond tree. Then said the Lord unto me, Thou hast well seen, for I will hasten my word to perform it.' In the Hebrew there is a play on words that is lost in their English translation. ' I will hasten my word to perform it ' is more accurately translated ' I am wakeful over my word to perform it,' and the Hebrew words for being wakeful and for almond tree are almost identical. Dr. Moffatt translates the passage in this way. ' Jeremiah, what do you see ? I said, The shoot of a wake tree. The Eternal said to me, You have seen right, for I am wakeful over my word to carry it out.'

The young prophet was to enter upon his work—the work which was to be to him a source of deep and lasting sorrow—the work which was to involve him in unmerited reproach and suffering—the work which was to bring him into ' perils from his own countrymen '—the work which he felt impelled to persevere with whatever its outcome as regards himself—fully confident in the unbroken wakefulness of the Lord and in the consequent fulfilment of His purposes.

4. It was a tremendous task to which Jeremiah was called—to be a prophet in such a time and to such a people. No wonder he shrank from it. His was not the prompt and eager spirit of Isaiah crying out, ' Here am I, send me.' Jeremiah was sensitive and shrinking. Yet what did he become ? God made out of this tender-hearted, gentle, and sensitive man ' a tower and a fortress.' He stood like ' a fenced city and an iron pillar,' assailed and persecuted, yet never flinching. Whatever his inward moods, revealed to us in his writings, his countrymen saw in Jeremiah a man of iron, neither to be intimidated nor cajoled.

¶ In his hero lecture on Cromwell, Thomas Carlyle has these words : ' Perhaps of all the persons in that anti-Puritan struggle, from first to last, the single indispensable one was Cromwell. To see, and dare, and decide, to be a fixed pillar in a welter of uncertainty : a king among men, whether they called him so or not.'

The Appeal of the Past

Jer. ii. 2, 3.—' Thus saith the Lord ; I remember thee, the kindness of thy youth, the love of thine espousals, when thou wentest after me in the wilderness, in a land that was not sown. Israel was holiness unto the Lord.'

JEREMIAH is here contrasting Israel's infidelity with God's faithfulness. ' I remember,' is Jehovah's lament, recalling in fond memory His choice of her and delight in her. The prophet also contrasts Israel's present infidelity with her past faithfulness, as seen idealized through the mists of history. ' I remember for thee the kindness of thy youth, the love of thine espousals, when thou wentest after me in the wilderness, in a land that was not sown.' The early Israel was not perfect ; none knew better than the prophet how imperfect it was. Then, too, were rebellions and back-slidings, and murmurings even in the wilderness. Still, their history is a record of greatness. With all the faults and failures revealed in the early story of the nation, there must have been a whole-hearted and generous heroism. God's love brooded over the youth of their race ; and they had responded sincerely. They clave to God, and went out like their father Abraham, not knowing whither they went, but strong in faith because they were assured they went with God.

1. It is God's love rather than Israel's which is here first of all emphasized. He would soften them with the thought of it, remind them of His watchful, sleepless care, and make them feel ashamed of their heartless desertion of Him now. But they, too, had once been faithful to Him in the kindness and glory of youth, in the love of the first espousals. ' Israel was holiness unto the Lord,' consecrated to Him, ' the first fruits of his increase,' and so protected by Him in loving care from all enemies. But, alas ! this idyllic relation is broken : the strong religious bond no longer unites Israel to God. The failure is not on God's part. ' Thus saith the Lord, What iniquity have your fathers found in me that they are gone far from me, and have walked after other gods—vanity ? ' Idolatry is vanity, emptiness ; for to the strong religious sense of a prophet idols were nothing, a ghastly simulacrum of the reality.

The folly of it oppresses the prophet. The shame of Israel's infidelity is increased by the thought of the poor choice they made. The insult to God might have been less if the new object of their love had been more worthy. The lover in Tennyson's *Locksley Hall* breaks out into scorn, not so much at his desertion, as at his desertion for such a poor unworthy rival, a clown whose grossness of nature will drag her down, and sings of the folly of choosing a range of lower feelings and a narrower heart than his. If she must be false, there would not be so much pain had she chosen a higher and a better. He would at least have been saved from the sting of insult and the sense of shame on her behalf. How much more is the feeling of scorn to a clear-seeing soul like Jeremiah for what is to him an infinitely more foolish and disgraceful choice! So contemptible does it seem to him to turn from the pure spiritual worship of the living God to the degrading rites of idolatry, nay, so astounding that he would expect to see the very heavens frown and the skies laugh with mocking irony, ' Be ye astonished, oh ye heavens, at this.' It is terrible blindness which does not see the highest, which cannot see the best. The insanity of the choice weighs on the prophet's heart. To choose the palpably lower seems such incredible folly.

Yet what common folly it is! Is there no counterpart of that folly in our own lives? Are any of us at this very time turning our hearts towards a lower ideal which we confess in our sane moments to be lower, choosing the part which our conscience tells us to be not the better part? Are any of us giving up the highest because it is too high, shutting our eyes to the light that would lead us upward and our ears to the manifest call of God? Are we letting in worldly and selfish thoughts and aims and ambitions, and shutting out Christ? Are none of us to-day making the great refusal?

To casual seeing, he was just the same
As he had always been : he dressed the same,
And walked and talked as he had always done.
But though he made no sign and walked securely
The usual round of everyday affairs,
He was no more the man that he had been
Than I am Julius Cæsar. For oft
Within his eyes I caught the look of one
Who bears a secret trouble at his heart,
And now I never see him but I think
Of the heroic path he might have trod,
And those dim peaks of his refusèd greatness.

2. Memory is one of the good angels of God recalling the past in the ethical interests of the present and the future. Sometimes it works through the failures and mistakes and follies and sins of other days, working in us shame and humility and repentance. Sometimes it works on other lines, not by a recollection of past failure and sin, but by a recollection of past faith and love and joy and peace. It reminds us of the kindness of youth and the love of early days and the first high thoughts and noble passions. We can be touched as truly and profoundly by the recollection of goodness, by seeing ourselves again in the mirror of the past as we were at our best. The contrast can move us, as the prophet sought to move Israel by that picture of their devotion when Israel was holiness unto the Lord.

God appeals to us as a *nation* by our past, by every noble struggle and every hard-won victory, by all that our fathers have won for us of liberty, by the standard that has been set to us, by every possession, material and intellectual and moral and spiritual, which we have inherited. It is all a call to prove ourselves worthy of a great vocation. The appeal of the past comes to us also as a *Church*, by the Christian centuries, by all the way through which the Church has been led, by the devotion and sacrifice and faith and love and tears and blood of all the saints. Every story of grace is a new appeal to us, to feel ourselves in the succession. Surely also God appeals to us as *individuals* by our past. He reminds us of His goodness and grace and love. There is perhaps the memory of a happy childhood, the patience and care and love and regard of parents and friends and teachers ; or it may be the recollection of innocence, turning back the page to the time when we looked out on life with pure eyes and unselfish thought. He would soften us by the memory. It is there, somewhere in that past, an appeal which moves the heart by the very contrast. It may be a time of decision when we, too, came to terms with God and knew ourselves to be in a loving relationship to Him. Is there in our past a sacred spot made holy to memory by holy associations, made noble by a noble aspiration, made pure by a pure resolve, made beautiful by the entrance into the heart and life of the King Himself in His beauty?

¶ Whenever Ralph Erskine felt his faith

slipping from him, he would go back in memory to a holiday he had once spent in his youth at Portmoak, when again and again God had drawn so near to him he could almost see and hear Him : ' yonder at the hillside, and yonder on the top of the mountain, and yonder in the east room, and yonder in the west room, and yonder in the low room, when He made my heart to go after Him.' [1]

The offence of idolatry by the Jews was a thousand times worse than the heathen's offence, for it was *apostasy* ; it was as the shameful breach of the marriage vow. Rightly to appreciate our own situation with regard to the past and all God's gracious love revealed in it, we need to use the same prophetic figures and to put something of the same moral passion into the words. When we have looked back to that sacred spot in our past, we have to ask ourselves with something of the same indignation, turning the edge of the irony to our own hearts,

[1] G. T. Bellhouse, *Our Sufficient Beauty*, 89.

will we commit the folly, the glaring infidelity of denying that sacred past ? One of the deadliest sins of middle life and of age is irreverence of the dreams of youth, sneering at early piety or early earnestness, declaring that then we were ignorant and foolish and full of impossible ideals, but that now we have seen more of life and know the world, and are too wise ever again to be entrapped into high feeling or burning zeal or self-forgetful devotion. It is a low deep when a man so views the past ; for he is hardening his heart against its appeal.

If God remembers, shall we forget ? If God recalls to us some such time of early faith and decision, when we fell in love with His will and lost our hearts to His life, when in the passion of a great resolve we counted all things but loss that we might gain Him, will we not use this revived recollection as a new opportunity, and turn to Him again, and once more give ourselves in glad and full surrender ?

A CONDEMNATION AND A HOPE

Jer. ii. 13.—' My people have committed two evils ; they have forsaken me the fountain of living waters, and hewed them out cisterns, broken cisterns, that can hold no water.'

ACCORDING to some, Jeremiah was a doleful prophet and forever dwelling, and forever enjoying dwelling, on the darker side of things. So accurate was this assessment judged to be that the word ' jeremiad,' meaning a doleful tirade, was coined, linking the name of the prophet with a particularly depressing form of utterance.

But such an estimate of Jeremiah is unjust. He was a realist, not a pessimist. He lived in times which were sadly out of joint and while he, as many false prophets did, might have cried peace where there was no peace, being an honest man he spoke honestly of conditions as they existed. If his utterances were gloomy on occasion, it was because the circumstances with which they were concerned were gloomy. If he spoke sternly to his countrymen, it was that he might awaken a consciousness of their mistakes and a desire to correct them. Robert Louis Stevenson, in *Weir of Hermiston*, speaks of ' love wearing the disguise of anger,' and that suggestive phrase fitly describes the prophet

Jeremiah's attitude to his people. It was because he loved them so deeply that he addressed them so frankly. It was because he cherished such a high opinion of their capacity that he castigated them so severely for their misdeeds.

On no occasion, perhaps, did he speak more frankly or with a greater sense of responsibility than on the occasion on which he uttered the words of the text. Conditions had become difficult. Responsibility was laid by his countrymen at this door and that—at every door, indeed, except their own. The prophet listened —and disagreed. If conditions were bad, he said, his countrymen and no one else must be held responsible. ' My people,' said the prophet, speaking in God's name, ' have committed two evils ; they have forsaken me the fountain of living waters, and hewed them out cisterns, broken cisterns, that can hold no water.' If it was a frank utterance, it was not without hope. If they had created the conditions by forsaking

God and by substituting lesser loyalties for their loyalty to Him, they could improve conditions by abandoning the broken cisterns which had proved unworthy of their trust and by restoring God to His rightful place in their affections.

The particular situation calling forth this utterance of Jeremiah's may have been forgotten long ago. But the relevance of his utterance has not passed with it. There are situations still, in the life of nations and of individuals, for which men and women try to lay responsibility at this door and that—at every door, indeed, except their own—and when it is one's bounden duty to declare, in God's name, that the responsibility must be borne by them and by them alone. They, like Jeremiah's contemporaries, must be told, sometimes, that they have committed two evils. They have forsaken the fountain of living waters and hewed them out cisterns, broken cisterns, that can hold no water. He, indeed, is the only realist who dares to make such a pronouncement. And if ever the world needed such realists it is to-day.

1. He must be singularly unaware of what is proceeding around him who is not aware that there are nations and individuals who have done precisely what Jeremiah charged his countrymen with doing.

God, the fountain of living waters, has been forsaken. Nations have quite openly abandoned belief in Him, and individuals have ceased to come to worship Him. The human heart is so made, however, that, while it may abandon belief in God, it must believe in something or in some one, and, while it may discontinue its worship of Him, it must find something or some one to worship. You may remember that, when Moses was called to ascend Sinai to receive the Commandments, he tarried so long upon the Mount that the Israelites grew impatient, and finally determined to have done with their leader and the God he professed to represent. But they couldn't live in a vacuum of unbelief. Accordingly, they requested Aaron to fashion a god whom they could see, and he, succumbing to their pressure, arranged that they should bring him their gold, from which he ultimately provided them with a golden calf. As it was then, so is it now. Men may declare themselves unable to continue to believe in God and to worship Him, but there the matter does not

end. Something or some one must be found to fill what H. G. Wells once called ' the God-shaped blank ' in the human heart. And both nations and individuals have found the something or the some one they have sought.

It was once reported to A. E. Whitham that a young Girton girl had declared to a Church assembly that ' public worship has no attraction for the young.' ' Is that quite true ? ' asked Whitham. ' What about those twenty thousand Italians who cheered Mussolini (who was then at the height of his power) in a square in Rome the other day ? Surely that was public worship. What about the thousands who cheered their football favourite last Saturday ? I should have said,' continued Whitham, ' that youth, and humanity generally, has so strong a desire to worship something that the very strength of the desire carries recognizable dangers. If men cannot find the true God to worship, they will worship tin gods—or gods with a good deal of tinsel about them.'

And that is the position. Nations may have abandoned their belief in God and many individuals may have discontinued their worship of Him, but even those who profess to interpret such facts as man's rebellion against tradition and his desire to emancipate himself from what they are pleased to call age-long superstition, cannot deny that nations and individuals have had to find something or some one to believe in and something or some one to worship. Nations and individuals may not be Christian, and may declare with some heat that they have no desire to be so described, but, in banishing Christianity, they have far from banished religion from their life. For their belief in God, nations have substituted belief in race and soil and the super-state. For the worship of God, individuals have substituted the worship of their fellows, or the worship of position or possessions or pleasure. ' My people,' said Jeremiah, speaking in God's name, ' have committed two evils ; they have forsaken the fountain of living waters, and hewed them out cisterns, broken cisterns, that can hold no water.' Precisely the same two things—though some may object to their being called evils—have happened in our day and generation.

2. There may be some, as we have suggested, who interpret the nations' banishment of God from their scheme of things, and individuals'

discontinuance of their worship of Him, as man's rebellion against tradition and his desire to emancipate himself from age-long superstition, but the fact which they, as well as we, have to face is that nations and individuals who claim to have rebelled and to have emancipated themselves do not present a very reassuring or convincing spectacle. We all know that nations that have instituted a religion of race and soil and the super-state have become intolerant of their neighbours, and quite indifferent to the suffering which the pursuit of their chosen aims may involve for others. Individuals who have substituted the worship of their fellows or the worship of position and possessions and pleasure for the worship of God don't give very satisfactory evidence of their new gods' power to satisfy the human heart.

The connexion between the policy of certain nations and the dissatisfaction experienced by some individuals and the gods they have substituted for the living and true God, is as clear to some of us as the connexion between the two evils his countrymen had committed and the conditions which prevailed was to the prophet Jeremiah. What he said, indeed, to his countrymen needs to be said afresh to every generation. You cannot forsake the fountain, something immeasurable, for a cistern, something measurable, without certain consequences following inevitably. You cannot abandon belief in a God who is infinite and whose love is universal for belief in a nation which is measurable and whose love is restricted without paying some kind of penalty. You cannot discontinue the worship of God and substitute the worship of your fellows without disastrous results. Small gods mean small ideals, and small gods can give but small satisfaction.

You may remember a poem of Alfred Noyes in which he speaks to a man who set his heart upon attaining riches, who sacrificed everything and every one to his pursuit of them, and who, his ambition realized, finds that, though he has gotten riches, he is without possessions more precious by far.

And after all the labour and the pains,
  After heaping up of gold on gold,
After success that locked your feet in
    chains,
  And left you with a heart so tired and
    old.

Strange—is it not—to find your chief desire
  Is what you might have had for nothing
    then—
The face of love beside a cottage fire
  And friendly laughter with your fellow-men ?

You were so rich when fools esteemed you poor.
  You ruled a field that kings could never buy :
The whisper of the sea was at your door,
  And all those quiet stars were in your sky.

The nook of ferns below the breathless wood
  Where one poor book could unlock Paradise . . .
What will you give us now for that lost good ?
  Better forget. You cannot pay the price.

It is the story of many an individual and many a nation. Abandoning the worship of God for the worship of something or of some one else, individuals have deprived themselves of the satisfaction which only the worship of God can bring. Abandoning belief in God for belief in race and soil and the super-state, nations have deprived themselves and others also of the loyalties which only belief in God can inspire. He is the only realist, and the only true friend of nations and of individuals, who makes that clear, who brings home to the hearts of men, collectively and separately, that responsibility for many of the conditions which exist must be laid at no door save their own. ' My people,' said Jeremiah, speaking frankly because he loved them, ' have committed two evils ; they have forsaken me the fountain of living waters, and hewed them out cisterns, broken cisterns, that can hold no water.' And wherever these two evils are still committed certain consequences still follow.

3. But, fortunately, our message does not end there any more than the message of Jeremiah did.

This utterance of the prophet, when it was properly interpreted, must have been seen to be the one bright star shining in a very dark sky, for, if it indicated how his contemporaries had created conditions which they all found irksome, it indicated, no less clearly, how they could create conditions much more desirable —by abandoning the cisterns they had created and by returning to the fountain they so foolishly forsook. The remedy was in their own hands. And, if nothing happened, they had only themselves to blame.

There are two things whose combined influence to-day may constrain our contemporaries to return to God. The first is the obvious and painful inadequacy of modern ideologies to provide a life worthy of men and women. Perhaps their very inadequacy, the fact that they have awakened hopes which they haven't been able to fulfil, may bring men and women everywhere to seek security not in a scheme of human devising but in a plan of salvation ordained by God Himself. The second thing is the persistent witness of men to an authority higher than man's. We cannot think too appreciatively of or give too fervent thanks for the stand taken by ministers of Christ in other lands, a stand taken at tremendous cost and sacrifice to themselves. They believe and declare that only one voice must be obeyed and that not man's voice but God's. Is it not just possible that their very stand, the fact that they are prepared to endure obloquy and loss and even death rather than be unfaithful to God Almighty, may put men in remembrance of One whose commands supersede those of His children ?

If nations and individuals have the courage to say as the prodigal, having come to himself, once said, ' I will arise and go to my Father,' the future for both can be and will be bright. With the restoration of God, the Infinite, the Immeasurable, the All-Loving, to His rightful place, the loyalties without which life is chaotic and miserable will return, and the peace which passeth all understanding will again garrison individual hearts and minds.

RODERICK BETHUNE.

The World's Supreme Need

Jer. v. 1.—' Run ye to and fro through the streets of Jerusalem, and see now, and know, and seek in the broad places thereof, if ye can find a man, if there be any that executeth judgment, that seeketh the truth ; and I will pardon it.'

IN this passage the prophet reveals his opinion of contemporary society at Jerusalem, and it is not flattering. He declares it to be a city of hypocrisies whose citizens in their lives deny the religious profession of their lips. He does not allege that there is any definite lack of outward or ritual observance. Indeed, Jerusalem at this time appears to have been what we would describe as a church-going city. Jeremiah, anyhow, acknowledges it to be a community which says, ' The Lord liveth.' It declares its corporate belief in the being and sovereignty of God, and no doubt, as is our own custom, would have considered it only fitting to associate with the celebration of its major civic festivals an act of public worship. But it is just this outward profession that stirs the prophet to passionate indignation, for the common life and individual practice of the citizens show up their faith as an unreality and their religion as a sham. ' Though they say, the Lord liveth,' cries Jeremiah, ' surely they swear falsely.'

Surveying the life of his generation, Jeremiah is dismayed by the contradiction exhibited between its profession and its practice. The people call upon God with their lips ; but whatever else may be characteristic of their general life, justice and truth, His attributes, are conspicuous by their absence. ' Find me one man who executeth justice and seeketh truth ! ' That is the prophet's challenge. He is convinced that the search for this individual will be a depressing process. It will go to and fro through the crowded streets, the busy squares, the broad places of the city, before that man be found, if indeed he be ever found at all. But, should the search unearth him, he will demonstrate the infinite worth of one good man to the society in which he moves and has his being. ' If there be found one that executeth judgment and seeketh the truth, I will pardon the city,' said the Lord.

¶ Diogenes is said to have sought for a good man in Athens with a lantern and a candle at noonday. Being asked what he was looking for, he replied, bitterly and abruptly, ' a man.'

¶ Goethe says : ' No greater good can happen to a town than for several educated men, thinking in the same way about what is good and true, to be living in it.'

1. The moral and religious teachers of mankind have consistently emphasized the supreme value of a good minority. And the central message of the Good News which came in Jesus Christ was its thrilling call of hope and encouragement to those who, following the highest light they knew, found themselves in a distinct

numerical inferiority with a hostile and cynical world against them.

Our Lord never told those who desired to follow Him that their lines would fall in pleasant places or that they themselves were destined to popularity. On the contrary, He was frank in warning men and women what association with His cause would involve, and that a readiness to take up a cross was a condition of allegiance which could not be avoided. To be a Christian meant to be allied with the few against the many and the mighty, and to be the declared champion of a moral and spiritual idealism against which the powers of selfishness and materialism had mustered their big battalions. A religious life, as a great French writer reminds us, is a struggle before it is a hymn. The disciple of Jesus, in the twentieth as in the first century, need expect from the worldling nothing but the treatment which the Master Himself received.

¶ Not so very long ago my mother and I were saying ' Good-bye ' to a husband and wife of middle age, mother and father of two children just at the most formative stage of life, who were leaving the country to begin life all over again on the other side of the world. That man had held a good post in business, but the day had come when he had been asked to do something of which his conscience disapproved. He said no, and he was told pretty plainly what the consequences of persisting in that attitude would be. He stood by his guns and they fired him, without a thought for the years of service he had given and the work he had done so faithfully. Not only did he lose his job, but the firm he worked with made it impossible for him to get employment in that line of business with any other firm in this country, and he had to sell up all he possessed, realize his assets, and set sail for a distant land.[1]

But our Lord always preserved a great understanding and compassion for that very worldling who hated Him, opposed and thwarted Him. He knew, what some of the official exponents of His religion at times forget, how hard it is for ordinary men to preserve amid the glittering deceptiveness of the things that surround them that sure vision and level judgment which recognizes what is seen to be temporal but what is unseen to be eternal. Faith in the Christian values as alone worth seeking is not come by

[1] D. P. Thomson, *Men Christ Wants*, 41.

easily. As a thing rises in worth, so correspondingly does its price increase. Yet the Gospel pages ring with that reiterated call, ' Be of good cheer ! ' He had overcome the world, and so would they who followed Him. He assured them that, however contrary might be appearances, they, and only they, who were true to His idealism were the lights of the earth.

Those who are moved to despondency because the appeal of the Christian Church does not apparently arouse a universal response, either in this nation or in any other, view human affairs from a wholly different standpoint from that which was our Lord's. Christ quite naturally expected His Church to find tribulation, and He would be the last to be surprised to find, in our own day, many empty pews where His gospel was purely and fearlessly preached. We learn from the New Testament that from the time when His position was realized to be spiritual and not political many turned and walked no more with Him.

2. ' Seek, if ye can find a man.' The world's sorest needs, despite the contrary assurances of many of our garrulous advisers, are neither political nor economic. Nor is the world's supreme need, as some have told us, for more first-class brains, desirable as such a commodity may be. We have by this time had evidence enough that first-class brains, unless allied with first-class character reflecting the mind of Christ, have a dangerous tendency to become the curse of society. The world's urgent need lies deep-rooted in a necessity for the development in individual lives of high moral and religious character.

Many of us, unfortunately, lose our sense of perspective as life goes on. We cease to recognize the obvious when we see it; we confuse life's greater issues and values. Our heads and our hearts become absorbed with our possessions and consumed by the lust for more. Yet, what shall it profit a man if he gain the whole world and lose his own soul ? Our common life, too, is often degraded by blatant and unashamed selfishness, by uninformed class antagonisms, and by a blind disregard of our duties towards our neighbours, who have rights as well as we. We are all more or less affected by such things, and have good cause to examine ourselves in order that we may see whether our outlook is that of free intelligent people or is twisted and distorted by environment, acquired prejudice, or inherited tradition.

There is also an increasing tendency in many departments of life towards self-centred aggressiveness, and our public activities, both secular and ecclesiastical, are frequently disordered and robbed of their fruitfulness by the reckless conduct of parties and sections who are out mostly for their own hand. What we regard as selfish conduct in the individual we must also repudiate in the wider sphere of our corporate life. 'It is of the utmost importance,' once said Lord John Russell, 'that a nation should have a correct standard by which to weigh the character of its rulers.' And to this we might add that the true greatness of nations lies in exactly the same qualities which constitute greatness in an individual.

Back again we are forced to Christ's centre of emphasis. It is the individual, and always the individual. The Kingdom of God is within you. 'The soul of all improvement is the improvement of the individual soul.' Back again we are forced to His advice to all who are concerned with the world's troubles and filled with earnest anxiety to alleviate and banish them. It is the little leaven that leaveneth the lump, so He insists again and again. Therefore —and this is the inexorable first command of His social gospel—be you yourself true to your faith, your work, your personal responsibilities, remembering that by one man the city will find its pardon.

Not in the clamour of the crowded street,
Not in the shouts and plaudits of the throng,
But in ourselves, are triumph and defeat!

3. But idealism itself, we have frequently to remind ourselves, must be conditioned by the wisdom which is from above. There is, for instance, much idealism abroad these days, enthusiastic and impassioned. It is a matter of grave urgency that we carefully examine it before accepting it as being wise in the sense in which Christ would define wisdom. Still, even when in our view misguided, it should always be listened to with respect. The ocean of our social and religious thought is disturbed to-day by many conflicting currents. Let us try to keep a big and warm heart for humanity, and have the sympathy and common sense to

respect genuine conviction and to realize that it is well worth our while to investigate the source and the value of all sincere ideas. The wind bloweth where it listeth, and we never know from what unexpected quarter comes the life-giving whisper of the Holy Ghost.

4. Whatever life may bring us, and whatever it may take away, we do not need to be with the crowd to have our own personal influence really effective. We must beware of accepting popular verdicts without analysis and scrutiny just because they are supported by numbers. Nor is established authority infallible. It poisoned Socrates, crucified Christ, and burned St Joan of Arc to death. That which matters is that we should follow God's light as we see it, in humility and honesty of heart. 'Light, more light!' cried Goethe as he died. 'Light, more light!' should be our prayer each day we live. Emerson was fond of insisting that the driving force of the world consists of ideas. It is thought that creates action. Those who seek the truth shall save the city.

There is nothing in the world so strong in influence as human personality. There is none of us but has owed something to the personal influence of some dear friend. It is the personality of Christ that calls forth all that is best in human nature—His courage, strength, and gentleness, His love and power, His sympathy and understanding, His mercy and His pity. Whatever we may question in this bewildering and mysterious world, let us never doubt the eternal influence of our own life and character. Amid the noise and tumult of affairs; when men, some of whom know no better, and some of whom ought to know better, requite our good with evil and our unselfish devotion with contempt; when the most cherished ideals and convictions of our souls can find no place even in the hearts of those we care for most; when loyalty to our faith demands of us misunderstanding, loneliness, and loss—well, let us look yonder to

those holy fields,
Over whose acres walked those blessed feet,
Which, nineteen hundred years ago, were nailed
For our advantage on the bitter cross.

And from Him, one lonely but gallant youth walking so bravely those Galilean fields, has come the peace of God to the restless hearts of men. Through Him comes that inward power which, inexhaustible, continually rejuvenates His Church on earth, which, itself the extension of His incarnation, seeks in all ages to draw men into Him. And because no institution, however holy and divine, can limit the operation of His grace, He lives among men everywhere, the light that is beyond all light, the loveliness that men dream of but have never seen and in this world can never see. He to whom all power hath been given in heaven and in earth is the source of whatever seeks to lift, to ennoble, and to beautify.

From Him is all that soothes the life of man,
His high endeavour and his glad success,
His strength to suffer and his will to serve.

There is no sphere of life, no enterprise into which the vicissitudes or responsibilities of our lot may call us, but in which He is, and remains for ever, the supreme standard of judgment, thought, and conduct. 'What would Jesus do?' is still the question which in things trivial and commonplace as well as critical and weighty each one of us ought daily and hourly to ask of his conscience and endeavour to answer in his practice.

In such an identification of our lives, our work, and our endeavours with His mind there is a security to be found in life and in death. We know ourselves to be safe amid the universe, since that universe is His, and He is able to keep what we have committed to His trust. Whatever we may have to leave behind us when we pass from these temporal scenes, we may be assured that the values of Christ and the dominion of His love will still endure. This, indeed, can give a glory and a splendour to all human toil and enterprise, and to every effort to elevate our character and to ennoble our desires. For though the tabernacle of this earthly house must one day be dissolved, and though this planet on which the human race has now its temporary home must eventually collapse into nothingness, the selfless exercise of our highest capacities and the courageous practice of all Christ-like virtues must inevitably be building for us elsewhere an House of God, not made with hands, eternal in the heavens.[1]

[1] C. L. Warr, *Scottish Sermons and Addresses*, 142.

Forbidden Battlements

Jer. v. 10.—' Take away her battlements; for they are not the Lord's.'

IT must have been a heart-break to the prophet that such a message as this was given him to declare. Jerusalem was the city of God. Over its fortunes in peace and war God had watched with peculiar care. Its enemies had been His enemies, its friends His friends. And now the enemy was thundering at the gates, and the city was drawing comfort out of the single thought that it was well protected. Those battlements—broad-based, firm-set, with tower and bastion—could defy assault and laugh at the invader. And then, uplifted through the city streets, came the harsh reiterated cry, ' Take away her battlements, for they are not the Lord's.' It sounded like a very cruel cry. As a simple matter of fact it was the opposite. Judah was staying herself upon securities that had no sanction in the will of heaven. And God commanded that they be swept away, not in hatred but in tender mercy, that Judah might be brought to lean again upon the strength of the everlasting arm. That was the cry which went ringing through Jerusalem. That cry has gone ringing down the ages. We hear it in individual life, and not less audibly in national and social life.

1. *The Bible.*—To begin with, let us think of the Bible, that Book to which our debt is infinite; that revelation of the love of God, crowned in the priceless gift of a Redeemer. It is the Book that comforts us in suffering, cheers us in battle, heartens us in toil. It is the only Book that never fails us amid all the change and chequer of the years, for it is higher than our highest thought, and it is deeper than our deepest need. In it we read the story of that sacrifice which is far too good to have been false, without which we cannot live and cannot die. Is, then, the Bible an inspired book? Ask the man who has proved its promises, and clung to them in sunshine and in storm. Ask the sinner who has found a Saviour there, in the hour when vain was the help of man. It is such things, and it is such things only, that are the valid proof of God in Scripture. It is not inerrancy, or verbal accuracy, or literal rendering of historic detail.

And wherever men have buttressed up the Bible by proofs which were never intended by its Giver, there has come the voice that once was heard in Judah, 'Take away her battlements, for they are not the Lord's.' That is what true research has always done—all loving, patient, critical inquiry. It has not touched the living word of God. It has removed the battlements God never built. And so it has drawn us nearer to that heart which is for ever throbbing in the Word, in whose mercy is our only hope, and in whose will our peace.

¶ 'From naïve acceptance of the Bible as of equal credibility in all its parts because mechanically inerrant,' says Dr Fosdick, 'I passed years ago to the shocking conviction that such traditional bibliolatry is false in fact and perilous in result. I saw with growing clearness that the Bible must be allowed to say in terms of the generations when its books were written what its words in their historic sense actually meant, and I saw that often this historic sense was not modern sense at all and never could be. There, like others, I have stood bewildered at the new and unaccustomed aspect of the Book. But that valley of confusion soon was passed. I saw that the new methods of study were giving far more than they were taking away. They have restored to us the historic Christ. They have led us to the abiding, reproducible experiences of the soul revealed through Him. They have given us His imperishable Gospel freed from its entanglements, the Shekinah distinguished from the shrine, to be preached with a liberty, a reasonableness, an immediate application to our own age such as no generation of preachers in the Church's history ever had the privilege of knowing before.'

2. *The Church.*—Or passing from our conception of the Bible we might turn our thoughts to the story of the Church. For this is the cry of every Reformation, 'Take away her battlements, for they are not the Lord's.' Our thoughts go back to the mediæval Church. What mighty defences she had raised around her; what buttresses and bulwarks she had built. Outside her boundaries there was no salvation: it was she and she alone who could give pardon. Her wealth was boundless, her civil power supreme; she could make monarchs and cast them down again; to be her favourite was to be blessed, and to be excommunicate

was death. Battlements of pride and place and power—battlements forged and fitted with such intricacy as to defy the batterings of time. And then, across the streets of Europe passed a heroic and prophetic figure, crying, as Jeremiah cried, 'Take away her battlements, for they are not the Lord's.' The strange thing is that they *were* taken away, such tremendous power is in prophetic voices! Her walls were ruined—her defences shattered—her pride and glory humbled to the dust. And once again, as long ago in Judah, that voice which seemed so treacherous and ruthless was the voice of the loving-kindness of the Lord. Out of the ruins of an earthly Church arose the form of a Church that was Divine. Faith revived, and the word of God was read, and the love of Christ became a great reality, and spiritual peace and joy came back again.

No longer do we grasp at temporal power to fortify the position of the Church. But is there not a danger lest our Church should seek to guard and fortify herself by battlements which the Lord will not acknowledge? When we think to prosper by organization instead of by the power of living faith; when the meeting for prayer is miserably empty and the entertainment is crowded to the door; when there is vulgar advertisement of flashy sermons, does not the cry go ringing through the Church, 'Take away her battlements, for they are not the Lord's.' Take them away, and give us back again a Church whose battlement is faith in God; a Church whose prayer is uttered from the heart, whose music is the simple voice of praise, whose preaching to the souls of sinful men is the message of the everlasting gospel.

¶ When Dr J. H. Jowett went to New York he found that, in general, the American churches were tremendously active, organized to a high degree, and apparently humming with life, but at the same time there was a deep and unsatisfied hunger for the Bread of Life. He wrote in a letter to a friend, 'I am learning to resist almost every hour of the day the tremendous forces that would push me here and there. I do not know what time ministers here spend in their studies. They are evidently engaged in a hundred outside works which must leave them very little time to prepare their message.'

3. *Individuals.*—But not only is that true of churches; it is also true of individuals. It

is true, for instance, of those strange reversals which come so often to the prosperous man. Sweet are the uses of adversity; sweet also the uses of prosperity. It is God's reward for faithful honest labour, and, being such, it is a blessed thing. Yet who has not seen and, seeing, sorrowed for, that fatal power inherent in prosperity to deaden character, and weaken faith. Wealth and comfort—how often these rise like battlements between the individual soul and God; and how often in these very things has a man thought to find his strength and safety. Then comes, in some unlooked-for hour, the sudden reversal, and the supports and pillars of his prosperity fall into ruin. And what is *that* but the prophetic voice crying across the life as through Jerusalem, ' Take away her battlements, for they are not the Lord's.' It is in hours like that men see again. It is in hours like that they feel their need of heaven. The battlements are gone, but God remains. Their only help and refuge is in Him. And so have many found, what Judah found, that the prophetic cry, which seemed so ruthless, has been the beginning of a blessed peace.

¶ To many, the loss of their money would be life's supreme catastrophe. Yet how many men have had to lose their money to find God : to cease living on money before they could begin to live on God. There are lines of mellow, ineffable beauty in Shakespeare which describe this transition. One has seen the thing happening again and again in the life of men one knew.

His overthrow heap'd happiness upon him;
For then, and not till then, he felt himself,
And found the blessedness of being little :
And, to add greater honours to his age
Than man could give him, he died fearing God.

4. *The Experiences of the Moral Life.*—Something, too, of the same kind is seen in the experiences of the moral life. We might think, for instance, of St Paul. Filled with the burning passion to be righteous, Paul had striven magnificently for holiness. Longing eagerly for peace with God, he had toiled heroically to be justified. And when his hope was dim, and when the fight was fierce, what unassailable battlements he had, behind which there was shelter for his soul! Circumcised the eighth day, of the stock of Israel, of the tribe of Benjamin; concerning zeal, persecuting the Church; touching the righteousness which is in the law, blameless. What fortresses of privilege and birth, to guard and shelter the besieged soul! Then came the hour when he met with Christ, as he was taking his journey to Damascus. In that great hour he saw his Saviour, and in that great hour he saw himself. And once again, right through that life of his, as through the streets of Judah long ago, rang out that old prophetic cry, ' Take away his battlements, for they are not the Lord's.' ' What things were gain to me,' he writes, ' these I counted loss for Christ.' In that hour he found all that he had been seeking—the inward peace, and the reconciliation, and the righteousness which he had sought in vain. All that his battlements could never give him, of safety and security and song, was given him in the hour he found a Saviour.

Now that experience of the great Apostle is still repeated in a thousand lives. Not by the privileges of their Jewish ancestry do men now build a refuge for their souls; not by the fact that they were born and bred of the stock of Israel and of the tribe of Benjamin. But none the less in the day of spiritual conflict, and in the craving for blessedness and peace, men still have battlements in which they trust. Sometimes it is rite or sacrament—sometimes that they are members of a church; sometimes that they have lived a virtuous life, or are men of honourable reputation. And how often, at this very hour, to those who trust in themselves that they are righteous, there comes the cry which came to the Apostle, ' Take away her battlements, for they are not the Lord's.' It may come in the dark day when sin conquered. It may come in the solemn hour of dying; that sense that all that we trusted in is vain, and that the walls we built to save us are in ruin. And it is then that we are cast on Christ, our only fortress and defence, who lived to inspire us, and who died to save us, and who is all in all to every one who trusts Him.

The Security of a People.

Jer. v. 10.—' Take away her battlements ; for they are not the Lord's.'

THE Hebrews were never entirely, or for more than a season, without their protesting voices.

There were always some men amongst them who would not be satisfied with any achievement on the part of their nation. If the achievement was frankly a wicked one, if it conflicted with some fine standard of the past, it came soon or late under the fierce denunciation of some one of themselves. And when the achievement was in itself good, even then there were voices from amongst themselves which declared that it was not so good as it might have been, and that, such as it was, it was nothing unless it became at once the stepping-stone or approach to something finer still.

It is this that makes them the people of God: their inability to accept as final, and as the best that God can do by them, anything to which they have so far attained. It is their idealism, their sense of something always beyond, of something always better, their sense that everything so far is but the approach and opportunity for something finer and more far-reaching; it is, as one of their own great writers put it, ' because God has planted eternity in the heart of man ' that to-day, when as a nation for long centuries they have ceased to be, the history of the Hebrew people, their public and political fortunes, and their own thoughts about themselves and about human life and about God, still offer to thinking men the best guidance in our own perplexities.

1. ' Take away her battlements, for they are not the Lord's.' Such was part of the message of Jeremiah to his country. There, once again, you have a prophet of Israel in his characteristic rôle, rebuking, in the name of God, not his enemies, but his own people; recalling them from certain defences or securities in which they were putting their confidence, assuring them that these would not survive the assault and test of time, that in any case it was not for the mere sake of maintaining such protections and fortifications that God had spared them in the past, or would support them in the searching time that was coming.

Now it is not unlikely that those very battlements which the prophet is asking the people of Jerusalem to abandon as being not the very line of defence which God would have them take, were battlements which in their day had served their purpose, battlements, it may even be, which had been erected under the inspiration of faith in earlier days. They had been neces-

sary for the security of the people once upon a time. The prophet's point is that they no longer afford such security, and that meanwhile their very existence, carrying with it a pretence of safety, is deceiving the people, hindering them from thinking out their whole position anew, and adopting a new attitude, a new policy, a new faith, such as alone will afford them, in the new time that is coming, that freedom from panic and alarm which the battlements provided in a crisis long since past.

There we come in full view of a great principle, a principle of such a kind that, if we can heartily perceive it and accept it, it may help thoughtful and religious minds to adjust themselves to the abandonment of watchwords and policies which seemed to offer security in old days, but offer no such security in this difficult and incalculable time. The principle is this: face to face with an immediate crisis, a man, or a nation, or a church, defends itself as best it can, spending its resources lavishly in order to arrest and beat back the immediate peril. One day the danger is past, the crisis is ended; whereupon the temptation arises that the man or the nation or the church continues to devote the best part of its thought to the strengthening and perpetuation of those measures which helped in the day of crisis.

For example, so long as Jerusalem was threatened only by local tribes—Philistines and the rest—the battlements round about Zion were probably sufficient. There are parts of our own country, especially in the Border counties, north and south of the Tweed and the Cheviots, where one still can see the ruins of old fortified houses, castles, and keeps. They served their day. Later, when feuds were no longer family affairs, but began to involve larger and larger aggregates of men—clans, then groups of clans, then a whole nation on one side or upon the other—the little fortified places no longer served, and thoughtful men on one side and on the other had to find some stronger security. The next step was reached when a *nation* fortified itself against a neighbouring nation. But later even that larger defence became obsolete, as one nation made alliance with other nations as being bound together by some old racial tie, or as being advocates and supporters of some common policy. And so we had *ententes* and alliances arrayed against each other until every nation on earth in our own day has had to take a side. And what we are seeing at the present moment, in all sober and reflective minds, is the searching for some method by which the whole world, and every honest community in the world, may be delivered from the terror and scourge of world-war.

The task is full of difficulty ; but we are here for no other purpose than to overcome such difficulties, and it is part of our very faith in God that if we ask we shall receive, and if we seek we shall find, and if we knock a door will be opened.

It was a hard thing that Jeremiah asked his countrymen to do—to dismantle the fortresses round about Jerusalem. For every order of things has its own supporters, and every change in the accepted order of things disturbs the habits of an ever-widening circle of people, who, acting upon a natural impulse, resent the change. And then, once again, it requires time and thought for people who have been saved from some earlier danger by a particular method to let go that method for the sake of another which is more spiritual, and therefore more nebulous, and at the best a hazard.

2. There is something in this ancient message of Jeremiah to his country which is applicable to ourselves, and to all the nations of the earth. It is a military axiom that the attack—if you give it time—can always overwhelm the defence. And there is no imaginable security in arms which, given time and a compelling moral reason on the other side, cannot be overcome. We had our Lord's word for that long ago. ' He who taketh the sword,' said our Master, ' shall perish by the sword.' He who buttresseth himself in any merely material security, and who thereupon presumes, will provoke—said our Lord in effect—from the surrounding world a force of the same quality, only vaster, keener, more passionate, which will overwhelm its antagonist.

Yes, it is a great principle. He that taketh the sword shall perish by the sword. He that useth an aeroplane for bombing purposes shall be terror-struck by his own device in other hands. And he who appeals to mere might as the arbiter of the human fate shall one day be brought to his knees by the very might which he, by his very existence, invoked.

Perhaps it is a perilous thing for us to say of ourselves that in the light of all that has happened it would appear that we and our allies have been an instrument in the hands of God to teach our enemies the truth underlying this solitary verse of Scripture. And yet it is hard to resist some such interpretation of world-events ; and in any case there is no room for pride. For to have been chosen by God as an instrument is not a proof at all that we ourselves are everything that God would have us be. It is part of the mystery of providence that God from time to time has made use of instruments which in their day were morally intolerable. He has made use of one great worldly empire to overwhelm another, because, so it must have been, to His all-seeing eye there was something *more* perilous, something more sinister for His future in the world, were one of these rather than the other to survive. But it is no proof that a nation is all that God would like it to be, or that, at the moment when He called it, it was all He would like it to be, that He asked it to perform a task.

There is a saying of Scripture that no word of God is of merely private interpretation. What God says to one man He says to every man ; and what God says to Germany He says to those nations, likewise, which have been used by Him to oppose and overwhelm Germany. And what is it that He says ? Well, in the light of this verse and in the light of this whole Book of Prophecy, what He says is something like this : it is the nature, or tendency of men as individuals, and of nations and empires, to put their trust in the visible signs of power to which, looking round, they can point. Now, from the very moment when a man or a nation looks round and celebrates to itself its tokens of surrounding power, from that moment a process, which the Bible calls the process of death, begins to set in. In some mysterious way that nation begins to be separated from the roots of moral soundness and permanence. Threatening, as such a nation does threaten, to disturb the moral peace of the world, the Universal Mind, or God, already begins to lay His plans to safeguard the true interests of the human race. Years may pass, a generation may pass, a century may pass ; but slowly the writing begins to appear upon the wall, and unless that man or that nation or empire takes fright at its own increasing solitude, that man or that nation or that empire must decline and fall.

Read the verses which lead up to the text and you will find a nation that had grown frivolous, extravagant, gross, paying no heed to the voice of God, trifling with certain sanctities in life, contemptuous of the moral wisdom of ancient and loftier times, intoxicated with arrogance, with pride, frustrating at once any private misgiving by looking round upon the battlements, as Nebuchadrezzar looked round upon the towers and palaces of Babylon. You will be made to feel that all the time there is creeping up to that nation something as stealthy as a fog, something which cannot be met at any one point and thrown back there, but something fatal, something in the atmosphere ; and it has all such an inevitableness that even as you read you know that the proud thing is doomed, and that, if this is God's world, it could not be otherwise.

What made the Hebrews the people of God was that they never were without voices which rebuked themselves ; and what makes us the people of God, and what will secure us increasing influence and, it may even be, a permanent place in this great world, is that we are ready to judge ourselves, and that we refuse to be satisfied with ourselves ; that we are ready to amend, to listen, and to learn ; our practice ever overtaking our ideals, and our ideals ever becoming purer and more humane ; in short, that we believe in God as Christ has made God known to us, and that we are not afraid to let the whole matter stand at this—that our place as a people shall rest not on the security of mere force, which in the long run is no true ' battlement of the Lord,' but that it shall rest, under God, upon the friendliness and respect and gratitude of all other peoples, because they perceive that what we stand for is something which must not perish from the earth.

¶ The foundations of our New Jerusalem depend not upon material programmes, but upon the acceptance of the ideal of love as the guiding principle of personal and national life.

That the change can be accomplished if we really desire it, and that the initiative can come from our own sorrowful but undaunted country I have never doubted, even in its darkest hours of complacency and self-seeking.

To-day, after witnessing London's endurance of its crucifixion without panic or vindictiveness, I am more than ever confident that the British people—provided that their innate decency is neither destroyed by the propaganda of hatred nor warped by excess of avoidable suffering—are as capable as any people in the world of accepting a way of life determined by love rather than by power.

We beseech thee to take us as we are, and of thy mercy make us what thou would'st have us be.[1]

Looking to the End

Jer. v. 31.—' What will ye do in the end thereof ? '

1. To look to the end is the mark of the wise man in every region of life. He is not content with present appearance ; he seeks out causes, and from causes knows something of consequences. A prudent man in business is not seduced by immediate success. He calculates what will be the probable ultimate result to his business. He looks farther ahead than the one particular transaction. He won't enter into a bargain until he sees what it is likely to mean in the long-run. The wise statesman is never a mere opportunist, accepting what turns up and making the best of it. He has often to do this, has often to limit himself to the practicable ; he has often to seize an opportunity which comes unexpectedly ; but to be a true statesman he must have more than a mere makeshift policy of using whatever happens to turn up. He has to look to the great ends in view, the great purposes of government, the ultimate issues of each step. The prudent man in every branch of activity is the man who is not easily led away by any specious attraction, but who consistently pursues an end which he has before him. To lead a shiftless, hand-to-mouth existence in any line of life is to invite ruin.

Now, there is a true sense in which we should live for the present, and take no thought for the future. ' Sufficient unto the day is the evil thereof,' and also the good, for that part. The man of faith will not be over-anxious and over-careful, but will live trustfully and humbly in the consciousness of the Father's love. But this disregard of the future is due to a higher regard. It is inspired by a larger end, seeking first the Kingdom of God, an end which relegates all other aims to their place of secondary importance. The man of faith is not feverishly

[1] Vera Brittain, *England's Hour.*

anxious about the things of to-morrow, because he has not given his heart to the things of to-day. His future is with God. His life will end in God. The man of the world lives his life in the present, and to-morrow can only be as to-day. He has no other life, no other source of joy reaching out to the future. The question asked of him is the question of which the conscience of man is clamant, the question suggested by all history, the very question of the prophet, ' What will you do in the end thereof ? '

But that is the very question to which the worldling shuts his ears. If he listened to it, if he asked himself what answer he can give, he would cease to be a worldling. The very essence of the worldly life is that it is blind to results, that it refuses to look at the end thereof. It ever prefers the present to the future, and refuses to make any sacrifice of present good for the sake of a larger future good.

¶ ' The worldly man,' says Bunyan, ' for a bird in the hand.' It is a marginal note which he appends to a scene in the Interpreter's House. ' I saw in my dream that the Interpreter took Christian by the hand and had him into a little room, where sat two little children, each one in his own chair. The name of the eldest was Passion, and the name of the other Patience. Passion seemed to be much discontented, but Patience was very quiet. Then Christian asked, What is the reason of the discontent of Passion ? The Interpreter answered, The governor of them would have him stay for his best things till the beginning of next year ; but he will have all now. But Patience is willing to wait. Then I saw that one came to Passion, and brought him a bag of treasure, and poured it down at his feet : the which he took up, and rejoiced therein, and withal laughed Patience to scorn. But I beheld but a while, and he had lavished all away, and had nothing left him but rags.'

2. The word ' end,' when spoken about human life, means more than the mere termination, the point where it ceases. It means an *end in purpose* as well as an end in time, that towards which it inevitably tends because its direction is fixed. In this sense the end of a thing is that for which it really exists, the result designed for it, the ultimate purpose. The end in time is merely the blossoming and the fruit of the end in purpose. The end of life therefore is not death, but the culmination of the kind of life. The end in time will only be the manifest declaration of what the end in purpose has been. The prophet's question therefore can be answered without needing to wait until the end in time ; for the end in purpose of your life can be revealed to you any moment as in a flash. What is the trend of your life ? What are the things on which you have set your heart ? ' Man's chief end is to glorify God and to enjoy him for ever.' What is your end ? The end thereof will be along the line of that discovery. You only need to be true to yourself in making that discovery to know what the conclusion must be. As in Rossetti's terrible sonnet on *Lost Days*—

I do not see them here ; but after death
  God knows I know the faces I shall see,
Each one a murdered self, with low last breath.
  ' I am thyself,—what hast thou done to me ? '
' And I—and I—thyself ' (lo ! each one saith,)
  ' And thou thyself to all eternity ! '

The prophet appeals to experience, he speaks to conscience, he asks what we can find out without fail, when he puts the question, ' What will ye do in the end thereof ? ' Ask yourselves, —What if the thing you have set your heart on were given you, what then ? You worship wealth, you long to be rich, you judge all things by the standard of money : suppose you attain to it, and get all that is implied in it, what then ? You are bent upon finding pleasure, getting the full measure of enjoyment out of life : suppose you get the overflowing cup and drink it to the very dregs, what then ? You must look at your life steadily and look at it whole, if you would get a true judgment of it ; you must see the end as well as the beginning. If you go straight on in the way where you are, what will you come to at the last ?

Is the end adequate, the end that is the mainspring of your life ? It may not be evil ; but is it sufficient ? Sufficient now and for ever ? Is it adequate as your answer to the question, What is man's chief end ? Is yours a life that moves to gracious ends, because it is hid with Christ in God ? Is yours a life self-controlled, because Christ-controlled ? Is it a life so shepherded by God that, whatever be the earthly fortune, only goodness and mercy can be the ultimate issue ? Or, is it empty of any high purpose, whose root is selfishness, whose motive is passion, whose end is destruction ?

Men speak indulgently of the thoughtlessness of youth ; and some of the young are putting away the personal application of all this on the ground that there is time enough to think of these things, and that meanwhile it is enough to rejoice in thy youth, and let thy heart cheer thee in the days of thy youth, and walk in the ways of thine heart and in the sight of thine eyes. But if you are ever to be thoughtful, if you are ever to make anything of life, when is there a fitter time than now to consider ? Not when habit has organised itself into life, and when tendency has hardened into habit. It is not for youth to be thoughtless—let age be if it may—but now, when destiny hangs on the decisions of these days and hours, it is the wilfulness of folly to shut the eyes and harden the heart. Rather there is infinite truth in the thought which lies at the heart of Goethe's profound couplet—

What a man desires in his youth, that he shall have in age as much as he will.

¶ There is a story of a young architect who for a long time had been engaged on the important work of supervising the erection of a great bridge. The work was nearing its completion when the architect was taken seriously ill with a nervous break-down. For weeks he lay in a state of helplessness, and it could be seen that all the time the thought that was weighing heavily upon his mind was the thought of the bridge. One day it was noticed that he had rallied a little, and one of the specialists suggested that it might be a good thing to take him to see the work upon which so much of his time and energy had been spent. So he was wrapped up and taken down very carefully to the river. They placed him in a small craft and rowed gently up the stream. Presently, as the bridge came full into view, all the young man's attention was absorbed as though he were studying every detail, and as they passed, at length, under one of the great arches he broke out with a joyous cry, ' Ah, that's it, that's it, that's what I meant it to be.' [1]

[1] S. H. Hedley-Perry.

The Conditions of Peace

Jer. vi. 14.—' They have healed also the hurt of the daughter of my people slightly, saying, Peace, peace ; when there is no peace.'

THE word of God which came to Jeremiah in the situation which he faced, is relevant to us in that which we confront. Judah was on the verge of moral and spiritual collapse ; the prelude to its physical downfall. Its society was disintegrated ; no man could be found ' to do justly or seek the truth.' Immorality was rife. The word of God was scorned. Beyond the national boundaries new political forces were emerging, and because Judah was morally and spiritually blind, she was politically following a disastrous foreign policy, for political insight depends on moral integrity. Yet priest and prophet alike were saying that all was well, crying ' Peace, peace,' when there is no peace, and the people loved to have it so. There is surely much that is relevant there, and we had better learn the truth and accept its judgment upon ourselves.

1. Rarely, if ever, are we deliberately and purposely complacent. Here and there may be men and women who turn from grim facts, but generally false and complacent optimism arises from false conviction, misplaced trust, confidence in the wrong things.

It is inspired by *over-confidence in our own powers*. It is a frame of mind paralleled in the modern man's confidence in science. H. G. Wood, in *Christianity and Civilization*, has made the significant distinction between the scientific spirit and the scientific attitude. Of the scientific spirit he writes : ' The love of truth, the resolve to face facts, to use reason honestly and fearlessly, from that the Christian faith must never be dissociated.' The scientific attitude, however, which asserts science to be the only form of knowledge, which scouts religion as an emotion, and claims that science can give all that is necessary to the ordering of our life and our world, this the Christian faith must oppose, for it is a subtle form of that pride which leads to disaster, for it seeks to usurp the place of God.

¶ Julian Huxley declares : ' I believe in science, and have faith that in the long run human reason, employing the scientific method, will enable us to control our destiny.

So, too, complacency rises from *confidence in material power*. Judah was playing a dangerous game in power-politics, trusting in the might of Egypt to save her from the attacks of the northern power of Babylon, but no deliverance could come that way. ' Then it shall come to pass that the sword which ye feared shall overtake you there in the land of Egypt, and there ye shall die.' That is not to say that there is no place for power, for the maintenance of justice and law calls for its exercise, but it is one thing to make power serve the ends of justice and peace, and another to decide by ' force majeure ' what those ends shall be. The bankruptcy of sheer power-politics has been illustrated again and again in Europe during the last five hundred years.

The other element of false confidence is closely allied to this ; it is *trust in material possessions*. ' They have denied the Lord and said, It is not he, neither shall evil come upon us, neither shall we see sword nor famine.' That is the Old Testament version of ' Soul, thou hast much goods laid up for thyself.' No one disputes the need for an economic solution to our distresses. But to use what the science of economics can do, we need to know what it cannot do. No expert handling of international finance, or trade, will heal our world's hurt by itself, and they who urge us to put our trust in that alone are false prophets, crying ' Peace, peace,' when there is no peace.

2. What, then, are the conditions of peace ? The understanding of them depends on our understanding the nature of peace itself : the acknowledgment that, like happiness and freedom, it is a by-product, something which God adds to men and nations as they seek to live by the truths which deposit peace. Just as happiness is granted only to the self-forgetful, and liberty only to the bond-slaves of the highest loyalty, so peace is added unto us as we seek the Kingdom of God.

It is added to those who obey the moral law, God's law. We Christians in our proper emphasis on the compassion, forgiveness and love of God, revealed in Christ, have been prone to speak of the gospel as superseding the Old Testament, instead of fulfilling it. The fact is that the gospel is significant against the background of that dispensation of Divine law. The road to Calvary leads first over Sinai, and if we only know what Sinai means as we look back from Calvary, so we only appreciate what Calvary means if we have passed over Sinai. The warping of conscience, and the disregard of the moral law mark the end of a nation, as of a person, however impressive their prosperity and success may seem.

Peace, too, is added to men and nations as they seek reconciliation. The Christian's task is not only to resist evil, it is to redeem men from it. Dr Farmer once pointed out the subtle difference between being peaceable and being a peacemaker. The one is a product of disposition, the other of will. Peacemaking calls for the establishment of the interest of justice, and all the precaution and negotiations of which men speak, but it calls for that activity to be inspired and formed by the motive of reconciliation, redemption, and restoration to fellowship of the offender. Christian teaching about love and forgiveness of enemies, far from being impracticable idealism, is strictly relevant to the task of the statesman, for an enemy is never truly vanquished until by some means he is changed into a friend.

¶ ' The great and abiding principle which is laid down by the Lord,' writes Dean Matthews, ' is that we should never allow the enemy to overcome our spirits to such a degree that we cease to love him and forget the bond which unites all the children of men. Though he may be filled with hate, we must resolve that he shall not reduce us to his level. We are to desire his good. But what is that good ? Surely not that he may continue in his hatred and aggression, but that he should be stopped in his mad career of self-aggression and be brought into fellowship.'

The Harvest of Thought

Jer. vi. 19.—' Behold, I will bring evil upon this people, even the fruit of their thoughts.'

To the prophets punishment was never a mere misfortune, an adventitious thing that came to some and missed others as by chance. It had an essential relation to life, the result of cause and effect as universal as physical law. It was not fortune ; it was fate. Not fate in the sense of a blind, resistless, remorseless force, but fate as the result of purpose, reason, law. They traced everything past the external appearance to the inward moral source, which alone gives consistence and true meaning to human life. They, no more than modern science, could conceive of anything as *causeless*. But they were not content to find out secondary causes and rest there. They saw the will of God as the inspiring force of Nature, the hand of God shaping history, the law of God ruling all life.

This inevitable consequence of cause and effect is the basis of all prophetic writing, and rewards and punishments are regarded as the product of the actual state of moral life. From the outside standpoint judgment is the result of conduct : from the inner standpoint it is the result of character. Conduct is character unfolding itself ; and character is the way a man thinks. From the one standpoint judgment is the fruit of men's deeds ; from the other it is the fruit of their thoughts. Isaiah puts the same message thus : ' Say ye to the righteous, that it shall be well with him : for they shall eat the fruit of their doings. Woe unto the wicked ! it shall be ill with him : for the reward of his hands shall be given him.' Jeremiah's statement is the same, only carried a little deeper to its source. Our destiny is the fruit of our doings and the reward of our hands ; and our doing is the fruit of our thoughts.

1. It is the fashion to speak of thoughts as of little importance in the review of a life. The opinions a man has, the creed he holds, the way he looks at things, the colour and bent of his mind—these are supposed to count for very little in determining religious value. Morality is made the standard of religion ; and morality is taken to be the things a man does, and the things he refrains from doing. That is a very external and wooden way of defining morality. The spiritual test of an act is its motive. There may be right acts with wrong motives : there may even be wrong acts with right motives. Robert Burns was a much better theologian and a better moralist, when he said,

> The heart aye's the part aye
> That makes us right or wrang.

Legality is not always equity for the simple reason that, except in special cases, it is not possible to make sure of motives, and so the law has to content itself with acts. But we know from experience how the best-intentioned man will sometimes blunder into mistakes ; and we also know that many an irreproachable deed may be damned by the cunning or deceit or crooked purpose at the bottom of it.

Christ's teaching was full of this inwardness of aspect. As opposed to the formalists, who had buried the spirit under a mass of outward observances and made the Law of none effect by their traditions, He showed that men were judged by the attitude of their hearts. It was held that if a man did not kill he was guiltless of breaking the commandment : but the Master taught that if hate was harboured in the mind the sin of murder was committed. With impeccable and respectable conduct, He showed that there could be adultery committed in the heart. Sinful deeds there were in plenty, but the root of the sin lay in the corrupted will, the depraved heart, the evil thought. We judge by our common rough-and-ready standards, and from our limitations it cannot be otherwise to some extent ; but God's judgment is not so limited. It is the fruit of our thoughts.

2. Again, it must be remembered that in the long-run as we think so will we act. Thoughts issue in speech and in deeds. The bent of a man's mind is the bent of his life. The way he looks at God and the world and life must determine his every act. Our Lord's statement is a general statement of fact, that ' a good man out of the good treasure of the heart bringeth forth good things ; and an evil man out of the evil treasure bringeth forth evil things.' There never was a more absurd and inept idea than the common one that it does not matter much what a man thinks and believes. By comparison nothing else matters. It is true that a man may hold certain opinions and speculations in a loose fashion without these affecting his life ; but that is because these opinions are not his true creed. They are really outside his mind. If they entered into the fibre and tissue of his thinking they would represent the exact man. We speak of convictions when we mean only vague impressions : we speak of creed when we mean only surface views taken on trust floating lightly on what we call our minds. But below the stream of what we show to the world there flows strong and deep the current of what we really think and believe ; and that is the measure of the man.

¶ One often hears it said that it does not matter what a man believes provided his life be right ; as if a stream might somehow be pure though its source be polluted, or as if we might expect a fine crop of grapes from a thorn-tree. The story of Joseph in the Old Testament teaches us rather that nothing is so practical as faith. When he was a child his heart was somehow drawn to God ; when he left home, a lad of seventeen, ' the Lord was with him ' ; when he stood before Pharaoh at thirty, the Spirit of God was in him ; and his habitual realisation of the presence of God was the motive-power of all his actions. It is evident that his religion was an inward principle, not a code of laws, a set of propositions, or an array of ceremonies. His creed—his central enthusiasm for God, the thing which he really believed—determined his life.[1]

3. We are tempted to miss the inwardness of life and religion, and so have shallow views of sin and punishment and redemption. Sin is not merely mistake, the neglect to observe certain rules ; it is a spiritual thing, and its roots go deep, past flesh and blood down to the very fountain of life. Sin is the foul creature from which springs the hateful brood which we call sins ; and her nest is in the heart. So repentance is made the gate to life because it touches the source. It means a sorrow that turns the heart from its old loves and lusts, and gives the life a new direction. When will we learn, therefore, that judgment is not arbitrary or incidental or capricious ? It is self-registering, automatic, the harvest of our life.

¶ ' Things,' Joseph Butler declared, ' are what they are, and their consequences will be what they must be.' That is the law, a law we are continually trying to dodge. It is in fact a law that never can be dodged, whose patient, persistent movement can be reversed only through the radical transformation of thought and conduct that is real repentance. Judgment begins within, in the darkened vision, the dulled imagination, in the slow, gradual deterioration of the soul ; but when at last the harvest has ripened it is transferred to the realm of the visible and the concrete.[2]

The wages of being good is not some recompense added on like a perquisite to a salary. Its highest wages is goodness itself. The recompense of being holy is holiness : the reward of being pure is purity. The punishment of sin is itself, its own loathly self. The penalty of a depraved mind is depravity. The retribution of an impure heart is impurity. Who will deliver you from the body of that death ? ' I will bring upon this people the fruit of their thoughts.' Well might the Proverb say with wistful solemnity, ' My son, keep thine heart with all diligence ; for out of it are the issues of life.'

Who is sufficient for these things ? Who can guard his thoughts and keep a sleepless watch at the citadel of life ? There is no safety for a man except by giving up his heart to the keeping of a stronger than himself, submitting his thoughts to the very thought of God, yielding his will to be conformed to the will of God, bringing into captivity every thought to the obedience of Christ. It is a process, a life-long work ; but it begins as an act of will, an act of faith, opening the door of the heart to the gracious Master who stands knocking for entrance. Where he has possession there is no room for any kind of evil. It cannot live in His presence. We know in fragmentary form how it is possible for one man to dominate another by his personality till the other thinks his thought, speaks his words, performs his will. So it is possible willingly to let Christ so dominate our every power that the same mind as was in Him is in us, His very way of looking at things is our way, His life is our life. That is the Christian ideal and the Christian task to have Christ formed in us. If His pure thoughts were our thoughts, could we ever be afraid to see the fruit of our thoughts ?

Good may ever conquer ill.
And love may walk where hate hath trod.
As a man thinketh so is he :
Rise then and think with God.

The Wisdom of the Bird

Jer. viii. 7.—' Yea, the stork in the heaven knoweth her appointed times ; and the turtle and the crane and the swallow observe the time of their coming ; but my people know not the judgment of the Lord.'

' IN the migration of birds,' says Professor Newton, ' we are brought face to face with the greatest mystery in the animal world.' How these little creatures find their way across continents and oceans without chart or compass,

[1] J. Strahan, *Hebrew Ideals*, ii. 122.
[2] H. Ingli James, in *The Rebel Church*, 67.

and how they sustain themselves for so long a journey without rest or food are problems that puzzle the most advanced students of natural history. But in the midst of what lies outside of the range of our present knowledge certain facts stand out in perfect clearness, and from these many instructive lessons can be learned. When the nights become chilly, and the leaves begin to change their sombre green into brilliant and varied tints, and the music of insect life dies away, these visitants of the air gather in great numbers round some old chimney-stack, or ruined building, and with a common impulse start for Central Africa and other friendly lands. So, when the call of spring-tide reaches them from our own coasts they return to us with the same instinctive wisdom and regularity. At their appointed time they know where to go, how to go, and the right moment at which to begin their long and adventurous journey. And the prophet, so quick to catch the intimations of Nature in all her interesting and mysterious ways, contrasts this bird-wisdom with the folly and stupidity of his fellow-countrymen who heed not the ' ruling of God.'

1. The first suggestion of the text, then, is that these birds of passage know *where to go to secure their safety and well-being*. In their flight to other lands they turn right away from those regions where misery, starvation, and death would be their lot, to countries which offer them hospitality, sunny days, and security.

We are all going somewhere, for movement is one of the great laws of life. We cannot stand still in any of our serious concerns. In this respect we are something like poor Jo, in *Bleak House*. When the policeman told him to move on, or be locked up, he replied : ' I'm always a-moving on, sir, I've always been a-moving on and a-moving on ever since I was born.' In a deeper sense than poor Jo meant we are all doing the same thing—we are always a-moving on. But where is our moving on taking us ? We know where the boy in the old story was going when he broke away from the restraints of home and kindred ; he was going to a country where shame and servitude awaited him ; to a life that wrung from his bleeding, broken heart the cry of unrelieved anguish : ' I perish with hunger.' Where are we going ? Many people— many young men and women—like these sagacious birds, know where to go. They know

where to go for their future safety and happiness. for the durable satisfactions of life, for their most wholesome and helpful pleasures, for the grace that sustains them in the hour of temptation and adversity. They know where to spend their Sundays, and hours of leisure. They know where to go in every time of need. Others, however, are not equally wise, and, like all foolish wanderers, their life ends in futility, disappointment, and often in the darkness of despair. They know not the judgment of the Lord.

¶ Dr Smellie, in *The Men of the Covenant*, says that high up in the Alps are two small lakes which lie in such close proximity that it is possible to throw a stone from one to the other. The one is called the White Loch, because its waters are light green in their colour ; the other is known as the Black Loch, because its appearance is gloomy and forbidding. The White Loch sends its overflow to the Adriatic, while the other is connected with the Black Sea. We look at the one, and think about the sunshine of Italy ; at the other, and are transported to the wintry Crimea.

From the same cradle's side,
From the same mother's knee—
One to lone darkness and the frozen tide,
One to the crystal sea.

2. Then these birds of passage know *how to reach their destination of security and well-being*. In their long flight they seem to have a wonderful sense of self-preservation. Except when crossing the ocean, where dangers to bird-life are few, they fly high ; sometimes beyond the reach of the naked eye. ' They have been seen through the telescope passing the disc of the sun six miles above the earth.' There, beyond the reach of the fowler's gun, they are delightfully safe. Of course, all birds do not fly with the same caution and instinctive wisdom. Those who send their pigeons for long-distance flights tell us that they lose many of their most valuable birds because they so often fly within easy reach of the sportsman's gun, or dash into aerials and telephone wires.

There is safety in elevation. Danger lies along the low margins of a worldly life. Safety is discovered in the higher altitudes. Lot was travelling along low levels when overthrow met him in Sodom. Judas had left the high altitudes of fellowship with his Master when his soul collided with covetousness. Peter was warming himself at the world's fire in the courtyard of the enemy when disaster overtook him. There is a familiar story which tells of a magnetic island and how it drew the great ship closer and closer to it, drew it out of its course, and without sound of hammer or noise the mighty ship fell into ruin and was swallowed up of the waves, for the mighty magnet drew every rivet and bolt and strewed the wreckage upon the sea.

¶ On the front of the old grey Abbey at Bath, is a sculptured representation of Jacob's ladder and, as in the Bible story, angels are passing up and down this ladder. I have often stood and looked at these angel-forms, and have always noticed that those at the top of the ladder are in a state of almost perfect preservation, while those near the bottom have lost, either their wings, or feet, or head. The latter suffer because they are within easy reach of the stone-thrower, and other mischievous and destructive people. And the broken heads and wings in real life belong, for the most part, to those at the bottom of the ladder.[1]

Our moral and spiritual well-being largely depends upon elevation—elevated thoughts, desires, ideals, pursuits. 'Whatsoever things are true, whatsoever things are honest, whatsoever things are just, whatsoever things are pure, whatsoever things are lovely, whatsoever things are of good report ; all excellence, all merit, think on these things.' For the man who sets his affections on things above, and not on things on the earth, high-toned things, as Moffatt calls them, will have no fear of the ' terror by night, nor for the arrow that flieth by day, nor for the pestilence that walketh in darkness, nor for the destruction that wasteth at noon-day.'

3. Again, these migratory birds know *just when to leave our shores for sunnier climes*. They appear to have learned by instinct, or some other power of which we have no knowledge, that there is danger in delay. With the first premonitions of coming winter they are on the wing to other lands where the prevenient mercies of God await them. To stay on when those warning voices have reached them, though tempted to do so by St. Luke's little summer, would be fatal. They evidently know the worth of timely action. Do we ?

[1] A. E. Phillips.

¶ No doubt many of us, in our reading of history, have come upon the tragic death of the Prince Imperial. When war broke out in Zululand he joined the British Army, and went out with others, one day, scouting. After getting very near to the enemy one of the company said : ' We had better return.' ' Ten minutes more to drink our coffee,' replied the Prince light-heartedly. Before the ten minutes had gone a band of Zulus came in upon them, and in the skirmish the Prince was slain. When the circumstances of his death were related to his mother she said : ' That was his great mistake from his boyhood. He never wanted to go to bed at night at the proper time, nor to rise in the morning. He was ever pleading for ten minutes more. When too sleepy to speak he would lift up his little hands, and spread out his ten fingers, indicating that he wanted ten minutes more. For this reason I sometimes called him Mr. Ten Minutes.'

The tender, but reproachful, utterance of the text was an attempt on the part of the prophet to avert a national calamity in the life of ancient Israel. He pleaded with his people for prompt repentance and timely action in view of imminent danger, but they turned a deaf ear to his voice, and suffered the full penalty of their sin and procrastination in a long and cruel bondage. Listen to them as they mourn over their folly and lost opportunities : ' The harvest is past and the summer is ended, and we are not saved.' Lost, through putting off to a future day what should be the most immediate, most urgent, concern of life. ' Seek first,' first in point of importance, and in point of time, ' the kingdom of God and his righteousness.' The harvest and the summer are still with us, but how long this happy condition of things will last no one can tell. ' Now is the accepted time, behold to-day is the day of salvation.'

¶ When he went on his first voyage to the north, Nansen left behind him waiting and anxious loved ones. Weeks and months passed without word from the north. One morning his wife found a carrier pigeon pressed against her window and, taking it in her hands, she discovered a message that all was well. The little bird had come home over the wild and wintry wastes of the ice fields with its message of love. It had followed the leading of its deepest life, the life which God had given it.[1]

[1] H. T. Kerr, *Old Things New*, 132.

Harvest Home

Jer. viii. 20.—' The harvest is past, the summer is ended, and we are not saved.'

HARVEST home is often a happy season. When all the dangers which have threatened the seed since it was put into the ground—drought and deluge, mildew and worm—have been escaped, and the last load has been secured, the sense of work satisfactorily done makes man feel contented and glad, with energy for a new start. But harvest home is not only a season of contentment and pleasure, it is often a time of serious reflection. There is something in autumn which seems to make us thoughtful. The days lose their radiance. As the sunbeams slant across the landscape and the birds become silent, and the leaves fall noiselessly to the ground, it seems so much like a parable of human life, descending to its end, that one cannot help looking back and sighing, and looking forward and trembling.

1. Each portion of life has allotted to it its own appropriate work. We are made to work ; we must be employed. The powers we possess at one time of our life are not the same as those we possess at another part of our life. The powers we possess should point out our work. In childhood we are dependent upon others. We are like soft clay, capable of being moulded into almost any shape. Then this is the season for education. And youth is a time of hope and ambition and ardent affection, when we feel we can do almost anything. That is a time we should not waste. It is motor-power which may drive the engine or be allowed to escape in noisy waste. And manhood is the time of mature strength, and sound judgment, produced by experience, when a home is to be made and kept comfortable and happy and good, for both wife and children. The powers and the circumstances of each period show what is the proper work of that period. The lesson from this is that each part of our life is a very solemn thing—that if we don't do the proper work of each at its own proper time we lose that which we can never find again. In some cases we may partially recover lost ground. But in doing it at the improper time we lose the chance of doing something else. If we do to-day's work to-morrow, when will to-morrow's work be done ? and what if, when the judgment comes, we are a day

behind ? Have we thought much about such things as these ? Have we felt that our life, however humble, has so much deep meaning in it ? Begin this thoughtful autumn-time. It is a special season for reflexion.

2. The next thing is that each period of life stands to the succeeding periods in the relation of a sowing time. Every day we are sowing and every day we are reaping. For in all work there is profit. We often hear people say it does not matter—it would have been just the same if we had not done it. But it does matter. It is not the same. Even the least and most trivial action alters things in its measure, and alters them for ever. From each action of ours there come up two harvests. First, whatever we do is done. If a man ploughs a field, the harvest is that the field is ploughed. If a man paints a picture the product is the completed picture. If a man tries to relieve distress or to make others happier, the gain is in distress diminished and in happiness conferred. He who sows wild oats will never reap a crop of good corn any more than he who scatters thistledown in his garden will produce roses or lilies. And thus that saying of the Bible is seen to be true, ' Whatsoever a man soweth, that shall he also reap.' What we put into the ground, that it is which springs up ; and that is the first and direct harvest of conduct.

¶ There is an old and well-known story which tells how Lokman the Wise, a slave, but also a wise man of Arabia, was sent one day by his young master to sow certain fields with wheat. He prepared the ground and sowed the seed, and left it there till it sprang up and grew. When it was well-grown he brought his master to see it. The master looked at it and then turned angrily upon the old slave. ' What is this ? ' he cried. ' I order you to sow wheat here, and there is nothing but coarse and worthless rye.' ' Sir,' Lokman replied, ' I sowed rye but I hoped and prayed that wheat would come up.' ' What do you mean by playing the fool in this way ? ' cried his indignant and wrathful master. ' Sir,' he said, ' you are constantly sowing in the world seeds of evil, seeds of selfishness, self-indulgence, and folly, and yet you seem to expect to reap the reward of virtue ; so in the same way I thought I might get a harvest of wheat from a sowing of rye.' [1]

But each action has a second harvest. It

[1] Ivor E. Newell.

consists in the reaction of conduct on ourselves. Not only does the man who ploughs the field have the reward of seeing his work completed and the field ploughed; but as practice makes perfect he is a better ploughman for his work if he has done his best; and a worse one if he does not care how he does it. The artist not only sees his picture, but he has increased his skill, and mayhap some new perception of beauty has dawned upon him while he has been working which eventually will produce a new power. The man who has tried to make others happy not only sees the pleasure he has given, but has also obtained by his conduct a larger, kindlier heart. So to every act there are two harvests: first, the thing which was intentionally laboured for, and second, the strengthening and even the creating of aptitude and power.

3. But if each period of life has its own appropriate work, and one period is a sowing-time of which the succeeding is the necessary reaping-time, in like manner this whole life of ours in this world has one peculiar all-important work, is one sowing-time; and the next life is the great reaping-time—the Eternal Harvest. Are we doing the work of this period? Is it clear to us what this work is? The work of this life is to be what we call ' saved.' Some people think that it is a fact of the next life, not the work of this. They think that it means to get to heaven; but it does not. It means to become heavenly, rather than to get into a place we name heaven. To be saved and to be safe are different things. Some men only want to be safe. They are quite contented to be idle, intemperate, and dishonest; but they would like to escape condemnation. But to be saved is to be delivered from all our badness, to have all our mean, greedy, brutal dispositions subdued and destroyed. It is to be saved that we are here; and that is to be ' cleansed from all unrighteousness.'

Is this all-important life-work making progress? The best time to begin it is in youth, when the heart is pure and the affections warm and generous and confidence unshaken, and the power of habit limited and plasticity perfect. The young should take advantage of this precious sowing-time.

But there are too many who, in middle life, have not begun this great work. With such it is summer. The green corn should be waving, but instead there is barrenness or the fruitless prodigality of weeds. The work of being saved is harder for them. The soil is hardening and drying up. They have lost time; and that they can never get back. But still the year is not over. Let them take hold upon the present, and put in some good seed. It cannot perish, and God will give the increase. And there are even those who have outlived the heats of youth and the steady strength of manhood, who begin to feel the inroads of decay, but who are without religion and all its guiding light and vital warmth; whose affections are chilled, whose faith in mankind is dead, whose capability of joy is withered away. An old man with icy heart and peevish temper and greedy craft, an old man who cannot pray, who cannot lean his broken strength upon God, is a sad sight—harvest past, the summer ended, and not saved.

Would'st thou the veiléd future read?
The harvest answereth to the seed.
Shall Heaven e'er crown the Victor's brow?
Ask tidings of the battle *now*.

The Celestial Surgeon

Jer. viii. 22.—' Is there no balm in Gilead; is there no physician there?'

LONG years ago Jeremiah faced a world of unrest and convulsion not unlike our own. And the question he then asked is like the questions we are asking to-day, in a mood bordering on despair. In a world where there is enough and to spare for all, how is it that so many are in want? With thousands of years of the experiment of living, where one would look for progress and peace, why does one devastating war succeed another, with the prospect of race suicide? Is there no medicine for a sick world? Is there no skilled physician to prescribe for it? Is there no daring surgeon to operate upon it?

We Christians believe that Jesus Christ has much that is vital to say to a sick world and a sick soul. Let us consider His credentials for such a task.

' A great surgeon,' it has been said, ' must have three gifts—the eye of an eagle, the heart of a lion, and the hand of a woman.' May we not ascribe these three qualifications to Jesus Christ, the Son of God?

1. *The Eye of an Eagle.*—No reader of the New Testament can fail to note Christ's unerring and instantaneous diagnosis of human ills. As a thoughtful writer has said—' Turning over the pages of the Gospels reminds us of the consulting-room of a famous physician. As the patients pass one after the other into the presence of the great man, one who had looked in casually on account of what he thought a slight ailment receives his death sentence ; and another who thought he was a victim of a fatal disease is relieved to find he is suffering from some common and trifling malady.' One can see this kind of thing happening again and again in the pages of the Gospels. We watch these people in Christ's waiting-room—the Rich Young Ruler, Nicodemus, the Woman by the Well, Matthew and Zaccheus and a host of nameless folk. We watch them coming in and going out. Here is a man who comes to Christ with a loud grievance. He has shared in a legacy which has brought family bitternesses, as legacies often do. What has the Master to say in the situation ? Will He reason with the domineering brother who has had more than his share ? Swiftly the eye of Jesus pierces through these irrelevancies to the trouble in the man's own heart. ' Take heed and beware of covetousness, for a man's life consisteth not in the abundance of the things he possesseth.'

Already the economist, the politician, the scientist are preparing for the salvage of a broken world. While they are busy with their stupendous and necessary tasks, the eye of Christ glances deep down into the desperate state of the body politic, and He has His own word to say. These racial hatreds, this class selfishness, the greed, the ambition, the inordinate love of pleasure which makes a business of it and so for ever defeats its own end—how shall these cancers be eradicated from the human heart ? *If Christ cannot help us here, who can ?* Woe be to us in the pangs of a post-war world if we refuse to pay heed to the diagnosis of the Divine Physician and proceed once more to build a new world on sinking sand.

So is it with the individual. Men shun this ' kind but searching glance.' All the while they know in their inmost hearts that there is no escape from the final word He pronounces on our self-centred lives. Let us place ourselves with perfect abandon in the hands of the healing Christ. Let us offer ourselves to Him as we are, without extenuation, without reserve. Let us bring into the white light of His Divine scrutiny all our inner unrest, our sloth, our indiscipline, our touchiness, our jealousies and littlenesses, all the wounds which shame would hide and, in His mercy, He will heal them all.

2. *The Heart of a Lion.*—The second qualification of a great surgeon is courage to operate. Recall that grim parable in which our Lord's inexorable sense of truth is arrestingly set forth. ' If thy right hand offend thee, cut it off, for your life. If thy right eye offend thee, pluck it out, for your life.' Stern words these, answering to life's stern facts. In countless hospitals in peace, in casualty-clearing stations in war, this kind of thing is a daily occurrence. What sane man would refuse to give a hand or an eye to save his life ? Christ stands to-day in the midst of a world gone wrong and makes His ruthless diagnosis of those ills that are the root causes of our present confusions and disasters. Beneath all the economic maladies He probes to those ever-recurring evils in the human heart that put us wrong with God and man. ' Wilt thou be made whole ? ' He asks, as He asked of old. Are we willing to pay the price in humbled pride, in patient investigation, in adventurous experiment, in just and severe reparation, whereby alone man may learn at long last to dwell in amity and justice with his fellow-man ? Only those who choose to linger on in the fool's paradise of wishful thinking will blind themselves to the life-or-death nature of the operation about to be performed on our national life before we can build a better world.

And this is true also of our personal life. In the heart of most men there are hidden compromises and secret concordats with sin which make a mockery of any hope of spiritual well-being. Needless to say, with everything that cannot bear the light of day, in business, in personal intercourse, in all the doublings and hedgings of our inmost heart, Christ, in His very love, is pitilessly surgical. ' Cut them off—for your life ' is His relentless formula. We do not pay a great surgeon to talk platitudes, to express sympathy, to suggest deluding hopes. We go to him that he and we may face the facts and deal with them.

Shakespeare has a great, comforting line—' There is no time so miserable but a man may be true.' That is to say, there is never a desperate entanglement into which we have been led by folly or sin but we may rise to our feet, trudge back to the point in our life where we first, consciously, went wrong and, in humble contrition, spread our inner treachery before the keen eye of Christ. To anyone with any real sensitiveness of spirit, there is no misery like secret estrangement from God. It is to be wrong at the centre of our being, and therefore wrong everywhere. And conversely, to such a one, there is no joy on earth like being restored to a calm and happy walk with God by the healing Christ.

> See the Wretch, that long has tost
>   On the thorny bed of Pain,
> At length repair his vigour lost,
>   And breathe and walk again ;
> The meanest flowret of the vale,
> The simplest note that swells the gale,
> The common Sun, the air, the skies,
> To him are opening Paradise.

3. *The Hand of a Woman.*—There is a scene in John's Gospel which describes as no other incident can the intimate touch of Jesus. Into the pure presence of the Son of God a poor, erring woman is brought, hounded on by a group of merciless Pharisees. As they snarl at her frailty and call down on her the last punishment of the Jewish Law, Jesus is overcome by their brutal inhumanity and hides His burning confusion by stooping to write upon the ground. Quietly, His piercing words go forth with deadly effect. 'He that is without sin among you, let him first cast a stone at her.' And again He stoops down and writes upon the ground. 'And they which heard it, being convicted by their own conscience, went out one by one, beginning at the eldest, even unto the last.' And so there are left alone the holy Christ and the poor, soiled woman. How perfect is His healing touch! 'Hath no man condemned thee ? ' He asked. She said, ' No man, Lord.' And Jesus said unto her ' Neither do I condemn thee. Go and sin no more.'

It is the glory of the Divine Healer that He has no stereotyped way of dealing with our spiritual maladies and diseases. Just as one is often impressed, in the company of a great consulting surgeon, with his calmness, with the thought that he is utterly at your disposal and is concentrating on you, so do we feel, in Christ's presence, that, in our fears and distresses, He offers to us personally all His Divine knowledge of the human heart. He has no ' cases.' He does not deal with Peter as He deals with John, nor with the young as with the old. Moreover, His methods are ever born of the insight of love.

¶ Says Victor Hugo of the good bishop in *Les Misérables*—' He understood how to sit down and hold his peace for long hours beside the man who had lost the wife of his love or the mother who had lost her child. As he knew the moment for silence, he knew also the moment for speech.'

Two thoughts seem to emerge from all this. The question arises for many of us as we take our shoes from off our feet, standing as we do on the holy ground of the personal suffering born of a cruel war. Do we Christians ever aspire to heal the sorrows of others ? Do we pray for the delicate touch of Jesus ? What a sphere of abundantly rewarding service opens up to any one so disposed ! The lonely, the bereaved, the anxious, men and women of broken hopes in business, in family, in heart—all these are ever with us, silent claimants for our sympathy and comradeship. May it not be our unique contribution to the war effort that we may convince these afflicted ones that they can lean on us in their Gethsemane ? To few of us will be given the power to explain to some one in mental travail the why and wherefore of all the ghastly tragedy of war. But to any one of us who would be done with self-seeking will it be given to put ourselves feelingly and whole-heartedly at the disposal of others in silent, healing sympathy.

¶ Lord Grey mentions an instance of his anxiety to find some simple word which might remain in the mind of those he sought to help. ' Some,' he said to a mother who in the first days of the war had heard that her son was missing, ' have more to lay upon the Altar than others.' [1]

The other thought concerns our own personal relationship to Jesus Christ. Is it an infrequent occurrence in life for men and women to put off a visit to a specialist, to live for months and even years in pining dread, then, in the end, to face the worst, to offer themselves to his skill, and to find that skill triumphant and their worst fears disappointed as they fare forth once more to enjoy life ? To-day, then, let us seek the Divine Physician with any or every dark fear that is keeping us from the joy and freedom of walking

[1] Frances Horner, *Time Remembered*, 152.

peacefully with God and man. So shall we take our place amid the multitude whom no man can number, whom He hath 'ransomed, healed, restored, forgiven.' [1]

The Tears of Jeremiah

Jer. ix. 1.—'Oh that my head were waters, and mine eyes a fountain of tears, that I might weep day and night for the slain of the daughter of my people!'

No other race can show a nobler dynasty of moral genius than the Hebrew; and in their long, troubled, revealing history there is no figure more heroic, none at once more tragic and triumphant than Jeremiah. Unfortunately his life has been misread; he has been made to appear as a lachrymose weakling, tender and tearful. He was indeed a man of sorrows and acquainted with grief, but he was no more a 'weeping prophet' because he may have written the Lamentations that bear his name than Tennyson was a weeping poet because he wrote 'In Memoriam,' or Milton because he wrote 'Lycidas.' If his head was a fountain of tears there was reason for it, because he was doomed to the saddest fate that can befall a great, true-hearted, clear-minded man—the fate, that is, of living in an age of decay, ruin, and disaster, seeing it all, warning his people against it, but powerless to stay or avert it.

1. *The Tears of a Patriot.*—Jeremiah was not weeping for his own sorrows. He might have done. He had many. And even a prophet may sometimes forget his people in the thought of his own troubles. When Elijah flung himself down under the juniper tree, and wished that he might die, his heart was full of the bitterness of a personal disappointment. There were times in Jeremiah's career when his own troubles overwhelmed him, and he poured out his soul in passionate reproaches to God. But here it is not for himself that he is weeping, it is for his nation. Jeremiah was big enough to feel the pathos of sorrows that were not his own—or rather, to make them his own through the power of a great sympathy.

The world's tears in the main are shed for personal troubles. For, naturally, we feel most keenly that which affects our own interests, or touches us through those we love. The mis-

[1] G. J. Jeffrey, *Christian Resources*, 52.

fortune that falls on our shoulders, the empty chair at our fireside—these are the things that draw our tears most readily. There is nothing wrong in that. The wrong is that some of us never get beyond that. We never break down the fences that mark off our personal and family life, and enter into the experiences of others. The most tragic poverty is that of the man whose narrowness of sympathy shuts him off from the joys and sorrows of his fellows. God has made us capable of going beyond the personal, and forgetting self in a warm and eager sympathy with others; and it is the sign of a big nature to be able thus to feel its oneness with the world outside and to carry communal burdens.

¶ Mary Tudor is reported to have said that, when she died, the word 'Calais' would be found written on her heart. Calais had belonged to the English for centuries, and was snatched from them in Mary's reign. She was a gloomy and cruel ruler, but she deserves credit for so losing herself in the national life as to feel a national humiliation so keenly.

Jeremiah was a true patriot. He rebuked his country, he threatened it, he opposed it—but he carried it on his heart. There is a spurious patriotism—an intolerant, bigoted, hysterical patriotism. From this counterfeit article we turn to the prophets to discover the real patriotism. They show us that love of country is not boasting about it, but suffering with it and for it.

Side by side with this picture of Jeremiah in tears let us place the companion picture of Jesus in tears. He was on His way to Jerusalem to be crucified, and He knew it, but that knowledge could not kill the love in His heart for it. 'Oh, Jerusalem, Jerusalem, thou that killest the prophets and stonest them that were sent unto thee, how often would I have gathered thee as a hen gathereth her brood under her wings—and ye would not.' Jeremiah and Jesus show us the patriotism of the breaking heart and there is no true patriotism that has not tears in it.

2. *The Tears of a Prophet.*—If any of Jeremiah's fellow-countrymen had heard his lament they would probably have laughed at it and at him. 'The slain of the daughter of my people —where are they?' they would have asked. 'Why, the nation is at peace. You are crying over imaginary troubles.' And they would have appeared right. Surely Jeremiah was foolishly

meeting trouble half-way, for the victims of war only existed in his own imagination. So it seemed, and yet Jeremiah was right ; far more so than the superficial scoffers who could not see beyond the facts of the moment. He had the vision which looks right into the heart of things, and which, because it sees the inner meaning of the movements of the age, knows what is going to happen. That is prophecy. Prophecy is not looking ahead, but looking into ; or perhaps we might say, it is looking ahead as a result of looking into. As Jeremiah pondered over the facts of the present—the shameless apostasy, the hollow worship, the false sense of security—there rose, vivid as an actual scene before him, the blood-red fields of slaughter on which their folly would be chastised ; and the sight filled his heart with a sorrow that tears could not relieve.

The prophet is one to whom God gives a clearer, deeper, truer vision than to the multitude. He is a seer. And the price he pays for his vision is that he gets nearer to the world's sorrow. Of course, his vision is not all sad. The deepest note of life is joy. But there is no way to joy but through the land of sorrow. The Hebrew prophets invariably predicted a happy future, but invariably it was to be reached through suffering.

When the two ambitious disciples begged for the highest places in the coming Kingdom, and Jesus met their selfish request with the solemn question : ' Are ye able to drink of the cup that I am about to drink of ? ' how startled they would have been if they had understood what He meant ! Not with such light-hearted eagerness would they have answered : ' We are able.' For what was the cup that Jesus was about to drink, and that He offers to share with His disciples ? Was it not fellowship with the world's suffering ?

Vision opens to us many and wondrous vistas —glory upon glory ; but if we are true seers and not mere dreamers, vision will show us the world's pain. In all the Jewish nation so near to disaster Jeremiah was the only man in tears because of that coming disaster, and God had privileged him to see the awful sight. Yes, *privileged*—for it is only he who sees and shares the world's sorrow that can help to heal it.

3. *The Tears of a Saint.*—It was the people's sin that most troubled Jeremiah. He could not but hold up the national life in the light of that ideal of righteousness which he had learned of God. And the sight of its blackness against that white background of purity filled him with shame and sorrow.

So long as evil remains in the world good men will shed tears. First of all for their own sin. We must begin there. When Isaiah saw the enthroned Lord in His ineffable holiness, the first impression made on his mind was of his own uncleanness, and before he heard the challenge, ' Whom shall I send ? ' his lips had to be touched with cleansing fire from the altar. There is a good deal of hollow and hypocritical moral indignation at the wrong-doing of other people, both in private and in public life—indignation that is worthless because it is unreal. Genuine moral indignation is healthy and helpful, but there is no virtue in it unless it is rooted in personal repentance.

But the good man, though he begins with deploring and fighting his own sin, does not stop there. He identifies himself with other sinners, and feels the pain of their sin. There is deep significance in the fact that Jesus was crucified between two robbers. Matthew says that thus the prophecy was fulfilled that ' He was numbered amongst the transgressors.' It was the outward symbol of a great inward fact—that Jesus, the Sinless One, had taken on His heart the burden of the world's sin. That is the way of redemption. It is the privilege of every man who has caught the spirit of Jesus to bear the sins of others on his heart. Such sorrow is the mark of Saviourhood. It is charged with healing power. Though the people little knew it, Jeremiah shedding tears over their sin was the mightiest redemptive force in the nation.

¶ He felt as his the starving of the poor, the shadow of curse on all, hard words, hard looks, and savage misery, and struggling deaths unpitied and unwept, rich brothers' sad satieties, the weary manner of their lives and deaths that want in love, and lacking love lack all, the heavy sorrow of the world, the horror of the things our brothers bear, the woe of things we make our brothers bear, our brothers and our sisters.[1]

A little later than Jeremiah another prophet drew a noble picture of a man who was wounded for the people's transgressions and bruised for their iniquities, who bore their griefs and carried their sorrows. We see the features of Jesus in

[1] H. S. Cripps, *The Death of St Francis.*

the picture ; but Old Testament scholars tell us that it was meant at first as a picture of Jeremiah or at least that it was his heroic tender figure that first suggested the great idea of vicarious suffering to which Jesus afterwards gave perfect expression. Jesus, a nobler, tenderer, more tragic and more triumphant figure than the prophet's—has wept for us. Does that mean nothing to us ? Does it not make us hate our sin, and bring us in penitent love to His feet ?

We have been wept over, and we should weep. Christ bore our sorrows and sins on His heart that we in turn, catching the passion of His Cross, might bear the sorrows and sins of others on our hearts. It is possible that our work for humanity may fail because, though it is earnestly and faithfully done, it is too hard, too mechanical, too soulless.

¶ In that lovely hymn of Bickersteth, based on the invitation of Jesus to His disciples to come apart and rest awhile, occurs this verse :

Come, tell Me all that ye have said and done,
Your victories and failures, hopes and fears ;
I know how hardly souls are wooed and won ;
My choicest wreaths are always wet with tears.

The world cannot accept the gospel of the Cross ; it still holds it foolishness. The world has a rival gospel—a gospel of blood and iron. There are tears in it of broken men, of widows and orphaned children, tears of misery and terror and shame—but the tears are not part of the gospel, they are the terrible fruit of it. That gospel has no note of redemption in it. In the Christian gospel it is the Saviour and not the sinner who goes to the Cross. There are tears in that gospel. God's tears, first of all, for a world of sin. Then our tears, as the love of God and the redemptive passion of Calvary sweep through our hearts.

The Balcony View of Life

Jer. ix. 2.—' Oh that I had in the wilderness a lodging place of wayfaring men ; that I might leave my people, and go from them ! '

1. PYTHAGORAS was once asked contemptuously by a Greek tyrant who he was and what was his particular business in the world. The philosopher replied that at the Olympic games some people came to try for the prizes, some

to dispose of their merchandise, some to enjoy themselves and meet their friends, and some to look on. ' I,' said Pythagoras, ' am one of those who come to look on at life.' Bacon, in telling the story, adds : ' But men must know that in this theatre of man's life it is reserved only for God and angels to be lookers-on.'

There are moments and moods when even a strong nature will feel tempted to escape, or to wish to escape, from the pressure of responsibility into a position where it would only be necessary to look on. Such was Jeremiah's case at this period of his career. He felt disappointed and disquieted with his age. He was at that critical phase of life when the first flush of enthusiasm, which throws men into eager contact with their fellows, has been succeeded by a profound sense of the corruption and self-will and greed which sometimes thwart an enterprise of religious or national reform. He had failed to carry the people with him ; he was unpopular ; and he was disheartened. At one moment he was ready to weep for his land. ' Oh that my head were waters, and mine eyes a fountain of tears, that I might weep day and night for the slain of the daughter of my people.' That is the anguish of a true patriot over evils which are being allowed to eat away the heart of a nation, over the rampant selfishness which forgets the rights and claims of God or of one's fellow-men, over the indifference of people to human pain and to Divine appeals.

But sensitive natures pass rapidly from pathos to irritation. Another mood now seizes Jeremiah. He longs to get away from the whole business. ' Oh that I had in the wilderness a lodging place of wayfaring men ; that I might leave my people, and go from them ! ' Now what does that cry mean ? Not simply the craving to escape from the sordid ingratitude and intrigues of men into ' God's free air and hope of better things.' Not simply the longing to exchange social treachery and the unrealities of the religious world for Nature's lonely, steadfast face in earth and sky, to hear nothing but the wind on the prairie and in the glens. Jeremiah does voice this disgust of a high-minded soul with the vices of a corrupt civilization, but his main thought is to be quit of responsibilities. He yearns for *a lodging-place of wayfaring men*. Not for a hermit's lonely cottage, nor for some hut of a recluse beside the Dead Sea, but for a khan or caravanserai. He was tired not so much of human beings as of responsibility for any of them. Out on the steppes, in a khan, he could still keep in touch with some currents of existence, and yet be no more than a cool, indifferent spectator.

¶ Lucretius, the Latin poet, commends those who seclude themselves in ' serene temples,' and hold themselves aloof from the busy life of the world :

But sweeter far to dwell remote, aloof
In some high mansion, built on Wisdom's hill :
Thence watch the errant crowd go to and fro,
Matching their wits, striving for precedence,
Toiling and moiling, hurrying night and day,
To rise to fortune and possess the world.

2. This corresponds to a mood which sometimes comes over us, a mood of dissatisfaction in which we would do almost anything to throw off our responsibilities for others in the home, the Church, or the State. We feel this whenever stupidity and selfishness get on our nerves, and when we think we cannot stand the strain any longer or be of any use to our immediate circle. Sometimes we can carry out our wishes. We can resign and withdraw from certain lines of service, if things do not go exactly as we want. But in many cases where we cannot alter our situation, the craving smoulders in the soul, and makes us cynical and superior, as if we had the right to be scornfully indifferent to the whole business.

It was not so with Jeremiah. His petulant irritation was only a passing mood. He recovered from it, as he realised after a while that God meant him to live among his kith and kin, suffering with them and for them as well as at their hands. In a passion of despair he broke out with the cry, ' Oh that I might leave my people.' But he did not leave them. He was too noble and generous at heart to become a mere looker-on. For this craving is a moral weakness. The heroic natures in every age are not seated on the balcony ; they are down among their fellow-men, bearing the strain and stress of their position, identifying themselves willingly with the people among whom it may have pleased God to cast their lot, and brave enough to meet

The fierce confederate storm
Of sorrow, barricaded evermore
Within the walls of cities.

¶ On the eve of his seventieth birthday Gladstone made this strange pathetic entry in his Diary : ' I am writing in the last minutes of the seventh decade of my life. This closing is a great event. The days of our life are three-score years and ten. It is hardly possible that I should complete another decade. How much or how little of this will God give me for the purposes dear to my heart ? Ah ! what need have I of what I may term spiritual leisure, to be out of the dust and heat and blast and strain, before I pass into the unseen world.' [1] He had then more than eighteen years to live. Within four months of writing those lines he was again Prime Minister. There lay before him more dust and heat and strain than had been crowded into the same number of years of his life before, and the mighty voice which had died down into these plaintive tones shook the civilized world again.

3. This heroic identification of himself with the interests of a faulty people marks out Jeremiah as a prototype of Jesus. When our Lord was on earth, some of His contemporaries were reminded of Jeremiah. ' Whom do men say that I am ? Some say, Jeremiah.' Why, we are not told. But for us Jesus resembles Jeremiah in this at least, that He did identify Himself, though in a far deeper degree, with the interests of a self-willed and rebellious people. He, too, shared their reproach and put up with their misunderstandings and ingratitude, in order to carry out God's purpose. He, too, had to meet and master the temptation to decline further association with their unfaithfulness. ' O faithless and perverse generation,' He once broke out, ' how long shall I be with you and bear with you ! ' There were moments when the incredulity and obstinacy of men were almost too much even for His great patience. But He triumphed over all such inclinations to disavow responsibility for His race.

' Men must know that in this theatre of man's life it is reserved only for God and angels to be lookers-on.' Must they ? Can they not win a better knowledge from the revelation of our Lord ? What does His life mean but that we have a God who is not content to be a looker-on, a God who identifies Himself to the uttermost with our eternal interests, a God who, instead of being our judge at the end and meantime the watcher of our little, foolish ways, enters into the

[1] Morley, *The Life of Gladstone*, ii. 597.

heart of our struggle through Him who came to bear our sins and carry our sorrows ? This is the gospel we receive from One who reminded men of Jeremiah—not of the Jeremiah who once longed to cast off his responsibilities, but of the greater Jeremiah who went back heroically to share his people's lot.

It is a gospel which forbids any despair of ourselves. After what Jesus has done and suffered on our behalf, we never can suspect that God will leave His people, as if He could no longer bear to have any part or lot in their ungracious lives. Christ is still one with our race in the redeeming purpose of the Father. He does not hold aloof. He is no looker-on at the little tragedies and comedies of our existence. He has made Himself responsible for us ; that is the strength and wonder of His gospel. He will not lose His interest in us, despite the errors and the emptiness of our days. He at least will never leave His people, such is the strong love and the long-suffering of His Heart towards us.

A Nation's Glory

Jer. ix. 23, 24.—' Thus saith the Lord, Let not the wise man glory in his wisdom, neither let the mighty man glory in his might, let not the rich man glory in his riches : But let him that glorieth glory in this, that he understandeth and knoweth me, that I am the Lord which exercise loving-kindness, judgment, and righteousness, in the earth : for in these things I delight, saith the Lord.'

1. TO-DAY no word of the prophets is of greater value than this word of Jeremiah from the Lord, in which the real glory of a nation is set forth. In what does true national glory consist ? Israel and Judah thought that it lay in the possession of three things—wealth, might and wisdom. A long peace had enabled them to accumulate enormous wealth. They had for that day a large army. Jerusalem was an impregnable fortress, so they imagined. And they had some clever statesmen who had concluded fine alliances or treaties with other powers. Nothing could be better. With such a trinity they were invincible. They made it their boast. Jeremiah brands the whole thing as false. He tells them that their supposed glory was their deadly peril. Their wealth excited the cupidity of other peoples ; their army invited a contest ; their statesmanship bred craftiness with its train of miseries. And to support his censure, he points to the darkening horizon and shows that Babylon and Egypt were gathering to the spoil. ' Your true glory,' he cries, ' does not lie in these things, but in another direction altogether. It consists in a spiritual response to God, who stands for loving-kindness, judgment and righteousness. If you would be secure you must delight in the things in which God delights.' In so speaking to his own people Jeremiah speaks to the whole world and for all time.

It is not necessary to labour the point that wisdom, might and wealth are real elements in the life of all progressive peoples. We need able men, strong men, rich men, in the fullest content of these words. This trinity of forces can advance a nation's life to an immeasurable degree. Wisdom, might and wealth, however, are only really useful to a people as they enable it to fulfil its providential mission in the world. And what is that mission ? It is to promote those things in which God delights, namely, ' loving-kindness, judgment and righteousness.' A nation has no other end than that. All its forces are given to it in order that it may discharge the mission assigned to it by God. For all nations exist by Him and for Him. That is the main truth we have to get home to the human conscience to-day. Each nation is a fraction of a large humanity which has its home upon the earth. But the earth itself is a fraction of something greater—the universe. And neither the separate nation nor humanity as a whole fulfils its mission unless it accomplishes the will of Him who is the Lord of all worlds.

(1) Look at *wisdom divorced from God*. By ' wisdom ' Jeremiah here means chiefly political sagacity ; but the word may be used to cover a larger field. Wisdom amongst a people is a most desirable thing, but when ' wisdom '—whether personal or political—becomes our ' glory,' our boast, and is distended to absurd dimensions, then it offers a great peril to a people. At the very best our fullest knowledge is but relative, partial, ever changing, and a mere fraction of what remains to be known. To make a god of it and to worship it is the most foolish thing conceivable. Knowledge and wisdom—which, after all, are gifts of God to us—are intended for the making of character, and were never meant to be ends in themselves. But no ' character ' is worthy unless at the heart of it there is harmony with the eternal wisdom, which, above all else, is marked by loving-kindness.

¶ It has been the tragedy of Europe during the

last few decades that it has had leaders destitute of morality and religion ; men who deemed their own cleverness sufficient to lead the world ; men who were so important in their own esteem that they imagined themselves to be the rulers of heaven and earth. The present calamities of the world are not due to the common people, but to their vain, boastful and unscrupulous leaders who have disdained all dependence upon the Divine wisdom and who have dragged mankind to the verge of the abyss.

(2) Look now at *might divorced from God.* By ' strength ' here Jeremiah intends, primarily, military strength. But, again, we may use the word to cover the entire range of brute force as employed by man. No wise person would make light of the advantages to a nation of a fine physical manhood. It is well that we cultivate the athletic qualities and that we seek to eliminate weakness from the race. But men are slow to believe that strength of this kind is not the highest kind of strength. At the best it is but brute force, which, as life wears on, gradually lessens, until it wholly fails. It is nothing to ' glory ' in, when it is remembered that man's highest distinction lies in the mental and spiritual realms. When might of any kind is placed under moral direction it becomes a great auxiliary of justice ; but when it is divorced from God, the source of all strength, and becomes a subject of vainglory, then it is turned into an enemy of ' judgment '—a contradiction of that in which God delights.

(3) Look also at *wealth divorced from God.* Jeremiah intended by ' riches ' not simply private wealth, but national material prosperity. Again, we use the word to cover the entire field. It is both idle and stupid to utter a tirade against wealth, which is inevitable where industry and commerce are efficiently conducted. Wealth has a great mission. By its means the arts and sciences can be developed and beauty cultivated. Placed under the empire of moral ideas, wealth can further the very highest human interests. It becomes a medium for securing human weal—wealth of life, thought and happiness. But when it is divorced from morality—that is, from God—it is converted into a weapon of injustice ; it opposes that in which God delights. Wealth perverted to selfish uses issues in all kinds of crookedness— the opposite of rectitude.

¶ ' No evil,' says the Greek poet, ' so great as money ever was current among mankind. This lays waste cities, this drives men from their homes, this trains and perverts honest souls, so that they essay deeds of shame.'

The book of history is open for us to read. Its pages are full of the stories of nations that have passed away because they have gloried in their might and wisdom and wealth and neglected those things in which God delights— loving-kindness, judgment, and righteousness.

¶ This is the moral of the history of Jerusalem. She trusted in herself. She relied on her own wisdom, riches, and might, and would not know the Lord ; and therefore she was destroyed. Thus she is a warning to every nation, and to every individual in every age.[1]

2. In what does the true glory of a nation lie ? In this one thing only—a complete spiritual response to God, who delights in loving-kindness, judgment and righteousness. This, the prophet says, is to ' understand and know ' the living God. The ' knowledge ' of God is something far above intellectual speculations about His Nature and His ' essence ' ; something far above philosophical and credal statements about His mode of being. To know God is to make the practical and affectionate response of the child to the Father, to be one with His purpose, to reproduce His Spirit. It is our glory that we can thus know Him, for we are made in His likeness and image, and Christ has come to reattach us to Him. To know Him is more than entering upon an intellectual quest after Him. It is to be penitent, to be trustful, to be obedient, to be co-operative. It is knowledge in life and with living results in life. Nothing is barren in this knowledge ; all is vital—it breaks forth as loving-kindness, judgment and righteousness. A nation ' knowing ' God in this manner becomes morally invincible. Its wisdom, might and wealth do not go astray ; they are all placed at the service of God for the service of man. Their uses are moral. Within such a nation, wars, injustice, bitternesses and crookedness automatically cease. There is nothing upon which they can feed. The forces of the nation become constructive, not destructive.

We must enthrone the ideal and refuse to abandon it. But we must do more. We are called to enshrine it within ourselves ; to adjust our own personal life to the purpose of God ; to

[1] Bishop Wordsworth.

seek the things in which He delights. We can do that, whatever others do. Let us vow, from this day onwards, that our sole glory shall be to know the Lord and to delight in those things in which He delights.

The Visitation of God

Jer. x. 15.—' They are vanity, and the work of errors : in the time of their visitation they shall perish.'

Luke xix. 44.—' And they shall not leave in thee one stone upon another ; because thou knewest not the time of thy visitation.'

1 Pet. ii. 12.—' Having your conversation honest among the Gentiles : that, whereas they speak against you as evildoers, they may by your good works, which they shall behold, glorify God in the day of visitation.'

IT is unfortunate that in English the phrase ' the visitation of God ' has acquired an uncomfortable and even sinister suggestion. When a man is struck with lightning or dies in some other way for which no one can be held responsible, the jury's verdict may be that he has died by the act or the visitation of God. But neither in the Old Testament nor in the New has the word any such gloomy association. As Cruden explains ' it means a coming for a special purpose, either to bless or to punish.' The prophet Ezekiel describes the process of this visitation in one aspect : ' Behold I will seek out my sheep and will deliver them out of all places where they have been scattered in the cloudy and the dark day. . . . I will seek that which was lost and bring again that which was driven away, I will bind up that which was broken and strengthen that which was sick, and I will save my flock.' That is the authentic visitation of God.

In each of the three phrases taken from Jeremiah, from Jesus, and from Peter an indication is given of what God does for men whom He comes to visit.

1. The hint which Jeremiah gives is that when God visits He at least *sees things as they are*. Our human seeing is always hindered by the haze of our likes and dislikes, our hopes and fears : we do not see things accurately, but often as we wish they might be, or as we fear they may be. In this tenth chapter we may observe how scornfully the prophet describes the process of manufacturing a god— silver is brought from Tarshish and beaten

into plates, gold comes from Uphaz into the hands of the goldsmith, purple and blue are required for the drapery ; but everything is the work of skilled craftsmen. Piece by piece the idol is built up by human hands, it is a manufactured article. But no one need suppose that the worshippers thus see their God : imagination plays its part in them, and fear of the unknown, and the power of ancient custom. Renan compares the worship of the Church of Rome, in which he was brought up, to a curtain of gorgeous brocade and cloth of gold—sumptuous and artistic and imaginative in its appeal ; but it is stretched across the black emptiness. If any hand were bold enough to pull the screen aside, the world would know that there is nothing behind ; but for the multitude the splendid illusion suffices, and its credit remains unchallenged. The same assertion might be made of the pomp and parade of other Churches, with their flourish of statistics which on paper look so well ; but what lies at the back of them ? What of substance is actually achieved ?

Aye, and what if God should visit ? asks the prophet : He will not be duped by the most elaborate of human devices, for His eyes are as a flame of fire. And thus of all manufactured deities and sanctities it is written : ' They are vanity, a work of delusion : in the time of their visitation they shall perish.' Makebelieves have no chance when God appears, and their judgment is declared as soon as they are seen.

But we must not think of God's visitation as altogether merciless and exposing, for it also brings to light, as Jesus tells us, a wealth of hidden virtue and unsuspected beauty. People who have always thought humbly of themselves, and whose neighbours have taken them at the same valuation, will then be seen shining like stars. Kind deeds, says Jesus, which you did instinctively and thought nothing of, will then be remembered ; for in His visitation God sees all things and all people as they are, and the stumbling, oft-discouraged man will then be acknowledged as God's friend.

2. When Jesus Himself spoke of this visitation He thought of God as coming not merely to see things as they are, but *to make them different*. Jerusalem's day of visitation arrived when God, with His help and wonder had

appeared—'God manifest in the flesh'; and to the same end He comes to us to-day.

In that age, as in our own, religion had grown largely formal, and though devout people prayed earnestly, the majority treated worship mainly as a matter of outward performance. The heart of man is great and spacious, needing big things to fill it, yet when God was offering them the greatest of all they were content to engage themselves with ritual.

The things offered were immeasurably great : in Luke's Gospel one lovely phrase is used to describe them—'the dayspring from on high,' a kind of heavenly dawn ready to break in upon the greyness of their bleak existence. As Paul puts it in one place, what happened in his life was only comparable to the creation of light—when the sun flamed up in the heavens ; or when, long afterwards, one day groping and feeling its way through the darkness and vapour that enshrouded it, there came a just perceptible dimness, a greyness less black than the dark, that flickered on earth's face, and stayed. Light had come ! And behind it trooped a whole infinity of unthinkable consequences— warmth, colour, beauty, life itself. 'And,' says Paul, 'that day God, who made the light once to shine out of darkness, caused it to touch my cold, dark, sterile heart.'

¶ Thomas Erskine of Linlathen, after speaking of the bewildering silences of God, makes this grand addition : ' He has not always been silent to me. . . . I have felt the power of His love, that God is love and that He loves me . . . yes, God has broken silence to me.' That was the visitation of God to Erskine—the unveiling of His heart, His proffered help.

But the mystery and the misery of human life is that to so many He makes approach in vain. To us it is given as a promise that ' whosoever knocketh to him it shall be opened ' ; but no such promise is given to the Lord and Lover of men, who continually is denied admittance. About many of us He has still to report : ' I was a stranger, and ye took me not in,' and on our side it is true that in a world visited and pervaded by the God of all fullness we remain obstinately poor.

3. When Peter speaks of the visitation of God he is thinking of a change of mood which it may work even in the unlikeliest of men. It was his lot to live when the tiny Christian communities were lost in a shoreless ocean of paganism. By word and by life the friends of Jesus did their best to commend their Master to a hostile world, but years ran away and there was little to show for all their effort. The cynical minister of a degraded Edinburgh parish once said that certainly one could make an impression on it, just as he might on a bowl of treacle so long as he kept his thumb in it ; but withdraw the thumb, and the dimple disappears. That was the judgment of a shrewd and witty man, but does it cover all the facts ? Peter, at least, was convinced that in many of these disdainful pagans to whom he had appealed there were unconfessed secrets of disquiet, which some day might transform the whole situation.

This discovery of latent possibilities in our human nature is not confined to religion : a miner of no particular credit will send his married companion up the shaft first for the sake of his wife and bairns, whilst he remains himself to die : a stewardess rushes back into the blazing cabin to drag through smoke and flame a stranger girl committed to her charge. It is magnificent, but we must not therefore think that these are of wholly different stuff from their fellows ; for possibilities of the same kind exist in utterly commonplace men and women about us, who pass through life without ever once disclosing what is in them. Only it is there, and on some fit occasion it may break through in splendour. That, certainly, was Peter's thought of the visitation of God. Grant that we Christians make little way, that our efforts are constantly baffled ; yet under the surface in these stubborn neighbours of ours the forces of God may be working, and some day their mood will change and our witness find a welcome. And they will glorify God in the day of their visitation.

This is what in our churches we should eagerly desire—a quickened sense in the hearers of the meaning of what has long been familiar. What makes the difference in a congregation between the eager and the slack is not their degree of knowledge but of discernment. The German poet Nietzsche exclaims with rapture in one place : ' Awake and listen, ye lonely ones, for good tidings are coming to fine ears ! ' ' If any man hear my voice,' said Jesus, ' and open the door '—that is the change of mood which Peter looked for and for which we ought to pray, when at length a man hears the Master speaking, and opens—and Christ Himself comes in.

St. Peter once : ' Lord, dost Thou wash my
    feet ? '
    Much more I say : Lord, dost Thou stand
      and knock,
At my closed heart more rugged than a rock,
Bolted and barred, for Thy soft touch unmeet,
Nor garnished nor in any wise made sweet ?
    Owls roost within and dancing satyrs mock.
Lord, I have heard the crowing of the cock,
And have not wept : ah, Lord, Thou knowest
    it.
Yet still I hear Thee knocking. Still I hear :
' Open to Me, look on Me eye to eye
    That I may wring thy heart and make it
      whole ;
And teach thee love because I hold thee dear,
    And sup with thee in gladness soul with soul,
And sup with thee in glory by and by.'

Our Attitude to Grief

Jer. x. 19.—' This is a grief, and I must bear it.'

THERE come times in people's lives when grief is such a great word that they cannot utter another—when the past is powerless, and the future is grey. What is to be done ? What is the solution of the bitter situation ? These questions concern us all, for we know that the grey thread of sorrow is woven soon or late into the fabric of every life, and we need to be, in some wise, prepared for the pain of the weaving. It will do us all good to meet and talk with a man who was prepared for his dark day. The shadow fell on Jeremiah's life and he said, ' Woe is me for my hurt ! My wound is grievous '—but he added, ' This is a grief, and I must bear it.'

1. Here we see a man of God in the hour of his adversity. ' Woe is me ! ' That is the one brief spasm of pain, that is the involuntary cry of the wounded heart ; but the man has himself in hand again very soon, and he says wisely, bravely, worthily, ' This is a grief—my grief—and I must bear it.' He was a prophet, and had not served God for nought. No man ever did. He had got beyond being frightened and bewildered and panic-stricken by the sorrowful surprises and painful changes of life. He recognized the place of grief in the mercy of God. Just as he would have said under other circumstances, ' This is a joy, this is a temptation, this is a duty ' ; so when the heart-break came he said, ' This is a grief.' It was a simple, brave admission that life must have its measure of sorrow, its chill shadows. He was not afraid of this word grief. It had some place in the great economy of the soul. It was not an enemy, not an interloper, not an accident. When the grey-clad messenger of sorrow crossed the threshold of his heart, and darkened the tiny room of life for him, he greeted him as one whose credentials were perfectly satisfactory ; only those same credentials were written in the cramped and crooked handwriting of pain, and in a language that it takes a man most of a lifetime to interpret.

That is what faith in God does for a man in the day of his great need. No panic, no flurry ; no ill-considered protestations. It makes a man quiet and self-contained, and dignified, and perfectly patient. The religion of the Old Testament (and infinitely more does this apply to the religion of the New Testament) dares to recognise grief—dares to accord it a place in the things that work together for good. Without the philosophy and inspiration of such faith, a man misunderstands his grief, resents it, questions its rights, refuses to believe that it can possibly serve a good and a lofty end. To the man of the world, sorrow is an intruder, it is a catastrophe. When it finds its way into his life, things are going wrong, and the best of life is imperilled. He is taken by surprise, frightened, perplexed, shaken. For the simple words of the prophet, ' It is a grief,' he substitutes an earthlier saying of his own : ' It is a mistake, a blunder, a cruelty, a hindrance. It does not belong to my life—it ought not to be here. How can I speedily be rid of it ? '

When the shadow falls on our life, as it certainly will fall, it will be something to know that the light that casts the shadow is the light of eternal love ; it will be much if, without misgiving, without panic-stricken cowardice, without blind resistance, we can say, ' It is a grief—it is my share of this world's sadness, bringing me nearer to my share of the other world's gladness.'

¶ The poet Southey's life was bound up in his son Herbert, who died at the age of nine. In the Fragmentary Thoughts occasioned by his son's death, broken fragments without connection, we catch echoes of his grief, but also of his Christian faith. Here are some of those fragments :

'Thy life was a day, and, sum it well, life is but a week of such days, with how much storm and cold and darkness !'

'Come, then,
Pain and infirmity—appointed guests,
My heart is ready.'

But the key to his victory is summed up in this fragment :

'My soul
Needed perhaps a longer discipline,
Or sorer penance, here.'

2. But further, after recognition must come submission. 'And I must bear it.' How may we gain this power of submission ?

First of all, by thinking upon God, who knows the whole measure and meaning of life's pain. How true the line we often sing, 'In every sorrow of the heart, Eternal Mercy bears a part.' God's good purpose runs through our saddened hours. It is then that pride dies and sympathy is born. But if we forget God we reverse this order of things. We grow narrower and colder and harder. We drift into cynicism and pessimism. We are the worse instead of the better for our tears.

Whether amid the things that grieve us we win a blessing or gain a curse, depends on how we bear them. We must bear the pain ; we may miss the benediction ; we must pass into the mists, but it is ours to say whether we pass out of them again into the lowlands of peevishness and ill-temper, or the uplands of large sympathies and braver endurance.

¶ In Fuchow there are three graves side by side. Two of them are the graves of the daughters of a widow in Australia. Those two girls went out as missionaries to China and they were both murdered. When the news came to the widow in Australia that her daughters had been killed, she was sixty-two years of age. Do you think she sat down and refused to have anything more to do with God ? Do you think she was resentful or bitter or cynical ? Let me tell you what that woman did ! She sold all that she had. She went to the place where her two girls had been murdered. She learnt the Chinese language, set up a school, and gave twenty years of service to China. She died at the age of eighty-two and was buried near her daughters.[1]

Again, we may become submissive by remembering that quiet submission is necessary if we are to do our bit of work in the world. The first impulse of a stricken heart is to accept the dominion of sorrow to the exclusion of all other claims—to draw down the blinds of the many-roomed house of life, shutting out all sunshine and sound. We cannot help obeying this impulse for a few hours ; but we wrong ourselves and our brethren if we continue to keep the blinds drawn and the door locked.

¶ The German poet, Heine, kept constant tryst with grief. His love for his father was like a flame in his heart, and long after his loss the poet wrote, 'I have tried for years to understand this loss, but never have I been able to overcome my grief at it.'

For one brief while we may give ourselves up to the luxury of grief, hearing only its voice, letting it range where it will through our life ; but that must not go on for long. When a sad heart makes idle hands, sorrow has missed its mark. We must not let life grow out of proportion—out of tune. God's work must be done in the world, and a brave man will go out to it, even if his heart be breaking. Perhaps it is well that the clamour, the claims, and the hard work, are always there waiting and calling for us. Indeed, there is so little time to grieve. Have you a grief ? Then ask God to help you to hide it in your heart, and go out and do your work. Very likely it will be better work than ever you did when life spelt joy—purer and more lasting.

¶ 'The occupation of work is the best thing for any one who has to bear great sorrow,' wrote Viscount Grey in December 1917 : 'If they have work in hand and strength to do it, and if they can sleep, the problem of how to endure life is solved for the present moment. Looking forward to the months and years that are to come is very dreary and depressing, but we do not live life in the lump, but day by day,

[1] L. D. Weatherhead, *The Eternal Voice*, 189.

and each day brings its own work and some expedient to help us.' [1]

If I should die, and leave you here awhile,
Be not like others sore undone, who keep
Long vigils by the silent dust, and weep.
For my sake, turn again to life, and smile,
Nerving thy heart and trembling hand to do
Something to comfort weaker hearts than
    thine.
Complete these dear unfinished tasks of mine,
And I, perchance, may therein comfort you!

Yet again, we can gain this grace of submission by thinking of the sorrows that other people have to bear. Face to face with our own heart's trouble—the dark figure sitting at the opening of life's little tent and blotting out half the sunshine—we have the splendid opportunity for developing that high courage that they must have who fight the battle for cheerfulness. There is a cheerfulness for which men and women have to fight, and in the many-sided battle of life there is nothing braver and worthier than that struggle. The coward says, ' This is a grief, and I must share it.' He presses many into the bearing of his burden. Every ear must hear his story, every one who looks in his face must read his trouble ; and never a day passes without his making somebody miserable. He is clamorous for sympathy, and there is no room in his soul for one thought concerning the heartache and pathos of other lives.

[1] G. M. Trevelyan, *Life of Viscount Grey of Fallodon*, 343.

¶ ' Self-pity,' said Dr William Brown of Harley Street recently, ' is a spiritual poison. The individual regresses, loses courage, and sinks into a state of depression. He blames himself, and has a feeling of unworthiness without being able to do anything about it. Even in the depressed state, when he seems to be blaming himself, the real trouble is his own lack of courage in facing problems.'

There is a nobler way of bearing grief than that. Listen to this story in the Old Testament. The Syrians were besieging Samaria, and the city was famine-stricken. Every one was wearing sackcloth as a sign of distress, save the king, and he still wore the bright robes that became his royalty. One day an awful scene, which scarcely bears repeating, caused him to rend his outer garments, and the people saw that beneath his kingly robe, he, too, was wearing sackcloth. Surely that was worthy a king. That is the royal way of bearing grief—without, the scarlet robe of cheerfulness—within, the sackcloth of a patient unobtrusive mourning. The clenched hand, and the tightened lips, and the grim, tense silence are not the signs of a man's triumph over his grief. That comes when the hand is stretched out to hearten his brother and the lips have learned the music of consolation. Let us go out of the darkened room of our experience with a smile and a song and a word of cheer. So shall God give back to us the light with which we seek to brighten other lives. This is the victorious bearing of grief. This is brave living. This is the triumph of religion.

FACING UP TO IT

Jer. xii. 5.—' If thou hast run with the footmen, and they have wearied thee, then how canst thou contend with horses ? and if in the land of peace, wherein thou trustedst, they wearied thee, then how wilt thou do in the swelling of Jordan ? '

THESE are grave questions, not easily answered. Addressed in the first instance to Jeremiah they were intended to check self-pity and brace the mind of the prophet. Addressed to us they are fitted to arrest the careless and to rouse us all to face up to the stern realities of life.

Jeremiah was manifestly of a sensitive and imaginative disposition, constitutionally timid and subject to dark forebodings. He had none of the natural boldness of his great predecessor Isaiah who, on receiving a vision of God and hearing a call for service, readily volunteered saying, ' Here am I, send me.' Jeremiah on the contrary had almost to be conscripted, for on hearing that he had been chosen from birth to be a prophet he shrank from his high destiny saying, 'Ah, Lord God, behold, I cannot speak : for I am a child.' His were no vain fears, for of all the prophets he had the most perilous and sorrowful ministry to fulfil, and his life was the most tragic of them all. Before he had gone very far he came up against the bitter opposition of his own people in Anathoth, his native town, and he felt very sore and discouraged over it. Then a thought flashed through his mind, which he recognized as a challenging Word of God, ' Will you faint at the first onset ? Are you going to let a little thing like that get you down ? How then will you face sterner foes, and how will you fare when you come into deeper waters ? If thou hast run with the footmen, and they have wearied thee, how canst thou contend with horses ? and if in the land of peace, wherein thou trustedst, they have wearied thee, how wilt thou do in the swelling of Jordan ? '

The expression, ' swelling of Jordan,' is rendered by modern translators as ' the pride of Jordan.' Down the broad valley of the Jordan there runs a winding strip of green which marks the course of the river. It lies deep below the general level of the valley, as deep in places as two hundred feet, and is a tangle of thick bush and driftwood which the river overflows in time of flood. This jungle is spoken of as the pride of Jordan. For instance Jeremiah speaks of a lion coming up out of the pride of Jordan, and it is held by many that in our text he is simply contrasting this jungle with more settled country. But the Septuagint renders the Hebrew by a Greek word expressive of the prancing of spirited horses, which would more appropriately indicate proud swelling waves than a jungle. The difference, however, is not vital, for Sir George Adam Smith, who prefers the translation ' jungle or rankness,' goes on to say, ' It is floods which have made the rankness, they fill this wider bed of Jordan every year.' [1] So we may retain the phrase, ' the swelling of Jordan,' which is the more expressive and is certainly more easily understood by the general reader.

Coming now to consider the teaching of our text and the application of its grave questions to ourselves we may find profit in seriously reflecting on two or three things.

1. *Don't raise such questions unnecessarily.*—

[1] *The Historical Geography of the Holy Land*, 485.

Many people who are imaginative and sensitive, as Jeremiah was, continually vex themselves by wondering what they would do if certain things were to happen to them. What if sickness came ? or bereavement ? or failure in business ? or loss of employment ? There is literally no end to such possibilities of trouble and sources of disquietude, and by raising them up as spectres before our minds we may keep ourselves in perpetual misery. Not without reason, therefore, our Lord has so expressly forbidden us to brood with anxiety on the possibilities of the future. ' Do not worry about to-morrow ; to-morrow will have worries of its own.' This counsel finds support in the homely wisdom of mankind, expressed in such proverbs as ' Don't cross your bridges before you come to them,' and ' Never meet your troubles half-way.' Take life as it comes, a day at a time, and you will find it manageable or at least tolerable. If we were asked to undertake a journey of a thousand miles on foot we should probably think it a formidable task, but going about our ordinary business and walking no more than three miles a day we more than cover the distance in a year.

Why then should we vex ourselves with the unknown possibilities of the future ? There are horsemen we may never have to contend with, swellings of Jordan we may never be plunged into. The brave and devout Colonel Gardiner, who fell at the battle of Prestonpans, said, ' I have had many troubles in my life ; most of them never happened.' Some gloomy person once put the question to D. L. Moody, ' Have you grace for a dying day ? ' To which Moody, with his robust common sense, replied that meantime he had no need for such grace, but only for grace to carry on the mission on which he was at the moment engaged. And sure enough, leaving the future in the hands of God, he came through all right at the appointed time. To his family gathered round his death-bed he looked up and said brightly, ' The valley of the shadow ! There's no valley here.'

On a dark night in 1918 an anxious father and mother were groping their way through a hospital camp in France to visit their son who was reported to be dying. In the hospital they found their boy much better than was expected, and as they came out with uplifted hearts, the husband turned and said with great emphasis, ' It seems to me there has been a great deal of unnecessary worrying.' How many will have to make a like confession at the close of this war when they reflect on all their needless anxiety about the safety of loved ones whom they have now received home again, safe and sound ! And doubtless the same confession will fall to be made by all who have passed beyond the troubles and anxieties of this present life, and are able now to see how many battles they fought with shadows and how many of their days were darkened by needless fears.

2. *When God raises such questions, face up to them.*—Life is a serious business, and the conditions of life under which God in His providence has placed us raise tremendous questions which imperiously demand an answer. What dangers and enemies must we encounter, and what deep waters must we inevitably pass through ere our journey is done ! There is, to mention only one, the stern and inescapable fact of death, which is naturally suggested to our minds by the prophet's phrase ' the swelling of Jordan.' But death is fearsome because it is the symbol of something far greater than itself—that *Mysterium tremendum et fascinans*, as Otto calls it, that tremendous and all-encompassing mystery which overawes while it fascinates the mind. The sense of this mystery has haunted mankind throughout the ages. The enigmas of birth and death, the uncontrollable ravages of earthquake and flood and fire, the stealthy ' pestilence that walketh in darkness,' the silent influences of the sky, have taught men, even the most primitive, that the foundations of this our earthly house are insecure, that there is a fathomless deep below as there is an infinite height above, that the known is but a tiny spot of light in the midst of the dark unknown, that all our civilisations are but as a woodman's clearing, hewn out and rescued from the wild, but liable to be overrun and swept away, that our boasted mastery over Nature is but a vain imagination for we are at the mercy of forces which carry us on in their iron grip to the inevitable end.

And so men, dimly conscious of this mystery and vaguely haunted by its fears, have tried to hide themselves from it, and have pushed away the hateful thought of it. Religion has been spoken of as wishful thinking. Nothing could be further from the truth. Religion arises through the pressure of the eternal upon the reluctant mind of man. Religious truths are not pleasing dreams with which man has fondly beguiled himself, but truths from which he cannot escape. It is the irreligious man who indulges in wishful thinking, who refuses to face the truth, who welcomes every excuse for denying the reality of the spiritual and the eternal. It must be said that modern man is specially prone to this folly. He hates solitude and stillness and dreads the dark. His is far from the mood of the patriarch lifting his eyes to the silent stars, or the prophet in the wilderness hearing the still small voice, or the shepherd communing on the hills with God. He is most at home in the throng of his great cities where his garish lights drive back the encroaching dark, and the roar of the traffic and the ceaseless blare of the wireless shatter the stillness, and the distractions of social life make an end of solitude. Thus entrenched he can imagine for the moment that he is safe. It is a poor defence, like that of sailors on a sinking ship who deadened their sensibility with strong drink. Thus they drift along on ' blind night seas without a saving star,' until, when evil days come and they are caught in the swell of some deep trouble, they are bewildered, often resentful, and even mentally upset. The most eminent psychologists are agreed in holding that here is one chief source of the prevailing nervous disorders of our time, and they affirm that such disorders cannot be permanently cured unless the patient find some foundation for his life. Surely it is not only a duty, but the highest wisdom, bravely and calmly to face up to the great realities of life and death. It is the vagueness of the unknown which magnifies its terror, like some ghostly phantom looming through the dark. More clearly seen it loses half its fearfulness. Tennyson speaks of one who

faced the spectres of the mind
And laid them : thus he came at length
To find a stronger faith his own ;
    And Power was with him in the night,
    Which makes the darkness and the light,
And dwells not in the light alone.

Is not that what we all need ? Then we must not vainly strive to escape from the inevitable, nor evade God's questioning, but face up to it and have courage to ' see life steadily and see it whole.'

3. Finally, *what answer can be given to these grave questions ?* Jeremiah, it will be observed,

attempted no answer. He would have been ready to say in all humility with St Paul, 'Who is sufficient for these things?' Doubtless also he would have agreed with the Apostle that 'our sufficiency is of God.' And what more could any of us say? Who would dare to vouch for himself that he has strength to bear the strain and face the tremendous realities of life and death? To sing with Henley,

I am the master of my fate,
I am the captain of my soul

may have a heroic ring about it, but it is a vain imagination. His proud protest that

Under the bludgeonings of Chance
My head is bloody, but unbowed

is 'a fine mouthful,' as J. M. Barrie says, but it breathes a boastful and defiant spirit that ill becomes a frail and mortal man. The wisest are the humblest; the bravest are least confident of themselves, but deeply conscious of their own insufficiency are most ready to look for higher help to see them through. Must it not come to this with all of us? Are we able in our own strength to win the battle of life? When we encounter the ultimate realities will they be too much for us or will we prevail? God alone knows, and unless He answer for us we can have no assurance from any other source.

And He *does* answer for us, is willing in His grace to answer for us all. He answered for Jeremiah. To that most sensitive and shrinking man He said, 'Behold, I have made thee this day a defenced city, an iron pillar, and brazen walls against the whole land. . . . And they shall fight against thee, but they shall not prevail against thee; for I am with thee, saith the Lord, to deliver thee.' By this assurance the prophet was braced to encounter and endure the uttermost, and by God's help he won through. 'And this is the victory that overcometh the world, even our faith.' Hear the witness of the Psalmist, 'God is our refuge and strength, a very present help in trouble. Therefore will we not fear though the earth be removed, and the mountains be carried into the midst of the sea.' Or listen to the triumph song of St Paul, as he defies all the embattled hosts and the swelling tides, 'I am persuaded that neither death, nor life, nor angels, nor principalities, nor powers, nor things present, nor things to come, nor height, nor depth, nor any other creature, shall be able to separate us from the love of God, which is in Christ Jesus our Lord.'

This assurance, resting as it does, not on human strength and resolution, but on the grace and power of God, is given even to the weakest of His people. How can they, in their weakness, hope to contend with horses, and how will they do in the swelling of Jordan? But His promise is, 'When thou passest through the waters, I will be with thee; and through the rivers, they shall not overflow thee.' And many have given their testimony that when they came to the deep places of life, and even felt they would be overwhelmed, they were sustained beyond expectation, and carried through. Of all Bunyan's pilgrims Mr Despondency and his daughter Much-Afraid were the most hag-ridden by fears, but when they came in the end to the brink of Jordan Mr Despondency's last words were, 'Farewell night, welcome day,' and his daughter went through the river singing.

Is this your hope and stay? Have you found a sufficient answer to the grave questions that life raises? When you come face to face with the inevitable will your resources be found adequate? Will your anchor hold? Listen once more to the message of Jeremiah, 'Thus saith the Lord, Cursed be the man that trusteth in man, and maketh flesh his arm, and whose heart departeth from the Lord. For he shall be like the heath in the desert. . . . Blessed is the man that trusteth in the Lord, and whose hope the Lord is. For he shall be as a tree planted by the waters.' If you have not yet faced up to the stern realities of life and found the answer to its grave questions, then we can only say in all sincerity, 'God help you,' for all other help will fail.

J. H. MORRISON.

The Problem of Human Character

Jer. xiii. 23.—'Can the Ethiopian change his skin, or the leopard his spots? then may ye also do good, that are accustomed to do evil.'

1. IT is a difficult question to answer. It is difficult, not because it is unanswerable but because there are so many possible replies;

and it takes some discernment to recognize the right one.

(1) A cynic might answer the question by saying that men are bound to act according to their own nature, and that you cannot expect much of the average man, human nature being what it is.

(2) A scientist might answer that, given a certain formation of the brain and certain physical surroundings, people must inevitably act in a certain way.

(3) A person with another outlook might say that life consists in accepting ourselves and the circumstances in which our lot is cast, and in making the best of them. ' Why *should* the Ethiopian wish to change his skin ? Isn't a black skin as good as a white skin ? And, by the same token, why should a leopard wish to change his spots ? A leopard's spots are beauty-spots ! No creature in the wild has a more handsome coat than the leopard. And the best of it is that its *utility* is as marked as its *beauty*. The leopard might like to exchange his spots for the tiger's stripes. But Nature has designed the stripes of the tiger to suit the habits of the tiger, and the spots of the leopard to suit the ways of the leopard. The tiger prowls along the ground among reeds and saplings : in the dusk his stripes look for all the world like the tall and slender stems amidst which he stalks, and he is scarcely distinguishable from them. The leopard, on the other hand, is made to climb trees. He lies full length along the bough waiting for the unsuspecting gazelle to browse upon the soft grass beneath him. His coat is so like the colour of the bark that his presence on the branch can scarcely be detected, whilst his black and irregular spots are exactly like the shadows of the leaves. If the tiger had the leopard's spots they would act as danger-signals and his victims would never come near him : if the leopard had the tiger's stripes the gazelle would see them from afar and fly in terror. The tiger's stripes are perfectly suited to the tiger ; the leopard's spots are the very thing for the leopard ; why then should either wish to change them ? [1]

The writer of the Book of Proverbs says, ' The conies are but a feeble folk, yet make they their houses in the rocks.' The conies accept the universe as they find it and the consequent handicaps it means for them. The rocks were there before them and were too great and strong for them to challenge. But the conies did not waste life in bemoaning their lot ; they accepted the situation as they found it and adjusted themselves to it in a brave and splendid way. Emerson says, ' There is a time in every man's education when he arrives at the conviction that he must take himself for better, for worse, as his portion ; that though the wide universe is full of good, no kernel of nourishing corn can come to him but through his toil bestowed on that plot of ground which is given him to till.' And, says Robert Browning in *Bishop Blougram's Apology* :

The common problem, yours, mine, every
        one's,
Is—not to fancy what were fair in life
Provided it could be,—but, finding first
What may be, then find how to make it fair
Up to our means : a very different thing !

We have to take the world as we find it, and ourselves as we find ourselves, receiving life gratefully and making the most of our limitations.

(4) But another person will answer that, while we must accept ourselves, it is wrong to acquiesce in ourselves and deny ambition. We are not to yield to a despondency that disables all effort, or make a virtue out of necessity as in *The Prisoner of Chillon* :

At last men came to set me free ;
I asked not why, and recked not where ;
It was at length the same to me,
Fettered or fetterless to be ;
I learned to love despair.
And thus, when they appeared at last,
And all my bonds aside were cast,
These heavy walls to me had grown
A hermitage—and all my own . . .
My very chains and I grew friends,
So much a long communion tends
To make us what we are.

It is because the Ethiopian is never satisfied with his skin, and the leopard never satisfied with his spots, that we go ahead and make progress. Complacency is a fatal gift. It is the noble dissatisfaction with existing conditions that has led the race from its primeval barbarism to its present culture.

¶ A workman once said to William James,

_____
[1] F. W. Boreham, *The Three Half-Moons*, 149.

the famous psychologist, 'There is not much difference between one man and another, but what there is is of great consequence.' It was a wise observation, for the difference is that one settles down without ambition while the other makes ambition the determining factor and allows no self-depreciation to make excuses.

2. But to come to the answer of Jeremiah himself. 'It might seem,' writes Professor Peake, 'as if he meant that evil-doing was as much man's nature, from which he could not escape, as the colour of an Ethiopian's skin or the spots of a leopard. But Jeremiah is not expressing so pessimistic a view of human nature as such, he is simply saying, with reference to the Jews, that they had grown so habituated to evil that it had become a second nature which it was hopeless for them to try to shake off. Jeremiah anticipates indeed an ultimate cleansing of Jerusalem, but, with sin so deeply engrained as the colour of an Ethiopian skin, and with a nature so trained and a will so inclined to wrong, it could be no swift process.' [1]

We cannot imagine Jeremiah, after all his preaching and appeals, saying to himself, 'What is the use of it all? Poor creatures, what can one expect, they are more to be pitied than to be blamed.' No, what he does say, is : 'You have by your own faults and follies made yourselves what you are.' His words contain a stern reproach, and that is their value for us. Instead of diminishing human responsibility they only intensify it. The very sting of the reproach lies in the fact that the illustration is so appropriate. Those addressed have so altered their nature that in its fixity and permanence it can be compared to the black skin of the negro or the spots of the leopard, with which the negro and the leopard have had nothing to do, and cannot help or in the slightest way modify; while they, on the other hand, have had everything to do with the colour of their character and the markings on it.

Now, probably, to most people who have thought over the matter, it will seem equally unreasonable to assert, on the one hand, that we, and we alone, are responsible for our characters and, on the other, to maintain that to all intents and purposes they are formed by outside influences, and by forces and factors over which we have no control. We are constantly

[1] *The Century Bible.*

hearing that our characters are to a large extent determined long before we can have any say in the matter ; and of course it is obvious that not only transmitted features, but training, home and social relationships, all sorts of influences which seem to lie outside our own individual personality, have had a share in moulding us and in making us what we are. In one sense our character is as much made for us as his skin is for the Ethiopian, or as its spots are for the leopard.

And yet, if we are healthy minded at all, both in judging ourselves and in judging others we, silently or openly, protest against the doctrine that our characters are for the most part the result of what is outside of ourselves ; or even if we do admit that such is the case, we make the admission very much in Jeremiah's sense. If a man allows his mind to be corrupted by reading certain books, or by taking up with a certain set, or gets into a certain way of looking at life owing to his habitual associations, no doubt the twist his character gets, or the set it takes, is the result of these outward circumstances, which from one point of view are in no sense of his making ; but all the same we invariably go on the supposition that he himself is there as well as the circumstances.

¶ We often quote, with approval, Robert Burns in his famous song, 'A man's a man for a' that,' for we see he meant that what makes a man is that he need not be the victim but may be the master of his circumstances. Or, as another great poet has put it :

A brute I might have been, but would not sink i' the scale.

But there is a truth suggested by the prophet's utterance even more important than the broad general truth of our responsibility for our character, the great truth, namely, of the persistence or continuity of character. It is only by degrees that our characters come to be what they are. We are every day, every month, every year, contributing to it. Every moral action, be it good or evil, increases its set in the one direction or the other, so that when we are face to face with evil or with good we have not to deal, so to speak, with the particular temptation or the particular call, but have behind us a solid force which determines us in the one direction rather than in the other. This is one of the most solemn truths of our spiritual life, and one which people who are ready enough to recognize their responsibility for their actions taken singly are too often blind to. It is only by a process extending over long ages that the skin of the Ethiopian has come to get its peculiar colour— it is only after countless changes that the markings of the leopard have come to have their fixed and peculiar form ; and it is only by a process extending as far back as childhood, and aided by a thousand acts on the part of the individual, that he comes to have this definite spiritual set we call character. He may vainly imagine that if circumstances were changed, or if some particular hindrance were taken out of the way, or some particular cause of provocation to unworthiness were removed, he would be a wholly different man ; but he has something far more permanent and solid to reckon with than circumstances or temptations or anything outward, namely, his own nature, this accumulation of past desires and actions and ways of looking at things, which make up character and of which he is himself the real creator, and which to the end he will have to reckon with.

3. When we come to realize this almost tragic truth of the permanence of character, we may sometimes be inclined in utter despondency to put the question to ourselves, ' Can the Ethiopian change his skin, or the leopard his spots ? then may ye also do good, who are accustomed to do evil.' But here, again, we must beware of falling into fatalism or despair. Just as in the case of the formation of character we must take ourselves into account as well as our circumstances, so here, while for our *warning* we are bound to realize the tremendous law of continuity or permanence, for our *encouragement*, for the free assertion of ourselves, for the sake of the gospel of Jesus Christ, we are equally bound to recognize the other great law of our moral life, the law of transformation of character.

Why should our Lord go on denouncing Jerusalem, weeping over it, if those children of the devil could by no possibility become the children of God ? Why should He keep Judas with Him to the last, if even his black heart might not yet be made white ? No one ever more solemnly and plainly laid down the great law of the permanence, of the continuity of character than did Christ ; and yet His whole saving activity was based on the other great and equally Divine law of the transformation of character—on the gracious, ever-hopeful belief that character can be fought with and changed.

Human nature cannot change itself, but human nature can be changed. Christ Jesus came into the world for that purpose, to provide an escape from the apparently inevitable, to give power to resist and overcome however unfavourable the circumstances, to bring into subjection things in life otherwise uncontrollable, to interfere with character so as to transform it anew. ' If any man be in Christ he is a new creature.' The gospel declares it. Human experience again and again proves it. ' If God be for us, who can be against us ? ' ' I can do all things through Christ who strengtheneth me.' For ' He is able to save them to the uttermost that come unto God by Him.'

¶ The success of prayer lies not in what God gives a man, but in what He makes him ; and if we could read the secret records we should meet hundreds and thousands and indeed millions of prayers thus successful—of men and women who by prayer have been delivered from every kind of bondage of sin and fear, of leopards who have completely and wonderfully changed their spots.[1]

An Absentee God

Jer. xiv. 8.—' O the hope of Israel, the saviour thereof in time of trouble, why shouldest thou be as a stranger in the land, and as a wayfaring man that turneth aside to tarry for a night ? '

THESE words are born out of dire calamity. Only those who have lived in the East, where the desert perpetually threatens and where rain is the condition of existence, can enter into Jeremiah's description of this great drought that had afflicted the land.

He depicts the gates—the gathering-places of the people—as black with the sackcloth of their grief and desolation. He draws the pathetic figures of the children returning from dry wells with empty pitchers and sorrowful hearts. He shows Nature driven through thirst to unnatural motherhood in forsaken calves, and the wild asses with staring eyes sniffing the wind for

[1] Sheila Kaye-Smith.

water. Unless it is the dramatic passages of the drought in Elijah's time to which Mendelssohn has wedded his immortal music, or the picture of the havoc of the locusts in the opening pages of Joel, there is perhaps nothing so poignant of its kind in the Bible as the passage before us here.

People were at their wits' end to know what to do. The only thing that could meet the need was rain, and to produce rain was utterly beyond the power of man. But what about God ? they asked. The rain is of God's creation. ' The rain cometh down, and the snow from heaven.' ' He sendeth the springs into the valleys that run among the hills.' Let us turn to God in penitence, and let us cry to Him for rain. ' Who can tell whether God will be gracious to us ? '

So they prayed to God for His help. But the situation remained entirely unaltered. The heavens were still like brass, and the sun beat down with the same unpitying splendour. They had appealed to prayer, and prayer, it seemed, had failed them. No one could do anything more ; people must simply wait until God changed His attitude and gave the rain His people longed for. But for Jeremiah to submit to this advice was impossible. He felt that men owed it to themselves to speak their minds quite frankly to God.

Jeremiah sees in his mind two things in antithesis, two things that ought to go together ; but now they stand in seeming opposition. The first is the world he lives in ; the world of Judah with the people he knows ; the cities and villages and steadings, crowded with people in great distress, and his sensitive soul was hurt ; hurt so much that he could not hold his peace. That sorrowful, suffering world haunted his mind with its pain. But, along with the sorrowful world, or rather over against it, standing, in fact, aloof from it, Jeremiah saw God as an absentee ; God as a mere spectator. ' A stranger in the land he once called his own ; a stranger who washed his hands of all responsibility for it.' ' A wayfaring man that turneth aside to tarry for a night ' ; a casual traveller who puts up His tent and stays where He is for the moment, but whose heart is far away, and who admits no kinship with the people He sees around Him. Nothing seems to arouse His compassion. He remains aloof and unaffected, a mere looker-on at the world's distresses. Jeremiah could not bear to think that the burden that weighed so heavily on him meant nothing at all to God. How could God bear to sit in heaven and see the misery of His world and yet never lift a finger to help it ? The thing to Jeremiah was utterly incomprehensible.

How can it be that God can reign in glory,
  Calmly content with what His Love has done,
Reading unmoved the piteous shameful story,
  All the vile deeds men do beneath the sun ? [1]

1. Many prophets and poets have felt about God exactly as Jeremiah did on this occasion. They have seen some gigantic evil, some terrible social wrong, and they have cried out fiercely against it. They have longed with all their soul to see it removed. They have cried to heaven for vengeance, and, when nothing has happened, they have denounced God. There in heaven is God, God with His wisdom and infinite power. But God does nothing ; He remains a mere looker-on.

¶ Recall that famous passage at the opening of *Sartor Resartus* in which Carlyle describes a city by night. ' That stifled hum of midnight, when traffic has lain down to rest ; and the chariot-wheels of vanity, still rolling here and there through distant streets, are bearing her to halls roofed-in, and lighted to the due pitch for her ; and only Vice and Misery, to prowl or to moan like nightbirds, are abroad.' ' Oh, under that hideous coverlet of vapours, and putrefactions, and unimaginable gases, what a Fermenting-vat lies simmering and hid.' And then Carlyle goes on to describe the picture in detail. Birth, death, happiness, misery, squalor, intrigue—he describes it all with a brilliance he never anywhere surpassed, and then he comes to his conclusion, or, rather, Teufelsdröckh, his hero, does. ' But I, *mein Werther*' I sit above it all ; I am alone with the stars.'

2. If we have to utter the prayer of Jeremiah, the fault may sometimes be our own. It was all very well for the people to ask God to come near them and not be as a stranger or an occasional visitor, but what welcome did they give Him ? Why should He tarry with men who had no desire to tarry with Him ? ' Thus saith the Lord unto this people, they have loved to wander, they have not refrained their feet.' Their own indifference was making it impossible for God to companion with them.

[1] G. A. Studdert Kennedy.

(1) *The picture of God as a stranger.*—Men love their country and their home. Heaven is God's home. If the land were not like heaven, God could not find a home there. That is the point with us. We need God, but do we want Him enough to make our land and our hearts His home? Can we say sincerely, ' Thy will be done in earth, as it is in heaven.' If we only call God in to get us out of difficulties, we can hardly expect Him to draw nearer to us. Jeremiah suggests the true approach to God. ' Why shouldest thou be as a stranger in the land?' We may make the words our own. We want things to be different from what they are. We want Christ in our life. He has been here, but we did not recognize Him. He did not feel at home. History has repeated itself. ' He came unto his own home, and his own received him not.'

(2) *The picture of God as a wayfarer.*—In our early days God is very near us, a friendly presence. But with many of us, this sense diminishes as the years pass by. Just as an inn is invaded, as the day progresses, by multifarious visitors, so does our life fill up with a host of new concerns. The thought of God is not so much argued away from our mind and heart; rather does it simply slip away and grow vague.

Our Lord more than once appeared in the guise of a traveller. It is said of Him that He was wearied with His journey. Once He could obtain no lodging for the night, as His face was as though He would go to Jerusalem. On the evening of His Resurrection day He fared better. He made as though He would have gone further, but His two companions constrained Him to stay with them that night. ' Abide with us, for it is towards evening, and the day is far spent.'

> A pilgrim through this lonely world
> The blessed Saviour pass'd.

The image of a traveller is not enough for us. A brief, an occasional visit from Him does not suffice. He wants to find in our hearts His home, to give us His perpetual Presence. ' Lo, I am with you all the days, even unto the end of the age.' His Presence continues with us, not as something fleeting and transitory, coupled specially with some moments of ecstatic transport, but unbroken, so far as it is unhindered.

God is *not* a wayfaring man that tarries for a night and then passes by ! We dare to correct this word of Jeremiah's. Nay, Jeremiah corrects it himself. No sooner has he sighed so plaintively about God than he turns within his soul and cries, ' Yet thou, O Lord, art in the midst of us ! ' God is never away. Though He seems to have visited us for a brief season and then departed, He is ever at hand, and asks of us only that we ' rise up and open the door.'

¶ Thou needst not seek Him here or there, He is not farther off than at the door of thy heart ; there He stands lingering, awaiting whoever is ready to open and let Him in. Thou needst not call to Him afar, He waits much more impatiently than thou for thee to open to Him. He longs for thee a thousandfold more urgently than thou for Him : one point the opening and the entering.[1]

3. The final answer to the complaint that God is ever a stranger or a wayfarer is in the Cross of Christ.

The Cross was an experience in time, but it represents an experience of God in eternity, an experience of God that is for ever true. God aloof from the world? God indifferent to its pains and wrongs and sins? Look at that Cross with open steadfast eyes and see if that is the impression we get.

> Inscribed upon the Cross we see
> In shining letters, God is Love.

Not goodness that stands aloof in pious contemplation, but love that suffers and gives itself in sacrifice.

(1) God suffers. The misery of the world is His, because He loves the world and longs to see it redeemed. ' In all our afflictions he is afflicted.' We cannot ever suffer what God does not share, and in the fiery hour of our deepest pain we may be sure that the Father's heart is quick to sympathize.

¶ Sir Oliver Lodge throws all his soul into a passionate passage that cries aloud that, though philosophers may scoff, what the human heart demands, and what, blessed be God's name, it finds in Christ, is a God who can yearn and love and sympathize and suffer. Yes, suffer ! Ah, with what suffering ! Can the insect with its dull insensitiveness ever begin to understand

[1] Meister Eckhart.

the agony of a man's breaking heart? I know that God foreknows all things; I know, unlike our puzzled and bewildered minds, He sees the end from the beginning; I know for Him there is no time nor space, no now and no hereafter. And yet and yet, how He is touched with the feeling of our infirmities, and how He is afflicted in all our afflictions only those know who have been in it with Him. It was no angel, cries a tried soul in the Old Testament, who helped me through my evil days, but God's own very Presence. No hand but His could have had a touch so understanding and so steadying. Don't talk to me, He says; I know. And, standing by the Cross, we also know.[1]

(2) The Cross proves not only the suffering of God; it also proves His triumph. Sin did its worst at the Cross; it contrived to bring to death the Lord of Glory; but the Cross was followed by the Resurrection, and that, to those who considered it, was the declaration of God's undefeated resources. The Cross is the pledge to humanity that God will never abandon His world, and the Resurrection that followed it is the pledge that victory, in spite of all, is assuredly His.

Jeremiah saw God apart from His world. But we see Him in Jesus Christ in close identification with it. The aloofness we speak of in God is due to our own limited way of seeing the problem. Let us come back again and again to the Cross, and in it we shall see that God is suffering with us and fighting for us, and out of His Cross our inspiration and victory will come.

God and Our Loneliness

Jer. xv. 17.—' I sat alone because of thy hand.'

IN the text the Hebrew prophet confesses the sense of loneliness. He feels separated from his fellows although he dwells in a crowded city. Those around him do not share in his deepest feelings. It is loneliness of soul, and yet he knows that this sense of solitude was not the result of chance. The Hand of God was in it, and there was purpose in this feeling of isolation. ' Only the wicked man is alone,' said Diderot, and there is truth in the remark. ' On the

[1] A. J. Gossip.

contrary,' adds Rousseau, ' only the good man is alone,' and that also contains truth. However we explain it, at times we feel around us ' the unplumbed salt estranging sea.' What the text suggests is that the experiences which make the soul solitary are not accidental things. We are alone because of God's Hand, and if we fail to recognize that, we miss the meaning and the message of these things. There are four experiences which come to all, and these bring this mood.

1. *The Loneliness of Responsibility.*—Every human soul has its life to live. Nothing can remove from our shoulders the responsibility for what we make of our lives. We may face this or shirk it, take life seriously or lightly, but in the deepest within us we acknowledge this responsibility. No matter how obscure our station, we have our influence. We are making it easier or harder for some one to see God's goodness. The way in which we live is helping or hindering that great power of grace which is in life. Our words and our deeds are like stones thrown into a pool of water, for the ripples spread ever outwards. We can refuse to admit the fact that we are responsible, but we cannot escape the result. We can drown for a little the sense that our life is ours and ours to answer for, but only for a little do we really forget, and back returns this devastating sense which separates us and makes us alone.

¶ ' Every soul in its sphere,' says Maeterlinck, ' has charge of a lighthouse.' It is ever on the fringe of things that lighthouses are set, in order that men may be warned of the dangers of the frontier, in order that they may at least know that here there is a risk of passing from an element that is altogether safe to one that is beset with infinite danger. Your opinion, even about what may seem trifling things, such as whether one has or has not the right to do what he likes with an odd pound-note or a casual glass of wine, may mean the opening or closing to another of a gambler's or a drunkard's grave. Every soul in its sphere has charge of a lighthouse.[1]

We are still alone, separated by the deep waters of personality from those around, but the loneliness has achieved its purpose if we have found through it the strength and succour of the Unseen. Man cannot live without God.

[1] Hubert L. Simpson.

Physically, mentally, morally, life and its responsibilities will break us if we have nothing beyond ourselves. God is the native atmosphere of the soul, and without God life becomes physically neurotic, intellectually lop-sided, spiritually cynical. But the loneliness of responsibility is not meant to destroy us but to lead us to what alone satisfies.

2. *The Loneliness of Consecration.*—' The man that God has touched,' observes Renan, ' is always a being apart.' The touch of God in the soul makes us alone. It is the solitude of the heights. There must come a time, if we are ever to grow up spiritually, when, as Newman says, ' there are only two things in the whole universe—our own soul and God who made it.' A home-sick farm-boy lies asleep on the hillside, and he dreams. The God of his fathers becomes his God, and Jacob is alone. Or, to take the most excellent example, we find the loneliness of consecration in the life of Jesus. The boy is lost, and His parents seek. In the Temple He is found, and lo ! Mary sees a new look on His face. He has outgrown the life of the home and family. The business of His Father He must needs do.

This loneliness of consecration belongs to youth. Only then is there the vigour and the freshness of the morning. Miss it then, and something is lost for ever. It is true that in any circumstance and at any age the burdened and broken human spirit can find the Eternal Saviour, but there is something about the consecration of the dawn which belongs not to experience. For God has so ordered life that the valour and splendour of our youth are the great opportunity. We may develop the impressions of our youth and confirm them through experience, but rarely will we look at the world afresh. Living can teach us many things. We learn thereby prudence and skill. We find out how to do things, but it is in the vision of youth we discover what to do. When the wonder of the world is breaking upon us, when life has a zest, when imagination can build its towering castles, when we can go forth to meet life, then it is possible as at no other time to feel that consecration which lights this earth with meaning and makes the glory of God manifest. The Lord God brings to the Eternal Kingdom each generation by its own path, and into the strange restless loneliness He calls the young soul in

order that it may see His face and find its Master.

' Christ with His lamp of truth
Sitteth upon the hill
Of everlasting youth
And calls ' to you.

3. *The Loneliness of Sorrow.*—There is another loneliness which comes into every life. He who has stood before the dark gates of death knows he must stand alone. When one who is dearer to us than life itself is taken from us, kind and compassionate our friends may be, real their sympathy, but the wound is in our soul, in our heart the stab. Alone we must climb the dark staircase to where there is light. When the disciples of John the Baptist came to Jesus with the bitter tidings of their Master's death, He said, ' Come ye yourselves apart.' And still God makes lonely in sorrow. The Hand of God is here. In the solitude of sorrow we see. Not in the brave light of the sun, but in the darkness, are the stars in their courses seen. ' I do not wonder at what men suffer, but I wonder at what they lose,' wrote Ruskin. How often has sorrow taught nothing, and the great lessons that might have been learned have been of no avail. The insight into life's meaning, the vision of sympathy have been lost because God's Hand was not felt. Through the gateway of our own sorrow we can enter into some sense of the largeness of God's purpose, and the Cross is to us more real thereby.

For from those ploughed up souls the spirit brings
Harvest at last, and sweet from bitter things.

Nathaniel Hawthorne suggests that God, having given man so many great and glorious gifts, lest this wonderful world should turn man's spirit into a clod, slipped in His gift of death. Do we find God there ? If not, hard and bitter will grow our lives. I sat alone because of Thy Hand. Alone with my sorrow, alone with the dark, gaunt things of life, away from the joy and converse, in order that I might be alone with God.

Feeble hands and helpless,
Groping blindly in the darkness,
Touch God's right hand in the darkness,
And are lifted up and strengthened.

4. *The Loneliness of Sin.*—'These wounds heal ill that men do give themselves.' And who has not wounded himself? The aspirations we had have been trailed in the mud. The failure of our resolution, the want of faith, the lack of charity. Our little weaknesses which we are too blind to see as sins. Such weaknesses, such sins of old brought Jesus to His Cross. And the sins of the world—the cruelty, the injustice, the bitterness. How can we say we have no part in them? They are but the outer darkness. The inner darkness of men's motives and desires shows itself outside in the sins and wrongs of society and the hates and bitterness of nations. We have wounded ourselves, and who can heal?

The utter and desolate loneliness of sin! Our deed has gone forth, and we see something of what it has wrought. And we are alone with this evil thing, with our broken life, our shattered aspirations, alone with this thing we did, and we see it now as sin.

> In the night, in the night
> When thou liest alone,
> Ah! the ghosts that make moan
> From the days that are sped:
> The old dreams, the old deeds,
> The old wound that still bleeds,
> And the face of the dead,
>   In the night.

But this is God's mercy and not the malice of Fate. It is to make men reach beyond themselves, and find the strength and the joy of forgiveness. Forgiveness is just seeking God's face, and learning how God has suffered and travailed to redeem. And in the Cross of Christ is God made known.

God who made us and Gods we make

Jer. xvi. 20.—'Shall a man make unto himself gods?' (R.V.).

1. THROUGHOUT the Bible there are two ways of speaking about God that at first sight seem in direct opposition. On the one side is the theological affirmation, God is and He made us. On the other side is the psychological affirmation, We make gods and serve them. 'In the beginning God created the heavens and the earth,' so the Bible starts, but throughout its course we keep running on another point of view. 'Shall a man make unto himself gods?' says Jeremiah.

This is not only ancient history. Few things go more deeply into our contemporary situation than this contrast between a theological approach to God—one Deity who made us—and a psychological approach to those elements in life which gain our devotion and become our gods. God made us—that is theology. We make gods and worship them—that is psychology.

Much of the unreality of our religious experience springs from our failure to note this difference and face its implications. We believe theologically in God. But does that necessarily imply anything about those inward deities that we really serve? Upon the contrary, a man conceivably might make drink his god, or money his god, or nationalism, or race, his god. Men who cherish bitter, menacing, anti-Semitism earnestly believe in God. And we Protestants would all consent: 'I believe in God the Father Almighty, Maker of heaven and earth.' This practical unanimity of consent to theological faith in the God that made us does not prevent our lives from being dominated psychologically by the gods that we make. Were Jeremiah to say to us again, 'Shall a man make unto himself gods?' we should have to answer: Jeremiah, that is what we are doing all the time; there is no habit more familiar in human life.

Let a man look down inside his own life. Who really is God there? Commonly not the theological God, belief in whom we may have inherited or persuaded ourselves to by argument, concerning which the New Testament itself says: 'The devils also believe, and tremble.' Commonly some psychological god is the real one, claiming the whole-hearted allegiance of our lives. Until a man has faced the god question thus, he has not been serious about it.

2. Let us take a further step, and try to describe those elements that constitute, in this deeper sense, a man's real god. Wherever a man discovers anything in life on which he relies, and to which he gives himself, his central loyalty—that is his real god. Those two elements always constitute the essential psychological meaning of one's genuine god: one's central reliance and one's central devotion. 'He restoreth my soul'—one way or another,

a man soon or late says that of his real god. ' Not my will, but thine be done '—one way or another, a man says that to his real god. That is why we say that a man makes the nation, or science, or art, or music, or some humanitarian cause his god. It can become his main dependence and his main devotion. When the god question is thus described in inner and psychological terms, it is no matter simply for church on Sunday ; it penetrates into the pith of every day's most common attitudes.

Theological atheism we often speak about. That means a materialistic philosophy that reduces the universe to the fortuitous self-arrangement of physical elements. But psychological atheism is much more intimate and penetrating. The psychological atheist has no God-experience within, no deep source from which he lives, no major loyalty for which he lives. One would hate to be a theological atheist and think the universe a mere matter of chance. There are such folk. Even the order, unity, symmetry, law-abidingness, and intelligibility of the cosmos leave them unpersuaded. They do not believe in the theological God. Yet how lovely some such people are ! ·As one watches them one sees that, while they do not have our theological God, in a profound sense they do have a psychological god. They have found in life a deep reliance and a deep devotion —some goodness, truth, or beauty they have found, some art, some science, some humane cause, some inner source of satisfaction from which to live, and some worth-while objective for which to live. We are sorry they do not believe in the Eternal God who made us, but sometimes one would like to show such people to some Christians, and say to the Christians, Look at them ! There, at least, as far as it goes, is a genuine God-experience. There, at least, is a deity, such as it is, that really commands a man's life. And as for us Christians, professional believers in God, who have inherited a faith in God or persuaded ourselves of it by argument, see how ineffectual that mere theological God is until he has become what in Christ he always seeks to become, a real, interior God, our inner reliance and our day-by-day devotion.

The practical upshot of all this is that this genuine God-experience is never inherited. It seldom lies at the end of an argument. It comes as a satisfaction meeting a profound personal need—often in some difficult crisis. Our experience need not be dramatic and critical, but there is nothing the Church of Christ needs more deeply to-day than men and women who have done more than inherit a theological God. How *real* is your God ? ' He restoreth my soul ' —does he mean that ? ' Not my will, but thine, be done '—does he mean that ?

3. Let us now take a further step and note the critical importance of this truth for the large affairs of the world to-day. In Hitler's book, *Mein Kampf*, there is presented with amazing frankness a man's soul and his philosophy of life. At the very heart of it, beating like a pulse in every paragraph, is this fact : that man has a god. Every time he thinks of that god his soul tingles, and to that god he has given the last ounce of his devotion. *Mein Kampf* is a story of one of the most absorbing god-experiences in our generation. But the god is the Aryan race. The only ultimate test of right and wrong, says Hitler, is whether a thing does or does not assist the ascending glory of that one supreme god. With unabashed frankness, he praises organized lying, mendacious propaganda, fitted to the passion, prejudice, and ignorance of the mob, if only it will help that race. That end justifies every means.

Let us not leave that matter stranded abroad with Hitler. No city that Paul ever travelled through, filled with temples to the deities of the Pantheon, was ever more replete with altars than is this modern world. And now, as in ancient times, the Christian gospel, when it keeps its purity, comes to this generation, saying, These are the gods that you have made, but there is one God who made you—all races, all nations, all classes, all men. Not Mars or Caesar, but the God of all mankind revealed in Christ, He alone is God.

If we should take that seriously it would be no mere matter of theology. Should we be earnest about that, it would shape and mould our attitudes as individuals and our policies as nations. The god question is very practical. See these gods that rend the world asunder ! They cannot save mankind. As a matter of most practical fact, they cannot save mankind. Many people to-day talk as though the present situation were denying the Christian gospel. Rather, it is confirming the Christian gospel. See these alternative and substitute gods ! ' By their fruits ye shall know them.' They cannot redeem the world. As a realistic fact, only one God can save the world : the God of all mankind revealed in Christ.

4. Finally, let us come back to our own individual lives and contritely confess the superficiality of much of our popular Christianity. You recall Charles Lamb's whimsical remark that his children were to be brought up in their father's religion, if they could discover what it was. It is not difficult to discover a man's formal, conventional, traditional religion. But how difficult it sometimes is to discover about a so-called Christian what his genuine, inner religion is, his real reliance and his real allegiance.

¶ Mr Julean Arnold, long attached to the United States Government service in China, tells the story of a Chinese bandit who was wounded in an encounter with some soldiers and taken to a Methodist missionary hospital. There after some weeks his broken leg mended and he was restored to normal physical condition. He was so grateful that he vowed that never again would he hold up a Methodist. Word of that vow spread through the countryside, so that whenever he did hold up any one the victim protested that he was a Methodist. So the bandit went back to the hospital to find out how he could distinguish a Methodist when he met one. They told him that a Methodist would always know the Lord's Prayer and the Ten Commandments. The bandit, therefore, memorized them in Chinese, and at the next encounter he exclaimed to the victim : ' You recite the Ten Commandments and the Lord's Prayer or Heaven help the spirits of your ancestors ! '

Do not think that all the gods we make are evil. They are not. The love of home and friends, great music, great books, great art, the loveliness we find in Nature, many a deep satisfaction in the human spirit, many a fine loyalty in human life—they are good. But to the Christian the God who made us includes them all, is the fountain of them all, overarches them all. Every lovely thing is a pathway to Him ; every lovely thing is a revelation of Him. We did not make Him. He made us—he ' inhabiteth eternity ' ; his ' name is Holy '—that is magnificent theology, but, continues the scripture— and this is the psychology of it—' I dwell . . . with him also that is of contrite and humble spirit.' [1]

<hr>
[1] H. E. Fosdick, *Living Under Tension*, 134.

The Blessedness of Trust

Jer. xvii. 7.—' Blessed is the man that trusteth in the Lord, and whose hope the Lord is.'

WE are not surprised to hear these words coming from the lips of this Old Testament prophet, for Jeremiah possessed a wonderful faith in God. Amid all the sufferings and calamities that befell him he never lost his faith. He lost almost everything else, even his life, for he met a martyr's death in Egypt—but not his faith. This wonderful faith in God filled him with confidence and serenity amid all the hardships of his life. He is speaking to us out of his own deep experience of God when he cries, ' Blessed is the man that trusteth in the Lord, and whose hope the Lord is.'

1. In the passage in which these words occur we find a contrast between the man who trusts in God and the man who relies on mere human aid. Over against the happiness of the man who knows God and lives in fellowship with Him, the prophet places the misery of the man who has no knowledge of the Eternal and who has only himself to fall back upon. Such a man, he says, is like a shrub in the desert that shrivels up quickly and withers away, because there is no moisture to feed it and nourish it. Happy is the man who trusts in God, but miserable indeed is the man who has only himself to fall back upon !

Nowhere in his Book does the prophet speak more directly to our time, for we are living in an age that is ' making flesh its arm.' The world has become secular. Men and women are relying solely on themselves. They are trying to manage their lives without the help of any power outside themselves, because they have ceased to believe in the existence of such a power. For multitudes God does not exist, and although many people are making a sorry business of life they do not seem to realize the cause of their failure. They say, ' We have our home, our friends, and our work, and science has given us a wonderful control over the forces of Nature. We do not need God, and we do not miss Him.'

¶ There is a story of a small boy who was asked if he said his prayers in the morning. His reply was : ' Of course not. I say my prayers at night because when I'm asleep I can't do anything. But when I'm awake I can look after myself.'

This brings us to the heart of the great conflict that is being waged in our day between the forces of light and darkness, between paganism and Christianity. When we examine this conflict we find that the forces of religion are confronted with three challenges.

(1) There is the challenge of *secularism*. Life has become an easier thing. Man's mastery over Nature is increasing every day. Science and machinery have given him a new sense of power. He does not feel the need of any Divine power outside himself.

(2) There is the challenge of *psychology* which seeks to show that there is no objective basis in reality for religious experience, that man's sense of God and his consciousness of Christ's presence are only illusions.

(3) There is the challenge of *humanism* which declares that there is nothing greater in the universe than man.

These are the challenges Christianity has to face to-day. It is not a new battle. We have just given new names to old enemies of faith and God. The same battle was fought in the time of Jeremiah. In vivid language he describes the misery of men and women who give way to the secular temper of their age. A curse on the man, he cries, who is relying on human aid, for he is leaning on a broken reed that will not only fail him but run into his hand and pierce it! And over against the misery and emptiness of unbelief he places the happiness of the man who has God to fall back upon. ' Blessed is the man that trusteth in the Lord, and whose hope the Lord is.'

2. Let us see, now, what this faith did for Jeremiah.

(1) First of all, for Jeremiah faith in God was *an outburst of joy*. ' Happy is the man,' he cries, ' that trusteth in the Lord, and whose hope the Lord is.' Happy! We do not usually associate that word with Jeremiah. We think of him more frequently as the suffering servant of the Lord. There was, however, at the heart of his life a great joy. He rejoiced in the knowledge that God was supreme in His universe and that God would have the last word. Evil might triumph for a day, but in the long run God would conquer. That faith filled him with joy.

To-day many lives lack this note of joy.

People are worried, troubled, and anxious. In all our churches there are people who are like an acrobat trying to walk a tight-rope. Their lives are full of strain, for they are always afraid they are going to fall off. If you ask them why they are worried, they will tell you they are worried about something in their home, or their business, or their personal relationships, or they may point to the international situation. But the cause of the anxiety is not really in their lives or in the international situation. It is simply their lack of faith.

¶ ' From the bottom of my heart,' wrote Luther to Melanchthon, ' I am against those worrying cares which are taking the heart out of you. Why make God a liar in not believing His wonderful promises, when He commands us to be of good cheer, and cast all our care upon Him, for He will sustain us ? Do you think He throws such words to the winds ? What more can the devil do than slay us ? Christ has died for sin once for all, but for righteousness and truth He will not die, but live and reign. Why then worry, seeing He is at the helm ? He who has been our Father will also be the Father of our children. As for me (whether it proceed from God's Spirit or from stupidity, my Lord Jesus knows), I do not torment myself about such matters.'

(2) Secondly, for Jeremiah faith in God was *an outburst of hope*. ' Blessed is the man that trusteth in the Lord, and whose hope the Lord is.' Again, we do not often associate the word ' hope ' with Jeremiah. We think of him as the prophet of pessimism and despair, and certainly the message God gave him to deliver was a message of doom. But it was not all doom. There was a break in the clouds. If the people would only repent and return to God, God could do anything. The vessel that was broken on the potter's wheel could be remade.

Like the other prophets, Jeremiah's face was turned with hope towards the future. Nothing is more remarkable in the Old Testament than this Messianic hope. Unlike the Greeks and the Romans, the Hebrew prophets placed the Golden Age in the future, and all their golden hopes were associated with the coming of the Messiah, the Divine King who was to set up a kingdom in which there would be no violence, strife, injustice, or war.

We must not lose this hope. There is much to discourage us in the international situation, in the drift away from the Church, in the paganism of our time. But the man who trusts in God never loses hope. Our God is the God of Hope.

¶ A soldier has described how suddenly one evening he heard a nightingale singing among the horrors of a battlefield in France. 'There was something infinitely sweet about it,' he wrote, 'as if the country-side were singing gently to itself in the midst of all our noise and confusion and muddy work. So that you felt the nightingale's song was the only real thing, which would remain when all the rest was long past and forgotten.'

(3) Thirdly, for Jeremiah faith in God was *an outburst of courage.* He was one of the most courageous men that ever lived. Many a time he had to stand alone. Many a time every one was against him. But he was never afraid to be alone for God.

That was the secret of his courage. By nature and temperament he was a timid, shrinking man, and if this timid, sensitive man became an iron pillar there must be some explanation. The explanation is—his faith in God. That was the secret of his courage. He felt that God was for him and that nothing, therefore, could be against him.

In the heart of each one of us there is both a hero and a coward, and what matters first and last is that the hero should triumph over the coward. The secret of courage is faith in God. Long ago Jeremiah made that discovery, and it transformed a timid, shrinking man into a pillar of strength and made him a hero ; and centuries later the Apostle Paul made the same discovery. 'I can do all things through Christ which strengtheneth me.' Faith in Christ gave him courage.

¶ A city minister tells of a young invalid in a tenement building who, because she also had made this discovery, was heard to say, 'Once I wondered how I could make the best of it. Now I wonder how I can make the most of it.'

How can we acquire this faith ?

We must remember that faith is not an entity. It is a relationship. We should not pray for faith and more faith, but for a greater sense of God in our lives. We should not ask for faith, but for the consciousness of God's presence. We must learn to pray. We must learn to read our Bibles. We must look for God in the events of our day and in our own lives. We must acquire a more vivid sense of His presence, and then faith will spring up in our hearts. The result of that faith will be joy, hope, and courage.

Heart Knowledge

Jer. xvii. 9.—' The heart is deceitful above all things, and desperately wicked : ' who can know it ?'

THE revised translation of the Old Testament gives a somewhat different rendering of the second clause of this text. Instead of the phrasing ' desperately wicked ' it substitutes ' desperately sick.' Sickness and wickedness are not quite the same thing, surely, though in this instance the prophet uses the word to indicate moral infirmity, and therefore we may fairly assume that some suggestion of culpability is involved in the use of the term ' sick.' ' The heart is deceitful above all things, and it is desperately sick : who can know it ? ' The idea intended to be conveyed is that the heart of man is not to be trusted, for morally it is in an utterly unhealthy state. It is no more to be relied on in its judgments and the advice it gives than the views of a sick man are to be relied on in regard to the affairs of life. When a man is ill, he is apt to take a morbid, distorted view of a situation concerning which, if he were well, he would think and feel differently. It is a wise maxim never to decide anything in an hour of physical depression, when vitality is low and the judgment goes awry. We think we see things more clearly than usual, but we don't ; we have got the whole situation out of focus ; we are probably entirely wrong in the conclusions at which we arrive. This is what the prophet here affirms of the heart in relation to all the higher issues of life. It cannot of itself be relied upon to give needful guidance to the soul.

By the heart, no doubt, he means the seat of feeling and volition. ' Keep thy heart with all diligence,' says the Book of Proverbs, ' for out of it are the issues of life.' ' As a man thinketh in his heart, so is he.' We read in Genesis vi. ' that the wickedness of man was great in the earth, and that every imagination of the thoughts of his heart was only evil continually.' On the other hand, St Paul tells us that ' with the heart man believeth unto righteousness.' The heart is that unfathomable depth in us all whence proceed our desires, aims, hopes, joys, and fears ; within it the springs of our motives lie concealed, sometimes even from ourselves. Disposition is of the heart ; so to an extent is character. That which stamps a man himself as over against everybody else, the individuality which distinguishes him from his neighbours, is very largely a matter of the heart. Reason is a superficial thing compared with it, for the reason can be overborne, cajoled, or altogether swept aside by the uprushes of passion which burst forth from the heart when it is deeply moved, like fire and lava from the crater of a volcano.

1. Now, does any man truly know his own heart ? We often speak of knowing one's own mind, and unless one is capable of knowing one's own mind when important resolves have to be made it is not possible to make much of a success in life. The men who do succeed are those who do not allow others to make up their minds for them, but who know exactly what they want and make straight for it. But it is a good deal easier to do this than to know one's own heart. We may think we are acting from one kind of motive on occasions when we are really impelled by another, and it is often a very hard thing to find out which. It is a task beyond the power of most of us to understand ourselves at times. There are moments of sudden illumination when we see in ourselves what was obscure to us before, and when they come we are as much startled as if we were looking into the heart of a perfect stranger. It is a curious and baffling thing to realize how little we know about ourselves—as to why we do this or that, or what we really think and feel about this or that, or in what way we should behave in certain eventualities. As a rule we do not know until we are tested, and then not infrequently the discovery is disquieting and humiliating to our self-love.

2. It is not only motives to which this general observation applies. It applies to everything good and bad that goes to make up an individual soul. Oliver Wendell Holmes used to say, ' I do not talk to tell people what I think, but in order to find out what I think.' We are like a vast continent with portions of the sea coast settled and cultivated, but with an enormous hinterland which has never been explored. How do we know what there is in that hinterland ? Perhaps rare and beautiful flowers and fruits are to be found there, but it may also be that ferocious beasts and venomous serpents lurk almost unsuspected in the forest depths. We are accustomed to order our not very remarkable course in life by means of a body of opinions and maxims which we sincerely believe to be our own. But the probability is that most of our convictions and assumptions about matters of conduct are not ours at all but have been supplied to us by the preceptors who had the charge of our upbringing, and by the society in which we live. If we had the courage to be ourselves out and out, we might be very different beings from the ones we imagine ourselves to be. What would we like to be and do if we had the chance and were able to give full vent to our inclinations ? Perhaps the results might startle our friends, not to speak of ourselves. What we really feel, what our actual tastes and tendencies are, what we are capable of both for good and ill goes largely unsuspected even by ourselves.

¶ It is said that Robespierre was in his youth of gentle, somewhat timid, disposition, beloved by those about him, and looked upon as a character in whom the kindlier virtues predominated. This was so even in his manhood. The families with whom he lodged in Paris during his rise to power were devoted to him, charmed by his courtesy and consideration for the feelings of others, and the many thoughtful and gracious acts he performed on their behalf from time to time. Yet this same man was a monster of ruthlessness, absolutely callous in the shedding of blood. It may be seriously questioned whether he himself knew this until the occasion came which revealed it to the world ; he might have lived and died with a reputation in his own small circle for the very opposite of the qualities on account of which he is now infamous.

3. There is one more point that needs to be mentioned here. It is that of the danger, peculiarly besetting religious people, of substituting good feelings for moral worth. One often hears the statement made by men of business that a very fervent, emotional type of Christian can be somewhat shifty and unreliable in his commercial dealings. A man who can display the deepest feeling in a prayer meeting may not be above taking a mean advantage in a business deal and he may not be the best of employers. Would it be right to dub him a hypocrite ? Not at all, any more than it would be fair to blame Christ-

ianity for his shortcomings. His religion does not make him an unfair bargainer or a hard master, as the case may be ; he is these in spite of his religion, and he is these because he does not really understand his own heart. While he is in a state of religious ecstasy he imagines he is as good as he feels, whereas he is nothing of the sort ; that is just what is amiss. And we can all be guilty of it, and probably all are in some degree. Do we never allow good feelings to do duty for good deeds ? Do we not manage to soothe conscience into slumber at times by cultivating sentiments unimpeachable in themselves ? Have we ever thought how somehow we can persuade ourselves that a bad thing in us is not really a bad thing, not very bad, not what it seems, although in somebody else it would be vile and unpardonable ?

¶ There may be coarse hypocrites, who consciously affect beliefs and emotions for the sake of gulling the world, but Bulstrode was not one of them. He was simply a man whose desires had been stronger than his theoretic beliefs, and who had gradually explained the gratification of his desires into satisfactory agreement with those beliefs. If this be hypocrisy, it is a process which shows itself occasionally in us all.[1]

We may deceive ourselves, but we cannot deceive God. We may be ignorant of what we truly are, but He is not ; He knows ; and nothing we can say or do will affect the verdict of His justice in the day when the secrets of all hearts shall be revealed and we shall know as we are known.

Who made the heart, 'tis He alone
  Decidedly can try us ;
He knows each chord, its various tone,
  Each spring, its various bias.

How can we obtain a heart void of offence towards God ? If we cannot trust it, if we are so liable to be betrayed by what it tells us, where can we look for the truth ? And even if we could, unaided, find the truth, how are we to make the heart obey it ? There is but one way that is efficacious. It is, to use the old evangelical phrase, to give the heart to Christ. Let Him have it, and let Him have it all. Give Him your undivided allegiance. You can at least make the sincere offering of your heart to Him ; you can tender Him everything ; you

[1] George Eliot, *Middlemarch*.

can make full surrender ; and then it is for Him to ratify and complete that solemn act of the will. ' Let us draw near with a true heart in full assurance of faith, having our hearts sprinkled from an evil conscience. . . . Let us hold fast the profession of our faith without wavering ; for He is faithful that promised.' And it shall be so that when Christ dwells in the heart by faith all that is not of Christ therein must go. The struggle may be fierce and long, but to enthrone the Saviour in the heart is to get rid of all shams and lies, all foulness and iniquity, and to become filled with the fullness of God.

Turn in, my Lord, turn in to me,
My heart's a homely place ;
But Thou canst make corruption flee,
And fill it with Thy grace :
So furnished, it will be brave,
And a rich dwelling Thou shalt have.

The Potter's House

Jer. xviii. 3.—' Then I went down to the potter's house, and, behold, he wrought a work on the wheels.'

NONE of the parables of the Old Testament has a more direct and personal, and at the same time a more general, appeal to us than Jeremiah's parable of his visit to the potter's house. While its original significance concerned Israel in its then state—for all the Old Testament prophets were first of all messengers to their own times— its meaning was by no means limited to its first application. Israel, as a nation, has passed away, whatever the future may, and assuredly does, hold for the dispersed in the matter of their national life. But this parable is a lens through which God is to be seen, the unchanging God of persons as well as of people, in whose hands are all our ways, and with whom we all have to do.

1. Let us look at the parable. The prophet is in a dilemma. The nation has broken away from God's protective law, has turned defiantly to its own ways. The external, material evils that have come upon it are as nothing in comparison with its spiritual apostasy. Unfitted, as it has become, to be the instrument of carrying out God's purpose towards other nations and unable to check its own momentum and reverse

its direction, its case looks hopeless, and Jeremiah is disheartened and voiceless. As he sees it, the situation is so bad that only a worse can come out of it. The nation can have no future except one of successive disasters and ultimate extinction.

¶ Those who have visited the Sistine Chapel of the Vatican, and gazed upon the masterpieces of Michelangelo will recall one fresco of the many that adorn the walls of that marvellous building. It is of the prophet Jeremiah. He is pictured there as this passage reveals him. We see the strong man bowed ; dejection is stamped upon his worn face as, head upon his hand, God's servant broods over the sins of his nation, their impenitence and his own impotence to deal with it.

But, under the Divine direction, Jeremiah went down to the potter's shop and watched the potter at his work, and there he saw what scattered his gloom, and restored his confidence, and gave him a message for the nation, which, had they but hearkened to it, would have changed the entire course of the people's history, and probably of the history of the whole world. He saw the whirling wheel, and the directing hand creating in clay the potter's thoughts. Vessel after vessel was swiftly fashioned and laid aside to be sun-baked, and then distributed for use. The inanimate material seemed to live under the potter's power to shape it from dull amorphousness into forms of beauty and usefulness. Then, as he gazed fascinated, something unusual happened. A handful of clay had evidently contained some hidden admixture, some bit of hardness, or, it might be, of over-softness, a tiny pocket of sand or of moisture—and the potter, for the moment, is beaten by it. He stops the rotating wheel by ceasing to operate the single treadle that controlls it, crumbles up the misformed vessel with his fingers, remedies the defect in the material, kneads it into plasticity again, restarts the wheel and, lo, under his hand it grows into another vessel.

This is a parable in deeds, not in words, for no conversation is recorded between the potter and his strange taciturn visitor, who stood and watched, and went away without purchasing anything or without even speaking. For Jeremiah had been too intent upon seeing and inwardly listening to talk. The operations of the craftsman had been teaching him profound lessons. In the materials handled by the potter,

and in the way they were manufactured by him, Jeremiah, with a mind like our Lord's, perceived a symbolic representation of great and central truths.

2. Let us stand beside the prophet in imagination and give our attention to the things that fell under his notice on this momentous occasion.

(1) First of all there is *the clay*. It is the raw material with which the potter works—the stuff of which each vessel, no matter what its shape may be, is composed. There resides in it the promise of becoming an object of usefulness or of beauty, once it has been subjected to the process of manufacture.

Our lives possess a similar capacity. There are possibilities in us that admit of being realized. Out of the undeveloped material there can be produced forms and modes of personality of the most diverse kinds. Like the clay, we yield to treatment. Our natures are plastic. Powers of body and mind and will, abilities of a physical, an intellectual, and a moral order manifest themselves. Character expresses itself, and more and more tends to stereotype itself on settled lines, and to harden into a permanent shape. Whereas in the early period there was little by which to distinguish one life from another, in the later peculiarities assert themselves, differences are conspicuous. We display our individuality not only by the features of our face, our height, our speech, our manner of walking, but in a multitude of characteristic ways, definable in some cases, but in others too subtle to be explained in words.

To compare this human life of ours to clay is not to state the whole truth about it. For clay is a substance passive and inanimate. But to us belongs freedom—a freedom which, though it is limited in its range, is nevertheless a real prerogative of self-determination within a certain compass. And reason is ours too—that Divine endowment whereby we are able to think, and construct a theory of the universe for ourselves, and plan what we shall do. And our natures are gifted with sensibilities also—we are susceptible to emotions and affections. Desires are kindled within us, hopes and fears sway us, our hearts know the pleasure of satisfaction and the pain of disappointment.

Yet, while between man and clay there is this great difference, they resemble one another in a certain respect. And it was that resemblance which came home to the prophet's mind. They are subject alike to effects being produced on them by a cause outside themselves. We know this about ourselves, that our lives do not consist of a series of experiences which we determine beforehand. The orbit of our career does not follow the path traced by our pre-conceptions and wishes. Things happen to us —bringing unexpected joys, or unlooked-for sorrows. Events take place in whose initiation and accomplishment we had no part. Perhaps we are apt to forget this fact about the circum-stances of our lives. Incidents of an ordinary kind, while they befall us in the character of unanticipated happenings, are not sufficiently unfamiliar to remind us of it. But when any great event takes place—any event, that is to say, which is fraught with serious consequences to us and ours, and which transforms our whole outlook ; when God asserts His power in our life either in His Providence or His Grace— then we realize that, in a true sense, we are clay.

(2) The second thing that arrests our atten-tion, as we stand beside the prophet and watch the potter at his work, is *the wheel*. The clay is set on the wheel, and the wheel moves with rapid revolutions. Up from its whirling centre there emerges the vessel, growing into definite shape moment by moment. The wheel is an indispensable implement in the craft of the potter. Its rotations are necessary to the production of the ware which he aims at manufacturing.

The wheel is life itself, the circumstances upon which our characters are fashioned. How ruth-lessly it seems again and again to deal with us. Yet as the clay remains nothing but shapeless stuff till it is placed upon the wheel, as the wheel with its swift revolutions is essential to the process of making an earthen vessel, so life, with all its ordeals and losses and perplexing events, is essential to the formation and fashioning of the character of man. It is not against these conditions in general amidst which we are placed that we are inclined to cry out. When the necessity of them is explained to us we are ready enough to recognize their inevitableness, and acquiesce in their appointment. Reality is acknowledged to be rational.

But it is not with the elements of a theory which has commended itself to our reason that we have to cope in our life from day to day. It is with the hard facts of personal experience— this event which has happened to us—not theoretical trials, but actual, grievous ones which make the heart bleed. It is against these conditions in particular that we cry out in ex-postulating anguish.

(3) But there is another object which meets our eyes as we watch with the prophet. It is *the hand of the potter*.

The wheel is not self-moved ; its rotations are controlled by the potter. And the strain and stress to which the clay is subjected as it sweeps round and round, and rises up in the form of a vase or a cup, like a plant growing from its root, are directed by him. No vessel in that booth made itself, or was made by the wheel. One and all took their shape, and were moulded after their respective patterns, under the skilled and experienced hand of the potter.

The hand of the potter is an emblem of the hand of God. We are apt to think exclusively of the wheel, and to ignore the hand. Whereas it is God who affects us with His providences, and seeks to mould us for His own purposes. The things that befall us, and from the occur-rence of which we shrink, the ordeals to which we are exposed, the disappointments that fill us with sorrow, are ordained by His Wisdom and Love. And such is His grace that, when by our folly or rebelliousness we mar His work, He is willing to take us again and refashion us with long-suffering patience.

¶ George Macdonald puts these words into the mouth of one of his characters who had been buffeted by inexplicable circumstances, and who, complaining to a friend about the hardness of her life, said in anger : 'Oh, I would to God I had never been made.' 'Why,' replied her friend, 'my dear child, you are not made yet ; you are only being made, and you are quarrelling with God's processes.'

Shall we not, then, seek to submit ourselves anew to the Will of God, and lend ourselves to the discipline and control of Him who delighteth in mercy ? The hand that guides our destinies— let us strive to believe it—is no iron hand of relentless force, violent in its smiting, as we are sometimes tempted to think. Its actions have been revealed to the eyes of men in the hand of Jesus Christ. It is the hand that took hold of a blind man and led him out to be healed, that was stretched out to rescue a sinking disciple, that was laid upon little children, that was pierced by cruel nails for our sakes. That is the hand which apportions the changing experiences of our earthly lot, and which gives and withholds in the case of each one of us. That is the hand which gropes around our hearts to touch into life chords of trust and assurance and obedience to-day. Oh! to have quickened within us a great and victorious faith in the Love which directs the working of the hand of God—to be able to say :

> So, take and use Thy work :
> Amend what flaws may lurk,
> What strain o' the stuff, what warpings past
>   the aim !
> My times be in Thy hand !
> Perfect the cup as planned !
> Let age approve of youth, and death complete
>   the same !

Seeing Life Whole

Jer. xviii. 3.—'Then I went down to the potter's house, and behold, he wrought a work on the wheels.'

THE Duke in *As You Like It* remarks : ' This our life . . . finds tongues in trees, books in the running brooks, sermons in stones, and good in every thing.' Jeremiah is learning this lesson here. The Spirit of God drives him down to the potter's house, and asks him to use his eyes, and learn his lesson.

But suppose we took some one else to the potter's house, and asked him what *he* saw ? Would he see what Jeremiah saw—and as he saw it ? No doubt, in Shakespeare's words, there are sermons in stones. But some people only see the stones. Indeed, most of the faulty criticisms of life and God spring from this. The eye only sees what it brings with it the power to see, and our faults of sight are the root of our faults of thought and outlook.

1. *Some people only see the Clay.* You show them a beautifully finished bowl, a dream of choice art : but all that they are certain of is— that it is made of clay. It may be a thing of beauty and a joy for ever : it may be like that Grecian urn in which John Keats saw beauty and God. But all this type of man is sure of is—

the clay. ' I tell you, I stood here and watched the man make it : and in spite of all your talk of beauty and purpose and plan, *it is only clay*. Yes, clay ! '

In this great potter's house, which we call the world, there are many beautiful things made by the glorious devising mind of the master potter. But there are people, some of them very learned —some of them scientists, some of them philosophers, some of them poets—and in all the wonders of the world and human life, they only see the clay. They always explain the highest by the lowest. They explain civilization, law, poetry, and dreams by a theory of electrons. They express health in terms of disease, mind in terms of matter, soul in terms of body, and man in terms of a gorilla.

¶ Balzac is famous for his minute knowledge of humanity, so we are told. And what is his verdict on us ? Ask Anatole France ! ' He showed with extreme precision all the functions of the claw, the jaw, and the stomach, all the habits of the man of prey.' Jaw, and claw, and stomach ; always these, but of trace of a soul, hardly a reminder !

We are linked, in God's mysterious ways, with the whole natural world in which we live. Mind is related to body, and, it may even be, controlled by it. This great world of growth has evolved from simpler things. We are of the world about us : and we have slowly struggled up, by God's spirit, from lowly forms. But this type of man, in explaining the mystery which we feel within us, *sees nothing but the lowly forms*. He does not see that you can never explain the higher by the lower, and that to trace obvious or suspected physical processes does not account for mental and spiritual facts. It does not lessen either us or the majesty of God to admit our connexions with the material world in which we are placed. But can we dwell amid the wonders of this potter's house of God—knowing the mystery of our own soul—and yet think that *clay* explains it all ?

2. *There are some who see only the Wheel.* We come into this potter's shop, and it is only the whirring, ceaseless, senseless round of things we see. This is life as we have known it—a great wheel on which we and our little world are placed ; and it goes round endlessly, senselessly, mindlessly. More people than Buddha see the world and human striving thus. What does it

all amount to—and does it not return where it begins ?

Into this world, and why not knowing,
Nor whence, like water willy-nilly flowing ;
And out of it, like wind along the waste,
I know not whither, willy-nilly flowing.

Now, it is right to admit the wheel. We can trace it in day and night, in the exact recurring of the seasons, in the succession of things throughout the ages, in the rise and fall of peoples and civilizations. But is that all ? Are we not losing facts merely in examining methods ? If it is only a wheel, does *chance* or *accident* explain anything of the things that must be explained ? The truth is—the wheel is only the method by which everything bigger is made possible. These great laws, whose unfailing regularity often bores us, are simply the necessary mechanism by which we live—we who are more than the laws, because we can question and comprehend them. And the one thing that we can be sure of is that the wheel—these laws—cannot be their own origin or explanation. A man begins to live when he sees that the one thing a law can't be is *mechanical*. Laws don't spring from chance, for chance can have no laws !

¶ Dan Crawford tells how a British scientist visited him in Central Africa and drew attention to some marvel in the jungle. ' The product of natural law ! ' he affirmed. ' And please, sah,' interjected one of Dan Crawford's negro converts who was standing by, ' please, sah, who made that law ? ' [1]

To see the wheel is good. To see only the wheel is as much ruin as it is folly. The man who sees the wheel without the Potter—the only eternal explanation, *mind*—is as much of a fool as he who sees the clay without the living, shaping spirit that gives it breath.

3. *There are those who, in a larger faith, see the Potter's Hand.* They admit Providence—in their tears they often must ! They see some dim purpose and power that masters things. Ah, yes, there is indeed a shaping hand ! Are not some of our souls raw from His touch ?

But they do not know anything further or deeper. They admit it all, but do so with shadowed eyes—puzzled and sore. Though they admit the process, they may see neither rhyme

[1] F. W. Boreham, *Boulevards of Paradise*, 70.

nor reason in it. Like Job they cannot account for their own bruises and disciplines : and when they think of the dear things that have been torn from them, the very pledges of happiness, it is with alternate bewilderment and rebellion that they face life. There is no doubt about the shaping hand ; it is *how it shapes* that hurts. Most people who have sorrow find God—but they often lose the Father.

No, glory be to God for all of us who see the shaping Hand. Is it fair for us to admit it gladly when it shapes for our good, and yet deny it when it hurts ? How often have we been shielded, through no merit of our own, from difficulties and dangers, and from sins and follies that would have cursed our peace ? And if now some of us are wistful, with unmentionable and unmeasurable accidents in our life, or with memories that are never assuaged by pious ' hopes,' is it just that we should deny the kindliness of the hand because it has hurt ? There is no meaning, no peace, no hope in a God who is not a Father. Such a God would be an irony. And we bless Jesus that we see God's face in His. In His tender love and mercy, we know that ' there 's a divinity that shapes our ends, rough-hew them how we will.'

Know well, my soul, God's hand controls
  whate'er thou bearest,
Round Him, in calmest music rolls
  whate'er thou hearest.
What to thee is shadow, to Him is day,
  and the end He knoweth,
And not in a blind and aimless way
  the Spirit goeth.

Making Things Again

Jer. xviii. 4.—' The vessel that he made of clay was marred in the hand of the potter : so he made it again another vessel, as seemed good to the potter to make it.'

' THE potter's house ' is generally identified with ' the potter's field ' which, St Matthew tells us, was bought, with the money paid to the traitor, as a burying-ground for strangers. It was situated in the valley of Hinnom to the south of Jerusalem, and it is said that the clay there is to this day suitable to the potter's trade. Jeremiah is sent thither to see a parable in action showing God's way of dealing with Israel. The nation was refusing to be moulded according to the design in the Potter's mind. To the stern prophet there was but one thing left for God to do—fling the marred vessel back into the mass of clay from which it had been taken, a shapeless, useless thing, without beauty or purpose. Jeremiah saw no alternative ; but God saw one. If the human artificer is at liberty to take the marred vessel of dead clay and shape it on a new pattern and design, cannot the Eternal Worker take the living, breathing clay of the nation of Israel, all marred and shapeless as its sins had made it, ' and make it again another vessel, as seemed good to him ' ? And so the prophet is taught that Israel is to have another chance. The resources of God's power and mercy are not yet at an end.

And the whole history of the world is simply the Potter making another vessel of the clay that was marred in His hand at the very beginning. No one can even imagine what must have been the beauty of His first design when the world of Nature issued from His hand and even He pronounced it very good. We cannot realize the beautiful, glad life man might have lived, passing from one lovely change to another still lovelier, until, having received all that this stage could give him, he rose into a higher and more spiritual, not by the sad process of decay, but by some natural and joyful process of ascension and glory. But the living clay refused to lend itself to the carrying out of the Divine pattern of the world. God might have shattered it at a blow of the hand that had shaped it, and made a new world from the beginning out of other material. But if we sometimes feel a certain pity for a spoiled thing, even if inanimate —a desire to pick it up and mend it again— how much more God for the living creatures He had made ! And so He would pursue His first purpose by means of another design. The whole history of mankind is just what the prophet saw—the Potter, out of the marred vessel of this world, making another as it seemed good to Him ; and when it is marred, as it is again and again, changing the design time after time, throwing nations, churches, individuals into new situations and fortunes, fashioning them into other vessels—not arbitrarily, as an inexorable fate, but according to His infinite wisdom and love.

1. We see it in *the life of nations*. Time after time Israel refused to be moulded after the pattern in the mind of God ; and time after time God made of it another vessel, by famine, war, pestilence, or exile, which, like the whirling of the potter's wheel, moulded, or sought to mould, the rebellious nation into some new shape that would still carry out God's original purpose in its election. Many nations have thus been marred in His hand—Greece, Rome, Spain, France ; but even when nations seem dashed in pieces like the potter's earthen bottle, it is more than possible that God is moulding them into other vessels for the fulfilment of His mysterious purpose of salvation. Let us hope that it is so with all nations, friend and foe, that have been shattered in the war. The history of peoples is made up of this constant moulding and remoulding of human clay in the hands of the Potter who bends above the whirling wheel of earth and time.

2. We see this as plainly in *the history of the Church*. We see it in the age of Constantine, when, persecution past, the Church made alliance with the world, was infected with its evil, and became in turn the persecutor ; and the Potter gave the marred vessel a new shape by setting the wild, whirling wheel of the barbarian invasions to play upon it. Or again, what does the very word Reformation mean but God taking the vessel of His own Church and making it another vessel—the same clay, but a new form ? And if we are wise we shall see this in many of those changes in the Christian Church which we lament. Some, no doubt, are changes of ruin. Yet often what seems to our alarmed eyes the marring of the vessel is only God Himself holding His sinful Church upon the wheel of the revolutions of the times and seasons, to give it a new shape and a new chance.

3. And the hand of the Potter is as busily at work in *the lives of individuals*. Take some of the great names, because their greatness makes it more easily seen. Jacob's duplicity marred the vessel which God meant to make, and on the banks of the Jabbok in the darkness of the night the hands of the Potter moulded him into a new vessel, broke his old reliance on his own cunning, and named him Israel. How terribly David's great sin marred the vessel, which was a man after God's own heart ! But the hands of the Potter took the poor marred thing and held it sternly to the wheel of pain, remorse, the

treachery of his friends, and the rebellion of his son ; fashioning another vessel out of which have flowed to penitents of every succeeding age psalms and prayers of sorrow for sin. Peter, marred with the denial of his Lord ; Paul, marred with his Pharisaic self-righteousness ; Augustine, marred with the sins of his youth —all these and a multitude that no man can number are witnesses to the truth of the prophet's interpretation of the potter and his wheel.

God takes also the humblest vessel of clay into those mighty and loving hands, and seeks to make of it another vessel. We mar our life in a thousand ways—by respectable worldliness no less than by wild prodigalism. In the very hand of the Potter we mar it—reared in Christian homes, taught in the Christian Church, we yet refuse to respond to His hand. And surely many of us remember critical times in our lives, when some sickness fell upon us, some ruin of circumstances, some strange unrest of soul, some fear of conscience, some hunger of the heart, something which seemed to break in life as if a new era had begun. And what should this be but ' the hands that reach through darkness moulding men '—the Potter refusing to fling aside the poor, marred clay as lost to life and use : for a little moment, indeed, crushing the spoilt vessel into shapelessness and apparent ruin, but only in order to set it once more against the whirling wheel of life, if by any means it might yield itself to the impress of another design ? That is what God is ever doing in the lives of men and women ; and blessed indeed are we if we recognize the hand and let it set us to the wheel.

¶ One of the masterpieces of Michelangelo is a colossal statue of David, nine cubits in height. There is an interesting story attached to it. A hundred years previously a huge mass of white marble had been brought from the famous Carrara quarries in northern Italy. A sculptor had attempted the work of carving it, and in so doing blundered badly and left his work unfinished. The block of marble was considered so marred as to be useless, until a century later, when Michelangelo looked at it and undertook to chisel it afresh, and with amazing skill he fashioned it into shape. The statue represents David going out to meet Goliath with his sling in his hand. The concave hollow left by the bungling sculptor in the side of the block was utilized by Michelangelo so as to form the curve of the slinger's body as his arm swept round to hurl the smooth stone from the brook at the oncoming giant. So that which had been considered a defect in the ruined marble was made use of by the master-sculptor to complete his design. His famous ' David ' is one of the glories of Florentine art.[1]

We have to do with no dark, inscrutable Fate, but with a wise, loving, and righteous Being, who stoops even to the point of accommodating Himself, as far as lies within His power, to our very sins, to our marring of the vessel, changing His design and making of us another vessel. St Paul says, ' O the depth of the riches both of the wisdom and knowledge of God ! how unsearchable are his judgments, and his ways past finding out ! ' And we may say with equal right, ' O the depth and the riches both of the mercy and grace of God ! ' For so marvellous is the love of God that often the new vessel which He has fashioned from the old one we have marred takes on a strange, undreamt-of beauty from the very change of design. We cannot help wondering if St Peter, St Paul, St Augustine could ever have had the same beauty of soul, humility, intensity of service, gratitude of love that gave all away, had they never marred the vessel at the first. The one thing necessary is that we yield ourselves, however marred, to the hand and to the wheel with a humble and glad surrender, for it is impossible to tell how beautiful God's new design for any of us may be, or what a vessel of honour He may make us—perhaps, as Browning says, a cup to slake His own thirst, the thirst which the Father of our spirits has for His children's love.

Maker of man, Thy pressure sure
  This grosser stuff must quell ;
The spirit faints, yet will endure,
  Subdue, control, compel.

The Potter's finger shaping me . . .
  Praise, praise ! the clay curves up
Not for dishonour, though it be
  God's least adornèd cup.[2]

[1] J. W. W. Moeran.
[2] Edward Dowden.

The Comfort of Dependence

Jer. xviii. 6.—'Behold, as the clay is in the potter's hand, so are ye in mine hand, O house of Israel.'

WE all shrink from the passages in Scripture which suggest the uncontrolled Sovereignty of God, for they, some of them, seem so far away from the Fatherhood of God. The emphasis is solely upon the untrammelledness of the Creator's will, in respect of His acts towards the creature. 'Nay, but, O man, who art thou that repliest against God? Shall the thing formed say to Him that formed it, why hast thou made me thus?' Can we imagine any statement more absolute, and more chillily stern, than that? As far as it goes, there is not merely no Fatherhood in it, but no statement of a moral principle of Sovereignty. It conveys solely the thought of a mighty Ruler, absolute and unconfined, doing that which seemeth Him good, fashioning this one to honour and that to dishonour, according to His mere good pleasure.

Such a thought of God as this is paralysing. What we need is the call to effort. Moreover, at a time when the social conscience is aroused, and men are gazing with new eyes on what seem to be the waste-products of the Potter's wheel—gazing curiously at those born (as it would seem) for pain and death, and even sin—a thought of God which tends, rightly or wrongly, to remove responsibility for the world's miseries from the shoulders of men themselves on to the Will behind the world, is a thought which we shrink from as unsupportable by our faith.

At the same time, it is not a thought to be forgotten, for it manifestly contains that which is true; and, moreover, contains that which is inspiring. It is not, when examined, so drear a thought as, at first, it seems. For within it there is not only the fact of formation, but the hope of re-formation.

1. But the simplest lesson contained in the image of the Potter's wheel is the old, direct one, that, in the last instance, in regard to life and sustenance and service and destiny, we are in God's hands. 'As the clay in the potter's hand, so are ye in my hand, saith the Lord.' That is manifest on the surface in Nature, Providence, and Spiritual growth.

(1) In Nature, one planteth and another watereth; but God giveth the increase. We plough the field and scatter the good seed on the land; but it is the power of life, inherent in Nature herself—the life in the seed, brought to new being by the 'burial and death of the grain'—that brings 'the green blade waxing mature.' That life we attribute, in the last instance, to the self-living One. In the beginning, He created the heavens and the earth; and constantly since then the physical world is sustained by continuous influxes of His power; through it, continually, the Divine Energy is passing. But of that energy we have not the secret. We have not even power over the servants of growth to more than a limited degree. We cannot control the winds; the rain ceaseth not at our bidding; we are no Joshuas to bid the sun stand still on Ajalon. The control of Nature is with her Maker. Here we are in God's hands.

(2) Still more vividly it comes to our minds in Providence that it is not in man that walketh to direct his steps. Let the older men bear witness within them. Remember the queer chain of accidents that settled you in this place and in your present work. As you look back, it seems as if you had neither art nor part in it. It just came so. Look on your own life; on the friendships that have given it meaning, on the work which dignifies it, on the successes which exhilarate, on the failures which develop your manhood; and see if this be not the exclamation on your lips, 'we are in God's hands.'

¶ F. W. Robertson of Brighton tells us how he became a minister. 'It was,' he says, 'through the barking of a dog.' He intended to become a soldier, but one night his dog barked so much that a lady who lived in the house next door, and who had an invalid daughter, wrote to him complaining of his dog. Like the gentleman that he was, Robertson called to apologize. Then he became acquainted with the people of the house, who introduced him to a friend of theirs, the Bishop of Cashel. In a talk with the Bishop one day, the latter advised Robertson to give up the idea of going into the Army and to become a clergyman instead. He did so. 'And so,' says Robertson himself, 'if my dog had not barked that night, I should now have been in the Dragoons, or fertilizing the soil of India.' 'Who can say,' he adds, 'that these things are not ordered?'

(3) But some will recognize the control of God

over them most clearly in the spiritual realm. There is a point when nothing more can be done. God must be left alone. Indeed, religious work is just to endeavour to bring souls into touch with God, and to leave them there. For it is God that giveth the increase. Some men know that well. For they have been suddenly gripped by the great Artificer. They remember that moment when, in a flash, it dawned on them that Christ's word was true, and the power of the truth held them mightily, and the unseen world momently became real. These tell you that, of a verity, we are in God's hands.

¶ 'One day,' says John Haime, the famous Primitive Methodist preacher, 'One day as I walked by the Tweed side, I cried aloud, being all athirst for God, "Oh that Thou would'st hear my prayer, and let my cry come up before Thee!" And the Lord heard; He sent a gracious answer. He lifted me out of the dungeon. He took away my sorrow and fear, and filled my soul with peace and joy in the Holy Ghost. The stream glided swiftly along, and all Nature seemed to rejoice with me. I was truly free.'

2. That, then, is the first and most obvious consideration, arising from the metaphor of the Potter. The second arises out of the thought of that which the Potter makes. He makes *vessels*; that is, He makes something for *use*. In the making, He determines the uses. Some are vessels of honour and some of dishonour.

Now, let this be our doctrine of election. God has imposed upon each one of us a service. He has strictly imposed it, by reason of the endowments which He has given us. And these services are very different. Some are more honourable than others, for the moment. They are dependent, so far, upon that with which we cannot in the least interfere; upon our original physical, social, mental, and spiritual complexions. In this sense, assent to the will of God is absolute for all.

But there is a darker suggestion here. A man may be a vessel in God's hands, used of Him and doing His work; and yet the man himself may not be God's. The Divine Power many a time gets service from evil men; sometimes indirectly but sometimes directly. Those that are not God's may be great in God's service. Wherefore, never be content with being useful in God's work. Never be content until He comes to dwell in the inmost, secret recesses of the heart.

3. The last consideration is one of pure gladness. Do not forget that Jeremiah uses this Potter's metaphor as a source of comfort, to teach us that He who formed can *re*-form.

It is curious that this metaphor of the Potter has almost always been used to convey to us a thought of our hopelessness and of our reasonable resentment against the God who made life so hard. We remember the often-quoted lines:

Ah Love! could you and I with Him conspire
To grasp this sorry Scheme of Things entire,
Would not we shatter it to bits—and then
Re-mould it nearer to the Heart's Desire!

At least we can say of this bitter-sweet outburst of the pagan poet that it precisely reverses the teaching of God's prophet, and the unveiling of His purpose given in His Son. In Him, One is given to us, who has proved unto death His willingness to conspire with us that this sorry scheme of things, which our own sick hearts have fashioned, may be remoulded nearer to His heart's desire. But here the Sovereignty of God sets its own limit. We must first assent to His work upon us. He will not compel. Are we to refuse that one condition? Nay, rather, assenting, we shall by Him be made like unto Himself.

A Name of Appearance and a Name of Reality

Jer. xx. 3.—'The Lord hath not called thy name Pashur, but Magor-missabib.'

PASHUR and Jeremiah started together, both were sons of priests, both had equal opportunities; and Jeremiah was not the one with less ability or feebler character. Yet Pashur found popularity and ease the way to overflowing success, while Jeremiah found poverty and pain, and the hatred which is much worse to bear, the only way to true manhood. The issue of it is that Jeremiah sits in the stocks, the object of scorn and ridicule to every passer-by, and Pashur is in a position to order it to be done.

Thoreau has a wise saying to the effect that he 'did not wish to practise self-denial any more than was quite necessary.' Neither Jeremiah nor Pashur wished to practise self-denial any more than was quite necessary. The sole difference between them lay in the kind of necessity each acknowledged. And that is the sole difference between any of us. What for us is quite necessary ? Is it only what is physically necessary—the compulsion of the body ; or is it what is spiritually necessary—the compulsion of the conscience ? What man calls us is chiefly determined by the former ; what God calls us— the infinitely more important consideration—is determined wholly by the latter.

1. In those old days people chose names for their children not by the sound but by the sense. The meaning, they thought, ought to be significant of the person who bore the name. To this significance of names Jeremiah refers in the text. The origin of Pashur has been sought in our day as far away as Egypt, but Jeremiah found it nearer home. Pashur, the son of Immer, he derived from ordinary Hebrew words which make them mean, ' Prosperity all Round,' the son of ' The Talker.' Let us think of it as one of those old Puritan names like Son of Humility Ford. Prosperity all Round Ford ! What an auspicious name with which to set out in the world ! What a popular name it would become, were English parents to take to saying what they think !

Then he was the son of Immer, The Talker. No virtue in him would ever lose effect from lack of a trumpeter, nor any promotion go past him for want of some one to keep asking for it. If our chief business in life is to get on, Immer, The Talker, is quite clearly the person to have for a father.

While Pashur was only a master of smooth and comfortable platitude, Jeremiah had the great gift of the preacher, the power of the winged, the unforgettable, word. Had he not imagination, insight, pathos ? And are not they the qualities which sway men, and make for success in any calling ? Alas for him, however, his name is not Prosperity all Round; the son of The Talker, but Jeremiah, ' The Lord shall Appoint,' the son of Hilkiah, ' The Lord is my Portion.'

Manifestly Jeremiah's first mistake in the way of getting on in the world was his father. To regard the Lord seriously as one's portion is apt to make a man forgo other more tangible por-

tions both for himself and for his children. And equally clearly his second mistake was with himself. His name was ' The Lord shall Appoint,' and the man who takes that seriously is very apt to find the Lord not appointing prosperity all round, but quite other things.

¶ ' The memory of my father is a sacred influence to me ; yet I can remember the day when I was hungry because of my father's conduct. I can remember my mother crying as she cut the last loaf, keeping none for herself, and gave us what there was,' wrote an elderly man. The father had been turned away from his business for refusing to do a mean and shabby thing. They gave him three days to think it over, and then he came home with no prospects and no money. The mother said to her children, ' It breaks my heart to see you hungry, but I will tell you what kind of a man your father is,' and she told them.

The son, far on in his years, testified : ' Many a time have I been tempted to do wrong, and then there arose before me the figure of the man who dared even to see his children suffer before he would sully his own conscience and sin against God.' [1]

2. There you have the secret of their lives. It lies in the necessities which determine them. Pashur will appoint for himself, and nothing will stand in his way except sheer outward obstacle. Jeremiah will have the Lord appoint, and everything will stand in his way that is not utterly veracious and just. Pashur will be defeated only if circumstances are too strong for him. No other necessity in the world could demand from him self-denial. But upon Jeremiah another necessity is laid of an entirely different order, one which makes circumstances a quite secondary and even unimportant consideration.

The difference appears at once in their preaching. Pashur is a shallow enough person, but one fact about mankind he has thoroughly grasped —the very far-reaching one that sugar is sweet in the mouth. He preached smooth things. But when Jeremiah preached he had no ear at all for the voice of his hearers asking for what they wanted. The sole voice he heard was the voice of the Lord appointing the truth. Then he had only awful, heart-shaking, soul-shattering things to say. ' Thus saith the Lord of Hosts : Even so will I break this people and this city,

[1] David Wlliamson.

as one breaketh a potter's vessel that cannot be made whole again.' Never in any age could that be popular preaching. We ought to be amazed at the moderation of Jeremiah's contemporaries in merely putting him in the stocks and dropping him into a pit.

¶ John Bunyan could have got out of prison any day by simply promising not to preach. Conformity looked easy enough, and it would have spared him the agony of making his wife and children suffer. But he remained in prison, saying, ' I must do it.'

3. There in the stocks in the high gate of Benjamin in the Temple Jeremiah sat all day a target for the gibes and the missiles of the thoughtless, scoffing, malicious crowd that thronged past. And there, when they had all gone, he sat solitary with his own thoughts all through the night, with the purple parallels of the lash stiffening on his back in the chilly night air.

It was an occasion for thinking seriously of one's life ; and Jeremiah thought of his as seriously as even Pashur could have desired. To lie like Pashur could not so much as enter into his thought. To be guilty of complicity in his country's fate, saying, ' Ye are all good and worthy people for whom God can have nothing but blessing in store,' was not conceivable for him under any pressure of violence. Might he not, however, hold his peace ? That might not give him the highest seat in the Temple with its popularity and honour, but it might at least save him from the lowest with its scourges and derision. His night of reflexion there makes him think of not making mention of God or speaking any more in His name, which was precisely the effect Pashur, having a due regard to his own skin, had confidently expected.

But, when Jeremiah thought of silence, it was as a burning fire shut up in his bones. He could no more be guilty of complicity in his country's ruin by criminal silence than by lies. He had no wish to practise self-denial any more than was quite necessary, but the final, irresistible, compelling necessity only God's word in his heart could lay upon him, not any word of man, however enforced with scourge or stocks.

¶ In Sir Walter Scott's *Fair Maid of Perth* there is a memorable conversation between Clement Blair, the priest, and the good Simon Glover. The latter warns Clement of the danger of giving voice to his doctrines, prophesying, if he does so, that it will inevitably cost him his life. To which Clement replies : ' Heaven be my witness, that I would comply in all lawful things, to conciliate the love and sympathy of my fellow-creatures ! It is no light thing to be shunned by the worthy as an infected patient ; to be persecuted by the Pharisees of the day as an unbelieving heretic ; to be regarded with horror at once and contempt by the multitude, who consider me as a madman, who may be expected to turn mischievous. But were all those evils multiplied an hundred-fold, the fire within must not be stifled, the voice which says within me—Speak, must receive obedience. Woe unto me if I preach not the Gospel, even should I at length preach it from amidst the pile of flames ! '

4. Even the longest night at length will pass. With the morning Pashur comes and, of his condescension and good pleasure, orders the prisoner to be taken out of the stocks. You see Jeremiah chilled, haggard, weary, with sleepless, burning eyes, and you see Pashur with the glow of sleep on his cheeks, and that sleek and spacious air with which success alone can endow its children.

But, suddenly, all is changed. The authentic high officer of God is Jeremiah. It is now Pashur's turn to sit white and haggard in the stocks. The fire goes from Jeremiah's bones into his eyes and his tongue, and he flashes out on Pashur : ' The Lord hath not called thee Pashur, Prosperity all Round, but Magor-missabib, Terror round About.'

What the Lord had called him had not concerned Pashur much hitherto, but the importance of it now came home to him with the insistence of the very physical force he understood. ' Thus saith the Lord, Behold I will make thee a terror to thyself and to all thy friends.' Before his sight they would fall by the sword, and he himself would go captive to Babylon and there be slain ; while the gain for which he had sold his soul would serve only to tempt the spoiler.

With good success in outward things and health and manifold activities and attention well fixed on what man calls us because of our reputation and standing in the world, the stress of life's tremendous issues may be long escaped. The notion that life is a business of taking up our cross daily may be so remote as not even to seem absurd, or become the pleasantest unreality, as when one hangs up a crucifix over the bed whereon his last desire is to suffer God to deal with his heart. But sooner or later every one's palace of illusion falls about his ears. Then nothing is of any practical concern at all except what God has called him, except, that is to say, what he really is and how it will ultimately fare with him amid the realities God appoints to try his spirit.

Other things being equal, we should all prefer to be Pashur honoured in the chief seat of the Temple to Jeremiah dishonoured in its lowest. To make light of ease and honour and prosperity is only a poor unreality. We are not even self-deceived, but are only offering ourselves a very foolish kind of incense, when we pretend that they have no value for us. But first let us be sure that other things are equal, especially the vital, the victorious, the impregnable things both for this life and the next. They are just what God appoints, the truth He requires us to utter, the deed He requires us to do, and such consequences of them as He requires us to bear. We have only to prefer what is good to what merely seems good and leave the rest to God. Then let our life be as easy and prosperous as God grants.

Look upon Jeremiah in the stocks in the high gate of Benjamin. Look upon a greater than Jeremiah. See Him spit upon, buffeted, nailed to the Cross. For us also that is what the everlasting wisdom and love may appoint. Our heart sickens at the sight. It is a terrible necessity this, to speak God's word, however unpopular, and do God's will, however unprofitable.

But if it is the bed-rock necessity of life, all the other necessities of chance and circumstance and age and death are at once put in a quite subordinate place. Even this life and this material world can in a quite amazing manner be put under our feet. Nor without this victory will there be peace, even the poor peace we have chosen, when God's authentic messengers of loss and pain shake our souls and drive us back upon reality.

The Seeming Deceptions of God

Jer. xx. 7.—'O Lord, thou hast deceived me, and I was deceived.'

WHEN Jeremiah first became conscious of being called of God to be His messenger in an evil time he was also impressed with the conviction that he would be divinely protected and made completely successful in all the duty he undertook. In the opening chapter he has placed on record what his expectation was in regard to this. He believed that God had said to him (not in actual spoken words, of course, but by the inner testimony of the Spirit) : ' See, I have this day set thee over the nations, and over the kingdoms, to root out, and to pull down, and to destroy, and to throw down, to build, and to plant. And they shall fight against thee ; but they shall not prevail against thee ; for I am with thee, saith the Lord, to deliver thee.' That was his commission, so he believed ; he was to protest in God's name against the iniquities and follies of his generation, especially amongst his own countrymen, and God on His part would see to it that no harm came to His servant and that his work should not fail. Well, we know what happened. So far from Jeremiah's labours having a triumphant issue, his was the saddest career in all the records of the great prophets of Israel. At the moment when he uttered the words of the text he was a prisoner in the hands of the priestly authorities of his own nation and had suffered the extreme of public humiliation and misery. He had been flogged like a common criminal and put in the stocks as a spectacle to all passers-by.

Try to enter into the feelings of this man when he saw the tragic outcome of his hopes and expectations. Things had not happened as he had been convinced they would. God had not protected him from misfortune and ill-usage. On the contrary, he had been subjected to the grossest ignominy, found himself an object of hatred and contempt, and, worst of all, his work apparently fruitless. It is little wonder that, plunged in the deepest melancholy and haunted by an overwhelming sense of failure, he should have cried, ' O Lord, thou hast deceived me, and I was deceived.' We know, looking back upon it all, that Jeremiah was not deceived. Every promise made him was royally fulfilled. He came through a sea of troubles safe and sound, and his word is living and powerful to this day. But the point is that to this great prophet there came an hour when heaven seemed to cheat him—' O Lord, thou hast deceived me, and I was deceived.'

1. There are times in the experience of most people when they are ready to say God has deceived them.

(1) Children begin with beautiful pictures of God, mediated to their imaginations by the loveliest symbols human experience provides, such as shepherd, friend, and father. Then they grow up to face life's tragic realities, and, seeing the incongruity between the sweet fatherliness of God that they have believed in and the cruel calamities life brings, they are ready to give up God. Then, coming to the church on Sunday and hearing us present our experience of God in terms of unalloyed security and peace, they cry, These people do not see the facts. Of course we see the facts ! How can one help it ? To feel that God is not living up to His good reputation is one of the most poignant, unescapable experiences His saints ever face. Who was it that cried on a cross, ' My God, my God, why hast thou forsaken me ? '—which is to say, My God, why hast thou deceived me ?

¶ In one of our Round Table Conferences in India a fine young Englishman, a leader among the group of business men who wanted better relationships between India and Great Britain, said in rather a disillusioned way, ' God let me down. My brother was wounded in the war. I prayed to Him that my brother might live. Any decent person would have answered. But He didn't and my brother died. Now I have no faith left. I do think that Christ was the greatest personality that ever lived. But God let me down, so I have no religion. I wish I did have one.' [1]

(2) In maturer years as well as in youth the confidence in God's management of life gets destroyed by events. There are individual tragedies. Marriages that seemed made in heaven are ended by what insurance men call an ' act of God ' ; promising children whom the world desperately needed are untimely carried off ; men rendering to the cause of God inestimable service are stricken down at the height of their strength, so that God at times seems to

[1] E. Stanley Jones, *Christ and Human Suffering*, 17.

be arrayed against Himself and to be fighting His own interests.

It is the feeling of fear and mistrust engendered by considerations of this kind that is distressing many sensitive souls and leaving them stranded in the general break-up of hitherto authoritative modes of belief and practice which is going on everywhere at the present time.

(3) Beyond such individual tragedies, moreover, men who have high hopes about the world at large—praying earnestly, working laboriously, sacrificing greatly for peace and justice—see the total drift of their generation set in against them until, far from being backed by the Eternal, their best efforts sometimes appear like whistling in the teeth of a hurricane. It is this that often breaks down the faith of men and makes them ready to say with Jeremiah, ' O Lord, thou hast deceived me, and I was deceived.'

2. Where does the trouble lie ? If we are to take our cue from Jeremiah, we will not hastily try to solve our problem by giving up God. It is not easy to give up God, for ' always there will remain deep, indubitable facts—the love of beauty, of goodness, of truth, conscience within, personal relationships that make love seem the most powerful force in the world, and great hours when the Eternal seems real indeed, and the world invisible shines through the seen—a whole series of spiritual facts which constitute man's life at its highest.

Oh, we're sunk enough here, God knows !
  But not quite so sunk that moments,
Sure tho' seldom, are denied us,
  When the spirit's true endowments
Stand out plainly from its false ones,
  And apprise it if pursuing
Or the right way or the wrong way,
  To its triumph or undoing.

There are flashes struck from midnights,
  There are fire-flames noondays kindle,
Whereby piled-up honours perish,
  Whereby swollen ambitions dwindle,
While just this or that poor impulse,
  Which for once had play unstifled,
Seems the sole work of a life-time
  That away the rest have trifled.

But if we are not to give up God, we shall have to give up some of our own attitudes. We shall have to give up a self-centred religion that thinks it is the chief business of God to keep us from trouble.

George Eliot, in *Middlemarch*, reminds us of old mirrors, which, after generations of polishing, are covered with innumerable, infinitesimal scratches, and she says that when, in the dark, a lighted candle is brought close to one of them, the markings arrange themselves in concentric circles around the image of the candle flame. So our lives become egocentric. We think of our friends, our family, our nation, our world, chiefly in terms of what we can get out of them. If, then, a man is religious, he brings God in, and his religious faith and reliance are added to the concentric circles. God's meaning for him lies in God's ability and willingness to save him from trouble. It is that picture of the Eternal which lets us down. But God never yet guaranteed to keep any man out of trouble, not even His Christ.

This universe isn't centred in us. This universe is centred in God, in whose eyes a thousand years are but as yesterday when it is past, and as a watch in the night. Let us play our small part ; stand what we have to stand. God is not letting us down because we suffer. Far beyond our beholding sweeps His eternal purpose.

God is greater, sterner, and more austere than our sentimental popular Christianity commonly suggests. If a man starts with a picture of the universe as run by a sweet, indulgent Deity, he is doomed to be let down. In saying this, one need not deny the gentle aspects of Christian experience. There are hours when the unseen Friend within makes real everything that Jesus said about the Father's individual care. It is true of Him that :

... warm, sweet, tender, even yet
A present help is He.

While, however, that is true, it is not the whole truth, and whenever partial truth is taken for whole truth dangerous fallacy ensues. The loveliest forget-me-nots are in the high Alps. They are beautiful, running their blue glories up to the very edges of the snow. But, lovely as they are, they are not the whole of the high Alps. The high Alps are towering altitudes with austere aspects that forget-me-nots do not exhaust. So is the great God.

3. Jeremiah recovered himself in seeing that there were loving purposes behind the so-called deceptions of God. That is one of the ways of God for strengthening and educating character. He leaves us, not because He is false, or because He has broken the promise of His help, but because, like a mother with her little child, He is teaching us to stand upon our feet. Had Jeremiah been ringed around with strength he never would have cried this bitter cry. Had his message been instantly and heartily received he never would have thus complained of God. But was it not the baffling of his hopes, and the world of sorrows he was called to bear, that revealed his depth and tenderness of character, and made him so true a forerunner of Christ ?

It is also one of God's ways to make us valiant, and to stir and rouse us to our best endeavour. Think, for example, of that first hope of Christendom—that the Second Coming of the Lord was near at hand. ' This generation shall not pass till all things are fulfilled ' : ' We which remain till the coming of the Lord '— that was the bright and burning expectation that shone in the heaven of the Early Church. But the years passed and Jesus did not come. There was no call of the trumpet ; the sky o'erhead was brass ; till some, deadened by the delay, began to murmur, ' Thou hast deceived us, and we were deceived.' We know to-day that they were not deceived, for Christ was coming though they knew it not. But without that burning hope could they ever have suffered and been strong ? They were mighty to dare, mighty to do and die, mighty to rise to the best and face the worst, because they lived on the margins of eternity. So does God strengthen us by what He hides not less divinely than by what He shows.

Again, this so-called deception is one of the ways of God to lead us on. There is a beautiful story of Dr John Brown (author of *Rab and his Friends*), that once, when out walking with some children, he found the little folk growing very weary. He might have scolded them, but he did not do that. He might have made promises, but he did not do that. He went to the thicket and cut half a dozen switches and made the children mount them for their horses. The children, beguiled by the wise and gentle stratagem, quite forgot how weary they had been. Would Israel ever have left Egypt had they not been beguiled by love upon their journey ? Would we ever have the heart to travel if we were not beset by stratagems of mercy ?

There are times when we are all tempted to say—Thou hast deceived us and we are deceived, but we shall find, if we only trust and wait till the day break and the shadows flee away, that what in our ignorance we called deceit was nought but the ingenuity of love.

The Good Old Times

Jer. xxii. 15.—'Shalt thou reign, because thou closest thyself in cedar ? did not thy father eat and drink, and do judgment and justice, and then it was well with him ? '

THE Latin tag, ' *laudator temporis acti* ' refers scornfully to the man who is always praising the olden days. The spacious times of Queen Elizabeth, heroic periods in the Church's story like the Reformation, shine in history in a golden light. Old men tell how summers were hotter and frosts keener when they were boys. Yet statistics give no corroboration, and reflexion on the horrors of past history leads to the conclusion that the world was at least as bad long ago as to-day.

But people do hanker after ' the good old times.' They turn from modern plays to Shakespeare, from jazz to old folk-tunes. Some of the most advanced socialism is inspired by the wistful looking backward to the mediaeval Trade Guilds and the time when the Church banned usury and undertook to fix a just price. And there is something wholesome in the desire to preserve or recover the finest elements of the past. In some connexions the recovery of what has been forgotten might be as valuable as the discovery of something new.

In one place Jeremiah, one of the most forward-looking men in his faith and hope, indulges in this longing for the good old times. ' Woe unto him that buildeth his house by unrighteousness, and his chambers by wrong ; that useth his neighbour's service without wages, and giveth him not for his work ; That saith, I will build me a wide house and large chambers, and cutteth him out windows ; and it is cieled with cedar, and painted with vermilion. Shalt thou reign, because thou closest thyself in cedar ? Did not thy father eat and drink, and do judgment and justice, and then it was well with him ? He judged the cause of the poor and needy ; then it was well with him ; was not this to know me ? saith the Lord.' He is contrasting the ways of two Jewish kings and he says the old king's ways were best. The modern craze in his day was the usual one with the newly rich, the appetite for vulgar display, new houses, spacious, elaborately decorated, expensive, with panelled ceilings and lots of scarlet paint. In former days men had been glad enough to eat and drink and live in simpler fashion, doing justice and loving mercy. ' Was not this to know me ? ' Jeremiah hears God say. The old times were plainer and they were holier and men were nearer God.

1. There was *virtue in simplicity*. Modern tendencies are towards over-elaborate luxury. Some years ago Glasgow gave as wedding-present to a royal lady a golden dressing-table. Whether beautiful or not, it had whatever merit lies in being not only useful but expensive and ostentatious. Even simplicity can be made costly, as a lady lecturing on domestic science knew who recommended striking a simple note in table decorations provided that it was obviously expensive. Those who cannot afford that style try for effect by the gaudy and tawdry.

Is it then altogether evil that to-day really simpler ways are unavoidable, and that, not merely for a year or two but perhaps a generation, living will be plainer and less luxurious ? A fashion designer has expressed the opinion that the discarding of frills and trimmings enforced by austerity rules has had the broad result that dress is of better design. Is it a pitiful thing if building is to be of Portal houses rather than luxury flats, and utility furniture does not run to cedar or red lacquer ? There is a correlation between plain living and high thinking, between luxury and selfishness and pride. It is certain that Jesus judged that the great danger in life was not to be poor but to be rich. A simpler life might make for greater interest in intellectual pleasures, and in justice and mercy. A life that was less elaborate might be holier and nearer to God.

2. Another good point the prophet recalls about the old times is their *more intimate*

personal relations. The old king, comparatively poor and plainly housed, was accessible to all and judged the causes of the poor. The prophet's idea is that one who lives in a grand house gets isolated from contact with common folk and away from the habit of dealing justly and generously with his neighbours. Those born rich are misled into a conviction that they have a natural right to be rich and maintain a certain style, although others, making perhaps a larger contribution to the needs of the community, are stinted ; and those who get rich by their own exertions or acumen think that they deserve all they get and that those who get less deserve less. These, though obvious fallacies, tend to be rich men's notions, and they cut away the roots of happy social relations.

One has the impression that personal contact was commoner and happier in former days than in an age of large combines and bureaucratic administration. Three thousand years ago Scripture tells that farmer Boaz came to his harvest field to see the reapers. ' The Lord be with you,' he said, and they answered, ' The Lord bless thee.' Forty years ago in a little Scots town the founders of its prosperity were still held in kindly remembrance. Rob and David they had been all their lives to their fellow townsmen even when by skill and energy and foresight and good fortune they came to own large factories and to possess very great wealth ; and the memory they left was of familiar homely acquaintances. So in a great Lanarkshire steel work living men have recalled wistfully the time when the concern was not a company, and when each man had, if he sought it, personal access to the chief, sure of a hearing and justice.

Like this personal interest of the employer was the personal pride of a workman in his craft. Of his father Sir Henry Jones in his *Memories* says proudly, ' A slack job never passed through his hands.' And of his own apprenticeship he recalls, ' The boots I made as a learner were handed round and praised or blamed just as if we were dealing with a work of art.' Whereas an experienced house painter said some years ago that he thought one reason why experienced men were not given jobs was not that they were too old but that they were too good. They had been trained to an ideal of workmanship that made them inevitably a little slower, and all that was wanted now was speed.

Enforced simplicity may bring back some of the personal note in life and labour that was getting lost. ' Water it with the dew of common poverty,' said Maurice Hewlett, ' and you will get one England again instead of a round dozen.' Officers get to know men better as privates than they did as employees or subordinates in civil life. Grand ladies become acquainted with their poorer neighbours in the queue. If poverty and hardship make for closer and more heart to heart contact it may bring a rich compensation for the loss of some amenities that fostered fastidious pride. Is not the simple life the life to which comes most readily the crowning touch of humble faith that makes it blessed.

3. In dwelling on the good old times one subject that comes inevitably to the mind is *Sunday Observance.* It is true that the English Puritans and the Scots took their stand on the Jewish regulations about the Sabbath and set aside Paul's declaration, ' I judge no man in respect of a Sabbath or a feast day,' and that to-day denunciations of people for doing harmless things on Sundays are futile. But the real question is whether people are making the best of a day that is part of their religious inheritance. ' I am amazed,' said Ramsay Macdonald, ' at many of my old friends who say that the Scottish Sabbath was a burden. I would like to see a state of society when every one preferred the old Scottish Sabbath to the modern French one, because in that state of society you would have great solid eternal foundations of character and self-command.' If Sunday practically disappears out of a man's life he is poorer just on the side he can least afford to lose anything. Those who wistfully recall quieter, holier Sundays are entirely right.

4. So one could speak of family worship and the family pew. But pass to one other matter —*the outlook on foreign lands.* A generation or two ago men had a really religious outlook on the world. Germany was for them the home of the Reformation, Palestine was the cradle of Christianity, America was where the Pilgrim Fathers found freedom to worship in their own way, Africa was ' Darkest Africa ' because the light of the gospel was there unknown. No doubt far more is known to-day about other nations. Palestine is a source of potash and a

first-class political problem. America is a melting pot for all races, a social experiment. Africa is a treasure house, for all its poverty, of gold mines and copper and diamonds and cocoa and palm oil. But is the old idea lost that the world of nations is a field for the gospel ' white unto harvest.'

Progress does not mean panelled ceilings and vermilion paint, or science or engineering, but to live nearer God. It is not material comforts and luxuries that make life nobler and constitute a better age. The good old times were not grander. They were simpler, more human, more religious. ' Is not this to know me ? ' saith the Lord.

R. W. STEWART.

A Noble Epitaph

Jer. xxii. 16.—' He judged the cause of the poor and needy ; then it was well with him : was not this to know me ? saith the Lord.'

THE prophet is here speaking of Josiah, King of Judah, who was personally devout and faithful, and whose reign was peaceful and prosperous. The context acquaints us with Jehoiakim, Josiah's worthless son, whose reign was defamed by selfishness and oppression.

The narrative suggests three points which we may consider.

1. The highest type of human character is the humane. ' He judged the cause of the poor and needy.' Jeremiah felt that he could pronounce upon Josiah no higher eulogy. Alexander Pope in one of his essays declares that ' the proper study of mankind is man.' But we may say that the proper study of man is mankind, and the rarest excellence of which we are capable is sympathy and helpfulness.

(1) The spirit of helpfulness is more admirable than the attainment of any measure of worldly power and glory. There are philosophies of life wholly devoted to glorifying the strong, the worship of power, the ' mailed fist ', the master morality. To-day, however, we have got so far on the path of progress that the powerful and selfish of any type will never again become the ideals of the race. The generous power that aids, guides, blesses, will increasingly be respected and esteemed ; but the selfish power that exploits the people for its own indulgence and aggrandisement is fast losing its black magic. More and more the lover of his fellows becomes the popular hero : and pity, graciousness, friendliness, kindness, sacrifice, are the qualities extolled and coveted. ' He judged the cause of the poor and needy ' is a grander epitaph than that he won battles, and carved a fortune.

¶ Napoleon was one of the most amazing personalities that have ever appeared on the stage of human affairs ; a man really great, since he changed the course of history, and left the world a different place from that which he found it. But when we ask whether his life was a blessing to the world, the answer is not for a moment in doubt. Is it not possible that, in the coming years, the name of Madame Curie, the French woman who discovered radium with its healing power, may be more deservedly celebrated than the name of Napoleon ? For she was a builder, not a destroyer. Fame is of two kinds, and there should be a separate roll for each. On the roll of those who have won fame by building up and not destroying human values, there would be inscribed from France the name of Madame Curie, and from our own land such names as Florence Nightingale, Josephine Butler, Dr Barnardo, Mary Slessor of Calabar, Grenfell of Labrador, with many others from other lands, who made the world a better place by their presence.[1]

¶ There is a fine story told in a poem by Sir Edwin Arnold about a Persian warrior whose praise was on every one's lips. The soldier had won many great battles, and was never known to fear danger. One day he was riding down a dusty road and there on the side was a poor old beggar trying to get a thorn out of his foot. After watching him for a minute the soldier got off his horse and taking off his gloves he pulled the troublesome thorn out and went on his way. The story tells that when the great soldier died he was received into heaven and saw a beautiful rose growing on a thorn. ' That,' said an angel, ' is the rose you planted when you took the thorn from the poor man's foot.' The soldier found to his surprise that his deeds in battle were unknown, but that one act of love was noticed.

[1] J. Colville, The Christian Highway, 33.

(2) More than this, the spirit of kindness is greater than genius. We must keep this distinctly in view, and resolutely contend that the kindly heart, the open hand, the self-sacrificing life, are more than the most brilliant brain. A determined effort was made on the part of a certain school to depreciate goodwill, compassion, philanthropy, as compared with dazzling intellectual eminence. Take one example. Bertram Dobell, in his introduction to Thomson's *The City of Dreadful Night*, observes : ' The only literature worthy to survive is that which reveals to us a nature superior to the commonplace aims and low ideals of ordinary humanity. Such a nature indeed may have many and great faults ; but we must needs take a deeper interest in a Burns or a Byron than in the most benevolent and blameless Lord Shaftesbury who ever lived.' If we do take such an interest, it is high time that we re-valued our values. There is something fatally wrong with a generation that exalts intellect above humanity. The verdict of Corot, the artist, is far truer. *The Imitation of Christ* was always on Corot's pillow, and he says concerning it : ' It has taught me that men must not be puffed up because they are emperors and add this province or that to their territories, or because they can paint and win a name for themselves. If these men are gifted more or less, I see no merit attaching to them. There is no glory compared to that of a St. Vincent de Paul and a Sister of Charity.' The primacy is of the heart. ' If I speak with the tongues of men and of angels, but have not love, I am become sounding brass, or a clanging cymbal.'

¶ ' I have lived a long time,' an industrial prince notes in a modern autobiography, ' and I have seen men and things in abundance. Out of my experience two truths shine with the brightness of the sun. The one is that goodness is more than cleverness and that kindness is the final possession.' [1]

Our ministry of kindness will be remembered when our cleverness and intellectual proficiency are forgotten. Thus does Wordsworth speak of

> that best portion of a good man's life,
> His little, nameless, unremembered, acts
> Of kindness and of love.

[1] A. Maclean, *Walk in the Light*, 36.

(3) Again, a gracious goodness is something more than formal righteousness. ' For scarcely for a righteous man will one die ; peradventure, for the good man some one would even dare to die.' No one would be in indecent haste to die for ' the Elder Brother,' but it is conceivable that one might be moved to sacrifice oneself for the Good Samaritan. We may be just, upright, consistent, punctilious, irreproachable, but is the spirit of compassion and helpfulness as pronounced an element in our life ?

¶ There are some kinds of good people whom you would walk blocks to avoid meeting. There are the conventionally good who, through a long lifetime having observed little rules of respectability, immoderately admire themselves in consequence, like the Pharisee in Jesus' parable : ' I fast twice in the week ; I give tithes of all that I get.' There are the negatively good whose goodness consists in having kept the lid clamped tightly down on their insurgent badness so that they are repressed and dried up and sour. How dreadful they are ! There are the censoriously good whose morality is all for export, who in endless interference with other people's business try to do us good. There are the narrowly good, who make an infinite to-do about infinitesimal matters of behaviour which do not matter much and who never get their eyes on the great ethical issues of their day, on economic justice and international peace.[1]

What a grand thing if the great mass of formal, conventional, self-regarding piety should suddenly acquire a new quality, and in addition to its rigid character should send forth throughout its whole neighbourhood the sweet-smelling savour of an active sympathy ! Such a ministry has God's own blessing. ' Thus saith the Lord, Let not the wise man glory in his wisdom, neither let the mighty man glory in his might, let not the rich man glory in his riches : but let him that glorieth glory in this, that he understandeth, and knoweth me, that I am the Lord which exercise loving kindness, judgment, and righteousness, in the earth : for in these things I delight, saith the Lord.'

2. The humane spirit is the condition of personal and national welfare.

(1) *Personal Welfare.*—' Did not thy father eat and drink, and do judgment and justice ? Then it was well with him.' The administration

[1] H. E. Fosdick.

of Josiah was marked by righteousness and benevolence, and acting thus he enjoyed life. Personally his was a happy reign. On the other hand, Jehoiakim practised selfishness and oppression. He set himself to build a great palace, and he built his palace with the sweat and blood of his subjects, compelling them to do forced labour without giving the labourers wages. He fed his pride and ambition at the expense of the needy. And it was not well with him. In life, unrespected ; in death unlamented, ' buried with the burial of an ass, and cast forth beyond the gates of Jerusalem.'

We cannot shut ourselves up to selfishness without defeating ourselves, without destroying our peace and joy of life. The ' blue bird ' which the whole world is chasing, makes its nest and wakes its music in the household that is at leisure from itself, that is alive to the sorrows and needs of its neighbours. To succour the poor, to befriend the ignorant, to visit the sick, to safeguard the weak, to show compassion to those out of the way, to hearten the struggler with adversity, is to know the Master's joy, the joy that no man takes from us.

Be useful where thou livest, that they may
Both want and wish thy pleasing presence still.
Kindnesse, good parts, great places, are the way
To compasse this. Finde out men's wants and will,
  And meet them there. All worldly joyes go lesse
To the one joy of doing kindnesses.[1]

(2) *National Welfare.*—The text reads, ' Then it was well.' Well with the Kingdom as it was also with the King. But Jeremiah predicts that it will not be thus under Jehoiakim. ' Woe unto him that buildeth his house by unrighteousness, and his chambers by injustice.' And the ominous anticipation came to pass in overwhelming national tragedy. National strength and safety are in justice, mercy, and goodwill. The stability of a nation is not in its commerce, manufactures, mechanical skill, and scientific knowledge, but rather in the general cultivation and exercise of the sympathetic feelings—in the rich considering the poor, in the cultured affording education to the untaught, in the strong befriending the weak.

¶ Alfred Russel Wallace writes, ' We should now clearly recognize the fact, that the wealth, knowledge, and culture of *the few* do not constitute civilization.'

3. The relation of this spirit to religious faith.

Our social duty is linked to the knowledge of God. ' Was not this to know me ? saith the Lord.' Note the close, the essential connexion between practical humanity and the Divine knowledge and fear ! That an enthusiasm for humanity has broken out from time to time outside the Church is true enough, but how far is it indirectly indebted to the Christian teaching from which it has been divorced ? Philosophical and social systems as taught by pure secularists boast principles which, directly or indirectly, have certainly been derived from Christianity.

It is as if a stranger should visit our Zoological Gardens, with its aviary full of sun birds and doves of the most gorgeous feather, or should visit Kew with its rare glowing blooms, and then conclude that this northern isle is strangely rich in its birds and flowers. They are foreign, adopted, living in artificial conditions, and the main difficulty is to keep them alive. So social sentiments are not native to many schools which now apply them ; those sentiments never emerged in pre-Christian civilizations, and if the atmosphere of the Christian Church were withdrawn they could not be kept alive.

¶ Dr T. R. Glover, writing of Athens in the age of Pericles, says : ' The horrible condition of the slaves in the silver mines of Attica is sometimes noticed by ancient writers, but there is no indication that it troubled the capitalists or the public conscience.' [1]

The revelation of God in the Old Testament shows His equity and gentleness to all His children, His special care for His suffering ones. In a dark savage world given up to the idolatry of power, teeming with slaves and cruelty, the tender humanity of the Jewish world shines forth a light from heaven.

In the New Testament we see our Lord turning with infinite compassion to the multitude, to the ignorant, the sinners, the sufferers, the burdened, the pariahs and paupers of His age. He showed, as it had never been shown before, the infinite worth of the meanest slave and of the guiltiest sinner. He sent forth His

[1] George Herbert.

[1] *From Pericles to Philip*, 44.

Apostles on the same errand of recovering the lost, and well did they fulfil their calling. They had no regard for the brilliant scenes and splendid things which furnish the purple patches of the pages of history; they were wholly occupied with the salvation of the sinner, no matter how abject his situation. Their Master opened their eyes to the sufferings and horrors of which the world is full, and He showed them that the path to truest glory was the mission of mercy, the proclaiming of the good news of pardon, blessedness, and immortality to all who cried from out the gulf of despair.

¶ In the work of a distinguished naturalist is recorded his long study of the vegetation of the Amazon. His chief object was the mosses. Glorious palms, superb orchids, famous lilies, are allowed to go by with hardly any notice; but in sickness, fatigue, and peril he was comforted by the discovery of a moss—the meanest, minutest thing on the landscape.

It is thus that we *know* God. Not in science or philosophy do we know Him, or in speculation of any kind, but in love, and sacrifice, and service. Not even in theology and worship do we attain the most vital knowledge of God, but in deeds of pity and self-denying love. The logic of love teaches more than any other logic. The best interpretation of Him whom no man hath seen or can see is to rescue those fashioned in His likeness. Thus we best know God, best please Him, best increase in His knowledge, and best prove to ourselves and the world that we know and love Him.

We must not give the shadow of sanction to the notion that philanthropy is as safe and efficient in the sphere of secularism as it is in the stewardship of the Church. We have the supreme example, the master motive, the habit of two thousand years. We rejoice in the work of humanists outside the Church, but still remember that philanthropy as a power and passion is native to the disciples of Jesus Christ. ' *Ye* are the light of the world.' May our light of love shine steadily and brightly until no dark place is left in the whole earth, and all classes and nations walk in the light of the Lord!

Jehovah-Tsidkenu

Jer. xxiii. 6.—' The Lord our righteousness.'
1 Cor. i. 30.—' Christ is made unto us . . . righteousness.'

RIGHTEOUSNESS of the requisite standard is not humanly attainable, but a name like this puts us on the way to its ultimate possession. Jeremiah uses the name on two occasions and in different references. On the first occasion it is the name of the ideal king—' This is his name whereby he shall be called, Jehovah-Tsidkenu '; the second time he uses it, it is the name of the ideal city or kingdom—' This is the name wherewith she shall be called, Jehovah-Tsidkenu.'

The ideal king is portrayed as being perfectly righteous in character, and as promoting righteousness throughout his realm. The ideal city or kingdom is depicted as being righteous altogether in its citizens and in all its conditions of life. The ideal state requires for its first essential an ideal government, or in more personal language an ideal monarch: ' A king shall reign in righteousness '—that is the first requisite of all righteous conditions. However difficult or apparently impossible the attainment of righteousness may be, the conscience of man has long felt that it is righteousness that exalts a nation, and that righteousness is the ideal state of being.

When Dr Alexander Whyte died he was described as the last of the great old race of preachers of righteousness. Those preachers of righteousness were in truth a great old race, Elijah, Isaiah, Amos, Jeremiah, Paul, Calvin, and others with them. They were men who preached righteousness as those who sought it for themselves above all recognition or reward, and as those who sought it for their society and generation as the true foundation of security and peace. They knew that perfect righteousness is of God and must be God-given; they had a profound sense of God, and preached and lived as if God were behind them and beside them.

¶ The deepest longing in us is born of the deepest need: oh that Thou wouldest rend the heavens, that Thou wouldest come down! Oppressed and afflicted by his own unrighteousness and the unrighteousness of others, man—every man—lifts up from the depths of his nature the cry for righteousness, the righteousness of God. Whoever understands him at this point, understands him wholly. Whoever can reach a hand to him here, can really help him. This is the reason that such prophets as Moses, Jeremiah, and John the Baptist are figures never to be erased from the memory of humanity. They uncovered to men their deepest need; they made articulate their conscience within them; they wakened and kept awake the longing within them for the righteousness of God. They prepared the way of the Lord.[1]

1. This saying of Jeremiah sets before us *the final and ultimate standard of righteousness.* When we consider any sort of moral situation we require some standard or norm by which to judge whether the things we consider right are adequate and appropriate or not; we want to know the measurements of the ideal, so that we may get the true requirements of the actual. It has been urged that where numbers of men are gathered together they have the right to agree among themselves as to what things may or may not be. In other words, they have the right to erect a standard of morality approved by themselves and adapted to their needs. But the world needs more than a number of nations living according to their separate standards; there must be one supreme standard, world-wide in its scope and rule.

There are some things that we may fix for ourselves, laws of local societies and institutions, wages and working hours. But there are some things that are fixed for us: the rising and setting of sun and moon, the ebb and flow of ocean tides, the coming and going of the wind, the rotation of day and night, seedtime and harvest, summer and winter; and in the spiritual world as in the natural there is somewhere an absolute standard as fixed as the sun, where right is right and wrong is wrong, and nothing can by any means mix them.

2. This name that the prophet gives to the ideal king and the ideal state, raises the further question as to *the source of righteousness.* Manifestly it is not found in ourselves; not alone because the Scriptures say so, but because our own hearts say so. 'None of us has strength to rise,' confessed Seneca, 'Oh, that some one would stretch out a hand.' 'To will,' the Apostle Paul cried, 'is present with me: but

[1] Karl Barth, *The Word of God and the Word of Man,* 13.

how to perform that which is good I find not.' Long and patiently he practised the plan of the Pharisees to attain righteousness. Sometimes he thought he had it or almost had it, yet it eluded the grasp of his eager fingers; then after repeated failure he abandoned the quest, because he had found some better way, he had found Some One who made His righteousness available for other men so that the man's hungry heart was satisfied at last and only craved—' That I may be found in him, not having mine own righteousness . . . but that which is through the faith of Christ, the righteousness which is of God by faith.'

¶ Bernard Shaw has pointed out that 'it is possible for a man to pass the moral catechism, Have you obeyed the Commandments? Have you kept the law? and at the end to live a worse life than the sinner who must answer Nay! all through the questions.'

¶ 'What should I do,' exclaimed Thomas Chalmers, 'were it not that it is written, "Christ died for the ungodly." Never am I in a better frame than when dwelling in simple faith on Christ's offered righteousness, and making it the object of my acceptation.'

We cannot keep all God's commandments, not simply because, as the Marquis of Lossie confessed when his life was nearing its end, he had not time to do so—we cannot keep God's commandments because we have not the ability to do so, even if we had the time; but, as the wise schoolmaster said to the Marquis, 'There is one commandment that includes all the rest, "Believe on the Lord Jesus Christ and thou shalt be saved."'

Jesus, Thy blood and righteousness
    My beauty are, my glorious dress.
'Midst flaming worlds in these arrayed,
    With joy shall I lift up my head.

3. The name has this further content, that it reveals to us *the secret of righteousness.* Martin Luther has discussed four kinds of righteousness. There is a political righteousness, that which implies obedience to the laws of the state and the principles of good citizenship; there is a certain ceremonial righteousness, which is attained by the observance of certain forms of ritual; there is also a legal righteousness which is obtained by a due regard to the Mosaic law, and the explicit commandments of God; and

there is a moral and spiritual righteousness which belongs to the inward life, as against these other purely external conditions of being.

Outward forms will not command the inward state, but the inward life can command the outward form. God requires truth in the inward parts. He sets up righteousness in the citadel of the heart, and out of a righteous heart are the issues of a righteous life. So the righteousness of Christ is not simply righteousness attributed to us. It goes beyond that, and becomes in present experience a righteousness communicated and possessed. ' The Lord our righteousness,' not the standard only, not a substitute merely, but the secret of being in which a completely new manner of life becomes an actuality.

This righteousness which Christ creates and cultivates in our experience is above the level of merely customary ways of living; it means a quality of life that is not subject to human opinion and fashion, nor accommodated to the spirit of the time.

Christ is the secret of that righteousness in every rank and level of life. He kept His own soul unspotted from the world; no life was ever more roughly handled or more severely buffeted or more persistently tempted, but He yielded at no point, and He is to troubled and tempted souls the strength and courage of righteousness. He is the inward motive and constraint of all those who make it the supreme business of their life, by all the aids that heaven lends to serious men, to practise the righteousness that approves itself unto God.

4. If the Lord is our righteousness we can possess a remarkable *serenity* about present and ultimate things. He will suffice for all time, present and future, and for all conditions. Men who have lived and died seeking this one prize, believed in it though it eluded them. Though they died before they attained it, they believed in it as if they were sure they would take up its quest again on the other side of death ; and if there were other worlds to conquer, they would conquer them too, and at last come to that promised righteousness, ' When we see him we shall be like him.' ' Henceforth,' cried one who joined in this quest with all his heart, ' Henceforth there is laid up for me a crown of righteousness, which the Lord, the righteous Judge, shall give me at that day; and not to me only, but unto all them also that love

His appearing.' The prospect was both peace and power to his life.

> Simple rule, and safest guiding,
>   Inward peace, and inward might,
> Star upon our path abiding—
>   Trust in God, and do the right.

God Afar Off and Near

Jer. xxiii. 23, 24.—' Am I a God at hand, saith the Lord, and not a God afar off ? Can any hide himself in secret places that I shall not see him ? saith the Lord. Do not I fill heaven and earth.'

IT is not clear what Jeremiah had in mind in these words, but at least they suggest this to us, and it is importantly true whether the prophet intended it or not : namely, that one way to keep the inmost conscience sensitive to God's will, one way to protect it against every influence tending to make it coarse and self-deceived, is to hold firmly before the mind both the *afar-off-ness* and the *nearness*, both the sublime transcendency and the intimate proximity, of God. The one with whom we have to deal is at once the Most High and the Most Near. Both thoughts are necessary, and necessary together.

1. Consider, first, the protection afforded by the awareness of God as afar off.

(1) There is, to begin with, the ever-present difficulty of distinguishing between what is the will of God and what is merely our own clamant desire. In the Old Testament the false prophets are frequently denounced for the way in which they continually led the people shamelessly and vulgarly to identify God's will with their own safety and success. Isaiah accused them of prophesying smooth things. Micaiah accused them of first finding out what the king wanted to be told, and then telling him it eloquently in the name of God. Ezekiel denounced them for saying peace when there was no peace. But it is a trick we can all use, even when we are not important enough to be set right by an Isaiah or an Ezekiel. Indeed, it is not a trick at all, but just a fatal and almost unconscious habit of the mind.

It is like an apparatus for magnifying vibrations, however small, which may be brought near it. When you enter the room, and the apparatus is turned on, instantly the silence is filled with a startling and awe-inspiring thunder. It might be the voice of a god. In reality it is your own heart-beats caught up and magnified a million times. So it is apt to be in our thought of God. He becomes merely a sounding-board to our own desires, giving them a power and an authority which they would not otherwise possess. How much of that sort of thing there is going on to-day needs no illustration.

What, then, is to protect us from such folly ? Well, it is at least a help to keep steadily before the mind the afar-off-ness, the transcendent sublimity of God. Isaiah kept on saying to Israel, in effect, Do remember that God is high and lifted up above all the circle of the earth, to say nothing of the circle of your own little life ; that His ways are not our ways ; that the chances are, to say the least, that the will of such a Being will *not* altogether coincide with our private ambitions and desires, or even the desires and ambitions of our nation.

In other words, we must come into God's presence when we want to know His will with a certain profound humility, a certain sense of the insignificance, and even irrelevance, of *our* ambitions to the purpose of one so vast in His wisdom and reach and power. It is at this point that worship becomes intimately related to the whole manner of our daily life.

(2) Then, again, there is the danger which ever besets the religious conscience of trivializing God, or, in other and more powerful words, of straining at gnats and swallowing camels ! It is a curious phenomenon this, and an examination of it might lead us to some important matters in the understanding of our own hearts. Perhaps it is our very sense of failure and incapacity that makes us so anxious to do over-time, if one may so put it, on things that seem well within our compass. If we cannot do the weightier matters, it is a good defence, the better for being an unconscious defence, to make a great fuss over the smaller things. Thus we mistake a peddling, finicky conscience for a true one, and are, as religious people so frequently are, austere and self-disciplined in a crabbed and singularly sterile way.

What we really need is a different vision of God and certainly a vision which includes more of His sublime transcendency and afar-off-ness. We should all do well to sit down and ask our-

selves at times what sort of God we really believe in, if we think He cares two straws about the things that occupy so much attention and excite so much controversy. Perhaps some of our ecclesiastical differences and debates would take at once a great leap forward towards solution. We may, perhaps, hope that that is one of the things which God will do for His Church through the vast evil and convulsion of our time ; namely, enable it to see certain matters in truer proportion, and so find unity in common penitence at the feet of the infinite and eternal God.

¶ In the town of Glarus, in Switzerland, the population is both Protestant and Roman Catholic. They use the same church. A curtain is drawn across the Roman Catholic altar at the conclusion of Mass and, as the worshippers leave, they say 'Good morning' to their Protestant neighbours who are coming in. It does not seem strange to the people. The custom of other Cantons seems strange to them. Perhaps it seems strange to God also.[1]

2. It is equally important, indeed indispensable, not to forget the God who is also near. It is all too easy, as the history of religion shows, to fly to the other extreme and ascribe to God such exalted sublimity that all effective awareness of His concern in the moral issues of man's so swiftly passing day is submerged. This can even masquerade as giving God honour, as a release from that primitive anthropomorphism which drags the Most High down to the level of our daily bread and butter ; yet it is really an even worse anthropomorphism thus to think of God as no better than a city magnate who has no knowledge of the woman who cleans the office steps. Jeremiah's thought is much sounder, for it is precisely the thought of God's afar-off-ness which forces this question from his lips : ' Can a man hide himself in secret places and thou shalt not *look upon him* ? '

Few things, indeed, are more striking in the prophets of Israel than the way in which they combine a profound sense of the unspeakable glory of God with an equally profound sense of the way in which that same God fastens His eyes on the smallest detail of conduct. God will not be satisfied with what Isaiah calls, in a powerful and almost cynical phrase, ' temple-trampling.' Rather He points to the landlord

[1] W. E. Sangster.

indifferent to his tenants' needs, to the expropriation of people from the land ; in short, to this, that, and the other social iniquity and injustice.

This also is a word for our own day, and to our own social evils and disorders. Walt Whitman says, 'I never ask the wounded person how he is, for I become the wounded person.' It has been often enough said that God's judgment rests to-day upon our whole civilization. But to say it is one thing, to feel it deeply, as deeply as we ought to feel in the presence of the judgment of God, that is another matter. To talk about His judgment on civilizations and remain unaware of His judgment upon *us* might, indeed, be just another way of insisting on the afar-off-ness of God and missing the searching challenge of His nearness.

3. Do not I fill heaven and earth ? The final answer is in Jesus Christ our Lord. Dr C. H. Dodd reminds us in his *Authority of the Bible* that 'in all religion there is a certain rhythm of movement between two poles of feeling—the feeling of the utter remoteness and strangeness of God, and the feeling of His nearness to men. He is the unknown, the mysterious, the " completely other " than man, and man must fear Him. Yet there is an irresistible impulse " to seek " God, and to experience His power—to come into communion with Him.'

(1) In the new world of Christ's creation that rhythm becomes life, and joy, and peace. Here in the Son of Man 'infinite distance into nearness grows.' The light of the knowledge of the glory of God shines in the face of Jesus Christ. Because He dwelt among us, we know that if there is a difference between us and God, there is also an affinity, and we who sometime were far off may be brought near by His friendship.

(2) In life's trials Jesus bridges the gulf between heaven and earth. When the depths are broken up, and we feel forsaken of the Father, it is the face of Christ, the Man of Sorrows, the Helper and Healer, which alone makes near. God is like that in the shadows—like Jesus. There is, too, the light that streams from the Cross, with its assurance that there is no depth so deep as to defy the reach of the Everlasting Arms.

¶ Arriving at a London railway station at midday, and depositing his bag in the cloakroom with the official whom he has come to

know, Dr. Hutton gives this transcript from real life : ' " Not bad," said I, " for so early an hour of the day ! I have come two hundred miles this morning ! "

' " I have been millions of miles this morning," he replied gravely ; " millions and millions of miles and back again."

' " Where have you been ? " I asked.

' " To the throne of God ! " he answered.

' " But He is not far from any one of us," I quoted.

' " He is a God far off and near," he answered in a tone which left me in no doubt that he had come to a difficult place.'

No one so far away as God,
Yet none who is so near ;
For He who this earth's acres trod
Wipes still the falling tear ;
Although His throne is far above,
He liveth yet, Incarnate Love.

(3) There is, finally, that deeper distance from God than space or circumstance can make —the moral distance between what He is, and what we really are ; between His infinite holiness and our sin.

But it is just here we find, or rather are found by, the wonder of the gospel of Christ, 'that matchless miracle of love.' That very feeling is the open sesame into the kingdom of heaven. Let that sense of distance but tremble into repentance and faith, and it vanishes, and in its place there comes the blessed assurance of acceptance with God. ' When he was yet a great way off, his father saw him . . .' Jesus Himself fills in the picture—God's love taking its own Divine initiative to deal with that distance, and bring such as are far off near by the power of forgiveness.

' Made nigh by the blood of Christ.' Yes, it is all there. He broke the banishing, separating power of sin in His life of selfless obedience. The Cross was the culmination, because the barrier had to be thrust back even there, right through the gates of death.

No one so far away as God,
Yet none who is so near ;
For lo ! twixt heaven and earth the rood
Uniteth sphere and sphere ;
In light of light the great God dwells,
But visiteth in lowliest cells.

The Language of Sincerity

Jer. xxiii. 36.—'Every man's own word shall be his burden' (R.V.).

1. In a letter to *The Spectator* Canon Streeter once urged in defence of the Buchmanites that it was a mistake to criticize its slangy turn of speech. What does 'life-changing' mean but 'conversion'? And if the word is fresh, all the better. What does 'sharing' mean but 'confession of sin'? And if it describes how a modern youth likes to unburden his soul to a friend, why not use the word? A 'quiet time' may seem a new-fangled way to speak of an hour of prayer, but why object? Indeed, what such examples may suggest is not that 'groupists' are wrong in using new phrases but that other people are too content with familiar language that has lost its vital force.

This question comes up in a curious place in Jeremiah. He is not only a poet but a psychologist who makes an intimate and profound analysis of the workings of the mind, and in this passage the artist with a matchless style throws aside all aim at beauty and sets himself in the simple, heavy, stodgy prose to make himself perfectly plain. There is a phrase of which he is sick and he wants every one to stop using it. ' As for the prophet, and the priest, and the people, that shall say, The burden of the Lord, I will even punish that man and his house . . . the burden of the Lord shall ye mention no more : for every man's own word shall be his burden ; . . . Thus shalt thou say to the prophet, What hath the Lord answered thee ? and, What hath the Lord spoken ? But if ye say, The burden of the Lord ; therefore thus saith the Lord : Because ye say this word, The burden of the Lord, and I have sent unto you, saying, Ye shall not say, The burden of the Lord ; therefore, behold, I will utterly forget you.'

This is a strange outburst. He harps on the words as if he wants to sicken people of the sound of them. He clearly wants to kill the phrase. Why all the fuss about this harmless, even pious, cliché. Why should any one not say, 'The burden of the Lord' as often as he liked ?

The answer is just that this *was* a cliché, and not simply in a literary sense. It was a solemn formula, a way prophets of old had given oracles, and it had become a religious catchword. People with really nothing to say assumed that if they began with these words it would rank as a prophecy. In Jeremiah's day there were swarms of false prophets. Their fault was not that they tried to mislead in any particular direction but just that they were religious humbugs with nothing fresh to contribute. ' They steal every one his word from his neighbour,' Jeremiah says. All they had to tell was second-hand ideas picked up from one another. Or else it was just drivel. ' I have dreamed, I have dreamed,' they said. But they imagined that if they began with this solemn old-fashioned pious phrase, 'the burden of the Lord,' it would lend authority and weight to empty words. So, just as to-day preachers are advised to avoid the pulpit voice and sanctimonious manner and speak simply and sincerely, Jeremiah calls on men of his day to drop the old stock phrase and get down to reality. Let them use the simple opening, ' The Lord hath answered,' that is as it might be put in modern fashion, ' This is what I am led to say.' With that pretentious phrase taken out of their mouth some noisy shallow talkers might dry up altogether, which would be no loss, but others, forced to start in a natural way without flourishes, might for the first time say something real and fresh and true of their own to which people could listen without being bored or put to sleep.

2. There is thus a lesson here for preachers. It is, however, not only in the pulpit but also in the pew that men think they are carrying on a living religion while really all that is in them is an echo or odour of orthodoxy without any fresh personal experience or vision. The sacred words of olden times can be dangerous by creating a contentment with the mere sound of them. Here is a test. If all the old words were blotted out or forbidden could you find a fresh way, a real way, your very own way of declaring your faith ? Genuine religion must use the language of sincerity.

(1) Apply the test to *prayer*. On a visit to a cousin one does not repeat the last conversation with him or consult a book for suitable sentences to address to a relative. The talk will arise naturally from the circumstances and activities of life. Yet in prayer how the familiar quotations from Psalm and Gospel and Prayer-book

are apt not merely to inspire but to circumscribe utterance. 'I suppose,' says Mr Gilby in one of George Eliot's novels, 'we are all "miserable sinners" in a manner of speaking, but I don't like to have it thrown at me as if I had really done anything.' People like him indeed prefer the traditional language, which by its very age and familiarity does not come home to them in any really personal way. Supposing instead of saying, 'I have sinned against heaven,' or 'I am unworthy of Thy mercy,' they could find words in which to make some real admission such as, 'I am greedy, I am close, I am hard on others and easy on myself,' though not better English, it might be a better prayer, hesitant and stammering yet meaning more than fluent paragraphs of devotional quotations. Say not, 'the burden of the Lord,' though it be a fine old holy phrase, 'but every man's word shall be his burden.' Were that the rule in devotion some prayers might cease, many be cut down to a few broken words, but would not the volume of real prayer that reaches heaven be increased?

(2) Apply the test, and fearlessly, to *theology and preaching*. 'Tell me the old, old story' must not forget the fact that the gospel was an amazing new story, and that it is not 'the same old story' unless it makes the same first impression of being good news. The genius of the Lord's Supper is that, while it is an ancient memorial, it is not dusty like an old relic, but, each time that it is spread, fresh and new. The declaration of the gospel should have this perpetual freshness. What makes some sermons and many books about religion dull and ineffective is that they repeat old-fashioned phrases that have lost the bite and grip they once had and convey no surprise or gladness. It is no attack on the meaning of the great theological words or even evangelistic catchwords that thrilled a former generation to acknowledge the fact that they do not get across to the contemporary mind. The man whose religion is real will be able to find fresh words, his own and modern ways of conveying the truth. The essential consideration in speaking of Jesus Christ and His work is to sound the note of reality, to express wonder and reverence and gratitude in words that come from the heart. 'Never quote,' said Principal Denney once to his students. 'It may be queer, but if you have anything to say people will feel it come to them with more power if you just say it yourself than if you quote Plato or Calvin or John Knox.'

That famous scientist and religious agnostic of last century, Professor Huxley, once found himself the guest one Sunday morning of a fellow scientist who was a Christian believer. His host said to him a little sadly as he started for church, 'I suppose you won't come.' 'No,' said Huxley, 'but may I make a suggestion. Will you stay at home this one morning and just tell me in your own words what the Christian religion is to you in your own experience.' How would you meet such a challenge? Would you quote Scripture or sermon? Or could you find some word of your very own to say. Say not 'the burden of the Lord.' Use the language of sincerity. 'Every man's own word shall be his burden.'

R. W. STEWART.

A MESSAGE FOR HARD DAYS

Jer. xxix. 11.—'For I know the thoughts that I think toward you, saith the Lord, thoughts of peace, and not of evil, to give you hope in your latter end' (R.V.).

MANY people these days are being called to undergo experiences which, had they been left to themselves, they would not have chosen. Some, because their country needs them for its defence, find their career interrupted; some, because of the price strife entails, are bereaved and desolate; and some, because a war like the present involves more than the fighting services, are confronting circumstances harder than they anticipated having to face. Such experiences— and little wonder—have altered the outlook of many towards life. Hearts that once were gay have suddenly become heavy. Men who were optimists have exchanged their optimism for pessimism ; and whereas they were wont to greet the unknown with a cheer, now they regard the future with some anxiety.

It was to a company not dissimilarly placed that Jeremiah wrote a letter and entrusted it to the hands of royal messengers. His heart went out to his compatriots who had been carried captive to an alien land, whose world as a consequence had come tumbling about their ears, and who were shaken and dismayed by all through which they had been called to pass. News of their heavy hearts, their pessimism, and their hopelessness had reached him. He felt he had a message to give them—not the glib, facile proclamation of some false prophets who endeavoured to hearten the exiles with promises of a swift deliverance which had no foundation in fact, but a message from God Himself, built firmly and securely upon a solid and reliable basis.

The content of his message is worth noting—particularly worth their noting who to-day are undergoing experiences which, left to themselves, they would not have chosen.

1. He began by assuring them that he appreciated the plight into which they had been suddenly plunged. To be lifted from one set of circumstances and placed in an entirely new set of circumstances was, he admitted, a disconcerting experience and one which was the harder to face because of the indefinite time it was likely to last. But, having made that admission, Jeremiah went on to suggest that the only sane policy open to them was to make the most of the limitations amid which they were set. With seventy long years ahead of them, let them, he counselled, live as near to their old ways as possible. Let them build houses and inhabit them. Let them marry and settle down. Let them, so far as their religious principles permitted, enter into the life of their adopted country and participate in whatever pleasures might come their way.

If, having got that length, Jeremiah lost something of his compatriots' attention we should not be greatly surprised. If some among them were inclined to follow his advice, others must have found it unpalatable since, recollecting the comfort and freedom they had so recently enjoyed, they had little heart to make the most of their altered conditions. All very well for Jeremiah to speak as he was doing, they may have said, all very well for him to counsel men in circumstances unfamiliar to himself to make the most of their new conditions, but why *should* they and how *could* they do as he suggested ?

Their reaction is not unlike our own when some, echoing Jeremiah's very exhortations, counsel us, whose career has been interrupted, whose homes have been left desolate, whose erstwhile prosperity has changed to comparative poverty, to make the most of things, and cite for our emulation the examples of contemporaries who, having seen the things they gave their lives to build, broken, have stooped and built them up again. Why should we, and how can we, make the most of things ?

It was, however, just here, when he raised such a question in his compatriots' minds, and, on that very account, was in danger of losing their attention, that Jeremiah proved himself a prophet of a quite different order from those who had made their glib and facile pronouncements. Having exhorted them to make the most of things, he went on to suggest how that was possible, to remind them of the faith that should sustain them amid their changed and difficult circumstances. Others had exhorted them to make the most of things—but they had offered no very satisfactory reasons why they should. Jeremiah exhorted them to make the most of things—and went on to tell them why. And if we, placed much as Jeremiah's compatriots were, feel impatient when told to confront our altered conditions with resolution, his reasons are worthy of our careful consideration.

2. You should, and you can, make the most of your altered conditions, declared Jeremiah, if you bear constantly in mind that God's thoughts towards you are thoughts of peace and not of evil, that His purpose for all men is good, that whatever befalls you befalls you within His universe, that whatever happens you cannot pass beyond the reach of His love and mercy.

Those to whom Jeremiah wrote may well have construed their exile as a sign of God's disfavour, or at least as a sign of His indifference. It was on that very account that many of them had no heart to do as Jeremiah had counselled—build houses and enter into the life of their adopted country. God, they were persuaded, was not in this experience with them.

Life had suddenly become meaningless and God very distant and altogether uninterested in their wellbeing. But Jeremiah's message must have set them thinking. What if, though appearances were all against such a thought, God was nearer them than they had believed and was prepared to vouchsafe them strength to triumph where they thought they must fail ? That, if it were true, put a totally different complexion upon things. They might not be able to see His purpose in permitting such a fate to overtake them, but they could trust Him to be with them now that they needed Him more than when life was as happy as a morn in May.

If we read our Bibles we shall find that that very faith with which Jeremiah sought to inspire the exiles is the faith which sustained many who were tested just as severely as we are being tested—the faith that God's thoughts towards them were thoughts of peace and not of evil, that His purpose for all men is good, that everything that befalls us befalls us within His universe and that whatever happens we cannot pass beyond the reach of His love and mercy. The hills are His, says the Bible, and so, also, are the valleys. His purposes for us are fulfilled by the joys that give us wings and, equally, by the disappointments that deepen all our living.

That is the faith which has enabled men in succeeding generations to make the most of irksome limitations and dark experiences. During the last war, Professor Farmer in one of his books reminds us, the black, irrational horror and cruelty of it all almost overwhelmed men's souls until they recollected that out of the world that had produced such horror and cruelty had come Jesus Christ, who, for men and their salvation, had given Himself to the Cross. It was the assurance He gave that God's thoughts towards men are thoughts of peace and not of evil that kept men sane and brave where they might have been cowardly.

' Make the most of things ? ' ask those whose career has been interrupted, whose homes have been left desolate, whose prosperity has turned to comparative poverty. ' Why should we and how can we ? ' The first answer is because the valley is part of the world as God made it and even there, if we really ask it, we can experience the comfort of His rod and staff.

3. But you should, and you can, make the most of your altered conditions, said Jeremiah to the exiles, not just because God has made it clear that His thoughts towards you are thoughts of peace and not of evil, but because He can give you hope in your latter end. Their exile would last, but it would not last forever. The seventy years might seem so much wasted time, but out of them God would gather a harvest that would be to their eternal enrichment. Why He should have permitted them to be carried captive might be a question to which, for the present, they could offer no answer, but some day they would know even as also they were known. What a faith with which to inspire men who felt that God was not in the experience through which they were passing, who were inclined to regard it as a meaningless interruption of their happy, useful lives, a catastrophe out of which no good could possibly come. If this faith of Jeremiah's had any foundation, then, through the very experience they were inclined to resent, God might well be fitting them for a fuller and richer life than they had yet known.

The attitude the exiles assumed towards their enforced removal from their native soil is the attitude many of us assume towards much that befalls us—that it is sheer waste, a meaningless interruption of our hitherto happy and useful lives, a catastrophe out of which no good can possibly come. That is why we have so little heart to make the most of our altered conditions. But let the thought of Jeremiah's God once take hold of us, the thought of One who has brought order out of chaos and light out of darkness, the thought of One who permitted Joseph to be sold into slavery and all the while fashioned him for a position of eminence, who led Moses by a way that he knew not until He made him fit to be the leader of his people, who kept Jesus in Nazareth for thirty long years until the time was ripe for the commencement of His mission, and those things we were tempted to consider meaningless interruptions, profitless catastrophes and purposeless changes appear in a different light. Out of such God may bring a harvest which will be not only to our own eternal enrichment but to the eternal enrichment of many more besides.

' Make the most of things ? ' ask those whose career has been interrupted, whose homes have been left desolate and whose prosperity has gone. ' Why should we and how can we ? ' Because as Christians this is our belief—that God does give us hope in our latter end, hope that the disciplines and disappointments of life are not meaningless and purposeless, but the means by which our own lives are enriched and His own purposes are fulfilled, hope that what is meantime mysterious will some day be revealed.

It must have been difficult for the exiles from Jerusalem to be other than heavy-hearted, pessimistic, and hopeless—until Jeremiah, understanding their feelings, furnished them with a faith. It must be equally difficult for many to-day to face their altered circumstances if they are not sustained by the faith which has sustained Christian men and women in succeeding generations. But, given the faith with which Jeremiah sought to fire his compatriots, there is not one of us but can face whatever confronts us with courage and endurance and patience. If this is God's world, then wherever we are He can reach us. And, if He can reach us, then every experience, sad as well as glad, will be made to yield its contribution to our own enrichment and to the fulfilment of His purposes.

RODERICK BETHUNE.

The Discovery of God

Jer. xxix. 13.—'And ye shall seek me, and find me, when ye shall search for me with all your heart.'

THE prior fact is that God is seeking us. He wants to make Himself real to us, to come very near to us, and reveal to us His truth and grace. We are not to think of Him as hiding from us; as withdrawn from us; as unwilling to be found. The Bible insists that He seeks us before ever we think of seeking Him. He takes the initiative. We love Him because He first loved us.

I sought the Lord, and afterwards I knew
He moved my soul to seek Him, seeking me;
It was not I that found, O Saviour true;
No: I was found of Thee.

Surely that is the significance of Jesus. In Jesus, God came into this world seeking us, wanting to assure us of His reality and nearness.

¶ Principal D. S. Cairns writes : ' I remember once in Japan seeing the great statue of the Buddha, and to it there came on pilgrimage all kinds of people—farm servants from the remote country, soldiers from the army, people of Japanese society, they all came there, thronging to this great, tranquil giant figure of the Buddha. Is that an adequate picture of God as you get Him in the New Testament ? The Cross is a far truer symbol. Here, we have One who does not wait for men to come to Him and find Him out ; He goes seeking them.'

1. *Can we have such an experience of God ?* Do we feel that God to us is, more or less, just a Name, without much real meaning ; just an idea in our mind, an abstraction ; just a cold, vague, distant something ? Never a real person with whose Spirit ours can meet ; never a majestic, gracious Presence ; never a real friend and helper ? And do we wish it were otherwise ? Do we want to know how God can become real to us ?

Then (1) we have to learn how to be alone with ourselves. ' Be still and know that I am God.' If we complain that God never speaks to us in such a way that we know it *is* His voice, frankly, how much chance do we give Him ? To use a wireless metaphor, is His voice not commonly jammed in our heart by the noisy, insistent interests that pre-occupy us ?

Perhaps we hate to be alone with our own thoughts. We would do anything to avoid that. We must escape from ourselves. We must have some company other than our own. But it is the wholly unanimous testimony of religious men in all ages that God is only likely to become real to those who take or make time to be alone with themselves, and with Him. Those who would fain hear God's voice, and know Him to be gracious and near, just have to insist on themselves doing that, somehow or other.

¶ How did Dr. Edward Wilson, when cooped up in the Antarctic in the narrow space of that little ship, the *Discovery*, keep alive his sense of God ? By first thing each day climbing up into the crow's-nest and there being still and listening.[1]

¶ ' Solitude,' said Landor, ' is the antechamber of God ; only one step more, and you can be in His immediate presence.'

(2) God will become real to us only as we set ourselves to do and to accept His will. Many

[1] G. T. Bellhouse, *Thinking It Out*, 110.

people, if they looked into their hearts, and were honest with themselves, would discover that, in the normal ways of life they neglect God altogether and only seek Him in time of trouble. The Unknown Soldier himself felt it shabby and put his thought into words in his verses *Christ in Flanders.*

We had forgotten You, or very nearly——
You did not seem to touch us very nearly,
Of course, we thought about You now and then,
Especially in any time of trouble.
We knew that You were good in times of trouble,
But we were very ordinary men.
And, all the while, in street or lane or byway,
In country lane, in city street or highway,
You walked among us, and we did not see it
    then.

We may all tend to make God a convenience, the servant of our purposes, at our disposal to give us this and that on which our heart is set. But God does not exist to do our will ; He has wanted us to do His will. That is the truth, the reality of our relationship, and until we face it, and act on it, then we won't be dealing with the real God at all. It is only as we bring Him into the situations of every day that He will become real ; only as we ask what His will is, and pray to Him for strength and light.

(3) Along the road of love we discover how real and near God is. God is love. That is His inmost nature. That is the real truth about Him. And since that is so, how can He ever be known, how can He ever be real and desirable to the selfish, unloving, hard, censorious heart ? He that loveth not, knoweth not God. Through loving service for other people the assurance of God's reality and nearness grows.

¶ Donald Hankey in his *Letters* tells how, as a young man, he sought, and sought in vain, for a sense of the reality of God. One day, when he felt like giving the quest up altogether, he seemed to hear a voice which said, ' If you would find your Lord, go and look for Him in His Vineyard ; you will find Him working there.' He obeyed that voice, and went to do what he could for Christ in the slums of Bermondsey, and there, in serving others, he was found of God. ' I do not think,' he has written, ' that I have ever felt God so near as at the bedside of a boy dying of consumption in a Bermondsey slum.'

2. *The condition attached to seeking and finding God.* We must search with all our heart.

In mythology there is the story of the Swan-maiden, one of the oldest stories in the world, its countless versions to be found in all parts of the world, its meaning pointing to the divine side of our human nature. The flight of a bird (disdaining earth and cleaving the skies) became a favourite emblem of divinity. It gave Mercury his winged sandals. It produced Odin's Valkyries, who flew to the battle-field to bear brave warriors to Valhalla. It explains the winged bulls of Babylon and the winged angels of the Jews. And it even suggested the hovering dove as the Christian symbol of the Holy Spirit. Moreover, the arduous search for the vanished bride has inspired numerous legends, such as Hercules bringing back Alcestis from the Lower World, or the quest of King Arthur's Knights for the Holy Grail.

In the story of the Swan-maiden a young hunter or shepherd watches a flight of swans alight on a meadow or by a lake-side, when they cast their feathers and become damsels who dance upon the grass or bathe in the water. The watcher steals the swan-robe of the fairest of them all, and thus secures her as his bride. But later, through some mischance, the wife recovers her plumage and flies away. Then must the desolate bridegroom travel to unheard-of lands, and perform superhuman tasks, before he can find and regain his lost love.

The message of the Swan-maiden myth is as follows : If we will look into our heart, we will know that each one of us believes that we ourselves are more than ordinary ; and that some special fortune awaits us in life—in fact, a Swan-maiden. Moreover, our conjecture is well-founded, for each individual is the dear and cherished child of God ; and Christ came to earth to demand for all God's children the opportunity of achieving the highest blessedness of which they are capable. Now, speaking generally, most of us do at times realize our dreams. Shafts of glory on occasion break into our lives ; and (as it were) through no particular merit of our own, a Swan-maiden takes up her abode with us. But we fail to retain her ! We take for granted such a heavenly visitation, and are at no special pains to cherish our precious prize. The result is that the glory disappears. And we can only recover our loss by seeking it with tears, and resolutely exercising that self-discipline and sacrifice which alone makes us worthy to possess what is of eternal value.[1]

(1) There is *prayer*. Prayer costs. It costs time. We usually divide our day of twenty-four hours in this way—eight hours for work ; eight hours for meals, and rest, and recreation ; and eight hours for sleep. It is not said where reading, and meditation, and prayer come in. And the reason of that is because, with most men, these things do not come in at all.

But we need time to prepare our hearts to seek God. And as life goes on, we come to discover that time is as indispensable and as important an element in all true prayer as is repentance, or faith, or reformation itself. Indeed, without a liberal allowance of time, no man has ever attained to a real life of prayer at all. So much is that the case that, instead of a few stolen moments now and then, it takes from some men all that remains of their time on this earth. Now that cannot, surely, be said to be bought cheaply which despoils us of so much of the most precious thing we possess ; and a thing, moreover, which is so fast running short with so many of us.

¶ One day a University student came to see me on the matter of prayer. He reminded me of an address which I had given recently and asked whether he had understood me aright that John Henry Newman and Andrew Bonar both gave two hours a day to prayer. I said he had heard me correctly. I went on to say that there was nothing singular about that so far as the saints were concerned, and talked to him of the devotional habits of other people who hungered and thirsted after righteousness and how, despite their exceedingly busy lives, they were prodigal with hours spent in prayer.

His bewilderment grew. ' What beats me,' he said, ' is how they filled up the time. It is hard to imagine how men with many duties to do could give the *amount* of time to it, but it is still harder to know how they used it, once it was set aside. I can't pray for ten minutes. I've tried. I kneel down every night and just ask God to forgive me for anything I've done wrong. I thank Him for His blessings. I mention mother and father and my other relations. I say a word about my friends, and the Church, and then I'm done. Sometimes I stay a bit longer, but my mind keeps going

[1] C. M. Chavasse, *Christ and Fairies*, 36.

off at a tangent and I've nothing more to say. Five minutes covers it. How people can pray for two hours beats me.' [1]

Prayer costs thought. God is infinitely the greatest and grandest subject of thought and imagination in all the universe and yet there is nothing in all the universe to which most men give less thought and less imagination than to Almighty God.

Prayer, once we take it in dead earnest, will cost us all our soft, and easy, and slothful, and self-indulgent habits. Nothing is so costly as that which is bought by prayer. But, on the other hand, nothing is so truly enriching as that is which is got and held by prayer, and by prayer alone.

(2) There is *holiness*. Every one of us has known occasions when it seemed natural to believe in God ; times when our hearts were filled with earnest longings after holiness, and a deep peace descended on our souls when we prayed. But is such blessedness a lasting experience ?

> Where is the blessedness I knew
> When first I saw the Lord ?
> Where is the soul-refreshing view
> Of Jesus and His word ?

Can it be otherwise as long as we leave religion to chance, and take no trouble to cultivate this amazing possibility of closest union with Almighty God Himself ? As in the legend of the Holy Grail, there is a world of high and brave adventure beckoning on the knight of the Cross who would gain the reality of the Presence of the ever-living Christ. Like Sir Percival he must meet and conquer the three great enemies of the soul—the World, the Flesh, and the Devil. With good Sir Bors he must find God in every-day life by doing his daily duty for the love of God alone. In the steps of Sir Galahad he must escape across the Swamp of Mortality and the Sea of Time, along the thousand arches of the Bridge of Prayer. But as he thus presses forward on his quest—resolved to persevere, whatever betide, until he find the Holy Grail of Holiness,

> Then move the trees, the copses nod,
> Wings flutter, voices hover clear :
> ' O just and faithful knight of God !
> Ride on ! the prize is near.'

[1] W. E. Sangster, *He Is Able*, 209.

In a word, we cannot unite ourselves with the supernatural unless we desire this Divine fellowship above all things, and bend all our powers towards the possession of God.

¶ The wonderful change that took place in the life of Charles G. Finney, the famous lawyer, evangelist, and Divinity Professor, was attributed by him to this verse in Jeremiah. 'I do not think,' he says, 'that I had ever read the passage, but I felt that it was the Word of God. I instantly seized hold of it with my whole heart. I was as conscious of trusting at that moment in the veracity of my God as I was of my own existence. "Lord," I cried, "I take Thee at Thy word ! Thou knowest that I do search for Thee *with all my heart*. I have come to this place for that very purpose ; and Thou hast promised that I shall find Thee ! " That seemed to settle the whole question. I felt that I had performed my vow.'

That low man seeks a little thing to do,
    Sees it and does it :
This high man, with a great thing to pursue,
    Dies ere he knows it.

.   .   .   .   .   .

That, has the world here—should he need the
    next,
    Let the world mind him !
This, throws himself on God, and unperplexed
    Seeking shall find him.

The Pilgrimage of Love

Jer. xxxi. 3.—' I have loved thee with an everlasting love.'

To every thoughtful and awakened mind the most vital of all questions is, ' Am I an object of Divine care ? ' When clouds are all around our lives we fail to see the Divine love shining behind. At such moments, when all is dark and we feel ourselves the sport of an unknown fate, there is wonderful power to soothe and enlighten in the old words of Scripture. ' I have loved thee with an everlasting love ' comes like fragrant balm upon our smitten heart, and awakens the slumbering chords of faith and hope.

1. We hear in these words the sound of the footsteps of a Divine Pilgrim moving along an everlasting road, seeking till He find. Time and eternity are the background and the scene of God's pilgrimage. All through the long history of man that love has existed, patient, waiting. It goes away back before creation, for ' everlasting ' is a mighty word. Woven into the story from before a million years, this almighty love lurks and hides and shows itself wherever mind and heart have looked. Long, long ago, He made a universe. Ages passed while the stars found their courses and settled into their unchanging roads. Amid the untracked vastness, the world emerged at length, a whirling mass, and for long ages it blazed and shrank and found its orbit.

Before the epic of creation the mind falters. God, as it were, hid within His world, waiting ; for the life that came had to learn to know Him, to look for Him. When man appeared at length, he was a poor creature yet endowed with capacities that determined his ultimate triumph over all. Still love waited and followed after.

Who knows in what far-off hour the dull heart of man first stirred to look beyond the world about him, and guess at a meaning and a home ! Perhaps it was when he first felt pity. Jerome K. Jerome says somewhere, that the original standard-bearer of the Lord was the man who first felt pity. Perhaps one day, when some hurt creature lay before him, his dull eyes grew troubled with a strange new pain not known before. And the love that followed after knew the first faint sign of recognition.

But man also had a long road to tread. All through the history of mankind the tale goes on through ages of trial and thought. Primitive man gave place to those higher in the scale until the great civilizations began to appear, to rise and fall—Egypt, Crete, Assyria, China and a score of others remembered or forgotten, down to Rome and the age that followed Rome. Unchanged, unchanging, behind the vast and splendid story, was the love that fashions all, and goes on seeking and waiting till the truth comes home to all mankind—' I have loved thee with an everlasting love.'

2. Through the long ages of his history, man also set out on his quest. There came to him the hint of a dream, the first thought of meaning in this vast impinging world. It was

as if his soul became slowly capable of hearing, or at least of listening for that deep tone that murmured through all creation.

Pity was his first step; he learned first through other men the thought of love—the thought that is not content within itself but must live in others. The quest had opened, man was getting a hint from the world that *He* was there, that He wanted them to seek Him.

Little by little, the glow of that love was perceived, isolated, recognized. A people learned through tribulation, and guidance not their own; prophets stood apart and listened and cried aloud. At length came Jesus Christ. The everlasting love could never be veiled any more for those who cared to look and serve. The long pilgrimage of God was met by the quest of man. In Jesus, they stood united, God and man, one, bound by cords of love. We have never fully interpreted that love, or Christ who made it plain. But the long mystery of creation was revealed, the Word hidden from before the foundation of the world was made clear. ' I have loved thee with an everlasting love.' To us, and to all the ages that shall yet unfold the power of it, Jesus Christ stands for God, as much as we can know, as much as we need to know.

> The manger where He lay
> New-born upon the hay,
> The bench at which He toiled,
> The hands His labour soiled,
> The simple words He said,
> The multitudes He fed,
> The grave by which He sighed,
> The Cross on which He died,
> His resurrection face
> Bright with celestial grace—
> All the long way He trod,
> Still speaks the love of God.

3. Can we look out upon the crowded world of to-day aright without the background of this eternal drama, and do we ever understand our life unless we interpret it by this Divine motive ? In our day, the world grows wise. We look back upon the long period of man's upbringing and think that we have at last attained. In our conquests of knowledge and material control our hearts easily turn away from God.

World commerce has brought the skill and produce of all races to our doors; the triumphs of science make life easier and fuller. We correct the mistakes of our forefathers, we press our inquiry into the secrets of creation, the vast and the infinitesimal alike reveal their mysteries, and show countless more beyond. Einstein displaces Newton, Rutherford lays bare the atom, Michelson measures light. The mind of man is wonderful. But the love of God has seen many an age of man like it, and has out-lasted and out-loved them.

His love is supreme. It is all-powerful. All men are compelled at last to acknowledge that its might is irresistible. The genius of man is great. He can chain the winds, utilize the vast forces of Nature at his pleasure, measure the stars in their courses, flash his thoughts from continent to continent, but to the resistless power of love he must bow. It is the river which has made earth's desert fruitful and its wilder-ness to blossom like the rose. It is the chain of gold by which the round world is every way bound about the feet of God. It is like the sun, in that its gracious power turns darkness into light and makes the waste places fertile. It alone satisfies the heart, and satisfies it the more the greater its dominion over the heart and life. So Michelangelo confessed :

> Painting and sculpture's aid in vain I crave.
> My one sole refuge is that love divine
> Which forms the cross stretched forth its
>   arms to save.

The Cross stands in our midst, the Cross where death and life meet, where is forgiveness, and healing for the great world's hurt, where is love when the world's love fails. There is an hour when the comforts of our rarest possessions cease. The man who has never felt it is a child still ; he is coming to the full estate of his soul when he is consciously seeking.

¶ Coventry Patmore, in his short poem, *The Toys*, describes his little son dismissed to bed with punishment, after some childish delinquency. Visiting his bed, he found that the sleeping boy with tears still on his eyelids, had laid out at the side of his bed his few treasures, counters and shells and coins, ' to comfort his sad heart.' Patmore continues :

> So when that night I pray'd
> To God, I wept, and said :
> Ah, when at last we lie with tranced breath,
> Not vexing Thee in death,

And Thou rememberest of what toys
We made our joys,
How weakly understood,
Thy great commanded good,
Then, fatherly not less
Than I whom Thou hast moulded from the
    clay,
Thou'lt leave Thy wrath, and say,
'I will be sorry for their childishness.'

Ever since God made the worlds He has looked for souls to love Him, has waited and travailed and suffered for our sakes. It is for us to bend our purposes to that mighty Will, not to be blinded by our own prowess, but to shape the life of society and nations so that love has sway, to be of greatest use to mankind because we ourselves have given over our lives to His control. All our noble purposes that flourish in an unwilling world are the moving of the eternal love. This is to learn salvation—to turn that age-long motive into the life of to-day.

God shall yet complete His pilgrimage; He who has loved shall see the travail of His soul and be satisfied in us. Though we have forgotten, He remembers, though we have scorned, He loves us still. This is the glorious gospel of the Blessed God. 'I have loved thee with an everlasting love.'

Nature and Grace

Jer. xxxi. 29.—'In those days they shall say no more, The fathers have eaten sour grapes, and the children's teeth are set on edge.' (R.V.)

1. THERE is a well-known saying to the effect that it is a greater thing to write the songs of a people than to impose upon them their code of laws. The influence of the metrical romance, or ballad, which is found in every primitive country where there is much curiosity and intelligence, but little reading or writing, is almost incalculable. The stories of the murder of Siegfried, told by the German ballad makers, the exploits of Athelstane by the Anglo-Saxon rhymers, the war songs of the fierce struggles of the Serbians against the Ottoman Power—all these have left their mark, for good or ill, upon the later history of these nations; the makers of the ballad poem, whose very names

are unknown to us, have done more than the law-givers.

And there is another kind of primitive literature which has no less influence, the popular proverb. Every nation has its proverbs, and it is interesting to note how they reflect 'the nation's best wisdom applied to the details of life.' A proverb has been defined as 'a brief saying which arrests the attention by its truth, and sticks in the memory through the felicity of its language'; and it would not be hard to show that they serve not only to reflect, but also to mould, the character of a people. The Scotsman's prudent, thrifty, reticent nature has not merely revealed itself in his national proverbs, but is in some degree the product of their common use.

But we have to remember that this influence may equally well be used for evil as for good. A foolish or wicked proverb may be a powerful force for the excusing of sin: a reference to the folly of spoiling the ship for a ha'porth of tar may be an apology for 'squandermania'; while the supposed necessity for a young man to sow his wild oats may help to expose a whole nation to the ravages of those insidious diseases which destroy the innocent child or wife as well as the sinner.

When we turn to the old Hebrew literature, while we note the extraordinary value of the good proverb, we find that the best religious teachers are fully conscious of the menace of the bad. We know how large a part of the development of Hebrew religion was the result of the conflict of the two great schools, those of the priest and the prophet; besides these two there was a third school, that of the Wise Men, which appears infrequently before the Exile, but which is well enough defined by the time of Jeremiah to be named along with priest and prophet: 'the law shall not perish from the priest, nor counsel from the *wise*, nor the word from the prophet.' They were the men who found their interests and activities in the sphere of practical morals; they were not necessarily deliberate coiners of moral aphorisms; generally they took those which they found in common use; for proverbs spring up naturally. A shrewd person one day says a shrewd thing in epigrammatic fashion; it is passed on, and polished and improved as it goes—a chip of experience hewn from life; and the mass of proverbs grows like a cairn to which every passer-by contributes his stone. So these men did not coin but collected, and our Book of Proverbs is one of the results of their labour, a Book in which the great principles of revelation are applied to the details of everyday experience. Not all have had to learn by heart, as John Ruskin was taught by his mother to do, long chapters of the Book of Proverbs, with which, as he declared, 'she established his soul in life'; but it may be that we have come to regard a proverb, even if it be not in our Bible, as almost a sacred thing, and a wise and sure commentary upon human life and experience.

But we can see plainly enough that even among the Hebrew proverbs there were some untrue or misleading sayings. Jeremiah does not conceal his distrust of some of the wise men. 'How do ye say, We are wise, and the law of the Lord is with us? But behold the false pen of the scribes hath wrought falsely.' And both he and his great successor, Ezekiel, exclaim with something like bitterness against what was evidently a popular saying of their day. Jeremiah says that in the coming days, when men shall have a new heart, they shall say no more, 'The fathers have eaten sour grapes, and the children's teeth are set on edge.' And Ezekiel, at a time when the national fortunes have fallen still lower, makes the same protest, 'What mean ye, that ye use this proverb concerning the land of Israel?' He is not, the people who use it are not, in any doubt as to the meaning of the words—they are clear enough; but just *because* they are so clear the prophet wants to know how they dare give them the particular application. Evidently they are being used simply as an excuse; and against that use he, like Jeremiah, utters an emphatic protest. And yet, surely, whether in Jeremiah's day or in Ezekiel's, there was some justification for their use. The national misfortunes were assuredly the result in no small degree of the miserable policy of the last generation. The sins of Manasseh had caused the destruction of the nation, and God *is* a jealous God, visiting the sins of the fathers upon the children. They were reaping what their fathers had sown.

But, as Jeremiah and Ezekiel agree, the proverb, as they used it, was entirely mischievous. For every man must pay the penalty of his own guilt; no one can shirk the moral responsibility which rests upon him.

2. Ever since Darwin's magnificent and painstaking induction made familiar the ideas of evolution, the problems of heredity have been quivering in our air. Not only the scientific man, but the social and economic thinker has them constantly in mind, and a whole class of fiction, frequently of a decadent type, is based on the idea that man is helplessly bound by his ancestry, that the iron hand of the past grips him. The sense of responsibility in man is drugged, and we need to protest against this slavery of the living to the dead, this reduction of man to the bondage of a blind sequence.

There is many a young man or woman going out into life, subject to the temptations of a great city, freed from the restraints and observation of home, who is tempted weakly to compound with sins of self-indulgence by urging excuse of ancestry or environment. It would be the most irritating folly to deny that our parents make a vast difference to our characters. There can be no doubt that the nature of our parentage makes a tremendous difference. But, remember, ancestry decides the *form* and not the *fact* of testing. And there is within us a something which recognizes our personal responsibility for passing the test. Every sane man in his quiet moments knows that it is he, and not his father, who is responsible for his sin.

We recognize, then, that we are the fruit of what has gone before; and yet we are sure that we are different from, say, the brood of pigeons which the fancier moulds. See that brood, and note how the fancier by careful selection and breeding will develop here the plumage sheen, there the crest, there the spreading tail, till apparently he can mould at will. In what way are we different? We are conscious of two great differences, one within and one without.

(1) *A difference within.*—When we talk of our heredity let us be scientific, let us take in every strain of the pedigree. We know how in every problem each factor must be carefully sought out, lest we miss that which decides. When you notice in a child some trick of manner or of feature, you will miss the explanation until you find some far-off uncle or grand-

father. So, when we speak of heredity, why is it that we so often mean the baleful and noxious and forget the good ? Trace your ancestry back—father and mother, grandparents, great-grandparents ; and then how soon the dark ! But trace backward till, by-and-by, the message of revelation comes home, we emerge into the light—' which was the son of Seth, which was the son of Adam.' Do not stop there, for the message which makes revelation worth revealing is still to come. ' Which was the son of Adam—*which was the Son of God.*' That is the strain in the pedigree that is so often omitted, and yet it is the dominant strain after all. Think what it means ! That there is something in us of God's own nature, some deep-seated power of choosing good, something at the back of all the wreckage of the sinful and debased that is Godlike, that can respond to righteousness. And with·what force can we come to the young man, conscious of stirrings to ill which he would fain tell himself are the result of sins before he was born, with what force can we come to him and point him back along the line of ancestry till we raise his bent form and thrill him with the glad news ' *which was the Son of God* ' ! This difference there is within us to mark us from the brute creation around.

¶ A favourite text of many secular writers is that ' the fathers have eaten sour grapes, and the children's teeth are set on edge.' They insist upon it that we can never start quite fair in the race of life, but are handicapped by the influence of dead men in the past and living men in the present. They speak of ' the melancholy captives on the road to Siberia, who each carry a link of the hopeless chain that binds them all together.' These writers do not always know, as the Bible does, that there is a heredity of grace as well as a heredity of nature—a heavenly Father as well as an earthly father—a ' Divine nature ' to supplant human nature.[1]

(2) *A difference without.*—God's Holy Spirit comes to give light to every man. Man has the power to respond, and God's Spirit brings the righteousness to which he may respond. A new power comes to the battered, bruised soul ; a new sense of dignity ; a new will-power develops, a new belief that its ancestry justifies faith in its destiny and belief in God's power.

[1] R. Stevenson, *Exposition of The Pilgrim's Progress,* 8.

Man never proves more royally the dignity of his own free-will than when he uses it by submitting it to the Divine will. For he proves then that his ancestry is truly operative in the highest sense. He feels the impulse of his higher nature, and he responds to it.

It is a grand thing to be a man. God leads each individual soul all by itself. He stoops down and takes it out of the tangled mesh of all the many lives that went to make it, and sets it fair and free in the dignity of its own individuality. He leads it to a lonely mountain peak made expressly for its climbing. And up this lonely peak God helps us to climb, often with bleeding hands and feet ; often He stoops to help with His strong arm when we are like to faint and fall. Higher and higher He helps us, and every breeze of heaven that rushes by is whispering to us, ' Child of God,' ' Child of God.' Higher and higher still till we stand upon the virgin peak with only God's heaven above us, and still the air around is thrilling with the whisper, ' Child of God,' till we can look up and answer, ' Father.'

¶ Oliver Wendell Holmes has a strange and perhaps unjustifiable novel entitled *Elsie Venner.* A girl is born whose mother has been bitten by a rattle-snake before the birth ; the child's nature is supposed to share the infection of the serpent. All through her childhood the two natures strive, the human and the coldly serpentine, till on the dawn of womanhood the true love of a man becomes hers, and, conquered by love, the last trace of venom disappears—and in the struggle the girl dies.

Which things are an allegory. I have been bitten by the serpent sin ; the poison is in my veins ; the conflict is continual. But as the battle sways to and fro I am conscious of the forces of God acting on me, and at last Love, the Love of the Cross, stoops to me, flings its arms around me, gets its own way with me, and as Love wins me the poison leaves me. And then, thank God, the parable fails, as parables of the spiritual always will fail. For it is not death that comes to my soul, but life, more abundant life, which overwhelms and transfigures me.[1]

[1] W. T. A. Barber.

The New Covenant

Jer. xxxi. 31, 33, 34.—'Behold, the days come, saith the Lord, that I will make a new covenant with the house of Israel, and with the house of Judah : . . . this is the covenant that I will make with the house of Israel after those days, saith the Lord ; I will put my law in their inward parts, and in their heart will I write it ; and I will be their God, and they shall be my people : and they shall teach no more every man his neighbour, and every man his brother, saying, Know the Lord : for they shall all know me, from the least of them unto the greatest of them, saith the Lord : for I will forgive their iniquity, and their sin will I remember no more.' (R.V.)

THE prophecy of the New Covenant is one of those great passages in the prophets—perhaps the greatest of all—which stand out from the rest and impress us by the wonderful spirituality of their tone, and by their evangelical character.

This particular passage has had a remarkable history and an equally remarkable fulfilment in the Christian dispensation, for it forms the basis, not only of our Lord's language concerning Himself and His work at the moment when His earthly ministry had reached its culmination, but of the very title given by the early Christian Church to the gospel it had to preach and the sacred literature wherein that gospel is enshrined—namely, the New Testament. It is from this passage that the designation 'New Testament' or 'New Covenant' is taken.

And when, at the institution of the Lord's Supper in the Upper Room at Jerusalem, hundreds of years after these words were written by Jeremiah, Jesus said, 'This is my blood of the New Covenant,' He was referring to the promise contained in the text, and the idea of which it is the expression.

So we see what an important saying it is, and what a notable part it has played in the spiritual development of mankind.

To judge from the context in which the words occur, they were uttered originally either on the eve of the capture of Jerusalem by the Chaldæans, or when the destruction had already taken place, and large detachments of the inhabitants were already on the road to exile. And so in the chapter from which the text is taken the prophet's thoughts sometimes go out in sympathy with his suffering and exiled compatriots, sometimes dwell in imagination upon a more blissful future when he pictures the exiled people restored to their homeland.

But what could be the use of restoring Israel if the disappointments of its previous history were to be repeated ? God had of old constituted Israel a people in close fellowship with Himself, but that constitution had failed to secure the expected results ; the mass of the people, at any rate, had failed woefully in their allegiance ; and God had at length been obliged to cast them off. And so, when the nation is once again restored, Jeremiah pictures the old constitution, or covenant as he calls it, as abolished, and a new one founded to take its place, furnished with conditions which will form a true safeguard against failure.

In every respect the New Covenant is to be a contrast to the Old. The law written upon tables of stone is to be replaced by the law written in the heart. The people may have the law written in material characters and yet not read it, or fail to understand what its significance might be. The law written in the heart will become, so to say, man's second nature, an inseparable part of his intellectual and moral being. Principles, again, will take the place of particular outward ordinances. Men will no longer need the law as something external to themselves, something prescribed from without, having no necessary hold upon them ; their inner nature will be brought into harmony with the will of God, so as to do what is well-pleasing in His eyes of their own spontaneous impulse.[1]

This is what Jeremiah plainly saw and published and thus made a place for evangelical religion six hundred years before Jesus was born ; but few people, even yet, are evangelicals at heart, and his word is never obsolete.

There are three aspects of the New Covenant given in the text where we see the new replacing the old and becoming the one eternal principle of religion and the only guarantee against moral failure.

1. It makes access to God direct, personal, individual. 'No man shall teach his brother, saying, know the Lord.' It sets aside intermediaries of every degree, and brings men face to face with God to know Him for themselves.

Now, in every age men have preferred to take their religion at second hand. In Israel,

[1] S. R. Driver, *The Ideals of the Prophets*, 44.

religion was mainly a national concern; God's relation was to the people as a whole, and every Israelite, however indifferent, shared in the benefit. The priests discharged their daily office, which kept things right for all, and a man needed only to perform some small ritual duties to keep himself in connection with the system. He did not need to be what we call a religious man himself; for if he observed certain occasions of feast or sacrifice, and followed certain rules of life, the system did the rest. That is the notion which arises wherever there is a priesthood, for the priest is one who manages your religion for you, going where you cannot go, and touching mysteries which are beyond your ken; and the efficient power is the mysterious grace of God, which resides in the Church as a whole, and which blesses all within the Church who comply with its external demands.

Many people may welcome the relief of a notion like that, and yet it is entirely alien to the religion of Jesus. It is commonly with strain that religion takes possession of a man's life, and it is with strain that it can be maintained, vital and uncorrupted. To see God for oneself, to open up the mind for the reception of His thoughts, to be exposed to the penetrating light of His presence—that is never easy; and the craven heart of man welcomes any expedient by which it can be avoided. To observe the ritual of religion, to take interest in the outward fortunes of a Church, or in discussions about its doctrines—these may be nothing else than expedients by which men conceal from themselves the fact that they are not religious.

The clearest mark of the new order of things, says Jeremiah, is that religion shall henceforth be taken at first hand. Jesus said, ' Have salt in *yourselves* '; do not be dependent for what keeps life strong and wholesome on influences outside of you. The religion which is worth anything is not what is told you but what you know of yourself. That does not mean that there is no room for teaching. Paul's understanding of what is contained in Jesus Christ is richer and more subtle than any of us could for himself have attained, for Paul had a surer insight and a more burning love. But if we know only what Paul says and have no answering knowledge in ourselves, even Paul will help us little. A man may be a heretic in the truth, as Milton says: and ' if he believes only because his pastor says so, or because the assembly so determines, without knowing other reasons, though his belief be true, yet the very truth he holds becomes his heresy.' It was proclaimed by Joel that God would one day pour out of His Spirit upon all flesh, even upon the servants and the handmaidens; for it is God's intention in the covenant that nothing in station or in lack of education or opportunity should hinder any man from knowing God for himself.

¶ So long as a man receives his Christianity on the authority of a church or a book—so long as it has not commended itself to his higher reason and moral sense, or reached his inner consciousness—he has no real hold of Christianity, he is believing only in his church or his book. There may be the most absolute belief in the infallibility of a Church or in the inspiration of the Bible, along with the most absolute unbelief in the doctrine taught by them, because the truth of the doctrine may be altogether undiscerned. . . . The Bible presents to our spiritual capacities their proper objects— the character of God, His relation to men, and His purposes towards them—and we then only receive the blessing which God intends for us in giving it to us when we apprehend those great things of which it speaks, and discern their eternal necessary truth; in other words, when our spirit actually meets God and we find that He is indeed a Father.[1]

¶ No heart can conceive that treasury of mercies which lies in this one privilege, in having liberty and ability to approach unto God at all times, according unto His mind and will.[2]

2. The second aspect concerns morals as the first concerns religion. All the moralists of Jeremiah's time believed in rules, and indeed it is seldom that a professional moralist escapes that snare. The condition in which Jesus discovered the Law in Israel moved Him to indignation, and yet things had come to that pass in a perfectly natural way. First of all there were the sacred Ten Words, then there were applications of these to the variety of actual situations, and rules were heaped on rules so that a man need never find himself

---

[1] Thomas Erskine of Linlathen.
[2] *The Golden Book of John Owen*, 240.

without a guide ; and the end was that men, whilst breaking no rule, were yet not good.

It is not the absence of fault that gives worth to any performance but the presence of some quality. Milton talks with scorn of the man who, in writing poetry, needs to count the syllables. That can be done, and verses can be knocked together by a sort of laborious carpentry, and those may like them who can. Rules have their place ; but a man will never make himself a gentleman by the most sedulous study of a book of etiquette, and a son will never, by the most dutiful performance, blind the eyes of her who asks only his love. No *almost* can ever mount up to the dignity and the spontaneity of the thing itself. In poetry, in courtesy, in affection, in character, it is something within a man that is controlling ; and he does not begin to make progress until his heart is gained for the work.

Few things in the Gospels are more astonishing than Christ's refusal to lay down rules for His disciples. They were ignorant and unlettered men, but He gave them no detailed guidance as to worship, as to behaviour, as to the constitution of the Church. ' Whatsoever ye shall bind on earth shall be bound in heaven,' He said ; ' whatsoever ye shall loose on earth shall be loosed in heaven ' ; that is, on the manifold questions of conduct and of duty I bid you judge for yourselves, for I will not settle them for you ; only, if you seek My Spirit I think you will judge securely. He swept away laws, says Seeley, in order to make of them a new race of law-makers. A man who could do only what he was told had little attraction for Jesus, who wanted men with courage and instinct to see their way, able to do what had not been done before, and to anticipate His mind in new conditions. Many are ready to follow a lead, liking to be told what to do and to see a limit marked for their observance, forgiving seven times, like Peter, and then being done with forgiveness ; but Jesus asked for men who, on occasion, could give a lead, and who would never be ashamed to stand alone.

¶ ' If you are exchanging measurable maxims for immeasurable principles,' wrote F. W. Robertson in a letter, ' you are surely rising from the mason to the architect. " Seven times ? "—no—no—no—Seventy times seven. No maxim—a heart principle. I wonder whether St. Peter *wholly understood* that, or got a very clear *conception* from it.'

That is what Jeremiah meant by having the law in one's heart. It implies a kind of instinct of the will of God, by which a man can guide himself apart from distinct directions, some better sense of what is noble in conduct.

3. When Jeremiah insists that every reformation begins in the heart, it might be objected— How is the heart to be made equal to the task ? Jeremiah has his answer—' I will forgive their iniquity, saith the Lord, and their sin will I remember no more.' The remedy is from above. The new order is to be inaugurated by a great act of forgiveness, in which all the heart of God will appear. In some public way He will treat the men who have refused Him as His friends, putting them all in His debt. Nothing short of that, as the prophet believed, will get at the obdurate hearts of men ; but at the touch of an unmerited forgiveness, gratitude will spring up within them, and love— the power by which men know God and the constraint under which they are drawn willingly to obey Him. Forgiveness brings to erring men new conceptions of what their God is like—a God who does not deal with His creatures on terms of strict, legal precision, but who pardons at His own cost, and gives them what they have not worked for. And the very sight of such a God is a real new birth, clearing and deepening all the faculties, and making obedience easy.

The prophet still lay in the shadow, and centuries had to pass before the Light of all the world was revealed, and yet we cannot much improve upon his programme. God does not leave us to ourselves in moral endeavour. The entire significance of the Christian evangel is that God in Christ has come to our relief. The whole meaning of the New Covenant is that the grace of God in Jesus Christ regenerates the moral nature, energizes the better self within us, and enables it to subdue the lower. ' For what the law could not do, in that it was weak through the flesh, God, sending his own Son in the likeness of sinful flesh, and for sin, condemned sin in the flesh : That the righteousness of the law might be fulfilled in us, who walk not after the flesh, but after the Spirit.'

¶ Olive Schreiner has a beautiful figure of the broken marble fountain by an Italian

wayside.   That fountain played no more ;
weeds and dirt had choked up the cistern ;
dry and desolate it lay in the sunshine, unable
to give a draught of water to any weary passer-
by. And yet the water was there all the time.
The spring from which that fountain had been
supplied was there as fresh and strong as ever
beneath the soil, finding egress in other directions, waiting to be drawn upon, ready to gush
forth the moment it received opportunity. All
that was needed was that the connexion should
be made, that everything that hindered its
entrance to the marble basin should be cleared
away ; then the fountain would flow once more,
flow probably as it had never yet been able to
do since it was built, flow from the exhaustless
reservoir that poured its flood down from the
everlasting hills.

A Profitable Investment

Jer. xxxii. 8, 9.—' Then I knew that this was the word
of the Lord. And I bought the field of Hanameel my
uncle's son, that was in Anathoth, and weighed him the
money, even seventeen shekels of silver.'

THIS is one of the most striking incidents
in the life of Jeremiah. It occurred during
his imprisonment in Jerusalem. His cousin
Hanameel came one day with an offer to sell
to him, as the nearest of kin, the ancestral plot
of ground at their native village of Anathoth.
This place was a sacerdotal settlement, and the
fields around it belonged to the priests as their
heritage. Ecclesiastical lands, according to the
Mosaic rule, could not be sold to a stranger,
and thus alienated from the tribe of Levi, but
a portion of them might be given or sold by
one member of the tribe to another.

In the Levitical household at Anathoth
Jeremiah was born ; and as the nearest heir of
the ecclesiastical patrimony, Hanameel appealed
to him to purchase it according to the provisions of the Jewish law. It was a strange
thing to propose, and a strange time in which
to make the proposal. The army of the
Assyrians was on the march to besiege Jerusalem ; they were ravaging all the country
before them. Anathoth lay on the great
northern road to Jerusalem, about four miles
distant from the city, in the direct path of
the conqueror ; and the fields around the city

of the priests would soon be in possession of
the enemy.

It was then that Hanameel urged his cousin
Jeremiah to take off his hands a property that
was exposed to such terrible risks. Dr. A. S.
Peake, in *The Century Bible*, says : ' the
reasons which prompted Hanameel's offer to
his cousin are unknown, but probably the
scarcity and consequent high prices and his
need of money had reduced him to the necessity
of selling his land.'

Also, in common with the men of Anathoth,
and particularly the prophet's own family,
Hanameel was bitterly opposed to Jeremiah.
Jeremiah had espoused what was at the time
an unpopular cause, and had aroused a general
unbelief and recrimination by his confident
prediction that the investing armies of the
Chaldæans would soon melt away and Jerusalem be free from the siege of the invader.

At such a time the property would be greatly
depreciated in value. He could not expect to
get the full price for it ; indeed, it was hardly
worth anybody's while to buy it. One can
therefore appreciate the noble disinterestedness
of Jeremiah. He would not take advantage of
Hanameel's necessity and anxiety to sell during
a time of panic so as to get a cheap bargain.
He gave the full price for the property.

Why did Jeremiah buy this land ? He did
not buy it because he was a sentimentalist. He
did not buy it because he was a patriot, though
he was the greatest patriot of his time. He did
not buy it because he was suffering from what
Chesterton has called ' the queer innocence of
old age.' He bought it because he saw that a
refusal to buy would be tantamount to denial
of his faith and repudiation of his prophetic
ministry of more than forty years. God had
said to him over and over again that though the
Israelites must go away to Babylonia for
seventy years, eventually he would bring them
back to that land and restore them to their
old privileges. He had preached that doctrine
up and down the land for years and had not
been believed, and he saw at once that if he
refused to back his faith with his money, and
to make sacrifices for it, his prophetic character
would be discredited.

Jeremiah knew quite well that the land he
was buying would fetch no price in the market
just then. It was the religious interest that
was supreme in his mind. The piece of ground

was small; but it stood for all that was most sacred in his own spiritual experience. Had he withdrawn from Hanameel's offer, he would have confessed himself to be as unbelieving as the great majority around him. In buying the field at Anathoth he was redeeming his own faith in the future and in God.

It seemed at the time as if the end of the covenant people had come; as if Jerusalem and the Land of Promise, with all their sacred institutions, were to pass away from them for ever, and to become the possession of their enemies. Every prospect was gloomy in the extreme. And yet Jeremiah, with prophetic foresight, looked beyond the impending calamity to happier times; and with all the forms and technicalities of legal conveyancing, as if the times were perfectly prosperous and assured, he purchased the field of his fathers from his faithless kinsman. And then, in a splendid oration, half prayer and half exhortation, he proceeded to show that this private domestic transaction was an acted parable of wonderful and far-reaching significance; for the purchase of his own ancestral field was an earnest of a coming time when every field in the land should be possessed in the same way, and the people should again sit each man under his own vine and fig-tree, with none to make him afraid.

¶ In *The Manchester Guardian* the following story is told. 'A man approached a woman on V-Day, and said, "That's a fine flag you have. How much did you pay for that?" "Sixpence half-penny," was the reply. "What?" he exclaimed. "But when did you buy it?" "The day war broke out," she told him.'

¶ No student of history can read the story of Jeremiah's purchase without remembering the story in Livy, when Hannibal's army was besieging Rome. The ground on which he had pitched his tent was put up at auction in Rome and bought at a great price. That was a fine thing, but the difference is this: Rome was sound to the core, it had military strength and value, while Jeremiah's Jerusalem was nothing in the world but a dump, absolutely defenceless and certain to go down. Yet Jeremiah risked his all on the promises of God, because he believed that God would eventually restore his people to the land.

At the very commencement of Jewish history is recorded the significant purchase of the cave of Machpelah by Abraham, the father of the faithful. That was a wonderful transaction, considering the circumstances in which he was placed. The whole Land of Promise was in possession of the aboriginal inhabitants; and he to whom it was promised was a pilgrim and a stranger within its bounds, owning not a foot's breadth of its soil. But, strong in his reliance upon God's word, he bought the field, and laid in it his dead, and thus took possession of it in the most sacred manner, in full assurance that the whole country would yet belong to his race.

It is the story of faith in all ages.

1. *Faith is an investment.*—'Faith is the title-deed of things hoped for,' is one of the papyrus renderings of a well-known verse which has had abundant and unforgettable illustration in modern history over and over again. 'We saw you going, but knew you would come back,' were the words in which the sore-tried inhabitants of Mons greeted the returning British soldiers in the hour of victory. Over and over again some sneering Hanameel has held the fortunes of the Faith cheap. And ever there has been some Jeremiah, who from the depth of his own prison has taken the scorner at his word and gladly paid the price of his unquenchable faith. 'Well, what about the prospects of foreign missions now?' his jeering captors asked of Adoniram Judson when he lay chained in a foul Burmese prison. 'They are just as bright as the promises of God,' was his swift and unhesitating response. The stock of the Kingdom of God unlimited is always safe to be held for a rise. There will always be investors even when the bottom seems knocked out of the market. They weigh out the seventeen precious shekels amid the laughter of an incredulous world. But they are like the man of our Lord's parable who, having caught a glimpse of gleaming gold where perchance the rains had washed away the soil, revealing the presence of unsuspected hidden treasure, went away and sought out the owner and offered him a fabulous sum for his field. And the ridiculous sum was eagerly accepted, the owner wondering at the lucky chance which had sent a madman to him with more money than brains. But he laughs longest who laughs last. And furnished with a spade from the Carpenter's shop at Nazareth he digs his field, gradually bringing to light all the treasure

hidden there, till at last his wild plunge is justified in the sight of all.

2. *Faith accepts the cost.*—' I weighed him the money,' says Jeremiah; but that was nothing compared to what life lived in this faith had cost the prophet. The suffering and the loneliness, the pain and the disappointment—these could not be measured or weighed; yet this was the cost of his faith.

¶ ' Who wishes to fight the evil spirit of His country must share that country's fate,' replied Carl von Ossietzky when counselled to flee from a Germany which was exacting a penalty for his love of peace. ' He that will come after me, let him take his cross and follow me.'

It is true in the great matter of *Christian missions*. We profess to believe in the ultimate and complete sovereignty and rule of Jesus Christ. We sing ' Jesus shall reign where'er the sun.' We believe that at His name every knee shall bow, that the kingdoms of this world will become the kingdom of our God and of His Christ. Our hopes for this are built on His own unique nature, on our belief that He is the Eternal Son of God to whom all authority has been committed in heaven and on earth; and on the inherent and infinite superiority of the gospel to the teachings of any other sage or faith. There are times in these modern days, when the prospects of His universal dominion do not seem very bright, and it would not be difficult to find people who do not share our faith and hope; and it would not be impossible to find people who mock at and deride it.

But we are expected to give some substantial proof of our faith. Everybody agrees that the times are critical for the Church, for organized religion and for the cause of Christian missions. The cost of maintaining all organizations of the Christian Church has very seriously increased and this, with the widespread indifference respecting religion, has made the situation extremely difficult. It is the time for faith and devotion to be ready to pay the price, the time for men and women of brilliant gifts and attainments to offer themselves, as, thank God, they are doing in some measure, for this splendid and blessed service. That was precisely what the pioneers in the pathway of the Christian faith did. In days when the Christian name and faith were scorned by the apparently invincible paganism of Rome—militarily triumphant throughout the world—and still more bitterly scorned by the Judaism that believed itself to be ordained of God and that spat upon the name of the Nazarene; in that day the brilliant young Jewish Rabbi Saul of Tarsus gave himself and all he was and all he had to the cause of Jesus, and gloried in sharing His reproach, and there can be no doubt that by his passionate devotion and bold and sacrificial service he saved the Christian faith. The modern situation, with all its difficulties, constitutes an appeal to all Christian people to give distinct pledges of their belief in the future of the Christian faith and the Christian Church, and emphatic proof of their loyalty and love. It is not enough to pray to God to vindicate His own cause in the earth. It is for us to vindicate it by our unashamed witness, our gifts and our open service.[1]

3. *It is a faith which God honours.*—How do we know? Because on man's capacity to respond and obey His call God relies for the fulfilling of His purpose in the world. We know because those who have committed their all to Him have proved and borne testimony in every age that He never leaves them nor forsakes them. We know because of One who belonged to God through and through, and who was obedient unto Death, even the death of the Cross; whom God highly exalted and to whom He gave a name which is above every name. We know because we receive from God not only the call to such a witness, we receive also the gift of power to respond. ' I knew that this was the word of the Lord.'

¶ Rev. F. C. Spurr tells the story of a young boy on his first visit to the sea-side. Greatly excited, he got his wooden spade ready for the great adventure. And when he looked upon the sea ' How big it is, Daddy,' he said, ' and what a splash.' But, next morning he had a great disappointment. The tide had gone far out. And all he could say now was ' What a shame '—as he cried because there was no splash. A little later however he had the thrilling experience of watching the tide return. ' Does the sea always come back like that after it has gone out?' he asked. ' Yes, my boy, always,' said his father—' always it comes back.' So when the Church seems to be facing

[1] C. Brown, in *CWP*, xcvii. 94.

an outgoing tide, it is well to remember that it has always a Come-back.

Power Limited by Purpose

Jer. xxxii. 17.—'Ah Lord God! behold, thou hast made the heaven and the earth by thy great power and stretched out arm, and there is nothing too hard for thee.'

THE confidence in God's power is here expressed with frankness and simplicity ; He is spoken of as the Maker of heaven and earth, One whose power is limitless and for whom nothing is too hard. This frank and unstudied confession is to be found repeated in many different ways on the pages of Scripture, and the truth it contains has been made into the first Article of the Creed. 'I believe in God the Father Almighty, Maker of heaven and earth.' So far, we appear to be standing on simple ground. What more natural than that men should attribute to God all power ? He who made all things must surely have been almighty in order to create the worlds. We feel it must be so. We are conscious of the immense play of forces by which the natural world is controlled, and when from that we turn in thought to the creator of all things, we feel sure that all powers must be subject to His will.

1. The first thought to which men came when they conceived one God and King over the whole world was that of His power. Men in earlier times were not always sure how God might use the power He had, but about the power itself they were certain. If evil came upon them they felt that it must come from God Himself. They did not understand the why and the wherefore of things, but they traced everything to the personal action of God. If the days were evil then God must be angry, and they sought to appease Him. If hardness entered into their lot they were sure it must be as a punishment for their sin. Their thought was absolutely simple. They might not understand God's ways, but they were sure that all the events which happened to them were God's ways.

Such was the creed of early times, of which we have the relic in their literature. To some extent, perhaps to a larger extent than we have imagined, it still persists. There are multitudes of men and women in all lands of the earth who trace the finger of God in all the things that happen in their lives. If evil falls upon them it is for some inscrutable reason, but they bow beneath it as coming from the will of God. It may be punishment, they think, or it may be discipline. Perhaps men have been growing forgetful of God, and God's power visits them to remind them He is King and Ruler ; but, whatever the explanation, it is not doubted that God is at work, and that His power orders all things.

Though dark my path and sad my lot
Let me be still and murmur not,
Or breathe the prayer divinely taught,
    Thy will be done.

If Thou shouldst call me to resign
What most I prize, it ne'er was mine ;
I only yield Thee what was thine :
    Thy will be done.

Should pining sickness waste away
My life in premature decay
My Father, still I strive to say,
    Thy will be done.[1]

2. Wherever this creed is found, whether in stated form or as a dumb spirit of submission, there is apparent in the modern world a deepening rebellion against it. The most acute religious problem of to-day is to relate the thought of God's power to the idea of His love, and to explain them in the light of present happenings.

Let us put the spirit of the time into the form of a question which is rising from countless hearts : 'How can omnipotent love be ruling over a world like this, where the earth is saturated with the blood of men, where cruelty abounds and sorrow blinds the eyes of women and children and everything is in a tragic muddle ? ' That is the acutest problem of all. Whenever you repeat that you believe in God the Father Almighty it seems to be a contradictory affirmation. 'If God is almighty,' men are saying, ' then He cannot be a Father ; if God is Father then surely He cannot have all power in His hands.'

        Beneficent
He is not, for He orders pain,
Or, if so, not Omnipotent :
   To a mere child the thing is plain [2]

[1] Charlotte Elliott.   [2] Thomas Hardy.

And let us remember that, while this problem has been heightened for all of us during the years of war, war itself did not suggest the problem. It was there in the years of peace. War is only one, even though it is the greatest, of those evils in the world against which we test the idea of God's omnipotence.

It is as unthinkable that God wills cancer as that God wills war. It must be the will of God that these evils should be swept away. The desire of eternal love must work for their removal. Explain their place in the scheme of things as we may, the true explanation cannot be that God sends them. As every instinct of good in the mind and heart of man is at work in the endeavour to overthrow them, so God must be at work. But at this point the problem becomes acutest. Why, if God be omnipotent, does He not use His power to abolish them at once? Why this delay while human wisdom and knowledge are summoning their resources to deal with them? That is the pressure of the problem as it comes home to the mind of the average man. Tell him that God is omnipotent and in face of such evils he is bewildered. Even though he feels vaguely that God must be silent for some strange and unknown reason, the thought of such a God is unreal to him. God is out of touch with all that is vital in his life and work.

3. The first step for us to take is to get rid of the crude idea of omnipotence. It is simply not true that God has the power to abolish evil in a moment and refuses to exercise it. He is not omnipotent in that sense. It is so easy for us to start with an abstract thought like that of God's power and say to ourselves that He could end the reign of wrong in a moment, and then, having said that, to wonder why He does not do it. Both the affirmation and the doubt are unreal; they are figments of our own imagination. We shall never arrive at any true understanding of God in that way. We must start, not with high-flown theories, but with tested realities. We must build our doctrines on history and observation and experience. The ways in which God has worked in the history of mankind and in our own little lives will give us the surest indications of what God is like and what His power means.

Suppose we start at that point in our search for knowledge of His power, what do we find? Look at history. With all the setbacks and reversions such as the recent war, history shows a consistent struggle upwards towards an increasing unity of life. You start with the family as the unit, then you come to the clan and the tribe, then onwards to the nation, and in the case of our own history to the empire of free nations, all pointing to the task which waits yet to be accomplished—a world federation of states. It is all one story which unfolds itself before our eyes as we open the pages of history.

Along with this you get progress in other directions, a growth of knowledge which gives men power over Nature and her forces, a growing control over such evils as disease and famine and pestilence, a wider interpretation of human relationship, which means a larger life for the individual. Superstition gradually gives place to knowledge, foolishness passes into wisdom, cruelty is succeeded by kindness. It is a slow movement, and progress is won at a cost. Do not imagine that war with all its devastation can obstruct that progress. Viewed in the larger light of history it is only like a tiny whirlpool in the middle of a flowing stream. Crises like this occur again and again in the story, and through conflict and stress further advances are made possible. Evil tendencies come to a head and receive a check; new principles are established and become part of the accepted order of things. This is the cost of progress, and again and again in history, as to-day, sacrifice has had to be paid as the price of advance.

When the Highest appeared in the garb of flesh, He obeyed the same conditions as His brethren have faced in all the ages. He was crucified and gave His life that the truth might prevail. But through His sacrifice the truth has prevailed and moved forward to a wider empire. It is all one story; that which you find in Christ you find in the story of mankind everywhere; that which you find in the story of men reaches its climax in Christ. There is no finer outline of history than Lowell's well-known lines:

Careless seems the great Avenger; history's
    pages but record
One death-grapple in the darkness 'twixt old
    systems and the Word;

Truth forever on the scaffold, Wrong forever
    on the throne,—
Yet that scaffold sways the future, and, behind
    the dim unknown,
Standeth God within the shadow, keeping
    watch above His own.

This is the consistent meaning of what both
past and present show. Are we not bound
through it to discover God's method of exercising His power ? He does not overpower men
by thrusting His will upon them. He does
not work from the outside, interposing to
change the current of things. Love always
works by the same method and always has
worked.

¶ It is said of William the Silent, that passionate lover of liberty and humanity, that his
amazing strength of character was evidenced in
nothing so much as in his quiet adherence as
long as possible to ' the more excellent way ' of
constitutional agitation against the tyranny
of Spain, in spite of the agony he endured in
witnessing the carnage wrought by the Holy
Inquisition, and the awful sufferings of an
outraged and persecuted people.[1]

It is the most superficial view to look for
God in the unusual and the extraordinary,
what we loosely call the miraculous. God is at
the heart of history, not present at occasional
moments. His work is accomplished in men
and by men and through men. It is God who
is striving through men for the establishment
of peace on earth. It is God who is struggling
through men for a truer order of society. It is
God who is coming to fuller light as truth
conquers error and knowledge scatters the
darkness. It is God's will that wins the victory
as men gain control of disease and lessen the
burden of suffering. That is the story of God's
power and the way in which He exerts it.

The purpose behind the method is a purpose
of God and could not be altered unless God
were to deny Himself, which is unthinkable.
His creation is established in freedom, and
without freedom would go to wreck and ruin.
We may try to imagine what the world would
be like if the possibility of evil were ruled out,
if God intervened to destroy it ; we may even
imagine such a world as a happier one than
this, but it would not be God's world or reach
the end He has in view. God created us to

[1] A. D. Belden.

determine things for ourselves, to have a real
and vital part in the story of life and its progress. He uses men as His workmen to arrive
at His thought through their minds, to express
His love, to carry His plan to its development
by the labour of their hands.

4. In a world such as this is there any meaning
at all in saying that God is omnipotent ? We
hold that there is. No doubt it is possible to
say that a world created in freedom is a risk
that may end in failure, that God's purpose
may be defeated. There are writers like
Mr. Wells who affirm that view of things and
say that God's victory depends entirely upon
man's will to achieve the highest. It seems a
logical view, yet confronted with it there is the
conviction that there is a power inherent in
truth which must overcome error, that love
must win the victory over selfishness, that the
will of God must prevail. Admittedly this is
faith not logic. Yet there is a certain amount of
evidence for such faith in human affairs. The
good may be at the mercy of evil for a time, but
it always rises again in power. The Cross is
never the last word.

Creation is not merely a reckless adventure
which may end in ruin. The victory of truth
and right, if slow, is sure. So we can say, ' I
believe in God the Father Almighty,' knowing
that because He is Father He will not assert
His power over against our freedom, but
knowing also that because He is God and
Father His power working from within ourselves will not suffer the splendid story to end
in pitiful failure.

Loyalty to Traditions

Jer. xxxv. 18, 19.—' And Jeremiah said unto the house
of the Rechabites, Thus saith the Lord of hosts, the God
of Israel ; Because ye have obeyed the commandment of
Jonadab your father, and kept all his precepts, and done
according unto all that he hath commanded you : Therefore thus saith the Lord of hosts, the God of Israel ;
Jonadab the son of Rechab shall not want a man to stand
before me for ever.'

JONADAB the Rechabite (or ' son of Rechab ')
is the person whom we remember in the story
of Jehu—whom Jehu passed as he was driving
furiously on his mission of vengeance upon
Jezebel, and invited to mount into his chariot
and come with him to ' see his zeal for the

Lord.' We are to think of him as one who, more than others, had been 'vexing his righteous soul' at the Baal worship and other attendant iniquities of Ahab's wicked house, and who would be welcomed by the avenger as a certain ally. Apparently he was not himself of the blood of Israel, but his tribe—the Kenites —had been from early times closely attached to the fortunes of the Chosen People. They had possibly become formally proselytes, but they had never given up the free desert life of their forefathers. They lived in tents in the wilderness of Judah and on the outskirts of the Holy Land. There is this feeling in Jonadab's charge to his descendants. He had himself, for a moment at least, tasted royal favour—had ridden with Jehu in his hour of triumph, and had earned, and probably received, the offer of high place in the new Court. But he had seen perhaps the hollowness and incompleteness of Jehu's reformation. He had seen the deep-seated, uncured vices of Samaria. And he laid on his sons and descendants the solemn charge to keep to their own simpler and purer and freer mode of life, to avoid the temptations of the life in towns, and the luxury, especially the luxury of strong drink, which he had seen to be a prime cause of its vices.

Three centuries had passed when the prophet Jeremiah found some descendants of Jonadab whom the stress of the Chaldæan armies, in the last days of the Jewish Monarchy, had driven for the moment to take refuge within the walls of Jerusalem.

It was a long time for a family tradition to endure, especially one which entailed an austere and unusual mode of life. They were in a different country. Circumstances had forced them to abandon part of their ancestral habits. There would have been much to excuse the abandonment of the rest. They might well argue that the rules fitting a desert life were one thing, the requirements of life in a large city another. Yet Jeremiah finds the descendants of Jonadab the Rechabite loyal to their tradition, living their old life as nearly as they can under the new conditions : 'We will drink no wine, for Jonadab the son of Rechab, our father, commanded us, saying : Ye shall drink no wine, neither ye, nor your sons for ever.'

1. The story speaks to us of *the sacredness of good traditions*—of the dignity, the solidity, the worth in God's eyes, of any community which can preserve the feeling of this, which can bind generation to generation by common ideals and purposes and sacrifices. What is the history of civilization but the history of races and nations which have, to some extent at least, possessed this power of linking the present to the past, of holding fast what is good, of clinging to custom, to order, to discipline, till God shows them indisputably that the time for change has come ?

The quality of loyalty to traditions is one which in theory is highly rated among us. It is the supposed basis of much of our national politics, one of the two great principles which we recognize as those by which communities live. To preserve and to improve, to reverence and cling to the past even as they trust and prepare for the future. It is our boast as a people that we think more than some other nations of the great legacies of bygone times, that we are more slow to trust novelties, to break with old habits, more patient of apparent limitations and inconveniences if they are part and parcel of a proud inheritance.

But our business now is not with politics in this restricted sense of matters of legislation and public administration. The public politics of a community, important and even sacred as they should be felt to be, are the outcome and expression of something larger and more vital still, of something in which all have part, even if they think they have no interest in political questions, of the ideals and purposes and habits of life which are prevalent in all classes among them.

It is here that the prophet meant the example of the faithful sons of Jonadab to tell on his Jewish hearers. It is here that his words of blessing and of warning may come home to ourselves. Is it true that good traditions are coming to have less hold among us, in our homes and in social life ? Is it true that the claim for personal independence—natural and with a good side to it—is yet to a dangerous extent lessening the wholesome discipline of family life, the restraints of custom, the regard for inherited standards ? Is everything coming to be felt, as it was not in the last generation, an open question, to be decided by individual taste and convenience—the observance of Sunday, the choice of the books to be read and topics to be discussed, the rules of social propriety, respect for authority ?

The inestimable value of good traditions, the duty and the dignity of clinging to them—these are truths written very large for us in the Bible. In the Old Testament, from the blessing of Abraham, the ' father of the faithful,' and the reason given for it : ' I know him that he will command his children and his household after him ; and they shall keep the ways of the Lord,' to the promise and the warning of the last of the prophets : ' Behold I send you Elijah the prophet before the coming of the great and dreadful day of the Lord : and he shall turn the hearts of the fathers to the children and the hearts of the children to their fathers, lest I come and smite the earth with a curse.' And in the New Testament, what else is the very meaning of the institution of the Christian Church, the ' pillar and ground of the truth ' ? What is the meaning of those words that come so often in the Epistles, ' hold fast,' ' hold the traditions that ye have been taught,' of the praises of order, steadfastness, obedience, of following good example, of bringing up children in the ' nurture and admonition of the Lord ' ?

2. There are two sides on which the exhortations and warnings appeal to us.

(1) They speak to us of *the community*. They bid us, for the sake of the community, shrink from helping, by the example of our own families or by the freedom which we allow in ourselves, to lower in any way or degree the standard of good which it has inherited—the sober household religion, the modesty and dutifulness of tone, the respect for wholesome customs and traditional pieties to which English life and character have owed, and owe, so much.

(2) But they speak also of *the individual life*. They appeal to all of us, but especially to the young. It is to them most that the conflict which sometimes is felt between inherited instincts and habits on the one side and the claims of fashion and the temptations of liberty on the other brings practical difficulty and dangers.

Who would not say to them : ' Cherish—cling to—the good traditions of your home ' ? All that is best in life—religion and its hopes and protection, good feeling, the sense of honour, unselfish purpose, conscience itself—all these things come to us in a great measure by inheritance.

One home is not quite like another, one is a little stricter, holds a standard a little higher and more exacting in one point and another. What shall we do when we first realize that difference ? What will wise and generous spirits do ? Will they be ashamed of anything in their home teaching and usage which seems, in the light of that new knowledge, peculiar, which goes beyond the fashion of their neighbours ? Will they carefully prune and pare away everything in the way of religious observance or of strictness as to speech or act which others about them have not been equally used to ? Or will they cling all the more closely, with a certain honourable pride, to home habits and traditions—not obtruding them, not necessarily expecting them of others, but content to go their own way as they have been taught, to deny themselves (if so it be) freedom which others take and think innocent, holding firmly their own ground, for memory's sake, for affection's sake, for the love of those who taught them all they know of what is high and true and good ?

¶ Ruskin comes to one's mind for the beautiful way in which he bore himself to his parents in the Denmark Hill home. ' He submitted,' we are told, ' without murmur to the rule of the house, which, on the Sabbath day, covered his beloved Turners with dark screens. This man, well past middle life, in all the renown of his principal works, who for a score of years had been one of the chief forces in the literature of the century, continued to show an almost childlike docility towards his father and his mother, respecting their complaints and remonstrances, and gratefully submitting to be corrected by their worldly wisdom and larger experience.'

The Indestructible Word

Jer. xxxvi. 23, 28.—' He cut it with the penknife, and cast it into the fire. . . . Take thee again another roll, and write in it all the former words that were in the first roll.'

THIS dramatic encounter between the king and the prophet divides itself into three scenes. There is first the quiet room in the city, where Jeremiah, ' shut up ' by man, is proving that ' the Word of God is not bound,' by dictating to his faithful friend Baruch a full record of his prophetic ministry. It is an account in which judgment and mercy intermingle ; but towards its close it becomes more and more threatening in its tones. The enemy is near the gates ! ' The axe is laid at the root of the tree ! ' Nebuchadrezzar draws nigh !

Nevertheless doom may be averted still. Let the king and his councillors give up their foolish trust in Egypt, ' that broken reed.' Let them throw themselves on the mercy of Nebuchadrezzar. Best of all, let them trust in God alone and cast away their idols and their vices and there is hope even yet that a remnant may be saved.

Eager that this hope may not be quenched, even at the eleventh hour, Baruch hastens with his ' roll ' to the temple courts, so that he may meet some of the chief men there, tell them of its ominous contents, and thus lead the king to listen to its message. He is successful in doing this. A royal council is arranged, and one of the ' princes ' friendly to Jeremiah agrees to bring the matter before the king.

This brings us to the second scene in the chapter. It is a splendid room in that ' ceiled house ' which, Jeremiah tells us, this puppet-king spent so much of his brief reign in building. His lords and councillors are round about him and the king sits before a fire, for it is winter time ; not improbably flushed with wine, for drunkenness was one of his vices. Jeremiah's roll is brought and the king directs his secretary to read it out. As he does so the king turns his face to the reader, listening at first with half-concealed contempt. But as Jehudi goes on with his recital of ' the thoughts that breathe ' and ' the words that burn,' the monarch's face changes in its expression from indifference to annoyance, from annoyance to anger, from anger to fury, until at last, losing all self-control, he rises from his seat, tears the roll out of the secretary's hand, hacks at it with his penknife, and then flings the tattered fragments into the fire, watching it consume to ashes there.

Once again the scene changes. We are back in Jeremiah's little room. Again the prophet speaks and again Baruch writes. It is the same words as before. Only this time ' other like words ' are added to it, and there is no suggestion to send it again to the king. God's word has been rejected, but it will not be abrogated. It remains indestructible. ' Heaven and earth shall pass away, but my words shall not pass away.' Such are the three scenes brought before us. What are they meant to teach us ?

1. *Gods Speaks to Man.*—This was not the first time He had spoken to Jehoiakim. When we read his brief biography we see that God sent him message after message.

(1) He did so *by giving him a good example.* His father Josiah was one of the noblest kings that ever sat on the throne of David. All his childhood he had that example pointing him to a better life. Yet, in spite of that, he was one of the worst of kings. ' He filled Jerusalem,' we are told, ' with innocent blood.' At a time when his nation was in its death-throes, he was spending his days in drunken revelry and oppressive luxury.

¶ In the old cemetery of Princeton University two graves stand side by side. One is the grave of Jonathan Edwards, the first President of the College and America's greatest saint ; the other is the grave of Dr Burr, his son-in-law, and a man also eminent for piety. You would have said that the child of such a parentage would have been a good man. Yet that child was Aaron Burr, who grew up to be an infidel and profligate who, after a life of infamy, died a miserable death.

Do not lightly esteem the blessings of a Christian home. Do not cut with a penknife that page out of the Family Bible which records a godly parentage. There is no message from God so potent as that which comes from a mother's lips. There is none which, if despised, is so fraught with disaster.

(2) Again, God spoke to Jehoiakim *by trouble.* He came to the throne in a time of national mourning. His father had just fallen on the disastrous field of Megiddo, in battle with the King of Egypt. His younger brother, whom the people had placed on the throne in preference to him, had been carried away captive to Egypt to see his native land no more. Under such circumstances we might have expected Jehoiakim to have been sobered. As he sat on the throne we might have thought he would have turned over a new leaf. But this was not the case. He rioted out his days in luxury, immorality and oppression, and when Urijah, a prophet, lifted up his voice in protest, he hounded him to death, dragging him back from Egypt, whither the poor man had fled, and

casting his dead body into a common grave. He would have done the same to Jeremiah; but the people rose in his defence. Bad as they were, they did not wish to have the blood of that great prophet on their conscience.

Jehoiakim's life illustrates the oft-illustrated fact that, if trials do not make us better, they will make us worse. It was wonderful that, after such a life, God should have sent the king any further message at all. And yet He did so. This 'roll' of Jeremiah is God's last message to him. It was chiefly a message of judgment; yet it was also a message of mercy, which, if he had even then listened to it, would not have been too late to save him, as it saved Manasseh. But he heard it not. 'He cut it with a penknife and cast it into the fire.'

2. *God's Word may be Rejected.*—The reasons which probably moved Jehoiakim in his treatment of God's word are undoubtedly still in operation in the case of many who, like him, reject the word of God. Primarily, Jehoiakim's reason for his treatment of Jeremiah's prophecy was that there was in the message so much which to him, a fast young man, bent on luxury and display, and endeavouring to combine wickedness with an easy and popular form of religion, *was not pleasant.* For Jehoiakim was 'religious' in his way; he liked preaching well if it was pleasant. We learn from the Book of Jeremiah that he had surrounded himself with not a few court-preachers; the prophet once and again refers to them in terms of tremendous severity. The king and the people said to them: 'Prophesy unto us *smooth things.*' And so they prophesied smooth things, according to the demand, and king and court no doubt applauded. If only Jeremiah had fallen in with the fashion, and had prophesied smooth things with the rest of them, the king would not have cut up his roll, or ordered his arrest. But Jeremiah was not a man of that kind. He told what God had told him was the truth, and he kept telling it; and when the king would not *hear* the truth, he *wrote* it and sent it to him. And the truth was just what Jehoiakim did not want to hear. He wanted the Lord by all means to be merciful to him and his people, but not at the price of giving up his sins. And so he rejected the word of the prophet, and no doubt persuaded himself that the prophet was a disloyal croaker in the pay of Babylon.

Just so is it still. The true reason of most scepticism is not found in inability of the intellect. It is found not in the head at all, but in the heart—in the will. Men still say, as they said in Jeremiah's day, and in so many words: 'Preach smooth things.' God is a God of love, they say. It will be all right in the end. All right? How can it be all right if your life is all wrong? Is it kinder to say, 'Peace, peace, when there is no peace,' than to tell you plainly in the words of the prophet, 'There is no peace, saith my God, to the wicked'?

3. *God's Word is Indestructible.* — Though God's messenger may be rejected, God's message remains. The roll of Baruch may be hacked and burned, but God's Word cannot be destroyed. When Jeremiah hears the story he sits down in his room and dictates just the same words to his secretary: only, Baruch remarks, 'There were also added many like words.'

What were these added words? As we read elsewhere, they were terrible ones for the wicked king. 'His dead body shall be cast out in the day to the heat, and in the night to the frost. He shall be buried with the burial of an ass, drawn forth and cast out of the city.' Four years after these words were spoken they received a tragic fulfilment. The end of Jehoiakim is obscure. He may either have perished in a foray outside the walls against the Babylonian armies which were then investing the city, or he may have died by the assassin's hand in some insurrection within the walls against his hated rule. At all events the words of Jeremiah were, we may be sure, fulfilled, else they would not have been recorded. His dead body was probably pitched over the walls or left outside them, lying there to rot in the sun like the carcass of an ass. He went down to

> The vile dust from whence he sprung,
> Unwept, unhonour'd, and unsung.

God's words may be rejected. God's Word cannot be destroyed. The burnt roll of the prophet remains with its mystic letters clear upon it, 'Nec tamen consumebatur.' The dead body of the contemptuous king lies out in the night, there to find a burial in the vulture's mouth and the jackal's teeth.

¶ When the Bible was first printed in England, the Romish bishops and priests tried to play Jehoiakim's game. They bought up all the copies they could put their hands on, and made bonfires of them. And what was the result? The printers used the money thus obtained to provide ten presses where there had been one, and the Bibles in the land increased fifty-fold.

Ebed-Melech

Jer. xxxviii. 7.—' Ebed-melech the Ethiopian.'

1. THE story of the kindness of Ebed-melech to Jeremiah is very winsome. Ebed-melech—the name means ' King's Servant '—was a negro belonging to a most unfortunate class of men-servants. The facts that he had access to Zedekiah, the King of Judah, that he had the courage to call Zedekiah's attention to the injustice and cruelty of powerful men in the Court towards Jeremiah, and that Zedekiah listened to Ebed-melech and was influenced by his representations in the prophet's favour, show that this son of Ethiopia was a thoroughly trustworthy man. He was really far better entitled to the name of ' King's Servant ' than the princes and courtiers who had worked on the feelings of the weak king to get put out of their way a man whose messages to the king and to the people were too frank and fearless. It is not title or office that makes a man honourable, but qualities of mind and heart and soul ; and Ebed-melech, a slave of a despised race, and belonging to a most unhappy class regarded with contempt, had a golden heart.

It is characteristic of the Bible, both in the Old and in the New Testament, that generous tribute is so often paid to men of no account according to the estimation of the world. It is this quality in the Bible that makes it such a democratic Book, a Book which makes its continual and eternal appeal to the heart of humanity. God's patent of nobility pays no regard to earthly titles of honour, or earthly grades of social distinction. The slave girl who called Naaman's wife's attention to the healing power of the prophet Elisha, the widow who nourished the same prophet out of what remained to her in her utmost poverty, the un-named ' poor wise ' man whose ' wisdom saved the city ' in the Book of Ecclesiastes, and a host of others have been given immortality in the Word that endureth for ever, while persons of the greatest importance in their day were passed unnoticed, and their names, as soon as the earth covered them, faded from human memory.

2. Ebed-melech is a most attractive character. We do not know if he had counted himself among the prophet's friends, or had paid more heed to the delivery of his messages than had the sneering crowd and powerful ones of the royal court. Even had he thought that Jeremiah was a truly inspired prophet of Jehovah, what did it matter to anybody what a black slave believed ? He was simply a piece of royal property, discharging the duties assigned to him in the midst of a licentious and brutal court, and yet, as in the days of Paul slaves of Cæsar in the Imperial palace at Rome listened to the gospel message which consuls and pro-consuls scorned, so among men of the lowest grade in the palaces of the Kings of Judah and Israel, in the most sunken condition of the nation, there were souls of the Ebed-melech type. Such men are the salt of humanity, and such men there are in all lands to-day.

The value of such men is recognized in many a village and little country-town church, in many a struggling church and mission in a slum district. They are ' King's Servants,' keeping their ears open for the whispers of the still small voice, and with feet eager to run on His errands. They are men of the warm heart, with that sympathy which makes men akin to Christ. Jeremiah in that filthy dungeon was left to rot, but God had still work for him to do, and we may well believe that Ebed-melech, a kindly soul, and, as we must believe, a pious soul, was chosen by God to be His servant and His chosen means to effect the deliverance of the prophet.

3. The fact that Ebed-melech was an Ethiopian suggests an interesting reflexion. The negroes were a race loathed, as a rule, by the Semites. They were the ' sons of Ham,' on whom, according to Israelite belief, lay the curse of God. But the story in this chapter shows that God was not going, even in those days, to leave the Ethiopians without know-

ledge and without witness. Ebed-melech was nearer to the heart of God than the most highly placed men of the race who boasted of their descent as God's most favoured nation from Abraham, Isaac and Jacob. We know to-day, from the story of African missions, that among the darkest sons of darkest Africa God has His Ebed-melechs. Moffat has told us and Livingstone and the Congo missionaries, and the missionaries of Uganda and God's white messengers to other black nations, that the African has a heart to feel and a soul to be saved as much as the white man. Among the Africans captured for Christ have been souls most noble who have played the part of King's servants among their own peoples, and to the white missionaries have proved themselves brothers beloved, sons of consolation, friends and helpers in every good work. What a King's son James Aggrey of Achimota was !

Ebed-melech has proved himself worthy of taking his place in the ranks of Christ's saints and Christ's co-workers for the redemption of humanity. Still, however, there are too many men of our own nation and Empire and of the United States who look upon Ebed-melech with contemptuous eyes. They dislike him, they criticize him, they will not travel with him in the same compartment of a railway train or sit with him at the same table in a restaurant. It may be hereafter, in that land where all earthly distinctions are obliterated, that Ebed-melech will stand 'nearer the eternal throne,' in a place of higher honour than those who shun him and will not worship with Ebed-melech in the same church.

¶ 'Some white men,' said Dr Aggrey once, 'ought to be transformed into negroes just for a few days, so as to feel and suffer what we suffer.'

¶ Two years ago Mr Learie Constantine, the well-known West Indian cricketer, was awarded damages in a British Court on the ground that he had been refused the accommodation reserved for him and his family for four nights in the Imperial Hotel, London. When he arrived he was told that he could only stay one night, and when he asked the reason the manageress said it was because of the two to three hundred Americans and Colonials who were staying there. At the time this incident occurred Mr Constantine was a Government employee looking after the welfare of West Indians who had been brought to Britain for war-work under the Ministry of Labour.[1]

The Spirit of the Cross

Jer. xlv. 4, 5.—' When *I* must destroy what I built, and when *I* must uproot what I planted, shalt *thou* seek great things for thyself ? ' (McFadyen).

1. ' WHEN *I* must destroy what I built, and when *I* must uproot what I planted, shalt *thou* seek great things for thyself ? ' That is a question which life puts to all of us, sooner or later. But there are two other questions which usually lead up to it. The first is, ' *What do you want ?* '—the question which challenges us as we stand on the threshold of responsible life. We choose a career, or drift into one. We enter on a friendship which may shape all our life. We begin to create the world of personal interests in which our chief recreation will be found. It seems as if a really adequate answer would require the knowledge drawn from a full experience of life. How can we tell what anything really is until we have tried it ? We stand like travellers at the parting of many untried ways, where to choose one is to reject the others, and to which there can be no retracing of our steps. Really to know what we want of life is no mean portion of life's wisdom. It was a pardonable exaggeration of Carlyle's to say, ' Blessed is he who has found his work ; let him ask no other blessing.'

Close on the heels of that first question, ' What do you want ? ' comes the second, ' *What will you pay for it ?* ' Again it seems an unfair question. How can any of us foresee just how much effort in muscle or brain it will cost him to reach the chosen goal of his journey ? Nobody knows what any particular experience will cost him until he has gone through it. We must go on paying for what we wanted, day by day. Each man learns the cost to himself. If any one cries, ' I don't want to be this, I want to be something else,' life is ready with the question in a new form, and retorts, ' Then what *do* you want to be, and how much will you pay to change over ? ' Most things are possible— even to be a saint—if we want them enough, and are ready to pay the inevitable price for them.

The third question is really that of the text :

[1] *Life and Work*, August 1945, p. 123.

'*What do you want it for?*' It usually lags behind the others, and is sometimes sprung upon a man in his middle-age, when he has largely attained his ambition, made his reputation, gathered his money. 'What will you do with it, now that you have got it? What was the secret motive all the time inspiring your energies'? This is the most difficult of the three questions to answer, because it deals with the subtle pressures, the half-conscious instincts, the dim desires, which we have never dragged into the light for self-judgment. How easily a man may go on persuading himself that he is inspired by high and honourable motives, by the desire to serve others, to make a genuine contribution to the world's welfare, to advance knowledge, to obey God—until he reaches a point at which the subtle tinge of selfishness is revealed to others or even to himself! That revelation may come through success, when a man no longer needs to pretend. But it may also come through failure, disillusionment, the embitterment of spirit that at last knows itself for what it is.

2. The question of the text was addressed to Baruch, the secretary of Jeremiah. He had answered the first two questions successfully. He had encountered one of the world's really great men, the finest of the Old Testament prophets, the large-hearted, tender-souled Jeremiah. Baruch's own heart had gone out in passionate discipleship to him, for here surely was a man to love and a man to follow. When Baruch met Jeremiah, he knew what he wanted. Not less was he ready for the second question, ready to pay the price of such discipleship in isolation, hatred, peril of life. He does not seem ever to have flinched whilst Jeremiah and he stood alone against a whole people. It was worth while to be the friend and companion of such a man as the prophet, and to feel sure of being on the side of God. But now came the third question, the acid test of the alloy of selfishness. It came through apparent failure. To see no result for all your work, to believe that it will all be thrown away—how hard it is to go on working still for the work's sake! For Baruch, the sorrow of this personal grief was mingled with sympathy with his country's fate: 'Woe is me now: for Jehovah hath added sorrow to my pain; I am weary with my groaning, and I find no rest.'

To such a man comes the Divine message, through the prophet's lips. The point of it lies in the contrast between the unshrinking spirit of God and the shrinking spirit of Baruch, yet beneath the contrast there is God's greatest gift, an offered fellowship. 'When *I* must destroy what I built, and when *I* must uproot what I planted, shalt *thou* seek great things for thyself?' It is the emphasis of the new translation which brings out this point. God has lavished His care on a people whose national existence He is now compelled to destroy. God is about to overthrow the very building His own hands have built through many centuries. God will uproot the very trees His own hands once planted. In Christian terms, the prophet's message gives a glimpse of the Cross of Christ in the heart of God, the eternal passion of self-sacrifice that is God's very nature, 'the authentic sign and seal of Godship.' To this sorrowful human heart, God Himself says, 'Behold, and see if there be any sorrow like mine . . . can you not forget your own demands, your little self, as I show you my heart of sorrow?' That is the greatest of all comfort, for it is the lifting up of a man's thought and vision to something far greater than himself, to a purpose of far-reaching horizon, to an interpretation of the universe in which his private trouble falls into its true place and finds its true comfort. The realization that there is self-sacrifice at the very heart of God gives strength, motive, vision, and, above all, the companionship of Spirit with spirit, in what would else have been a lonely world.

¶ François Coillard of the Zambesi, at the very close of his work, when bitter disappointment had clouded all his life, wrote as follows: 'It seems to me that it is only now that I have some slight glimpses of what love is—true love, the Love of God, which loves unselfishly, without calculation, without response: which loves in spite of hostility, ingratitude or even hatred. God *is* Love. O my God, live in me, that I may live with Thy life and love with Thy love.'

3. The spirit of the Cross is a *spirit*, and not a formula. 'To become stereotyped,' it has been said, 'is to fail in life.' To live by a spirit is much more difficult and sometimes more dangerous than to conform our lives to a set of maxims, a code of rules. But surrender to cir-

cumstances and to public opinion is again and again challenged by the essential Christian emphasis on the spirit of the Cross. The Christian is always in need of the Apostolic warning that life cannot be reduced to a set of petty rules—' Touch not, taste not, handle not.' On the other hand, the spirit of self-denial ranges from the mere courtesies of everyday intercourse up to the great heroisms. Think of Jesus in the Pharisee's house, watching with half-humorous pity the unseemly jostling for the best seats. His little parable of good manners—' when thou art bidden, go and sit down in the lowest place '—is not simply a contribution to a Palestinian book of social ' Don'ts ' ; it is the application of the spirit of the Cross to the little things of life. There is no finality in such a spirit. We do not exhaust its meaning in some choice of a vocation once for all, like that of the monk or the missionary. Those who make a worthy choice at the outset find that the ideal of it continually expands, and makes ever new demands upon them. There is a fine, though simple enough, example of this in the Labrador experience of Wilfred Grenfell. He tells us how his work as a medical missionary had brought him to a home where the mother lay dead and the father dying. Next day, he had to improvise a double funeral, and then found himself, as he says, with five little mortals sitting on the grave-mound. ' We thought we had done all that could be expected of a doctor, but we now found the difference. *It looked as if God expected more.*' So Grenfell had to establish his Children's Home. That is the essential quality of the spirit of the Cross. God expects more, and both the glory and the rebuke of the Christian ideal spring from that Divine expectation. To face that continued demand is one of the most real difficulties of the Christian conscience. Where am I to draw the line between legitimate personal comfort, honourable ambition, a respectable standard of Christian living, on the one side, and on the other, the sternly haunting word, ' Seekest *thou* great things for thyself ? ' If I do draw such a line, God's finger wipes it out.

4. The spirit of the Cross, then, is the characteristic spirit of Christianity. This is the genuine spirit of the Church of Christ. Underneath all the differences of the successive generations and nationalities, all the peculi-

arities of organization and utterance and even conduct, we could find no more universal and characteristic feature of the genuine tradition of our faith than that of the spirit of the Cross. Whether we think of the message or of the method, of the religion or of the morality, it is this note of self-sacrifice, Divine and human, this acceptance of suffering for the sake of the Divine purpose, which makes the true Church one. The supreme sacrament of the Church is the sacrament of apparent failure, for in the sacrament of the Lord's Supper we proclaim, we ' preach,' the Cross of Christ, the Cross which was failure before it could be success. The history of the Church may often show the lamentable absence even of the ideal, but also shows its continual re-emergence and frequent realization. The spirit of the Cross is not confined to the visible Church, and some of its finest examples lie beyond the borders of any organization. Yet it is the Church which best nurtures that spirit in ordinary men and women. It is the Church as the fellowship of that spirit which preserves and hands on the great tradition of it, and in this sign alone can conquer. The fellowship of the Church is built on what has truly been called that right of the weaker over the stronger which is part of the moral structure of the universe. It is built on the principle enunciated by a notable French writer, ' Nothing is lost when we make an offering of it.'

Such a fellowship of men, by its very nature, proclaims that fellowship with God on which it depends for very existence. All human sympathy, all social consciousness, all generous service, spring from a human nature which God has created in His own image. They belong to man as truly as the self-seeking instincts, with which they are so often in conflict. But, because of this conflict, they need the constant reinforcement of the fellowship of God, in whom there is no such conflict, since it is of His very self to give Himself. Morality always needs, indeed always implies, some sort of religion. Life is ultimately a lonely business, and loneliest as it moves upwards. But that upward path, at every step, brings a clearer vision of Him who so loved that He gave, Him for whom living is giving.

In some deep sense it must be true that the Cross of Christ is the age-long Cross of God Himself, whilst sinning and suffering man works out his troubled course and attains his destiny. It must be true, for there is no solution to the problem of human suffering, save in the Divine. This is the clear teaching of the Bible, in the Old Testament as well as in the New. We have been listening to a prophet comforting his disciple by the thought of a fellowship with God in suffering. This is the essence of the gospel. God's love shrinks from no sacrifice that it may save to the uttermost. The spirit of that Divine sacrifice can animate every honourable career, and consecrate every worthy ambition, but it is also the secret of that inner peace for which every human heart seeks, the peace which Jesus offered on His Cross.

¶ Dear Lord, who bore so much for me, grant me Thy nature, that I, in my small way, may bear a little, a very little, for Thy needy world, that I may be made comformable unto Thy death ; that my life, held against the tremendous background of Thy Cross, may not clash with it, but may rather match with it : that the pattern I see there on Calvary, in big, may run on—very little now, but still the same pattern, unchanged and unbroken, through all the nothings that make up my days.[1]

False and True Greatness

Jer. xlv. 5.—'Seekest thou great things for thyself ? seek them not.'

BARUCH, a man of noble birth and the secretary and friend of Jeremiah, seems to have expected to have either important office in the state or, more probably, the gift of prophecy bestowed upon him. His ambition is destined not to be gratified, and the prophet here warns him of the fact. In addition to the burden of the sins and sorrows of his country, which afflict him sorely, he must learn to repress the desire to be anything more than the attendant upon him whose gift of prophecy he may not hope to share.

To play a prominent part in the impending crisis, to be the hero of a national revival, to gain the favour of the conqueror whose coming he announced, this, or something like this, had been the vision that had come before him, and when this passed away he sank into despair at the seeming fruitlessness of his efforts.

[1] A. J. Gossip, *Experience Worketh Hope*, 121.

In the great purposes of God most of us, like Baruch, can only play a small part. If desiring to do some great thing for God and His Church carries with it a willingness to do something little, if God so wills, such desire cannot but be well-pleasing to God. But if such desire implies unwillingness to fill a little space and discharge a little duty, that is another matter. And sometimes there is a tendency, even in good, sincere souls, to assume that fidelity in little things is of a different quality from that which is needed in what are regarded as the great things of life. Against the soundness of that assumption our Lord said, ' He that is faithful in that which is least is faithful also in much ; and he that is unjust in the least is unjust also in much '—meaning that in His judgment true fidelity in things great or small is the same.

All service ranks the same with God :
If now, as formerly he trod
Paradise, his presence fills
Our earth, each only as God wills
Can work—God's puppets, best and worst,
Are we : there is no last nor first.

Say not ' a small event ! ' Why ' small ? '
Costs it more pain that this, ye call
A ' great event,' should come to pass,
Than that ? Untwine me from the mass
Of deeds which make up life, one deed
Power shall fall short in or exceed ![1]

1. *Mistaken Measurements.*—We are constantly attempting to put a value upon our own deeds and those of others. Some we call great, others we call little. The distinction is not entirely baseless, though after all it is but superficial.

¶ The Russian dramatist, Tchehov, in a play called *The Three Sisters*, puts the following words into the mouth of one of the chief characters : ' And it's curious,' says Vershinin, ' that we can't possibly tell what exactly will be considered great and important, and what will seem paltry and ridiculous. Did not the discoveries of Copernicus or Columbus, let us say, seem useless and ridiculous at first, while the nonsensical writings of some wiseacre seemed true ? '[2]

We fancy that influential situations and

[1] Browning, *Pippa Passes*.
[2] ' Philemon,' *From My Window*.

special occasions are indispensable for the expression of superior qualities and graces, when, in fact, they are not at all essential. The provincial architect may think that his potential genius remains undiscovered because he has never had a palace to build ; the village musician may impute his obscurity to the accident of not having had an opportunity to play a cathedral organ ; and many suppose that the fine or strong qualities which they think they discern in themselves remain undemonstrated because of the absence of rare stimulation and opportunity.

Such reasoning is generally mistaken. Superior intellect asserts itself in the extraordinary way in which it deals with ordinary tasks and occasions. The modest daisy was sufficient theme to secure for Burns a place amid the immortals ; a single string stretched on a wooden shoe was all that Paganini needed to demonstrate the master minstrel ; and a bit of canvas a few inches square was ample to certify to all generations that Raphael was the prince of painters.

And is not all this equally true in relation to character ? Surely here we do not need great things to prove great qualities ; for moral power, richness, and grace declare themselves in a way that cannot be overlooked or denied in stations and actions which have no other greatness. As Waller writes,

Circles are praised, not that excel in largeness,
    but th' exactly framed.

2. *The Greatness of Little Things.*—It may be admitted that the occasional deeds of splendour done by men or women of exceptional gifts may be more arresting and that they are more applauded, but they are not to be compared for their effect upon the general happiness and well-being of society with the deeds that are daily and hourly being done by the less gifted of our fellow men.

¶ As Henry Martyn entered the senate house at Cambridge to compete for academic distinction there flashed across his memory the words, 'Seekest thou great things for thyself ? seek them not.' He says, 'I obtained my highest wishes, but was surprised to find I had grasped a shadow.' He lives to-day, not by the 'great things' of learning, but by that which looks little in the eyes of the world, his humble walk with God.

Does not God Himself discover His unequalled perfection in the perfection of little things, common things, fugitive things ? That God is greatest in His smallest creations philosophers have long understood, and modern science furnishes abundant confirmation of this view. The microscope, certainly not less clearly than the telescope, reveals the glory of God. Minute things are as exquisitely constructed as the most gigantic, and the things of the moment are as superb as everlasting orbs. The dew of the grass rivals the splendour of the diamond ; the wing of the moth is as marvellous as that of the golden eagle ; the bubble on the stream duplicates the grace and glory of the firmament.

¶ As Robert Browning has it in his dramatic lyric 'Saul'

I but open my eyes,—and perfection, no more
    and no less,
In the kind I imagined, full-fronts me, and
    God is seen God
In the star, in the stone, in the flesh, in the
    soul and the clod.

Or that fine conception of William Cowper in 'The Task'

                    One spirit—His
Who wore the platted thorns with bleeding
    brows—
Rules universal nature. Not a flow'r
But shows some touch, in freckle, streak, or
    stain,
Of his unrivall'd pencil. He inspires
Their balmy odours, and imparts their hues,
And bathes their eyes with nectar, and includes,
In grains as countless as the sea-side sands,
The forms with which he sprinkles all the
    earth.

And as God manifests His infinite greatness in small and common things, so we may reveal the utmost depth, loftiness, and refinement of moral and spiritual life in the most commonplace and monotonous vocation. We can prove our love to God in small sacrifices, as at the martyr's stake ; our courage by witnessing for Christ in daily life, as much as by bearing witness before kings ; our patience by smiling away the worry of common days, as by bowing to some bitter tragedy ; and we can as clearly demonstrate our enthusiasm by small, continuous efforts in an obscure circle, as by some heroic exertion on a great occasion.

For thirty years the life of our Lord was entirely uneventful. He lived in a village, mixed with peasants, wrought at the bench, dwelt in a cottage. There was no great trial, like the temptation in the wilderness; no moving triumph, like the palm-strewing; no ecstasy, like the Transfiguration; no humiliation, like the crown of thorns; no grief, like Gethsemane. Without dazzling episodes, striking situations, or tragic sorrows, without the dramatic, or the miraculous, He grew into the fullness of that supreme character which commands the admiration and reverence of mankind. It is most encouraging to know that the noblest life attained its last completeness in the simplest scenes, unprompted, undisciplined by anything extraordinary.

It is an ordinary thing to read the Bible, to pray to God, to attend the sanctuary, to maintain and extend God's cause in the world. It is an ordinary thing to provide for one's family, to be kind and considerate to one another. It is an ordinary thing to be sober, truthful, honest, and industrious. The greatest man in the world is no more discharged from such ordinary things than the smallest is; and when great things come off at the expense of these, and a man thinks himself too brilliant to waste his time upon trifles, God spurns his great things. If we are to abide the final judgment of God, ordinary duties, however seemingly small, must be faithfully discharged.

3. *The Bearing of this on Personal Religion.*— There have always been those who, instead of accepting the simple plan of salvation through repentance and faith, have turned away from it like Naaman. They have imagined that the measure of the Divine gift is by a standard of their own. ' If the prophet had bid thee do some great thing, wouldest thou not have done it?' something in keeping with our position, and the superior quality of our moral virtues. But ' all the fitness He requireth is to feel our need of Him.'

We can conceive it possible that God might have imposed conditions much harder than simple faith. How very thankful should we be He has made the way so easy—that we have only to ' take the blessing from above, and wonder at His boundless love!'

¶ ' I must confess,' said Dr Chalmers in his later years, ' that I never have so clear and satisfactory a view of the Gospel, as when I regard it as a simple offer on the one side, and a simple acceptance on the other.'

False and True Ambition

Jer. xlv. 5.—' Seekest thou great things for thyself? seek them not.'

IT is common to speak only in disparagement of ambition, to regard it as an unmixed evil. And a great deal that is very forcible and very true has been said with the object of warning people respecting the danger and fascination of this deluding passion. For example, that exquisite sentence written by Queen Caroline Matilda of Denmark with a diamond on one of the windows of her Castle of Flensburg, ' Give me innocence, let others be great,' or those well-known lines of Charles Kingsley, ' Be good, sweet maid, and let who will be clever.' We all recognize the truth as well as the beauty of these expressions, and no doubt the advice here given is perfect for some people, yet we must not take it as the universal teaching of religion on the subject of human ambition. For religion does not require us to suppress all ambitious desires. The object of Christianity is not to extinguish, but to guide, elevate, and purify our natural instincts.

1. Ambition is a condition of success. If at school we see a lad whom nothing can spur into competition with the other boys, we naturally do not look for proficiency in such a scholar. We say he is deficient in ambition. In the same way, a man who has narrow aims and limited interests need not expect a successful future, for greatness seldom overtakes us unawares. In no profession does a man leap into distinction without conscious effort on his own part, however circumstances may favour him. Ambition, then, is a condition of success, since it inspires the hope and determination necessary to secure strength of purpose and constancy of aim. The leading spirits of the age who constitute the moving forces in the world of mind are invariably men of strong aspiring nature, whose disposition and habit it is to look ahead. Our best books, our greatest

discoveries, our noblest institutions are due to the resource and energy, the daring and enthusiasm of such men.

¶ Let the ambition to discover the North Pole lay hold on Peary and no obstacles could defeat him. For over twenty years he made it his ambition to plant the Stars and Stripes at the North Pole, until, as he said, ' I long ago ceased to think of myself save as an instrument for the attainment of that end.'

We may have too readily accepted the attitude to ambition as historically represented in old monasteries, where men turned their backs on this world's ambitions and hopes, and counted themselves holy for so doing. That same attitude is represented in some forms of evangelicalism, as in hymns like,

Oh, to be nothing, nothing.

The idea behind that familiar conception of Christianity is that ambition is to be crushed, and the consequence of that attitude has been a pallid and sickly kind of Christianity. If a man prays too hard, ' Oh, to be nothing, nothing,' he may get exactly what he asks.

When, however, one turns to those great lives which have been the glory of the Christian movement, it is plain that they are handling ambition in another way altogether. William Booth, founder of the Salvation Army, was a man whose figure looms the larger the longer we know it, as mountains look greater when we retreat from them. But his own phrasing of the motive power which drove him down into the slums of Darkest England to work for folk whom everybody else had forgotten, was this : ' the impulses and urgings of an undying ambition ' to save souls.[1]

It is also told of the famous preacher, C. H. Spurgeon that, in his early days, he thought of applying for entrance to a College. An appointment was made for the Principal to meet him. Punctually, young Spurgeon called and was shown into a room where he waited two hours. At length, venturing to make inquiries as to the unreasonably long delay, he was told that, through the mistake of a servant-maid, the Principal had also been in another room waiting, and, thinking that the young man had failed to turn up, had gone away. Spurgeon was greatly disappointed. But, on his way across a

[1] H. E. Fosdick, *Twelve Tests of Character*, 147.

Common, a voice seemed distinctly to say to him—' Seekest thou great things for thyself ? seek them not.' And there and then, he decided to follow other plans than those at first intended.

But Spurgeon did not renounce ambition. His decision was to renounce only worldly ambition and devote himself entirely to his Master's service. Ambition is not wrong in itself. Ambition is only wrong when set upon unworthy objects or from an unworthy motive.

2. Two lessons are included in our Lord's teaching on this subject—one on *humility*, the other on *service*. There is such a thing as greatness, Christ seems to say ; but it is the greatness of humility, the greatness of littleness. He is truly great who, with a man's power and influence, has a child's heart and life. But there is also the greatness of usefulness. Our Saviour teaches that there is a legitimate province for ambition in the words, ' whosoever will be great among you, let him be your minister,' that is, your servant. We ought then to be ambitious to *serve*, but if we care only to excel, our ambition is unworthy the disciples of Him ' who came, not to be ministered unto, but to minister.'

(1) *Humility*.—A great many people read this verse as though it were written, ' Seekest thou great things ? seek them not.' But in omitting the words ' for thyself,' they leave out the clue to the meaning of the whole verse, the very words upon which all the stress ought to fall. Baruch, to whom the words were addressed, is blamed not because he seeks great things, but because he seeks them *for himself*. He is blamed not because he is ambitious, but because the object of his ambition is a purely selfish one.

The ambition to overtop our fellows, to have more than other people have, to be more than other people are, has left a bloodstained trail across history. If one wished to suggest a name or a life in which ambition had freest and most unrestricted reign it would be the name of Napoleon. In Napoleon ambition, insatiate and unconcealed, had undisputed sway. He waded to his throne, as has been said, through the blood and tears of millions and shut the gates of mercy on mankind. He allowed no scruple of affection to stand in his way if he wished to add one more jewel to his crown. And after all, what did it amount to ? We know him now. Many even of his contemporaries knew him then : the French who suffered because of his military ambition, as much as the rest of Europe, knew him as a man who had sold his soul, as it were, that he might gratify his lust for power.

It is true that the general good may even accompany self-seeking. A great historian has said : The best work in the world, perhaps, is being done by men who are scrupulous as to aim but unscrupulous as to means, yet who in their very self-seeking manage to benefit the human race. But if the self-seeking were out of account would not the benefit to the human race be incalculably greater ? It is selfishness which is the bane of ambition. 'Seekest thou great things for *thyself*? seek them not.' Weed out the selfishness and we turn this powerful auxiliary to human zeal and energy into a faithful servant, whose office it is to assist us in the path of duty and honour.

¶ Carlyle puts clearly the distinction between the true ambition and the false. 'Let me say that there are two kinds of ambition, one wholly blameable, the other laudable and inevitable. . . . The selfish wish to shine over others, let it be accounted altogether poor and miserable.' 'Seekest thou great things for thyself ? seek them not.' This is most true. 'And yet I say,' continues Carlyle, 'there is an irrepressible tendency in every man to develop himself according to the magnitude which nature has made him of, to speak out and to act out what nature has laid in him. This is proper, fit, inevitable ; nay, it is duty, the duty of duties. For man the meaning of life here on earth might be defined as consisting in this—to unfold yourself, to work what thing you have the faculty for. It is a necessity for every human being, the first law of our existence.

(2) *Service.*—The end of all ambition and individual development is service.

Why is it that some men have been granted special gifts and special advantages ? Is it because they deserve these privileges ? Is it that they may secure the greatest measure of happiness and enjoyment ? That may be the result, but it is certainly not the purpose. Every gift and opportunity placed within our reach is not for our own advantage, but the benefit and advantage of others. We are simply trustees of privilege.

If one is gifted athletically and excels upon the football field, the object of that gift is not fulfilled unless he contribute it to the composite skill of the whole team. In the same way our intellectual gifts were given us not for the purpose of getting individual marks, though that may seem their proximate purpose at present, but rather that we might devote them to the welfare of the polity at large. And so, too, if we have received from God the gift of Christian faith, *the* object of this faith is lost if it is simply concentrated upon our own soul ; our ambition must be to share with others its comfort and support.

For we must share if we would keep
  That good thing from above ;
Ceasing to give we cease to have :
  Such is the law of love.

Nothing alters our whole outlook upon life so much as the realization that life's highest law is the law of service, and that everything was created for that express purpose. All about us the law is continually at work. The vegetable world dies in ministry to the animal world, the animal world in its turn ministers to the needs of man, and man must needs live and labour and die in the interests of his fellows. We are created for service. 'Usefulness is the rent that each of us must pay for the room he occupies upon earth.'

3. True ambition is to live out what is in us for the sake of Him who gave us life. It is a wonderful, it is even an awful, thought that God Himself finds fulfilment through what we are. God's work is being done, God's thoughts and purposes are being realized by apparently commonplace men and women. We are each a unique product in the universe, and there are unmeasured possibilities before every one of us. Each of us, all of us, are citizens of eternity.

There is a Divine idea pervading the visible universe, the spirit of truth and beauty and good. Every one of us is called to reveal and express that Divine idea in some fashion. For us it is embodied in Jesus Christ. And the life that is given to Christ is well invested. It has produced the best results in the history of human character. Paul might have opened any door to fame, and who knows where that brilliant Jew might have stopped if he had entered the service of the Cæsars? But the Christ crossed his path, and this ambitious, zealous, burning soul changed to something else; Saul the persecutor became Paul the apostle, and this was his verdict when the evening came—'I have fought the good fight, I have finished my course, I have kept the faith.'

We are here to choose the life wherein we can throw our best energies for God, not to drift into a destiny but to have a vocation, a vocation for God, to consecrate our powers to that which is higher than self, in the same spirit of Him who said in His prayer, 'For their sakes I sanctify myself.'

'Seekest thou great things for thyself? seek them not.' Seekest thou great things for God? Go on. Live out all that God has given us as His trustees. 'Seek first the kingdom of God and his righteousness, and all these things shall be added unto you.'

Dwell Deep

Jer. xlix. 8.—'Dwell deep, O inhabitants of Dedan.'

THE Dedanites were the men of the desert who had developed to be the commercial travellers of their day. In long caravans they conveyed the treasures and the products of the East to the ports and cities of the West. They were the middle men of Asia Minor, a community which, like the City of London, devoted themselves, not to the growth of corn or the making of fabrics, but to the transmission and the exchange of goods. They were, therefore, busy, alert, always on the move. One of their routes passed through the land of Edom. Now, the judgments of the Lord were about to fall upon that wild and haughty land. So the message of the prophet to the inhabitants of Dedan is, 'Flee ye, turn back. Stop your caravans and retire out of the track of destruction. Dwell deep—that is, abide in the depths of the desert, hide yourselves in the caves of the wilderness, keep in remote and safe fastnesses far away from the march and the fury of the conqueror.'

It was as if the prophet used to them words which are familiar enough to-day: 'Take cover.'

We also live in perilous times, and the words, though not in the sense in which the prophet used them, fit our own situation. The busy, exacting, enterprising world around us is making exorbitant demands upon heart, and mind, and will, so that we have little leisure or energy for the things of the spirit.

So these ancient words—'Dwell deep, O inhabitants of Dedan' gain for us a new meaning. It is very necessary for us to be told to 'dwell deep,' to seek security against the many assaults upon our spiritual life.

1. How is this security attained? It is easy to say, by religion. But what does our religion mean to us? The vast majority of the people of this land are, no doubt, influenced by many Christian principles. The Church of Christ, with all its failures, has managed to implant respect for certain Christian virtues such as show themselves in care for the weak, respect for women, a love of truth and an admiration for integrity and justice and freedom in our midst. But though these are noble acquisitions, the real guiding and controlling idea in most people's minds is just a regard for certain traditions of conduct which are governed by the general sense of what we call decency in living.

But this sportsmanlike attitude as a philosophy of life, this general sense of decency, is too superficial; it has to do with the surface of life, and its danger is when it occupies the whole attention, and we forget that the surface is only the top layer and that it is what lies underneath that really matters. Consequently, any crisis which breaks up the surface, however painful to traditional ways of thought, may do actual good if it drives us down to fundamentals—in a word, teaches us to dwell deep.

Take, for instance, the case of such a thing as *liberty*. To be free has been an essential element in our life. But the whole conception of freedom is now challenged in large parts of the world, and we are being driven down to consider what we mean by freedom. When men are asked to die for freedom, they begin to want to understand, as never before, what this freedom is for which they are called upon to sacrifice themselves.

Or take *progress*. Till more recent times progress was assumed to be almost an automatic process. Things were getting better—the standard of life rising—mankind was on the up-grade. It only needed more education, enlightenment, and so on, and we would make the world a fine place, and achieve our own salvation. But somehow the process has faltered, and men have become bewildered and are asking : Is there really any underlying justification for a belief in progress ? If so, what is it ?

¶ A few years ago the Crystal Palace was burnt down. For nearly ninety years, since the great Exhibition of 1851, that Palace had been virtually a temple dedicated to the Victorian dogma of inevitable progress, and now it is a wreck of rubble and twisted iron.[1]

Here we touch the very nerve of religion. Men have extolled justice and mercy and honourable dealing and truth and loyalty, and have thought that these could be taken as obviously desirable and excellent without—*and this is the point*—relating them in their mind with God. In many cases, perhaps, they have disbelieved that He existed in any real and vital sense. They have thought that all those fine qualities could exist and control men by their own weight and impressiveness. But when God goes out of the picture all these fine qualities have no binding force. And they will less and less have binding force until men get down to the depths, and recognize that the underlying foundation and reason for all these excellencies is God, whose will and purpose is that they should be the reflection of His character in human hearts.

¶ Here is a fragment of conversation from John Galsworthy's *Maid in Waiting* : the girl, Dinny, is talking to her mother, Lady Cherwell. ' I suppose there is an eternal Plan,' she says, ' but we're like gnats for all the care it has for us as individuals.' ' Don't encourage such feelings, Dinny,' says her mother, ' they affect one's character.' ' I don't see,' replies the daughter, ' the connection between beliefs and character. I'm not going to behave any worse because I cease to believe in Providence or an after life.' ' Surely, Dinny—' ' No ; I'm going to behave *better* ; if I'm decent it's because decency's the decent thing ; and not because I'm going to get anything by it.' Whereupon her mother asks, ' But why is decency the decent thing, Dinny, if there's no God ? '[2]

[1] Norman Tubbs, *A Modern Pilgrim's Progress*, 10.
[2] J. S. Stewart, *The Strong Name*, 129.

2. There is the same message in the words ' Dwell deep ' for those who sincerely believe in God, and the accent must be placed on *dwell*. If any one had the whole force of evil directed against him it was our Lord. And yet He never had the slightest doubt of the ultimate victory of those very forces of good which in His mind sprang and emanated from God alone. God for Him was no mere ' bundle of abstract nouns loosely tied up in impersonality.' He had a will, a purpose, and a plan for the world He had made, and that purpose would be fulfilled. It was because Christ dwelt in the depths of that certainty that He moved through life to His Cross with a poise and a power which nothing could upset. Beneath all the changes and chances of this fleeting world He had grasped the one invariable constant, and that was God. Upon that His soul reposed. Here was the secret of His unruffled calm. But He did not use that fortress of the soul merely as a refuge, though it was that. Rather He used it as the station from which the power which could transform the world could issue forth. And if for Him, why not for us ? It all depends upon whether we, too, are willing to dwell deep. It needs but the steady and constant direction of our mind and will and heart, for God is there—undoubtedly He is there, if we will go far enough to find Him in the deep.

¶ Lord Rosebery declares of Dr Chalmers that he might be immersed in preaching, speaking, organizing, ' with the dust and fire of the world upon his clothes ' but ' always he carried his shrine with him.'

We live in an ambiguous world, so many things seem haphazard and irrelevant to our highest interests, and we are in danger of living in a haphazard way ourselves, taking things as they come, letting things drift, without making sure of a settled meaning for life, to give it rest and confidence. We need to dwell deep. We are so prone to become victims of the day's news, to be swayed by opinions, to be governed by circumstances rather than by a central and controlling purpose.

¶ As the pearls of the House of Austria, when they grew dim and tarnished, could renew their glory only by being sunk in their native element again, so our soul also will grow tashed and dull and faded, unless day by day, we sink it also deep in God.

A doctor says to his patient—' You need a change : you are run down, a change of air and scenery will help you.' It is not that the doctor is advising us to run away from life, evading its responsibilities. He simply wants us to disentangle ourselves for the time being from the complexity of things so as to come back to them with recovered strength. And Jeremiah is a doctor of the soul who urges us to get a background for our spiritual life, shaking it free from the embarrassment of surface things. That is the benefit of a Church service. It is the blessing of a Church building enclosing us for the time from the outside world. The vast world with its secular routine, its economic values, its exhausting interests—these all lie outside for the time being. We have to face them again ; they do not constitute our deepest life, but they are necessary. But we come to worship to realize anew that man's real possession is in the winning of the soul, in getting to our deep and native shelter, in laying hold of those spiritual faculties which deal with the fundamental and incontrovertible, so that when we go back to the world we will maintain our true rank and destiny. Therefore dwell deep.

3. Dwell deep by making religion the power of an endless life and not the convention of an outward form. It is much easier to adopt a form than to create a life, and it is the peculiar danger of those who are brought up in religious homes. By a divinely planted instinct we tread in the foot-tracks of our parents and imitate them in their religion as well as in their speech and action. The peril is that we may have the outward form of their piety without its inward power. It is right and necessary that the religious life should organize itself into habits, but it is imperative that a living stream of religious experience should flow unfettered through the soul.

We are the children of Eternity. Just now we are ' dwellers in tents,' with ' no abiding city,' but we belong to the city whose maker and builder is God and so can sit loosely to the passing temporary world.

A great bereavement befalls us. The fountains of the great deep are broken up and unexpected meanings are given to our petty lives. But beneath the deep is another deep. The calamities of life drive us back upon God. There is a peace that passeth understanding and transcendeth earthly experience. It is only God that can produce that. The supreme value of affliction is that it enables the soul to dwell deeply, rediscover its God, and thereby prove its royal independence of the lapse of time and the fell lot of circumstances.

¶ The picture that Edmund Gosse, in *Father and Son*, gave of his childhood was coloured by prejudice, because he himself had travelled so far from that Plymouth Brother home of his. Yet all the more impressive is the witness he bears to the real happiness of his parents, the lightness of their touch upon life, their gay enjoyment. They found matter for mirth in the simple affairs of daily life, and even in the externals of their own religious observance. There was a sort of guileless, innocent gaiety about them. When bitter tragedy came, their son testifies how they met it with serene tranquillity. But it is to their joy he first bears witness, their gaiety. And he himself reveals its secret. ' My father and mother lived so completely in the atmosphere of faith, and were so utterly convinced of their intercourse with God, that they could afford to take the passing hour very lightly.' [1]

[1] F. B. James, in *The Methodist Recorder*.

THE IMPORTANCE OF AN ATTITUDE

Jer. l. 5.—' They shall ask the way to Zion with their faces thitherward.'

' WORDS from the teeth out,' someone has bluntly said, ' mean nothing.' Just as truly might it be said that the hand without the heart is of little use. For the attitude we assume in saying and in doing things is of first-rate importance. And all of us are conscious of that. All of us have uttered words upon occasion behind which there was no sincerity ; and their hollow sound, echoing in our hearts for days afterwards, has rebuked our attempt to make men feel that we cared for them more than we actually did. All of us, too, have known ourselves undertake some task in which our hearts could not honestly be said to be. How limply we performed the task and how ineffectively !

Now, because we are each conscious of these things, we can place ourselves with little difficulty in the atmosphere in which the words of the text were spoken. Israel's history had been unhappy. Subdued by Babylon, she was taken captive to an unwelcome exile. There, amid alien customs, difficulties were encountered which had a detrimental effect upon Israel's faith. Some compromised, or thought they did, worshipping *both* the God of their fathers *and* the gods of the land of their enforced adoption. Others tried pathetically hard to be true to the old faith. But both uttered words meaninglessly and undertook ceremonies in which their heart could not be said to be. God could do little, they felt. And they said their prayers never expecting the least of them to be answered.

A new day was dawning, however, Jeremiah saw. The triumph of Babylon was coming to an end. Men and women who had once trusted Jehovah would be driven back upon Him. With a rediscovered sincerity they would begin to seek for Him. Not with so many empty words, but with pleading, passionate prayers would they ask to be brought to Him. Not doubtingly would they petition to be restored to Zion but with faith would set themselves in its direction and trust that some day their feet would stand upon its familiar ground. ' They shall ask the way to Zion with their faces thitherward,' said Jeremiah. Words would begin to be uttered with sincerity ; hearts would be joined to hands. Then, said Jeremiah, God in His love and mercy would give Himself freely to His people.

In so speaking to his people, Jeremiah has reminded us of one cardinal principle of all true religion. Here, as in all other departments of life, words spoken without sincerity, actions undertaken without the support of the heart, are worse than useless. Religion can be productive, the Kingdom of God can be built, only when a specific attitude has been taken up by men and women. ' Ye shall seek me and shall find me,' saith the Lord, ' when ye shall search for me with all your heart.' And shouldn't we say, if we were scrupulously honest with ourselves, that sometimes we have hindered ourselves in spiritual things and have kept back the progress of the Kingdom of God in ourselves and in others because we have asked the way to Zion with our faces turned from it ? The attitude we assume, we cannot too emphatically impress upon ourselves, is of paramount importance. Unless we are careful of the attitude we assume, indeed, religion must prove unproductive and the Kingdom of God remain unbuilt. We must ask the way to Zion with our faces thitherward.

1. This principle to begin with stands in the forefront of all seeking for and worship of God. We must come to a certain attitude before, seeking, we can find Him. If we would find God, in other words, we must begin with the faith that He can be found.

In other departments of our life, says one writer, ' we only seek because we believe that what we seek will be found. No one tries to get at truth, philosophic, historic, scientific, unless he believes that he is capable of recognizing truth when it is found. The thinker believes that the human mind was made for truth and that truth comes to reward the search for it. *The faith is first, then the search, then the justification.*' Correspondingly, if we wish to be sure of God, we must assume the attitude that is fitting. That is what the Scripture means when it says, ' He that cometh to God must believe that he is and that he is the rewarder of them that diligently seek him.'

Frequently, with anything but their hearts turned towards God, men and women have inquired the way to Him. They declare they have listened to and have read all the proofs of the existence of God but, withal, have not found Him. But bare words of themselves will not suffice. God does not lie at the end of an argument. Proofs of the existence of God have led few into fellowship with Him. Men and women who read them with never a thought that God *can* be found just cannot hope to be convinced and brought into His company.

We must confess that we, too, have frequently participated in public worship with anything but *our* hearts turned towards God. Our participation signified we were asking the way to Zion ; and yet, though we took part in hymn and prayer, we found the service as unproductive as could be. Indeed we went out of the sanctuary feeling in no way better or stronger or holier. When we think of our fathers, how they were lightened and their faces were not ashamed, we do well to remember that they fulfilled a certain condition. The Bible says they 'looked unto him.' They assumed the particular attitude which Jeremiah emphasized. Thou, says the Psalmist,

> For thou art God that dost
>   to me salvation send,
> And I upon thee all the day
>   expecting do attend.

Unless then, like them, we come with some sense of our need of God, with faith that He can be found, all that is said and done must prove fruitless so far as we are concerned. But to those who wait, expecting, God comes in all the wonder and mystery of His love. We must ask the way to Zion, therefore, with our faces thitherward, if the services of God's House are to be helpful and inspiring.

2. What holds in seeking for God, holds, too, in the communion with God we call prayer.

Most of us do pray. We were taught some simple petitions when we were children which, now that we have grown older, we have exchanged for others. Yet, solemn as the words are, how frequently do they appear so many hollow sounds, lifeless, ineffective, achieving nothing. How frequently do we rise from our knees content that we have kept a tryst we should have done ill to forget, but without hope that what we have done will be of the slightest avail in the living of the ordinary day.

Now that, of course, is not as it should be. Prayer, we cannot but see when we examine His life, was for Jesus a great source of strength and encouragement. It was the breath of His life ; the secret of His unending vitality ; the inspiration of His ceaseless quests. Why is it that some of us find so unproductive what Jesus found so strengthening ? Let us be scrupulously honest with ourselves. Are our faces towards Zion when we ask the way thereto ? Is there any endeavour on our part to aid God in answering the prayer we make to Him ? Petitions which are uttered with meaning at the time and yet which we do not support by giving God room and opportunity to work in our life, are simply bound to fail. Petitions to be brought nearer Zion will not bring us one whit nearer that goal unless there is also in us a living desire really to be and to do according to the will of God.

That earnestness and sincerity of Jesus must be made ours if prayer is to become for us all that it should and can become. Not until we ask the way to Zion with our faces thitherward will prayer achieve in us and for us all that it can and should achieve.

3. And, further, this principle conditions the progress of God's Kingdom.

The Gospels tell of a particularly likeable young man who came running to Jesus one day asking, ' Good Master, what must I do to inherit eternal life ? ' ' Sell all that thou hast and give to the poor, And come, follow me,' said Jesus. But the young man turned sorrowfully away, for he had great possessions. It said something for him, certainly, that he saw something in Jesus which made him want to be like Him. But his inquiry was not backed by any determination or willingness to sacrifice. When the answer given was seen to involve a strenuous endeavour and a personal sacrifice he seemed less in earnest to pursue the goal he once thought he should like to reach.

Don't we sometimes congratulate ourselves that we are concerned enough about the state of the world and the neighbourhood about our own doors to *discuss* how Jesus' principles would make a difference in things and men ? We attend, like many of our fellows, conferences and services and ask what hundreds more are asking—the way to Zion. But how many of us have our faces thitherward ? How many of us are keen to make a personal sacrifice to bring the ideal nearer ?

' Eagerly, sympathetically, approvingly,' says one writer, ' the Jews listened to Paul, when arrested, giving his defence until he mentioned his being sent as a disciple to nations far away —to the Gentiles, the heathen. Then it was all over. Bang went the door of their minds. For in that statement he touched sensitive nerves—their pet prejudice of aversion to the Gentiles, their sense of race superiority and special privilege. Nations far away ? Indeed ! And so the cordiality of the hearing ended instantaneously with the cries : ' Away with such a fellow from the earth. He ought not to be allowed to live.' ' In our hearing of the gospel,' continues this writer, ' many of us are exactly like the Jews in their hearing of it when it was first proclaimed so many centuries ago. We listen up to the point where the gospel preached or taught clashes with our favourite aversion, our profit or our privilege. What is the point at which *we* stop listening to the teaching of Jesus ? we should ask ourselves. The very act of asking it and searching honestly and frankly for an answer will be a means of growth in grace and of extending the kingdom of God.'

That is perhaps a startling and disconcerting utterance. But it is nevertheless one which we each would do well to put to our own hearts. When do I stop listening to the gospel of Jesus Christ ? Do I cease making inquiries, cease to be zealous about things when demands are made upon my privilege and comfort and ease ? When it looks as though I were being asked to make some personal sacrifice do I turn sorrowfully away like the man of the gospel story ? Or am I so much in earnest not only in discussion but about my share in building better conditions and better men that no call to sacrifice however demanding ever falls upon my ears in vain ? These are questions we ought to put to our hearts, for we cannot too clearly understand that the men and women who have been of most service to Christianity have been those who have spoken with sincerity and who have joined hearts to hands.

Religion, let us remind ourselves, will only become real, and the Kingdom of God will be steadily and surely built when we, as followers of the Nazarene, ' ask the way to Zion with our faces thitherward.'

RODERICK BETHUNE.

God's Unlikely Instruments

Jer. li. 7.—'Babylon hath been a golden cup in the Lord's hand.'

IF there was one city in the world that seemed to be independent, it was that city of Babylon. It was magnificent in its equipments, ruled with consummate ability, strong with the most powerful army of the time. It worshipped its own gods, and was contented with them ; it had nothing but scorn for the poor deities of Israel. Its cup *was* golden, there was no doubt of it. But the prophet, inspired, saw that there

was a Hand grasping the cup. ' Babylon hath been a golden cup in the Lord's hand.' It was golden, but for all that it was God's. It was He who had raised it up ; it was He who held it ; it was He who would hurl it, violently, to the ground.

1. We learn, then, that beyond the sphere of grace stretches the wide sphere of instrumentality. God says to Cyrus, ' Thou art my battleaxe ' ; God says to Nebuchadrezzar, ' Thou art my servant.' These men were strangers to the promises, bowing in worship to the gods of heathendom ; yet ' thou art *My* battleaxe, Cyrus ' ; ' thou art *My* servant ' —they were all the instruments of Almighty God.

Now sometimes the blindest eye can see how exquisitely the instruments of God are fitted to the task God has in hand. We feel that infinite wisdom is at work, the tool has been chosen by a master-hand. In the story of Scotland, for example, go back for a moment to Reformation times, and remember that Scotland was a feudal country, a land where kinship and blood and birth meant everything. Then think of the exquisite choice of God in the first preacher and martyr for the truth. The blood of kings was in the veins of Patrick Hamilton ; the greatest in the land were kin to him ; and that gave an impulse to the gospel of Jesus Christ that would have been wanting had Hamilton been base-born. And there is not a land, and not a life, but could give signal instances like that of the perfect choice of God.

But is not the general rule the very opposite ? Here or there starts up some striking instance that reveals the perfect wisdom of God's choices. But far more often we are arrested differently ; we are staggered by the very strangeness of God's instruments. He is using means we never thought He would employ ; He is using the last men we should have dreamed of. We are face to face in the whole sweep of history with the unlikely instruments of God.

(1) Think, for example, of the instrument which He used to keep alive the knowledge of His name. A man could not do it ; it required a nation ; God's name is too great for one man to hold in trust ; but of all the unlikely nations in the world, surely Israel was the most unlikely. Shall the vivifying truth of all the ages be committed to a horde of slaves in Egypt ? Is it

these men gathering the stubble yonder, and crying out under the taskmaster's lash—is it they who are to guard the knowledge of God that is to be crowned in the great gift of a Redeemer? To a human eye that seems the worst of choices, and yet that nation was the chosen of God. Israel became the instrument of heaven. It was Israel that was the cradle of the Christ. Through wandering and war, through storm and sunshine, she was shaped and polished for most exalted use. Surely a most unlikely instrument, but for all that the instrument of God.

(2) Now if Jesus of Nazareth be the Son of God, we shall expect to find Him adopting the same procedure. And Paul, in a passage of very lofty eloquence, has preached this doctrine of unlikely choices. For God, he says (and he is thinking of the gospel), hath chosen the foolish things of the world to confound the wise; and the weak things to confound those which are mighty; and base things, yea the things that are not, to bring to naught the things that are. It is the wonder of heaven's choice of instruments for winning the triumphs of the Saviour's cause.

And has not the world wondered at it? It has been the perpetual marvel of the ages. We might surmise from His very methods that Christ was Son of God, whenever we think of His choice of the disciples. Twelve men, provincial and unlettered—and all the world against them in the battle. The poetry of Greece, the arms of Rome, the institutions that had grown grey with time, the thought that had taken centuries to build, passions and vices, and the blight of atheism—that was the world, and against all the world, Peter and Andrew, and James and John, and Thomas. It was a strange choice, yet it was very Godlike. It was like the choice of the slaves in the fields of Egypt. Yet by such men, inspired by the Holy Ghost, victories were won that changed the world.

2. That, then, is the doctrine of unlikely instruments. Now every doctrine has its practical bearings. What, then, does that inexplicable feature of God's choice mean for us?

(1) Well, first it guards us against putting limits upon God. Who shall dare say what powers may not be used by heaven, if even Babylon be a golden cup in the Lord's hand?

We are so apt to have contracted views. We are so prone to think that God will only work by means of instruments we should have chosen, that when He contradicts us, and works in other ways, we are blind to the presence of the Divine in it. Give a wide sweep to sovereignty. Remember that His ways are not as ours. You think that He is coming in the whirlwind? Hark! He is whispering in the still small voice. You say that the winnowing-fan is in His hand, and behold, the bruised reed He will not break. That is the first use of God's unlikely instruments. It makes us watchful, open-hearted, very humble. We must be alive to possibilities of usefulness, or the chances are we may be missing God.

(2) And, second, it should make us very strong when we are called to any little service. 'I am not fit for it; I am the last man in the world for it'—quite right! probably you are; but so was Israel, and the Lord called Israel; and so was Samuel, and the Lord called Samuel: it is a kind of way God has of working. The men who think that they are fit for anything are very seldom fit for God's work. But the men who cry, as Jeremiah cried, 'Ah, Lord God, I am a child, and cannot speak'—it is such men whose lips are touched with fire, whose hearts are emboldened, and whose way is opened. For God is not bent on glorifying us; God is bent on glorifying Jesus. And the more men see that the power is all of Him; the more men feel, knowing our poor equipment, that this or that is the doing of the Lord, the greater the praise to an ascended Saviour. We may take it that that is the deepest of all reasons for the unlikely instruments of God.

¶ One day Brother Masseo said to St Francis: 'I wonder why the whole world runs after thee more than after others, and all men want to see thee and hear thee and obey thee? Thou art not fair of body, thou art not deeply learned, thou art not of noble birth—why does the whole world run after thee?' When St Francis heard this, he rejoiced in his soul and turned his eyes to heaven, and stood a long time thus, with soul lifted up to God; and when he came to himself he kneeled down and gave thanks and praise to God, and turned to Brother Masseo and said to him with great spiritual power: 'Do you wish to know why this happens to me? Do you wish to know why the whole world runs after me? For I knew that thing from the all-seeing God, whose eyes see the good and the bad over all the earth. For these most holy eyes have nowhere seen a greater, more miserable, poorer sinner than I ; because in all the earth He has found no more wretched being to do His wonderful work, which He wishes to have done, therefore He has chosen me, so as thus to put to shame the noble, the great, strength and beauty, worldly wisdom, that all may know that all power and all virtue come from Him and not from creatures, and that no one can exalt himself before His face ; but he who praises himself, let him praise himself in the Lord, for His is the honour and the power for ever and ever.' [1]

[1] J. Jörgensen, *St Francis of Assisi*, 74.

LAMENTATIONS

INTRODUCTION

1. *Name.*—The ancient Hebrew title of the Book is *'Eykhah*, and this is the title which is found in Hebrew manuscripts and in all printed Hebrew Bibles to this day. It is the first word in the Book, and it means ' How ! ' This is the custom followed in the naming of the five Books of the Law, for example, Genesis (Hebrew *Bereshith*, ' in beginning of '), Exodus (*We'eleh shemoth*, ' and these are the names of '), Leviticus (*Wayyiqra'*, ' and he called '), Numbers (the fourth word is used, this being the first distinctive word, *Bemidhbar*, ' in the wilderness of '), and Deuteronomy (*'Eleh had-debharim*, ' these are the words '). In two other cases, namely Proverbs (*Misheley*, ' the proverbs of ') and The Song of Songs (*Shir hashshirim*), the full titles form the first verse, and the opening word (words) of the verse has been used.

In the Talmud and in Rabbinic writings generally the title is *Qinoth* (Lamentations), a title which is descriptive of the contents. This is the normal Hebrew custom outside the Law. It is followed everywhere by the Greek translators, who sought even for the Law to give titles which were readily intelligible to the non-Hebrew reader. The old Septuagint title is *Threnoi* (laments), translated by the Latin Fathers as either *Lamenta* or *Lamentationes*. The old title is found in Codex Alexandrinus (fifth century A.D.) and in the first hand of Codex Vaticanus (fourth century A.D.). This ancient Greek title was latinized by Jerome according to his usual custom, and becomes *Threni* in Latin. The other great Greek Uncials have the title *Threnoi Jeremiou*, which Jerome translated into *Lamentationes Jeremiae*, and this gives rise to the title of the English versions, ' The Lamentations of Jeremiah.' The title *Qinoth* was known to Jerome, but his choice of title was due to the Septuagint *Threnoi*, and not to Jewish Hebrew traditions. In titles, which he latinized, and in the order of books, he followed the Septuagint, partly because for four centuries it had been the Bible of the Christians, and

partly because his first two translations into Latin were from the Greek.

2. *Place in the Bible.*—There are three Jewish traditions as to the order of the books of the Hebrew Old Testament. The most common order is that of the German MSS., where the Five Rolls (*Megilloth*) are found together, either next after the Law (as in the first printed Bibles), or, more properly, amongst the Writings (Hebrew *Kethubim*, Greek *Hagiographa*) next after the three poetical books. The *Kethubim* is the third section of the Hebrew Bible, the other two sections being the Law and the Prophets. In this German tradition the order of the Rolls is Song of Songs, Ruth, Lamentations, Ecclesiastes, Esther. This is the usual order in modern printed Bibles. The Spanish (*Sephardi*) MS. tradition has the Five Rolls together, but with Ruth first and Song of Songs second. This is due to an attempt to put the Rolls in what was held to be the correct historical order. This tendency is more marked in the Talmudic tradition (*Baba bathra* 14b) where the order of the *Kethubim* is Ruth, Psalms, Job, Proverbs, Ecclesiastes, Song of Songs, Lamentations, Daniel, Esther, Ezra-Nehemiah and Chronicles.

In the Septuagint tradition the attempt to put the books in their proper order has been carried so far as to neglect the three great divisions of the Hebrew Bible. Both Ruth and Lamentations are reckoned amongst the Prophets, Ruth to follow Judges, since its setting is in that period, and Lamentations to follow Jeremiah because the Book was supposed to have been written by that prophet.

The Hebrew tradition which keeps the Five Rolls together, reflects the use which was made of them in the synagogue. They were read on special occasions of the year, Song of Songs at Passover, Ruth at Pentecost, Lamentations on the ninth of Ab (in 1945 this is July 19), the anniversary of the destruction of the Temple, Ecclesiastes at Tabernacles, and Esther at Purim. It will be noticed, therefore, that the German order is truest to ancient usage, and is due to the liturgical use of the Rolls.

3. *Contents of the Book.*—The Book consists of five poems, each complete in itself and independent of the others. The first four are alphabetical acrostics, in which each verse begins with successive letters of the alphabet. The last poem, though it contains twenty-two verses as a one-verse acrostic would demand, is not an acrostic, though C. J. Ball held that this was its original form. His proposed restoration involves such considerable changes that it is unlikely to be the case. The Jews, however, did actually reckon this last poem as an acrostic. The Rabbinic commentary on Lamentations (*Lam. Rabba*) says that the seven acrostics (the count is seven, because in chapter 3 there are sixty-six verses, and each letter of the alphabet is in its turn thrice repeated) remind us of the seven sins of Israel, whereas the acrostic form reminds us that Israel sinned from *aleph* to *tau* (*i.e.* from A to Z ; in Greek it would be from *alpha* to *omega*, ' the first and the last ').

The first four of the poems, then, are acrostics. The first, second and fourth poems each contain twenty-two verses. Each verse is of two lines, and the first line begins with the proper letter of the alphabet, *aleph, beth, gimel,* and so forth. The third poem is composed of sixty-six verses, each a single line, and each group of three lines beginning with the same letter. The fifth poem has twenty-two one-line verses. It has been recognized from ancient time as being different from its predecessors, since in the Vulgate it has a title of its own *Oratio Jeremias Prophetae* (The Prayer of Jeremiah the Prophet), and this is found also both in the Syriac (Peshitta) and in the Arabic Versions. There are eight other acrostics to be found in the Old Testament, Psalms xxv., xxxiv., xxxvii., cxi., cxii., cxix. (the great six-verse acrostic on the Law), cxlv., and Proverbs xxxi. 10–31, which Toy happily named ' The ABC of the perfect Housewife...' There are also remnants in Psalms ix.–x., and in Nahum i. A curious feature of Lamentations ii., iii., and iv. is that the letter *Pe* precedes the letter *Ayin*. This order is not peculiar to these three acrostics. It has been suggested that this was the original order in Psalm xxxiv., and Septuagint has this order in Proverbs xxxi.

It may be that the original alphabet had the order *Pe* before *Ayin*, but *Lam. Rabba* finds in it an occasion for a little homily, namely, that *Pe* (which also means ' mouth ') was placed before *Ayin* (which also means ' eye ') because Israel spake with the mouth what the eye had not seen.

The first poem has two equal divisions, the poet being the speaker in the first half and Jerusalem in the second half, though in each case there is an interpolation from the other speaker. The author of this poem had not the facility which is shown in poems ii. and iv. The whole poem tends to consist of separate verses, as though the poet achieved ' acrosticity ' at the expense of a proper development of his theme throughout the whole poem. Verse 12 has achieved an appreciation which has been denied to the rest of the poem. It is probably the best verse from the literary point of view, and its use by Handel in *Messiah* has given it increased prominence.

Poems ii. and iv. are of much greater literary excellence, and bear all the marks of the vivid experience of an eye-witness. They are probably by the same author. In each poem the responsibility of the religious leaders and the suffering of the small children are emphasized. The verses are detailed and specific in their references.

The third elegy is generally regarded as being below even the first in literary excellence, as though the task of beginning the three successive lines with the same letter of the alphabet has been altogether too much for the author. The tendency is for each line, even of a triad, to be separate from the rest. Nevertheless what the poem lacks in cohesion, it makes up in the excellence of many of the separate lines, for example, 22 and 23, 24, 26, 32 and 33, etc. There are many lines in this chapter which still provide encouragement and spiritual strength in a way which verses from the rest of the Book do not.

The fifth poem, which is not an elegy or a lament, deals with a situation which existed later than the actual destruction of the city. Its literary standard is good, being in this respect better than the first and the third elegies. Its abiding spiritual value is far below that of the third elegy.

4. *The Authors, and their Dates.*—The ancient tradition is that the whole Book, four laments

and one prayer, was written by Jeremiah the Prophet. It dates back probably to 2 Chron. xxxv. 25, which reads : 'And Jeremiah lamented for Josiah ; and all the singing men and the singing women spake of Josiah in their lamentations to this day, and made him an ordinance in Israel : and, behold, they are written in the lamentations.' The identification doubtless rests chiefly upon Lam. ii. 6 and iv. 20. It is probable that the Chronicler is referring to these poems (though his reference need not have included the fifth), especially since the reference to the ' ordinance,' *i.e.* regular annual recitation, seems to refer to the custom of reciting the Book on the ninth of Ab. Josephus (*Ant. Iud.* X. v. 1) is even more specific in his reference. The tradition is in the Talmud, in the insertion at the beginning of the Book in both Septuagint and Vulgate, and in Jerome's comment on the lamentations in Jerusalem mentioned in Zec. xii. 11. The insertion in Septuagint reads : ' And it came to pass after Israel had been carried away captive and Jerusalem had been laid waste, that Jeremiah sat weeping, and he lamented this lament over Jerusalem, and said.' Instead of the last two words the Vulgate has ' and with a sorrowful mind, sighing and moaning, he said.' The Targum has ' Jeremiah the Prophet and great Priest said.'

It is possible that Jeremiah should lament with tears over Jerusalem ; cf. Jer. ix. 1, xiii. 17, xiv. 17. There is a certain amount of similarity of language (*see* Driver, *Introduction to Literature of Old Testament*, 9th edition, p. 462). On the other hand, it is generally agreed that there are considerable elements which have little association with the prophet. Poems ii. and iv. have affinities in language and attitude with Ezekiel, whilst associations have been detected between i. and v. and Deutero-Isaiah, and iii. has points of contact with some of the later psalms. The political attitude of iv. 17 is contrary to that of Jeremiah, who always held that it was folly to look for help from Egypt. Other passages which are difficult to reconcile with the teaching of Jeremiah are ii. 9, iv. 20 with its reference to Zedekiah, and v. 7.

The probability is that the first four poems were all written by men who were acquainted with the teaching and style of Jeremiah, but were somewhat later so that they were influenced by the work of the other two great prophets of the sixth century. Lam. ii. and iv. are probably by the same author, a man who himself experienced the tribulations of the last days and the horrors of the final disaster. The date is (say) about 580 B.C. Lam. i. is somewhat later, *c.* 540 B.C. and by a second author, Lam. iii. by a third and belongs to a period after the Exile, perhaps in the fourth century, though some would say in the early Greek period (*i.e.* before 300 B.C.). The last chapter, the Prayer of Jeremiah, might belong to any age. Loehr, Budde, and Driver would make it the middle-exile period, *c.* 550 B.C., but Peake places it at the end of the Exile. Ball suggests ii. and iv. in the Persian period (early, but Cheyne, end), i. later, iii. Greek but pre-Maccabæan, and v. in the Ezra-Nehemiah period, a scheme which is generally followed by Cheyne. Some scholars, however, would put the whole Book late, holding that the siege of Jerusalem is not that in the time of Nebuchadrezzar, but one by Antiochus Epiphanes in 170–168 B.C., or that by Pompey the Great in 63 B.C. This position is argued by Duff (see Peake's *Commentary*, p. 496), and is followed by some moderns, but the weight of opinion is against this position. The general attitude is that of Peake, as outlined above, and this is the opinion of Oesterley and Robinson in their recent (1934) *Introduction to the Books of the Old Testament*, except that they are prepared to admit any date for Lam. v. It may indeed be as late as Pompey.

5. *Metrical Structure.*—This is important because the first four of the poems are in the famous *Qinah*-rhythm. The story of the study of this particular rhythm goes back to Lowth (1787), who noticed the unusual length of these verses, the fact that they were of the type of funeral dirges, and that, whilst the end of the line is full and strong, there is also a break beyond the middle of the line. The study of this curious halting rhythm was continued by Keil (1836) and Budde (1882), and the best modern exposition of it is to be found in G. B. Gray, *Forms of Hebrew Poetry* (1915), 85–120. The peculiar halting effect of the 3 : 2 rhythm can be seen with advantage in the excellent translations of Lam. ii. and iv. in George Adam Smith, *Jerusalem* (1908), ii. 274–283. A similar effect has been achieved by S. T. Coleridge in the more tragic parts of his *Ancient*

Mariner, with his verses which alternate with four and three stresses. It is not necessary to assume that the 3 : 2 scheme is rigid, since there are variations whereby, for instance, a 2 : 2 line is found. We deprecate, both here and elsewhere, that slavish and Prussian regimentation in which so many modern English critics follow those German scholars who rewrite Hebrew poetry in order to secure accurate rhythms. They forget the charm of those variations which every poet of the first excellence adopts to enhance the beauty of the whole.

6. *Bibliography.*—The books on Lamentations which are accessible to English readers are scanty. The most useful is the commentary which is found at the end of Peake's *Jeremiah,* ii. in ' The Century Bible ' series. The article by C. J. Ball in the *Encyclopædia Britannica* (11th edition), xvi. 126–129, is itself a small commentary. There are full discussions in Hastings' *Bible Dictionary* (J. A. Selbie), in the *Jewish Encyclopædia* (E. G. Hirsch and M. Loehr), and in the *Encyclopædia Biblica* (T. K. Cheyne), though this last needs to be read with that discretion and reserve which is to be applied to all Cheyne's later work. Some useful material is to be found in the Cambridge Bible Commentary on *Jeremiah and Lamentations* (A. W. Streane), but this is ultra-conservative just as the article on Lamentations in Peake's Commentary (A. Duff) is ultra-radical. See also Driver, *Introduction to the Literature of the Old Testament* (8th edition and later), and the Introductions generally, including the article by W. Robertson Smith in the *Encyclopædia Britannica* (9th edition).

NORMAN H. SNAITH.

The Cry for Sympathy

Lam. i. 12.—' Is it nothing to you, all ye that pass by ? behold, and see if there be any sorrow like unto my sorrow.'

THIS Book of Lamentations is a book of five poems, five dirges, five laments, over the desolation of the Holy City. The first, in the first chapter, gives us a picture of the distress of Jerusalem after its siege by the Chaldæans. The city is pictured as a widowed and dis-crowned princess, a widow bereft of her children,

sitting solitary in the night, weeping sorely. It is the utter lonesomeness of the city that is so vividly presented, the streets without traffic, the tenantless houses, emptied of all the stir and tumult of life ; and in this desolation she sits, helpless and hopeless, abandoned to her memories and her despair. She sits, and the night comes, and still she sits. She does not stir. The tears come in the silent solitude of the night, and there is no one to wipe them away. What a picture in contrast with her past ! She was not always a lonely widow, but a proud princess, a happy mother. So the poet speaks ; and then the deserted city herself takes up the lamentation. It is here that the text comes in, when the dirge is taken up by the desolate daughter of Jerusalem. She begins with this heart-piercing cry to the thoughtless passers-by. This is her complaint against indifference. The solitary widow pleads for something more kindly and tender and sympathetic. ' Is it nothing to you, all ye that pass by ? '

1. This is a **very** common feeling and a common cry. How painfully we feel the awful indifference of the world ! It is a strange feeling we sometimes have when we come out from the darkened room into the light of day—out from the sick-room into the street. See the bright, busy, noisy, laughing world, heedless of the man dying there. How indifferent the great world seemed to our sorrow ! The bustle and activity did not rest for a moment because we were sad, and the noise and laughter seemed harsh and pitiless. We were inclined to protest against this unresting business ; we wanted to protest even against the happiness of other people. How true it is of every heavy trial when we feel the weight of it, and see the world not feeling it at all ! ' Is it nothing to you, all ye that pass by ? '

2. But there is another thought here. The cry is not our own but another's. It is not our complaint against the cold world, but the complaint of others against us. For this is what life is like—an endless procession along the great highway ; and there are always those who sit apart in sorrow and those who pass heedlessly by. We are ourselves in the rush of the traffic of the world ; and when we are engrossed in our own errands and pursuits,

how little we are aware of what is happening beside us. We go past cares and sorrows, disappointments and bereavements, pain and sickness every hour of the day ; and voices we do not hear are whispering as we go, ' Is it nothing to you ? ' In ordinary life men mostly know very little of each other and care very little. Every man for himself. Personal interests are so engrossing, and personal cares so pressing, that we see little of what goes on beyond the circle of our own immediate affairs.

Now surely this text is meant to remind us of this—that the human heart has a great craving for sympathy. Among men the instinct of a sufferer is to crave sympathy—from a friend, if possible, but if that may not be, then even from a stranger. And we are not to say, ' Oh, it is only sympathy ! ' It is the sympathy that is prized. We hardly know how much it means sometimes—to be considered, thought about, not forgotten.

¶ Dame Nellie Melba had a great love for her father and one of the most touching stories in her book [1] is that of her return to Australia, after she had achieved fame, to find that he had been smitten with a stroke while she was on her way home. Coming back to London, Melba writes : ' On the day I arrived from Australia . . . I was summoned to see Queen Alexandra. The first thing she said to me was, " And how is your father ? We were all so sorry that your home-coming should have been so sad, and we have thought of you so much." Others of my friends—true friends they were, too—had forgotten that poignant little episode ; but Queen Alexandra had not forgotten. She knew the subject that was nearest to my heart, and she was the first person to ask me. I felt inclined to kiss her skirts.'

3. The lesson is not far to seek—that we should do our part to diminish the feeling of neglect, of indifference, to bridge the distance between those who sit by the wayside and those who pass by. Not that we can really make every distress we encounter our own, but we may learn to feel more, to be more ready to comfort. What we need is the sympathetic heart.

Think of Christ and mark His ways. He was no lonely hermit, no dweller in the desert. His life led Him along the ways with men. He was

[1] *Melodies and Memories.*

found where men were busiest. He was ever ' passing by.' But ' as He passed by,' how keen His eyes were for those who sat by the wayside ! Never a longing look cast towards Him remained unanswered ; never a sight of suffering met His eyes which did not touch His heart and win His help. Yes, His sympathy was perfect. That made Him all He was.

And what can we ask for ourselves but more of His spirit in us—quick and sensitive and responsive ? Opportunity will guide us for the rest, if His spirit is ours ; and we shall learn that this is the secret of the happiest life. Not the happiness that comes from giving a wide berth to the sorrowful sights ; not the kind of life that is a conspiracy to keep sorrow out of sight. No, it is strange, but it is true, that the happiest men and women in all the world are those who can share best and who do share most the sorrow of others. Our own burdens become lighter the more we share the burdens of other men. In the words of a great writer : ' We can have the highest happiness only by having wide thoughts and much feeling for the rest of the world as well as for ourselves.' Wide thoughts and much feeling—yes, much feeling.

¶ In the common room of Magdalene College, Cambridge, two portraits hang on the wall, facing each other across the table, portraits of the two men who shared the zest of life to the fullest and who fought hard for life's prizes. One is of Pepys—sleek, satisfied, kindly, sensuous ; a man who cheerfully tried to skim the cream off life's surface for himself and measurably succeeded. The other is of Charles Kingsley, who also delighted in life beyond most men, but whose heart burned like a flame in sympathy with the wrongs and sorrows of the poor, and who gave himself, like his Master, in generous devotion to all who needed him. And his face, lined with love and pain, is of one who looked ineffably far beyond the getting and spending of life's pleasures. It is not so much that one man had a different philosophy from the other, though this was true, as that one man lived in the closest contact with the spirit of Jesus, and the other instinctively avoided any contact with Him more intimate than that of formal religion. But the world to-day, in its present mood, recognizes in good-natured Pepys the despair of society, and in Charles Kingsley, with all his limitations, the power that can lift it out of its despair.[1]

4. This very chapter in Lamentations ends in an appeal to Heaven. When the passers-by are heedless, the stricken city turns from man to God for pity ; and this is the message of the Cross. If our sorrow is nothing to those who pass by, it is something to God who is afflicted in all our afflictions. That figure of the Crucified is the embodiment of the seeking love of God, of His compassion humbling Himself, identifying Himself with the world's sorrow. It is the last expression of that Divine sympathy which stoops and dies to save and bless. It is the refuge of the stricken-hearted, and the hope of the sin-laden and weary. Do we not see it as we read the Bible from the beginning ? God is coming nearer and nearer, entering more deeply into the life of man, taking upon Himself ever more of his conflict and burden, till at last in Christ He is here beside us carrying on His heart our load of sorrow and of sin. Christ is not ashamed to be our Brother, suffering with us, suffering for us, repenting for us with a sorrow we could not give to God. No, He could not pass by. This is the Priest who never passes by, the heavenly Samaritan who stoops to bless us. It is the perfection of sympathy ; and it saves.

When we truly know what it means, when we ourselves are saved by such a sympathy, it makes a difference as we look upon our brothers. It cannot be denied that this story of the Cross has changed the world and the ways of men, as these have been softened and sweetened by thoughtful, tender sympathy. The charity of the Cross makes us charitable, and we love because He first loved.

God sets it before us again and again in Word and Sacrament. The centre of our faith is the Cross—the sorrow that saves the world. It is the sorrow it most concerns us to remember. We would not forget its immense meaning for the remission of sins, but let us not forget that it saves us only as it makes us like Him who loved us and gave Himself for us. Beside that Cross, believing in that Christ, we cannot keep our pride and selfishness, or live any longer unto ourselves. ' We must love Him, too, and love like Him and try His works to do.'

[1] H. Kingman, *Building on Rock.*

The Passion and the Passer-by

Lam i. 12.—' Is it nothing to you, all ye that pass by ? behold, and see if there be any sorrow like unto my sorrow.'

THESE words have long been taken as peculiarly applicable to the Passion of our Lord.

> From the throne of His Cross, the King of
>   Grief
> Cries out to a world of unbelief :
> ' Oh, men and women, afar and nigh,
> Is it nothing to you, all ye that pass by ? '

1. The leaders of men in any high and serious enterprise know how hard it is for them to get the rank and file to regard rightly the main issues. It is so easy to pass by. It is equally easy to be indifferent to and to ignore the claims of God on our life. We may be engrossed in the many details of living, until the great aims of life itself are crowded out. The business of life keeps us so busy that we cannot spare time to deal with God and religion, and the things of the Spirit. We cannot concentrate mind and soul on the great claim of God, expressed in the Cross, to the love and loyalty of our life.

Others cannot give their attention to Calvary because of the sin that holds them. They have no interest in spiritual things ; they are caught in the high tides and swirling currents of evil, and are swung past the Cross with scarce a thought to spare for the Divine Sufferer who hangs on it.

Others, again, will pass by that Cross, and see only a cross-tree of wood and a man dying. This death is but one of the historical incidents, to be appraised in the same way as the death of any other good man, whose death has no vital significance for them. This Cross has had a great influence on the lives of millions, and has distinctly contributed to the history of men. But now its significance is spent. It is as a tale that is told, and its power is gone. They regard it as but a pathetic account of how a man was done to death because of his loyalty to the truth as he saw it, and because he did not take ordinary precautions to safeguard himself against the machinations of his enemies.

2. The whole world has to *pass* the Cross of Christ, and in doing so men are compelled to

pass judgment on that Cross, and in doing that they pass judgment on themselves.

God is not far away. An earthly king spends most of his life away from his subjects. Those who would see him must take elaborate trouble to catch a glimpse of his august majesty. Not so with God, the King of Kings and the Lord of Lords. We meet Him in Nature. He is there calling to us, seeking to win our hearts, desiring to enter into communion with us, trying to awaken a response to His friendly overtures. We cannot take a walk abroad but we meet Him, if we have eyes to see Him.

How close God is to us in the lives of our fellows, and in the ordinary experiences of the day. Surely a man must be a dullard, or a sinner, or a cheap cynic, not to feel and find the presence of God in the happenings of his own life, or in that of his fellows.

¶ Sometimes in Nature we, like Wordsworth, feel a Presence that disturbs us with the joy of elevated thoughts, as though all the things we see were the signs and tokens of a world invisible and real. Sometimes within ourselves a Presence rises, not to be denied, as though some Self greater than ourselves were seeking to win our allegiance from the selves we actually are. Sometimes among our friends we see troubles conquered, handicaps surmounted, spiritual victories won, until a soul that the world seemed about to conquer rises conqueror instead, strange, invisible resources coming to his help. And sometimes we see friends face death and, lo ! the world invisible appears to welcome them

> . . . as if some fair city were one voice
> Around a king returning from his wars.[1]

It may be contended that God is not manifest in Nature, and less so in men and women as we know them. But surely it is clear that on the Cross, if never before or since, God has manifested Himself. There He bared His heart to the world. God may or may not have won our allegiance, but at least He has tried, has emptied Himself, as it were, and taken up His abode with men in that life and death of Jesus. We may or may not give Jesus our hearts, but the Cross of Christ is one—nay, the greatest— fact in the history of the world. We may pass by that Cross, but it is there for us to pass by.

[1] H. E. Fosdick.

We may ignore the Cross, but to discount and dismiss it from our life is impossible. Look at the crowd around the Cross as you pass. A little band is there of those who do care. Men and women, among them Jesus' own mother. They are baffled and well-nigh broken with sorrow, but they have seen the vision. They are changed men and women ; they would find it difficult to tell us, could we question them as they gaze, what it is that He has given them. But they will go away from that hill, and after a little while will be trudging along the main arteries of the world of that time, preaching the forgiveness of sin, and the promise of a new life because of this crucified Man.

There are those round the Cross, and very near to it, who frankly do not care. Some cry in derision, mocking Him in His agony ; others gamble and curse to the very moment of His passing. Others, the priests, are satisfied with their work, as satisfied as it is possible to be with sin—for doubtless there were some who had misgivings about what they had done, and feared that they would hear again of this day's work. And there were still others, of whom it can be said that they did not care at first, but by the close of the day had learnt to care. There was the thief on the cross who in his dying moments turned to his Lord ; the Roman soldier who came to guard at the command of Cæsar and ere the day was done had at least heard faintly the call of the living God.

The band of those who do care about the Cross of Christ is an ever-growing band. The forces of God are on their side, and the sun and the dawn are with them. The day of their struggle and warfare may be a long one, and alas ! many times they will break from the ranks and flee, but they will come back to the standard and fight until the day is won for God and His children.

Dare we pass by that Cross, that Passion of our Lord, as but an idle spectacle without significance to us ? Are we so strong, so sure of ourselves, so confident that we can meet all the contingencies and possible catastrophes of our mortal and changeful life, that we can afford to spurn this proffered help and strength ? Is our burden so light, has sin so little hold on us, that we have no need for Him to aid us, and no need for Him to forgive us ? Thus to ignore and leave the Cross means that we must carry our burden alone. God wants to come into our life to increase its joy and to share its weight and its burdens—and we will not ; it is nothing to us ; we pass by !

¶ In *Gold Cord* Miss Amy Carmichael quotes a little-known poem of Traherne's as recurring to her persistently :

His earnest love, His infinite desires,
His living, endless, and devouring fires,
Do rage in thirst, and fervently require
   A love 'tis strange it should desire.

We cold and careless are, and scarcely
   think
Upon the glorious spring whereat we
   drink.
Did He not love us we could be content :
   We wretches are indifferent !

'Tis death, my soul, to be indifferent ;
Set forth thyself unto thy whole extent,
And all the glory of His passion prize,
   Who for thee lives, who for thee dies.

' " 'Tis death, my soul, to be indifferent "—that is surely a deathless word,' she adds.

And to those of us who say we do care—how careless we have grown, how heedless and forgetful we have been ! Let us gather round the Cross once more, and pray that it may mean more than ever to us ; that its consolation, its revelation, its promise for this life and for the life to come, and its appeal for our loyalty and fellowship in His suffering, may be to us the source of spiritual strength and vision. May we walk in the light of that Cross that leads, at the long last, to the abiding light of the never-ending day.

THE GOD WHO NEVER FAILS

Lam. iii. 23.—' They are new every morning.'

THIS is the kind of statement that gives the Bible its unique and unrivalled place among books. Born out of first-hand experience, the words are one man's testimony to the reality of God's grace. Burdened by many and great afflictions, which of himself he was incapable of enduring, he won through in the end because of the constancy of God's providence. His mercies and compassions, he declares, were new every morning, and, because of that, he who, left to himself, must have been over-whelmed, was made more than conqueror. Where else, except in the Bible, is such encouragement given to burdened men by burdened men ? It runs through both the Old and the New Testaments like a golden thread—the assurance of men and women who once bore the heat and the burden of the day to men and women who bear the heat and the burden to-day that, if we rely sufficiently upon God, we can and will be brought through the direst of life's experiences, the most exacting of moral struggles, and the gravest of calamities. What happened in their case, they affirm, can happen in ours. Of ourselves we may be as incapable as they were of compassing all that life asks of us, but God and we together should prove an invincible combination.

If all this seems platitudinous and vague to those of us for whom life is, in some sense or another, hard, and who are looking for suggestions as to what faith in God really means and for practical hints as to how best we may face life's responsibilities, the Bible, let it be said, does not leave us without the suggestions and the practical hints we profess to seek. Nowhere is that truer of the Bible than here. When this man wrote, ' They are new every morning,' referring, as we have already noticed, to God's mercies and compassions, he was not only paying tribute to the constancy of God's providence, but indicating how he himself lived and how, so living, he became more than conqueror.

1. First, the text suggests that *he learned to live a day at a time.*

It was, doubtless, a difficult lesson to learn. He, like many burdened men, probably besought God to remove his burden for good and all.

When his prayer went unanswered he, like many more in a similar case, probably grew depressed. But his eyes were opened at length to this fact that, if he wakened every morning to the old responsibility, he was carried through each day without fail. According to each day's need, so was each day's grace supplied. So clear did that become as he surveyed his life that he confessed to himself and to others that, but for the constancy of God's providence, he could not have come so far.

The art of living a day at a time is one we all must learn. And a most difficult art it is. All of us who are burdened would fain see the burden removed once and for all. Those of us who are engaged in a moral struggle—and which of us is not?—would fain see the fight finished and done with. The fact that the same burden will have to be carried to-morrow and the same old battle will have to be fought gets us down, and sometimes, because God does not answer our prayer for immediate and complete deliverance, we are forgetful of and indifferent to His present, daily mercies. One day during Spring when the sun shone from a cloudless sky I chanced to pass a man to whom I remarked on the beauty of the day. 'Aye,' he replied, in a mood scarce befitting the sunshine, 'but we'll pay for this yet!' How many of us are like him! We cannot see the glory of the present because of the heavy weather we are sure we shall encounter later. The fear of what may lie ahead prevents us from accepting our present mercies. We have got to realize that God gives His mercy day by day, that each day's needs are met by each day's grace. That is the principle upon which He has constructed life and it is a principle we were wise to accept.

A friend of mine has a suggestive sermon in one of his volumes which he entitles 'Hoarding Forbidden.' 'Long ago,' he reminds us, 'in their journey to the Promised Land, the children of Israel found that no man was suffered to possess an unfair advantage over his comrade in the matter of food. In a difficult part of the journey God provided them with iron rations —the mysterious manna, which had this property, that, if a man gathered more than a day's supply at a time, the surplus rotted on his hands.' It was natural, perhaps, in spite of the condition laid down, that some should want to see more than a day ahead and equally understandable that they should endeavour to make provision for to-morrow as well as for to-day. But all attempts to circumvent the rule were defeated. Without fail, what they gathered beyond one day's needs rotted on their hands. If, however, they complained that provision for the future could not be made, this they could not deny, that the daily supply never failed. God's mercies and compassions were new every morning.

Surely such an incident, like the testimony of the author of the Book of Lamentations, was left on record for a purpose. Many of us, when to-morrow comes, must return to a burden we have carried for years or to a battle from which we gain but short release. We may have asked, somewhat impatiently, with Christina Rossetti, 'Does the road wind up-hill all the way?' and when the answer, 'Yes, to the very end,' was given, we may have grown, understandably, depressed. But this is the assurance which men of faith give us, which those who once bore the heat and burden of the day give to those who bear the heat and burden to-day, that, if the road winds up-hill all the way, God leaves no man to his own resources. His mercies and compassions are new every morning. Learn, they seem to counsel us, to live a day at a time.

2. But if this man learned to live a day at a time, *he learned to leave the future to God.*

He had had trying experiences and the likelihood was that his experiences would become not less but more trying in the future. Human, like the rest of us, he might well have found the uncertainty of the morrow somewhat unnerving. But one great fact allayed his fears and enabled him to contemplate the future, if not with complacency, at least with confidence. Morning by morning the needed strength had been ministered. It was of God's mercy, he had to confess, that he had come so far successfully. Had he any reason to think that God, who had brought him thus far, would suddenly desert him? Had he any ground for believing that God, who had matched His mercy with his needs, would make inadequate provision in the future whatever his future needs might be? Surely if the past argued anything it was this, that, no matter what might happen, the necessary strength would be forthcoming. 'His mercies and compassions,' he whispered to his sometimes discouraged soul, 'are new every morning.' Therefore, if there were new needs, there would be new measures of God's grace.

The assurance with which he sustained himself in respect of the future was the assurance with which the greatest apostle of Jesus Christ continually sustained himself. In that great passage in his Epistle to the Romans in which he proclaims his belief that nothing will ever be able to separate him from the love of God in Jesus Christ he argues from the past to the future, from what God has done to what He is bound to do. ' He that spared not his own Son, but delivered him up for us all,' he says, ' how *shall* he not with him freely give us all things ? ' It was unthinkable that God, having gone thus far, would not go farther still. His giving of Himself in Jesus Christ was an indication, not of the limit, but of the nature, of His love. Therefore let the future have no terrors for him. God's grace would be sufficient however great and however demanding the need.

We have discovered little from our reading of the New Testament if we have failed to discover in such words an invitation to argue in our own life from the past to the future. Many of us are apprehensive of the future because we think insufficiently of the past. In all our lives, and not less in the life of our nation, we have been given many tokens of God's faithfulness, and that we have reached this present hour is entirely of His mercy and of His mercy alone. Have we any reason to think that God who has brought us thus far will suddenly desert us ? Have we any ground for believing that God, who has matched His grace with our needs, will make inadequate provision in the future ? Learn, say the great souls of the past, not only to live a day at a time, but to argue from the past to the future.

3. But if this man learned to leave the future to God, *he learned to think of God as capable of meeting any situation that might arise.* His purposes, he came to believe, could never be defeated. Whatever circumstances might arise He could and would turn them to the advantage of His cause and Kingdom. His power and inventiveness were never exhausted. His mercies and compassions were new every morning.

If it is necessary that we learn to live a day at a time and to leave the future to God, it is equally necessary that we should hold such a belief. There are many to-day who do not doubt, who cannot in the face of the facts doubt, that God in the past turned many disadvantageous circumstances to good account, but they honestly cannot see any parallel in the world's history to the conditions at present prevailing and are of opinion that all good Christian folk can do is cherish the memories of ' the good old days ' when God's hand was made abundantly manifest. Let such folk read the words of this testimony, ' God's mercies and compassions are new every morning,' until they are imprinted indelibly upon their minds and memories. Conditions may look singularly unpropitious to us, and that any good can emanate from them may seem a hope without any foundation. But let us not forget that, though some things are impossible with men, they are possible with God.

In the course of the last war, in 1916 to be precise, when it was difficult to believe that things could ever right themselves again, Professor James Hope Moulton, the prominent Greek and New Testament scholar, delivered a series of lectures in America. In the course of one of them he told of a friend, stricken with what proved to be his last illness, whom he had visited. ' He was,' said Professor Moulton, ' a scientific florist, who had been many years supplying the market of Manchester with beautiful cut flowers. He told me how he had tried very hard indeed to produce a particular tulip. He wanted to get this tulip double, and he wanted to get it pink. He tried all his known methods. He succeeded in getting it double, but the double flower was white, and to get it anything but white seemed to be beyond his power. One day a sudden storm came up. He went quickly around his hot-houses to see that nothing should be left that could be whisked up by the wind and break the glass. He picked up all the loose boxes he saw, but he overlooked one, and this one was taken up by the wind and a great gap was made in the glass. The cold, icy blast poured through the greenhouse. When he went to the greenhouse the next morning he found that this new flower upon which he had worked so long was pink ! ' God,' went on Professor Moulton, ' has His own ways of producing His perfect flowers. Sometimes the icy blast of affliction will do what all other methods fail to do. Weariness and despair after years of bloodshed produced the conditions under which it was possible for the Gospel to come.' And it may well be that the weariness and despair which will follow the present experience will produce the conditions under which it is possible for the Gospel to run and be glorified. God has turned worse situations to good account, and what He has done He can do again.

This testimony of a man to God's constant mercy is perhaps the tonic word that many of us, oppressed by personal as well as by world problems, badly need. Let us, therefore, repeat his words until they are imprinted indelibly upon our minds and memories and the faith in God which characterized men of old characterizes us in like fashion—' His mercies and compassions are new every morning.'

RODERICK BETHUNE.

Freshness of Life

Lam. iii. 23.—' They are new every morning.'

SOMETHING new. Is not that the undying craving of our nature ? Under some name or other, freshness is what we are continually seeking. And when we get down to a really healthy instinct of human nature, we may be quite sure that God did not furnish us therewith if He had not somehow intended to satisfy it. ' They are new every morning,' says this writer, rejoicing over the freshness of God's mercies.

We cannot doubt that, like a true Jew, when he spoke of God's ever-new mercies, he was thinking first of the external mercies that bore witness every morning of the love of God for His children. He was thinking of the constant renewal of health, the hourly growth of harvests, the continual care of Jehovah for the chosen people, that made the nation's most silent history a poem in the patriot's ears—of all these things certainly, but certainly also of something deeper than all these, of the way in which God Himself, who to the spiritual nature is always His own best mercy, was for ever coming to him with the freshness of a new approach, and making his life new with the newness of the everlasting life. It is the perpetual newness of the religious experience which must have most stirred his soul, and made it open into this unexpected flower of gratitude. ' The Lord is my portion, saith my soul ' ; and the next clause sings, ' therefore will I hope in him.'

1. One of the higher forces that preserve the freshness of human life, that keep the colour and spring and buoyancy in a life up to the very end, is *a strong personal friendship*. To be a Christian is to love, to serve, to imitate Jesus the Christ—not merely to recall a departed Teacher and to try to remember His commandments, but to live with a living Friend, to gather out of His present life present warnings and inspirations, to let Him guide us in all the little and great doings of our lives. ' I have called you friends,' He says. ' Lo, I am with you always.' Personal friendship with Him is the heart of the Christian faith. And the soul which, in its dealing with Christianity, has laid hold of this its most essential character, and has found its religion most purely and most consciously in the personal service of Christ, is the soul to which its religion is the source of never-failing freshness.

Think how the lives of the first disciples must have been changed in regard to their freshness from the time that they knew Christ ! Many and many an evening Peter and James and John must have rocked in their boat on the lake, watching the sun sink below the hills that lay behind Capernaum, and wondered whether it would always rise on days as monotonous as these that they were living. But from the time that they looked up from the nets that they were mending, at the sound of the strange, sweet, authoritative voice that called them, and left their nets and followed the Stranger, we are sure that such wonderment was gone. They began to find life all new. Life and death both became to them full of those deep, pregnant meanings that are always thrilling us as we read the New Testament. They began to live eternal life, as they loved to call it, by which they meant not merely life that is to last for ever—which is sometimes all that we mean by it—but life that, in every moment of it, was fresh and deep and vital with the Divine companionship of Christ. ' This is life eternal, to know thee, the only true God, and Jesus Christ whom thou hast sent.' The personal friendship had transfigured their dull routines and filled their mortal life with the fire of immortality.

¶ Do you think the first disciples were ever bored in the company of Jesus ? They were ashamed of themselves often, mystified and puzzled and taken out of their depth quite frequently, sometimes furiously excited, occasionally even frightened—but bored ? Never. What a thrilling Companion He was ! They would have gone through the world with Him if He had asked them. And when, after Pentecost, He did ask them, right through the world they went. He is the same thrilling Companion still. You never know what romance may happen next, when it is the Christ of God who is with you on the road.[1]

2. Another element of constantly fresh life is *work*. The captain and the working crew of a ship never feel the monotony of a voyage as it weighs upon their idle passengers. To them each hour is filled with responsibility and work. It is the sharp, full days when, as the man says, he has ' not time to turn round,' in which he ceases to want to turn idly on his pivot and goes straight forward to some purpose, and forgets that life is dull. Every morning his work is at the door, calling to him as if it, too, were a living friend, to come and take its hand and follow it to happiness. Where is the chance for him to grow weary ?

¶ When Charles Lamb was released for life from his daily drudgery of desk-work at the India Office, he felt himself the happiest of men. ' I would not go back to my prison,' he said to a friend, ' ten years longer, for ten thousand pounds.' He also wrote in the same ecstatic mood to Bernard Barton : ' I have scarce steadiness of head to compose a letter,' he said ; ' I am free ! free as air ! I will live another fifty years. Would I could sell you some of my leisure ! Positively the best thing a man can do is—nothing ; and next to that, perhaps good works.' Two years—two long and tedious years—passed ; and Charles Lamb's feelings had undergone an entire change. He now discovered that official, even humdrum work—' the daily round, the common task '— had been good for him, though he knew it not. Time had formerly been his friend ; it had now become his enemy. To Bernard Barton he again wrote : ' I assure you, no work is worse than overwork ; the mind preys on itself—the most unwholesome of food. I have ceased to

care for almost anything. . . . Never did the waters of heaven pour down upon a forlorner head.'

I am glad a task to me is given,
　To labour at day by day ;
For it brings me health and strength and hope,
　And I cheerfully learn to say :
' Head, you may think ; Heart, you may feel ;
　But, Hand, you shall work alway.' [1]

Christianity gives zest and freshness to life by furnishing it with abundant work. Is there one of us who does not feel that every little stroke of work that he has consented to do for his Lord has come back into his life with a reflow of fresh delight in living that was a thousand times its reward ? Work that we do for God—and, thank God ! He has filled His world with chances of it—brings us near to Him, and makes our friendship with Him more complete, and brings refreshment into our weary lives. ' Thy mercies are new every morning.' Yes : for every morning this great, noisy world, crowded with sin and poverty and sorrow, wakes from its uneasy slumber and cries out to us for help. Each morning we may do something for Christ in His brethren ; and, when we come to die we may wonder whether, in a world where vice and want are not, there can be any such chances of labouring for Christ as have made us perpetually happy here.

If we want an illustration of this, we need only look at the Lord Jesus Christ Himself. In profound reverence let us believe that the weariness of the Saviour, when He was here upon earth, was again and again consoled and lightened by the work for the Father that He loved to do. Was not that what He meant when He said that His meat and drink was to do the will of Him that sent Him ? When He was tired and sat by Jacob's well, was it a new fatigue or a great refreshment to open the fountain of the water of life to the poor woman ? Why did He sweep aside the officious thoughtfulness of His disciples to get at the children who needed His blessing and the blind man who needed sight ? Was it not that He wanted the joy of helping them ? When His life was heavy, He lightened it with work. And so He lived a human life here, ever fresh with the constant communion of Divinity. ' My father

---

[1] J. S. Stewart, *The Gates of New Life*, 24.

[1] Louisa M. Alcott.

worketh hitherto, and I work ';—that was the channel of the intercommunion of their One Life.

Do we not see that, since we also are permitted to work with God, we, too, may live in fresh and vital union with Him which shall be an echo of the Christhood, of that perfect union in which He and His Father were One ? Not only for the little that it will do for the world, but for the great need we have of it ourselves, may we be more faithful, earnest workers with God.

To do for others in some sort
  What Thou hast done for me,
Since in such work Thy saints have found
  A closer walk with Thee,—
This will my Father glorify,
  This happiness will bring ;
For, serving others, I shall find
  The way to serve my King.

Patient Hope

Lam. iii. 26.—' It is good that a man should both hope and quietly wait for the salvation of the Lord.'

THAT the man who wrote these words was at the time, and had long been, in great trouble and perplexity, is evident enough from the immediate context. It would, however, be a mistake to regard him as beaten down by his trouble and hopelessly overwhelmed. For while on the one hand he speaks of himself as ' filled with bitterness,' as not consumed only because of ' the Lord's mercies,' on the other hand he can see in the future, drawing ever nearer, a deliverance that was certain and would be complete. Accordingly he introduces into the midst of his complaints some unhesitating little verses : ' The Lord is my portion, saith my soul ; therefore will I hope in him. The Lord is good unto them that wait for him, to the soul that seeketh him.' Good therefore it is that a man—his country wrecked, his home broken up, his most cherished hopes apparently doomed to utter disappointment— even then, ' it is good that he should hope and quietly wait for the salvation of the Lord.'

But the words of the text have a much wider application than to the particular circumstances of the writer or to the Israel of that day. They are apposite to the case of every one who is perplexed because, for instance, the expected deliverance from sin in his own life does not come as he thought it would. Or the petition he offers for some good of which he conceives himself to be in great need, is not granted. Or the revival in his work, for which he has conscientiously wrought to the very last ounce of his strength, does not seem to be even on the horizon. We want to know what is the spiritual good of having quietly to wait and hope so long.

It is almost unnecessary to say that there is no thought in the text of any man having to wait until God is willing to bestow upon him the primary gifts of pardon and peace and forgiveness. It can never be good for a man to wait for the salvation which, by His free gift in Jesus Christ, God is so willing and eager to bestow. The despairing who cry for pardon, the weary and heavy-laden who ask for rest of heart, the lonely who seek the fellowship of love, are never kept waiting for the fulfilment of their desires. The prodigal is welcomed before he utters his prepared confession. The Evangel of Christ bears the ageless superscription that ' now is the day of salvation.' In this respect, indeed, it is never God who keeps men waiting, but men who keep Him waiting.

But, in regard to that aspect of God's mercy which is concerned with the strain of our present discipline, with the anxiety of future uncertainty, with the weariness of unremoved burdens—it is in that realm of life the prophet says it is good to hope and quietly wait for His salvation.

1. It is by waiting upon God that we come to know God with that knowledge which is the foundation of all character. It is only by being forced to wait upon God that some of us ever do wait on Him. We are naturally impatient, we are naturally impulsive, we naturally chafe at anything like slowness ; and God, by withholding the answer for which we have looked, keeps us at His feet in order that we may come to know Him. He is infinitely more concerned in the making and re-making of our lives than in the gratifying of our minds. He is infinitely more concerned in making us men and women of His own pattern,

and to deepen His life in our souls, than to gratify some of the desires which we often express in unconsidered prayer. For we cannot come to know God, and inferentially we cannot come to know ourselves, in an hour.

¶ One of Ruskin's pupils once said to him, 'The instant I entered the gallery at Florence I knew what you meant by the supremacy of Boticelli.' 'In an instant did you?' was the somewhat withering reply. 'It took me twenty years to find it out.'

It is told of D. L. Moody the famous evangelist that he was buried on a hill-top outside Northfield because it was there he had spent much time, waiting upon God. A friend of his, wondering why Moody chose that spot, sat one early morning looking from his bedroom window towards the hill. At first all was dark, and then the dim light began to dawn, and he watched the black clouds slowly drifting over the hill. Gradually a change came, the clouds were tinted with gold, a soft and delicate light broke across the hill, turning the clouds from ominous symbols into a roof of golden lamps, hung in the sky. Then the whole scene shifted again, as the sun rose above the hill, and a new day was born. If he had not waited he would have given a wrong verdict of the hill and those clouds. And thus he understood Moody's practice of going to the hill of New England: for there, in waiting, he discovered how God transformed the clouds of one's forebodings, and always opened up the threshold of a new day with new meaning to all who cared to hope and wait.

In both Nature and art there are things that must be allowed to grow upon us. Many people fail to feel the influence of Niagara at the first visit. The senses do not waken to its forces and scale themselves to its proportions in an hour. The visitor needs to see it in the sunrise and to see it in the sunset, to watch it from the Canadian and to watch it from the American side, to see it from the rapids and to see it from the whirlpools, to stand above it and to stand beneath it, to listen to the witchery of its roar at all hours of the day and night, till every nerve seems magnetized and every fibre tense and tremulous with sensations that are too large for it. Only then are its supreme qualities felt and recognized. And God must keep us long in His presence if we are to see His beauty and feel the transport of His power. We cannot know God by brief attendances in His presence.

¶ Scientists often spend years, sometimes a whole lifetime, in making an important scientific discovery. Then can we expect to discover spiritual beauties by spending only five minutes every day in quiet and prayer? [1]

God is preparing us, by keeping us waiting upon Him, worthily to receive, to interpret, and then to use the gifts He will yet give in answer to prayer and in fulfilment of His word.

2. Many of our prayers must be passed through the refining medium of God's wisdom and love; many of them must be edited by God before they are answered. For well-intentioned prayer is not always well-informed. Like those who made requests of the Saviour, God often has to say to His children, 'Ye know not what ye ask.' If some of our prayers were immediately answered, the consequence would be almost certain moral and spiritual disaster. There are men and women, for instance, who pray for power, while their real objective is pre-eminence. What they really mean by power is that which will make them prominent in His service. When our motives are altogether unworthy of the words we express, we have to be kept waiting until God turns upon us the searchlight of His love, and learning the untrustworthiness of our own impulses, we yield to that gracious Spirit who makes intercession in us according to the will of God.

Not only in regard to the *motive*, but in regard also to the *content* of our prayers God has to keep us waiting. We may have seen children who have been utterly spoiled by the weak good-nature of parents who gave them at once everything they wanted. For human love may be entirely lacking in wisdom. But the love and wisdom of God are one. When He keeps us waiting for secondary mercies, it is in order to make us know the value of the primary and spiritual. We have to learn that God's ' No ' is just as much an answer as God's ' Yes.' We have to learn that God's ' Not yet ' is just as truly an expression of Divine love as God's ' Immediately.' The day will come to every one of us when we shall know that God's silence was in reality His most loving speech to us. For we shall see that while seemingly

[1] Sadhu Sundar Singh.

inactive God has all the time been working in us, bringing us into moral correspondence with His will, which alone capacitates men to receive His gifts.

¶ Rabindranath Tagore, the Bengali poet, was stating a profound human experience, when he wrote : ' My desires are many and my cry is pitiful, but ever didst Thou save me by hard refusals ; and this strong mercy has been wrought into my life through and through.'

3. Faith can only be trained by being tested. As a man's muscles are only hardened by exercise, so his faith only becomes strong and ultimately invincible by being subjected to the discipline of strain. If God can afford to wait, so can we.

¶ ' Bishop,' asked Carlyle of Wilberforce, ' have you a creed ? ' ' Oh, yes,' replied the Bishop, ' I have a creed, and the older I grow, the firmer it becomes. There is only one thing that staggers me.' ' And what is that ? ' inquired Carlyle. ' It is the slow progress,' answered the Bishop, ' that that creed seems to make in the world.' ' But,' said Carlyle, ' if you have a creed, Bishop, you can afford to wait and bide God's time.'

Of course, there is nothing in common between quiet waiting upon God and lethargic indolence. True waiting upon God expresses itself in the expenditure of every energy of the soul at the clear directions for whose interpretation we do not need to wait an hour.

It would be supine folly in these days of tremendous opportunity to be content to ' wait upon God ' to open doors, to ' wait upon God ' to enlarge opportunities, to ' wait upon God ' to organize success and influence for us, while we ourselves did nothing, sat back complacently without disapproving evils or assisting in action against them, saying— everything will be all right in the end. Paul speaks about the patience of hope, but he never meant us to take him as saying—' I hope so : why worry.'

¶ In one of the most dramatic scenes of the Exodus, where the Israelites are caught with the unfordable Red Sea to front and the pursuing Egyptians behind, Moses goes apart to pray. The reply which he receives from Jehovah is startling. It is nothing less than a rebuke for having prayed : ' Wherefore criest thou unto me ? speak unto the children of Israel, that they go forward.' It is as though God were saying, ' I have everything prepared for your aggressive action. I have done the last thing that I can do, until you resolutely take advantage of it. It is your move ! You cannot obtain by prayer what comes only as the reward of work.' Such a rebuke many of our prayers deserve. We forget the proverb : ' If wishes were horses, beggars would ride.' [1]

It is only when we find ourselves in the grip of the inevitable and have no power to help ourselves—only when we have used our own best endeavour and find ourselves hemmed in by the insurmountable—it is only when after following consistent courses of obedience to God and consideration for the rights and interests of others, we find the problem still outgrows our power to grapple with it ; it is only then we are justified in a tranquil and untroubled waiting for God's delivering hand. ' Stand still and see the salvation of God ' is a word that fits into the rare emergencies of our lives, and has Divine authority behind it when we are walking in God's clearly prescribed paths. But it is just as far as we sustain the character of diligent, true-hearted, and faithful servants, that we shall find it ' good for a man to hope and quietly wait for the salvation of the Lord.'

We are not here to play, to dream, to drift ;
We have hard work to do, and loads to lift ;
Shun not the struggle ! face it ! 'Tis God's gift.
Say not, ' The days are evil ! Who's to blame ? '
And fold the hands, and acquiesce—oh, shame !
Stand up, speak out, act bravely in God's Name.
It matters not how deep entrenched the wrong,
How hard the battle goes, the day how long ;
Fight on ! fight on ! to-morrow comes the song !

[1] H. E. Fosdick.

The Yoke of Service

Lam. iii. 27.—' It is good for a man that he bear the yoke in his youth.'
Matt. xi. 29.—' Take my yoke upon you.'

THE yoke is that crooked beam of wood put on the necks of oxen by which they draw the cart or the plough. It is the symbol of service, of submission to another's will. We do not go far in this life when we find some one seeking to lay a yoke on our shoulders. Nature and society assume that we have come here to do something ; that no man liveth to himself. Most of us rise each morning to put on some one's yoke.

There is no calamity in this. No sympathy need be expended over the fact that this is a life of service. The calamity would be the idle, the useless, the yokeless life. For, next to sin, idleness is greatest in its influence to disintegrate the powers of body, mind, and conscience :

An angel's wing would droop if long at rest,
And God Himself inactive were no longer blest.

1. The poet says that it is good for a man to bear the yoke. It is good for the man himself. Aside from the product of his activity, aside from the gain that may thus come to others, the chief good is what the yoke does for the development of his own powers of body, faculties of mind, virtues of character. The poet says that it is good for a man to bear the yoke in his youth. Our own mature experience confirms the statement. For then the powers of body and mind are pliant, capable of adaptation, of strengthening and toughening for the service until service becomes easy, becomes a second nature to us. Coming to the breezy summit of middle life, we look back upon many things with regret ; but no man regrets the good honest hard work he performed. That, and the results of it, are his own. He may have been disappointed, and robbed of much by the way, but he cannot be robbed of the discipline and the character which he earned through bearing the yoke. For ever that is his. When the father would lay the yoke of business on the shoulders of his son, the young man may be reluctant to bear it and be restive under it ; but when the son, now capable and efficient, sees his father touching the seventies and wishes that the older man might take things easier, he does not know how to approach him on the subject. He will ask some mutual friend to suggest to his father the wisdom of letting the younger man bear the burden. Even the friend scarcely dares make the suggestion because he knows it will grieve the veteran's soul. For with whatever reluctance we may take up the yoke, we generally lay it down with regret ; it has become life and character and joy to us.

2. On the very threshold of the Christian life, we meet this yoke. Among the first words Christ has to say to us is, ' Take my yoke upon you.' Here, too, no man liveth to himself. The Christian life also is one of service, of submission. Christ is very frank about this, He allures no man to follow Him by false pretences. When men would follow Garibaldi to the liberty of Italy, he warned them that there would be hunger and thirst and fatigue, battle and wounds and death to be endured. Pizarro, in leading his veterans to the conquest of South America, drew a line across the deck of his ship, pictured the hardships and burdens men would have to bear who would go with him. He invited those willing to follow him on these conditions to cross the line to his side, and permitted the others to go back to Panama. Those who would follow must be willing to bear the yoke. When men would follow Christ, He frankly said, ' Take my yoke upon you '—the yoke of service, of self-denial, of submission. ' He that taketh not his cross and followeth after me is not worthy of me.'

¶ ' How hard it is to be a Christian,' cried Browning in the opening words of his *Easter Day*. To-day some people are trying to make it more easy. So they are discreetly silent about the yoke, and the cross, and the denying of self, concerning all of which Jesus spoke so plainly—while they make the most of the joy, and peace, and comfort of the gospel. The experiment, however, does not seem to be very successful. Chivalrous souls would be more drawn by the spirit of adventure in response to a trumpet-call to battle than to listen to these soothing songs of ease.[1]

The yoke of Christ in its more specific sense means three things. (1) First, that we are *to*

[1] W. F. Adeney.

confess *Him before men as Saviour and Lord.*
Each has his own theory on this matter of the
public profession of Christ, and his arguments
to establish that theory. And one man's
theory may be as good as that of another ;
but Christ, also, has a particular theory and
argument about it. Those who professed to
be His disciples He immediately sent out to
be witnesses for Him ; that which they heard
in the ear they were to declare upon the
house-tops ; they were to give what cup of
cold water they had to give in the name of a
disciple of Christ. Christ was emphatic about
this matter. ' Whosoever therefore shall confess
me before men, him will I confess also before
my Father which is in heaven. But whosoever
shall deny me before men, him will I also deny
before my Father which is in heaven.' That is
Christ's theory and argument, and they must
be allowed to outweigh ours whatever they
may be.

He is listening ; does He hear you speaking
of the things of earth,
Only of its passing pleasure, selfish sorrow,
empty mirth ?
He has spoken words of blessing, pardon,
peace, and love to you,
Glorious hopes and gracious comfort, strong
and tender, sweet and true ;
Does He hear you telling others something of
His love untold,
Overflowings of thanksgiving for His mercies
manifold ?

.   .   .   .   .   .

Yours may be the joy and honour His redeemèd
ones to bring,
Jewels for the coronation of your coming Lord
and King.
Will you cast away the gladness thus your
Master's joy to share,
All because a word for Jesus seems too much
for you to dare ? [1]

(2) The yoke of Christ means that we are
to obey His commands. Now Christ commands
nothing which is not ultimately for our own
good, and we know it. A life lived in accord
with His commands is the ideal life, that which
we most admire in others. To obey His commands should be as easy and as natural for us
as for the tree to bend to the influences of the

[1] Frances Ridley Havergal.

wind, and rain, and sunshine of the successive
seasons. Yet Christ calls this obedience a
yoke because He knows, and we know, that
there are selfish and self-willed tendencies in
us leading the other way. Every child, however amiable, knows what it is to meet his
father's commands with an expressed or an
unuttered ' I will not.' And this tendency of
our nature we carry into the region of our
religious life. To overcome it and to make the
will of Christ the law of our souls requires the
stooping of the shoulders and the taking on
of the yoke of obedience.

(3) The yoke of Christ means that we are
*to submit to His dealings with us in His daily
providences over our lives.* At first sight this
might seem no hardship ; He is wise, He is
kind, He is our friend, His plans for us must
be for our good. It would appear that we
should be the happiest of creatures in taking
each day what that day might bring, knowing
that it is sent or controlled by One who seeks
only our best. But Christ calls this submission
a yoke because there is in each of us an
independence, a constitutional wish and will
to plan our own lives, to shape our own course,
to arrange our own circumstances, to forecast
our own future. When our plans are interfered
with, when our pleasures are interrupted, when
our prospects are disappointed, it is not always
easy for us to say, ' Not my will but thine be
done.' It is of the nature of a yoke. Christ
Himself knew the weight of this yoke when,
that night in Gethsemane, He said, ' Let this
cup pass from me.' If we would see the deepest
depth and the highest height of the character
and example of our Lord, it is in that supreme
conquest of His own will brought into perfect
submission to the will of the Father.

But this yoke does become easy because we
bear it not from constraint, nor from mere
authority, but from love. It is said of Jacob
that for seven years he bore the yoke of Laban's
service for the sake of Rachel, and that the
years seemed to him but a few days for the love
he bare her. There is no love, however, like
that which the saved man bears to the Lord
who saved him. It is stronger than that which
binds husband to wife, parent to child, friend
to friend. It has carried the yoke through fire
and death. It is as strong to-day as it ever was
to carry the Christian through similar tests.
This public profession of Christ, this obedience

to His commands, this submission to His will is of the nature of a yoke ; but we bear it not from necessity, nor from obligation, nor from duty, but from love. The cares, the anxieties, the labours that we endure for our children are a yoke which we put on every morning and which we do not always put off at night. We have carried it since they were born and will bear it while we live, yet we do it not grudgingly, or complainingly, but for the love we bear them. As Burns puts it, in his poem 'To Dr Blacklock':

> To make a happy fire-side clime
> To weans and wife,
> That's the true pathos and sublime
> Of human life.

When our love for them is reciprocated by their love for us, the yoke becomes doubly easy and our burdens light. Herein is love, not only that we love Christ, but that He first loved us.

The Reluctant God

Lam. iii. 33.—' For he doth not afflict willingly.'

MANY years ago in an art exhibition in Munich there was a picture by a French painter which excited a great deal of interest and discussion, not so much on account of its artistic qualities as because of its subject. The picture was called ' Destiny and Humanity.' In the upper part was shown a face of great beauty and majesty, but so shadowed that the eyes were the only clear feature and they were of steel blue, piercing, unwavering and unheeding. In the lower part of the picture was a forest of hands, raised in the attitude of supplication and demand, hands of toil, delicate, bejewelled hands, little children's hands and hands that had ceased to entreat and clasped the revolver or the knife. But the more terrible feature of the picture was the eyes in the dimly-seen face above, pitilessly calm and unmoved, indifferent to the beseeching crowd. The artist had painted a face without the possibility of pity, or a suggestion of sympathy.

There are times when we are tempted to share the mood of the painter. Why should there be such a mass of undeserved suffering ?

Why should the innocent suffer ? Why does God ever permit the unspeakable horrors of war ? Many prayers were made for this one and for that, hearts were longing to welcome him home, yet he never returned. There are some who have lost sight and others who have lost mental vigour and health. From how many troubled hearts and homes throughout the world to-day there rises the insistent question, ' Why should this happen ? Why should these troubles come ? '

¶ Here are some sentences from a letter which Earl Grey, after his wife's death, wrote to a friend. ' I am having a hard struggle. Every day I grasp a little more of all that it means. Just when I have got my spirit abreast of life, I feel and understand more sorrow and sink again. Sometimes it is like a living death ; and the perpetual heartache, which has set in, wears me down.' [1]

How easy to think of God as if He were indifferent to the suffering of men, a God Almighty but unfeeling, a heartless Force rather than a Divine Father. When this bitter mood shadows us or our fellows, what can we say on behalf of God ?

1. This first. Over against the black cloud of mystery there is a bright cloud of mystery. The Cross on Calvary meant the Cross in the heart of God. The gift of His Son meant His own identification with human suffering and human need. The coming of the Son of God and His death of suffering meant sacrificial love in the Godhead. The suffering of the Divine sacrifice involved the suffering of the Divine Giver, God suffering on earth and in heaven. Humanity is not the only sufferer. It is not men alone who give up their beloved ; God, too, has given up His well-beloved Son. So over against the mystery of human sorrow we set the greater mystery of the Divine Sorrow. The excess of mysterious light dispels the mysterious darkness. That is the difference Christ has made.

But with this clue in our hands, we can grope our way farther. If God has allowed the sorrow of earth to reach His heart, we can take the ground which this ancient poet had reached without the fuller revelation and say, ' He doth not afflict willingly.' Whatever fruit this discipline of suffering may produce, however

[1] J. S. Stewart, *The Strong Name*, 127.

needful affliction be as a tool for the finer shaping of the human soul, we cannot easily gain present healing under some sudden, devastating calamity unless we gain this confidence, that it grieves Him to put us to grief, that He does not afflict willingly, unthinkingly, unpityingly, even when the affliction is to draw us nearer to Himself and to our fellows. Is it possible for us to believe in this ?

2. If we are to build up a right assurance and not trick ourselves into believing a beautiful lie, let us begin with the circumstances from which these words sprang. One man believed in the reluctance of God to give pain, one man had enough daring and insight and faith to say, 'God doth not afflict willingly.' From what a pit of despair this voice comes. The chapter in which this sentence is found describes not merely intense suffering but also the misery of being unheard. In the seventh and eighth verses we read : ' He hath hedged me about that I cannot get out : he hath made my chain heavy. Also when I cry and shout, he shutteth out my prayer.' Yet the man who wrote that, and much like it, comes to a place where the worst sorrow is healed and he can assert his new-found certainty that God not only cares for us but feels with us. Surely this man has the right to speak. It is from the depths not from the shallows that he comforts us.

He does not stand alone. There runs throughout the progressive revelation of the Old Testament a similar thread of thought. Rudimentary the conception and anthropomorphic the words, but how impressive the culminating assurance that judgment, whether it be penalty or discipline, is God's strange work.

Think for instance of the recurring phrase that God is ' slow to anger.' Make what deduction you please for Old Testament imperfect views of Divine indignation and then realize the alleviation which the brief daring phrase brought to one believing patriot after another as he saw his nation under the chastisement of God. Either in this form or in the beautiful word long-suffering, we find the same thought recur in the Books of Exodus, Numbers, Nehemiah, the Psalms, Joel, Jonah, and Nahum, to mention no others. It outweighs the suggestion of quickness to take offence contained in the word ' jealous.' It asserts that anger against His people is not easy to Jehovah. One poet dared to put it in a still stronger way, saying in the seventy-eighth Psalm ; ' Many a time turned he his anger away, and did not stir up all his wrath.'

Clearer still shine out two sentences infinitely comforting when we contemplate the indignation of God. When speaking by His prophet Ezekiel, He safeguards His judgments against misrepresentation. ' I have no pleasure in the death of him that dieth, saith the Lord God ' ; and again with added emphasis ' As I live, saith the Lord, I have no pleasure in the death of the wicked.' It is as if the God of Israel feared that He might be identified with Moloch, lover of human slaughter, therefore He would have this assertion made for Him. ' He delighteth in mercy,' wrote the prophet Micah. And Ezekiel here declares, ' He delighteth not in punishment.'

This then is the argument beaten out by these believers, as they were taught the mind of God. If God be reluctant to afflict men for their sins, how much more reluctant He must be to afflict them for their perfecting. As this poet puts it, when we translate exactly, ' He does not afflict from the heart.' The stroke must fall, the calamity must come, for our own good and the world's, but His heart is not in it. His heart is with our broken joys and shattered hopes. He would deliver us were there another way to reach His perfect end. All this the Old Testament says to us.

3. We gain a strengthening confidence when we use the analogy of human fatherhood which our Lord has taught us to use.

It happens only too often that a child must undergo an operation and is old enough to know something of it and to fear it. Yet for the child's health, perhaps for his life, it is necessary. Possibly the child, as the dreaded hour of leaving for the nursing-home draws near, hides himself or resists and has to be carried to the motor-car and again from the car to his bedroom in the home. In a little while, the operation takes place and the surgeon's scalpel cuts into the child's body and blood flows and pain is certain.

Suppose an uninstructed spectator of the scene. What will his thoughts be ? He will feel outraged at this apparent cruelty of a parent, compelling his child to a bed of pain.

If it be explained to this observer that the father has sought to assure the child that the pain is a necessity for health, still if he is obtuse he may say, ' Well, I cannot understand such hard-heartedness in a father, forcing a child to such a shock and suffering.'

But what a misreading of a human father's heart ! He hates the compulsion which is needful, would willingly bear the suffering himself, indeed does bear it as he carries the tender little body to the place of pain and waits for the surgeon's verdict.

If this be true of an earthly father, and his purpose of kindness be belied by outward facts, how much more true of the Heavenly Father with His larger wisdom and still more compassionate love. Appearances may be against Him, but have we not the right to say, arguing from the earthly analogy, ' He doth not afflict willingly ' ?

4. For the final confirmation of any conviction concerning God we must always turn to Jesus Christ.

Consider one parable, one lament, and one prayer of His and see how these confirm the growing conviction of our hearts that God is reluctant to put us to pain. Read again the parable of the vineyard and its vine dressers. Remember the thrice-repeated opportunity through a thrice-repeated request for the fruit of the vineyard. We regard this rightly as an aggravation of guilt for there was a threefold refusal with mounting proofs of rebellion and malignity as each successive messenger is cast out and mishandled. But consider the other side, the reluctance of the landowner to inflict punishment, as Jesus pictures him. He makes a fourth attempt, risking his best treasure as he sends his son to claim what is legitimately his own. He does not act swiftly, or punish as he might by law the first refusal or the second or the third. No, breathing through the familiar story is this long-extended patience with the ill-doer. Clear before our eyes is the long-suffering of the Father.

Jesus did more than teach us concerning God. He showed us God. ' He that hath seen me, hath seen the Father.' Behold then the rejected prophet lamenting over Jerusalem. What are the words of His lament ? ' How often would I have gathered thy children together as a hen gathereth her brood under her wings and ye would not.' The rejected helper is not swift to become the judge. ' How often ! ' Let the words contend against every misrepresentation of God. In them lies the truth of His long-suffering. ' He doth not afflict willingly.'

The precise point before us, however, is not God's aversion from punishment but His reluctance to put His faithful and trustful ones to pain. Here once more the example of Jesus aids us. Not only does He present the essential character of God to us. He also presents human nature, perfected and unshadowed by sin. In Gethsemane He shrank from the cup of suffering which He saw the Father about to offer Him. Thrice He asked that if possible the other way of sacrifice might be found, even while He submitted His will to the Father's choice. His confidence never wavered while His entreaty to be spared if possible, what in anticipation was agony, was repeated. We too have our Gethsemanes, little Gethsemanes it is true, but affrighting and desolating to us. Can we doubt that a shrinking, obedient Christ meant a reluctant Father in heaven ? Can we doubt that for us, too, in our dark and shadowed hours when we seek to adjust our wills to God's, His pity is at work ? We must drink the cup but it is put to our lips by a reluctant God.

¶ The Rev. H. Clifford Vincent tells of a soldier in the first World War who, after a long spell in the front-line trenches, became so worn out by the inevitable stress and strain that he made up his mind to desert. Accordingly, one dark night he put his decision into practice. Making his way back through the communication trench, and dropping into shell-holes to hide from discovering lights, he found himself at length on the road leading from the line and began to grope his way along in the thickening darkness. At length he came to what seemed to be cross-roads. He was afraid he might choose the wrong way, and find himself back in another part of the line, and be taken. He must make sure. Suddenly he felt the bottom of what he thought was a sign-post, still standing. Up this he painfully swarmed, and, clinging to one of the arms he sought and found in his pocket a stray match. Striking it he held it up over his head, and, behold, he found himself looking into the face of Christ. He had climbed a wayside calvary. He hung there stunned by the vision and it was only the match burning his fingers that brought him back to his senses. He dropped to the ground, and did the one thing such a vision prompted, he made his way back to the front line.

Long years ago, as earth lay dark and still,
   Rose a loud cry, upon a lonely hill.
While in the frailty of our human clay
   Christ, our Redeemer, passed the self-same way.

Still stands the Cross, from that dread hour to this,
   Like some bright star above the dark abyss,
Still through the veil, the Victor's pitying eyes
Look down to bless our lesser calvaries.

Justice

Lam. iii. 35, 36.—' To turn aside the right of a man before the face of the most High. To subvert a man in his cause, the Lord approveth not.'

JUSTICE is perhaps the most widely discussed virtue to-day. It has been defined as rendering to every one his due. It is the virtue of a man, not as he stands alone, but as he stands in society; and as he cultivates this virtue, he has to keep his eye on all the circles of society in which he stands, such as the family, the city, the nation, and the Church. It comprehends the mutual duties of parents and children, husbands and wives, brothers and sisters, friends and neighbours, clergy and laymen, employers and employed, rulers and subjects, and others too numerous to mention. If any one in all these relationships were a model man, then he would be a perfect man, and hence Justice has often been treated as if it were the whole of virtue; and even Aristotle, in an unusual outburst of enthusiasm, says: ' It is more beautiful than the morning or the evening star.'

When Justice is defined as rendering to every one his due, that might seem a very simple affair, but it is not so simple as it looks; and this we immediately begin to realize if we ask what is due to any other person, because the question always slips in, ' And what is due to me?' That is what makes it so difficult to keep the balance straight—the bias in favour of self. We may say, with the American Declaration of Independence, that every human being has the right to life, liberty, and the pursuit of happiness; but instantly questions arise like these: Has a man a right to life who has taken the life of another? Does not the pursuit of happiness by one man often involve the misery of many other men and women? In fact, we cannot find out what is the due of any one, and especially our own due, without close and careful inquiry. We must be educated ourselves in many schools, and learn the lessons which are taught there.

Let us consider four of these schools of justice.

1. *The Law of the Land.*—That every one should get his due is so essential to human welfare, that in every country in the slightest degree above the level of barbarism, the very best brains have been set to determine what justice is, and the united strength of the community to enforce it. In ancient Rome, for instance, the Twelve Tables were set up in the market-place, that every one might read them, and there, in the plainest words, the citizen was told his duty, and was made acquainted with the penalties of transgression. In our own country and in other civilized countries, picked men are brought together in Parliament, who spend their time, year by year, defining what justice is. Law Courts are set up; judges and juries sit; lawyers plead, to bring special cases under the general laws which Parliament has enacted; and prison and punishment exist for the purpose of bringing home to the general mind the majesty of justice.

¶ The story of the development of our Courts of Justice is a long and interesting one. In early days the King in Council was a sort of Court of Appeal for the whole realm. ' Day and night,' says the biographer of King Alfred, ' he was busied in the correction of local injustice: for in that whole kingdom the poor had no helpers or few, save the king himself.' A hundred years after the Norman Conquest we get the real origin of Trial by Jury, and a few years later, the King's Court was divided into the still existing Courts of King's Bench, Exchequer, and Common Pleas. Another hundred years, and the Court of Chancery was established to right grievances in cases in which the rigid law became injustice. About the same time in each county, Conservators of the Peace were appointed, with the duty of seeing that the laws were enforced, and life and property secured. The powers of those local magistrates were soon extended, and they became known by the name they still bear, ' Justices of the Peace.' [1]

These institutions in our midst form a school, to which we are all sent, that we may learn to give to every one his due. And on the whole the lesson is learned almost as completely as the lesson of nature by which we in childhood are taught not to stand in the way of a falling body, or bring our hand too near the fire.

2. *Public Opinion.*—In all civilized countries the justice of the law of the land is an inheritance from many centuries. In our own law extremes of wisdom mingle, derived on the one hand from the classical nations, and on the other hand from our Teutonic ancestors. And yet, in spite of all that has been done, and is being done, from year to year, the law of the land is an imperfect embodiment of justice, and a man may all his life keep out of the clutches of the police, and yet be an extremely unjust man. There may be holes in the law of the land. And it is not always the biggest things that the law of the land has arranged for, and passed over those that are comparatively trifling. On the contrary, the law very often strains at a gnat while it swallows a camel. For instance the law will deal with you most stringently if you touch your neighbour's purse, and it may not say a word to you if you break his heart. That shows the need there is for a stricter school of justice than that of the law of the land, and it is provided by public opinion.

The law may never have one word to say to a man; yet society may know him to be guilty of deeds which it intensely despises, and will not allow to be committed with impunity. It does not fine or imprison, but it turns its back on him. He loses his character, and the doors through which access are gained to the pleasures and honours of life are shut in his face.

3. *Conscience.*—There are holes in the net woven by public opinion, just as there are in those woven by the law of the land, far worse

[1] *Belief and Life*, 1932, p. 101.

than that even. There are many cases in which public opinion commands things it ought to forbid, and in which it forbids the things that it ought to command. The appeal from it is to the conscience of the individual. If a man is doubtful about what is right and what is wrong, let him simply ask, What ought I to do? and if he is really willing to do what he knows to be right, he will very seldom be without the right answer. This often is a far sterner tribunal than either that of public opinion or the law of the land. The great interest of religion is to strengthen the conscience, so that a man may feel that in its presence he is standing before a more august judge than if he were in any Court of Law, or than if he were surrounded by a whole theatre of spectators. It was to the conscience Jesus was appealing when He said : ' Whatever ye would that men should do to you, do ye even so to them.' That is the soul of justice.

4. *The Justice of Christ.*—Jesus was the heir and successor of the prophets. He denounced wrong with a plainness never elsewhere exemplified in the world. He gave many rules of justice, and this golden rule among them. Yet that was not the principal lift He gave to justice. It is well to understand that. There are things that make it easy to give to any one his due, or even perhaps a little more than his due. When a city is favoured with a visit from royalty, all the traffic is suspended, and the citizens, with one accord, put everything they have at the service of their royal visitors. There is not a town in the world where the well-dressed do not receive more courteous treatment than the ragged. That is human nature.

What Jesus did to secure justice for the common man was to raise the estimation of the common man. None can take in the teaching of Jesus Christ without recognizing that the humblest belong to that humanity which He took into His heart, and for which He sacrificed His life. And if thus we look at our fellow-creatures through the eyes of Jesus Christ, if we see God in them, then we have a new and the finest of all reasons for treating them with justice.

¶ The French scholar, Muretus, a Protestant exile from Toulouse in the sixteenth century, fell seriously ill in Lombardy, and was taken to a pauper hospital, where he overheard the physicians who were consulting about him say in Latin, not thinking that the pauper could understand that tongue of the learned : '*Faciamus experimentum in anima vili.*' ('Let us try an experiment with this worthless creature.') And from his bed the sick scholar startled them by murmuring : '*Vilem animam appellas pro qua Christus non dedignatus est mori ?*' (Will you call worthless one for whom Christ did not disdain to die ? ')[1]

God's Sovereignty

Lam. iii. 37.—' Who is he that saith, and it cometh to pass, when the Lord commandeth it not ? '

THESE words form part of a moving elegy pronounced over a comparatively small and weak country which had been overrun and devastated by the mightiest military empire in the world in the sixth century B.C. While it is not true that history ever does exactly repeat itself, it is remarkable nevertheless how often the same kind of situation tends to recur in international relations ; for all this might have been written about Norway or Denmark or Holland to-day. Here once again we had a mighty and ruthless neighbour rushing upon a people who had given him no just cause of offence, and whose numbers and resources were utterly unequal to the task of resistance, although heroically exerted. Here, too, we saw a country overrun and pillaged, its towns and villages destroyed, its inhabitants terrorized and enslaved, its homesteads given up systematically to fire and flood. Militarism does not seem to have changed much in character in two thousand five hundred years. But the religious poet who thus sings his sad song of lamentation over the sorrow of his native land says a strange thing about it which must be equally applicable to the conditions of the present day. After specifying a number of dreadful things which he had witnessed, such as the cruel treatment of prisoners by the invader, the daily perversion of justice, and the vast amount of private tyranny that was going on, he adds, ' Who is he that saith, and it cometh to pass, when the Lord commandeth it not ? ' In other words—and surely it is a daring thing to say—none of all this could have happened except by the permission of God.

[1] H. S. Coffin.

1. Our first proposition, then, is that *the Divine Sovereign tolerates evil*. Do not imagine for a moment that evil happens in spite of God. Nothing of the sort. It could not possibly happen unless He consented that it should happen. And why does God tolerate evil ? Simply because He has given men free-will— the power of choosing right or wrong—and though men may misuse that gift, He will not take back what He has given. God might have made men mere machines, driven smoothly like perfect engines along the iron rails of destiny. But God did not want machines. He had enough mechanism in His universe. He wanted men—men made in His own image, created after His own likeness, capable of moral growth ; men who could know Him and love Him and commune with Him and obey Him and be made one with Him at last for ever. And therefore He made men free. And although men abuse that freedom to injure one another and oppose the will of God, He will not withdraw the gift that He has given.

¶ Friedrich of Germany, when dying, confessed, ' I have grown weary of ruling slaves.' And our Lord will not be satisfied with a less noble sovereignty. It is not the forced subjection of slaves that He desires, but the glad surrender of loving hearts.

God is the Sovereign King, the Moral Governor of the universe, who deals with the peoples of the earth as responsible moral beings, as free-will agents. If they choose to sin, He does not violate their free-will, but allows their sin to have its natural and inevitable fruit. The grim and ghastly tragedies being enacted in Europe and elsewhere, are but the operating of the inexorable law, ' Whatsoever a man—or nation—soweth, that shall he also reap.' The nations have sown the wind, and are reaping the whirlwind.[1]

2. Our second proposition is this. The heavenly King, it is true, tolerates evil in a measure ; but *He also exercises His power to limit and set bounds to evil*. There is a bound to the iniquity of both men and nations. They may work their evil will and prosper marvellously for a time ; then suddenly they are pulled up. They find themselves up against a decree, ' Thus far and no farther.' They are unable to go on ; and if, in spite of all resist-

[1] J. O. Sanders, *Light on Life's Problems*, 8.

ances, they persist in trying to go on, then they are courting their own destruction. Is not that the lesson of the fall of mighty empires ?

Think, for instance, of the Roman Empire in its latter days—an empire grown so corrupt that one of its own historians says, ' We have come to this pass, we can suffer neither our vices nor their remedies.' What happened ? Why, from the ends of the earth came swarming myriads of barbarians, to annihilate an empire that had become too rotten to be tolerated. And who led them to the assault ? Who marshalled those savage armies, and guided them safely on their wanderings, and concentrated them at the point where the work of vengeance was awaiting them ? Charles Kingsley has answered the question. ' Shall I not believe,' he writes in a lecture on the Gothic invasion, ' shall I not believe that, though this great war had no general on earth, it may have had a general in Heaven ; and that in spite of all their sins the hosts of our forefathers were the hosts of God ? ' Or think once again of that colossal man, Napoleon—how strong he was, how brilliant he was, how successful he was, and how unscrupulous he was. And then recollect what Victor Hugo said of Waterloo. ' Was it possible for Napoleon to win Waterloo ? We answer, No. Why ? Because of Wellington ? No. Because of Blucher ? No. Because of the rain ? No. Because of God. It was time this vast man should fall. He had been impeached before the throne of the Infinite, and his fall had been decreed.' [1]

3. This brings us to our third proposition. The Divine Sovereign proves His sovereignty most especially in this, that *He not only limits evil, but uses it for good, and actually turns it into blessing.* Now is not this a wonderful demonstration of God's power ? Who but God could compel the very wrath of man to praise Him, and make evil itself contributory to well-being ? Does this strike us as mere accident, as a mere lucky result of a chance combination of circumstances ? Do we think that it comes about anyhow—without reason and without design ? Nay rather, when we study history, and see how constantly progress is made, not only in spite of wrong, but positively by means of wrong, are we not forced to recognize a Higher Government of the universe ?

[1] F. H. Dudden, *The Heroic Dead*, 21.

Take, for instance, war itself. God is putting forth His power to bring good out of that evil. It is war that is teaching us the common-sense necessity of an enduring peace ; it is the rapid advance of scientific ingenuity under the pressure of war that is teaching the paramount importance of living together as a family, for, with its manifold devices *used* in anger *against* the family idea, hell will be let loose still hotter, and we have had enough of hell, for sure.

Amongst many other things, there is one factor that has made a world-war, such as we have experienced, possible—it is the factor of proximity. We are all living next door to each other, and in suburbia, if we are at loggerheads with our next-door neighbour, life can be pretty hideous. The proximity that makes for community, can, if handled selfishly, make for chaos. So, the selfishness rife in the midst of proximity which made the war, is making us also see the need of community. It is either co-operate and *live,* or isolate and *die.*

The ungainly mammoths of the prehistoric age have perished, and why ? They believed in isolationism, they lived solitary lives, they hunted alone. But we still have the birds, because they flock, the bees still make honey for us, because they hive, the ants still swarm the garden paths, because they live in colonies. Wiser creatures than the all-brawn-no-brain creation, they said, as it were, we will do things *together* because we shall get *more* things together. We shall be co-operators ; we shall have a federal union. And living on the basis of sharing, of community, these creatures still live busy and useful lives.

Surely the fact is becoming obvious more and more, that, as nations, we shall be unable to have anything we want unless we have it *together,* neither can we be saved at all unless we be saved *together.*[1]

¶ ' A day will come,' said Victor Hugo, ' when you, France, you, Russia, you, Italy, you England, you, Germany, all you nations of the Continent shall, without losing your distinctive characteristics and your glorious individuality, blend in a higher unity to form a European fraternity . . . a day will come when bombs and bullets shall be replaced by ballots, by the universal suffrage of the people, by the sacred arbitraments of a sovereign senate. A day will come when a cannon shall be exhibited in our

[1] N. N. G. Cope, *The Night is Ending*, 14.

museums as an intrument of torture is now, and men shall marvel that such things could ever be. A day will come when we shall see those two immense groups, the U.S.A. and the United States of Europe, extending hand in hand over the oceans exchanging their commerce, their industry, their art, their genius, clearing the earth, colonizing the deserts, ameliorating creation under the eye of the Creator.'

Then shall all shackles fall ; the stormy clangour
　Of wild war-music o'er the earth shall cease ;
Love shall tread out the baleful fire of anger,
　And in its ashes plant the tree of peace.

Self-Examination

Lam. iii. 40.—' Let us search and try our ways, and turn again to the Lord.'

THESE words suggest that we are ignorant of our real selves, and that it is only by some serious effort that we can come to a true self-knowledge, for that is what the writer implies when he represents the distressed people resolving to ' search and try ' their ways. Easy as it may seem in words, experience proves that nothing is more difficult in practice than to fulfil the precept of the philosopher, ' Know thyself.' Self-examination, honestly undertaken, is a painful task and requires a great deal of courage to carry it through. It is at the same time a difficult and delicate task. We may well find it depressing instead of bracing if we approach it in the wrong spirit.

1. The ordinary healthy-minded Briton dislikes analysing his own feelings and appraising his own worth. He prefers to live on the outside of things—decently, of course—and take his moral condition for granted. And, indeed, this is preferable to the opposite extreme—the behaviour of people who are always thinking about themselves. There is an egotism even of self-abasement. Our Lord Himself expressly and emphatically condemned this religious self-centredness. Dwelling upon one's own virtues and vices, occupying one's mind with that theme to the exclusion of all else, was, He said, only a form of self-love. That was why He condemned the Pharisees. They were too self-conscious in their religion.

¶ Richard Baxter is a past-master in the art of self-examination. No man can read Baxter's books without finding all the secrets of his soul laid bare. It is like taking a lantern and flashing its light into the cracks and crevices that have been undisturbed for years. He searches the soul until the soul cries out for mercy. But, in his later years, he makes a significant and instructive confession. ' I was once,' he says, ' wont to meditate most on my own heart, and to dwell all at home, and look little higher ; I was always poring either on my sins or wants, or examining my sincerity ; but now, though I am greatly convinced of the need of heart-acquaintance and employment, yet I see more need of a higher work ; and that I shall look oftener upon Christ, and God, and heaven, than upon my own heart.' [1]

2. Religion can have too much of what Shelley calls ' the dark idolatry of self ' which by idle self-reproach and much brooding over the past can destroy our joy and peace and our power to serve our fellows. Still, in spite of all that, self-examination is a duty. The word self-examination is not so much in use to-day as in earlier times, but it is a duty as binding to-day on all of us as in the days gone by—and a duty to be performed in a wise way.
¶ We know far more about the world to-day than our fathers did. We know a great deal more about peoples and lands far beyond the seas. We live in a world that is infinitely richer and fuller and more mysterious than the world in which they lived. What could Thomas Boston in lone Ettrick know of all the pageantry of nations ? There was no telegraph along his valley. It was but rarely that he saw a paper. And yet, is there one of us who knows as much about the human heart as he did ? We have a greater knowledge of the world than our forefathers had, but a lessened knowledge of ourselves.

By all means use sometimes to be alone ;
Salute thyself ; see what thy soul doth wear ;
Dare to look in thy chest, for 'tis thine own,
And tumble up and down what thou find'st
　　　there.[2]

It is very possible for a man to drift into ignoble ways almost without being aware of the

[1] F. W. Boreham.　　　　[2] George Herbert.

fact, until perhaps some great calamity pulls him up. There are many people who seem to think they need not trouble about the registering of moral gain and loss which is always going on. They are, on the whole, well-meaning, they may even count themselves good Christians, but they do not put forth much effort to be any different from what they are. They just go on from year to year living the life they have to live, discharging their appointed tasks, bearing their sorrows, fighting their battles with circumstances, passing through changes in business or domestic relationships, but hardly ever pausing to ask how the inner life is going on. And yet it is going on ; no more than the outer man does the inner man remain the same from day to day. It is sometimes said that temperament never alters, that native disposition never undergoes any radical change from the cradle to the grave ; and, no doubt, that is true ; but it is not true of character. Character is altering all the time for better or worse in its reaction upon all that enters into experience. We are all rather apt to assume that that is not so in an ordinary way because we do not feel it, the changes take place so subtly, so insensibly. Every word we have spoken, the thoughts we have harboured, every deed, mean or magnanimous, that we have done, have been depositing themselves under the surface of our personality, and there building up character. And one day it will be matured and finished ; and we be ready for the destiny which is inevitable for that into which we have made ourselves.

> Fool ! All that is, at all,
> Lasts ever, past recall ;
> Earth changes, but thy soul and God stand sure :
> What entered into thee,
> *That* was, is, and shall be.

' Let us search and try our ways.' Whither are we going ? What is our life tending towards ? We have each a history—what kind of a history is it ? We have a character of our own—what is its quality ? We are thrown into all sorts of relationships with our fellow-men—how do we conduct ourselves in the midst of them ? Who is the better or the happier for our being in this world ? If we were to pass our motives and conduct in review for even one day, how much could we say was according to the mind of Christ ? Could we honestly challenge His in-

spection ? The years pass rapidly ; and meanwhile—what are we making of them ? Our life —what does it look like ? Our character—what is its influence ? We can take the name of Christ upon our lips and be a stranger to Him in our heart. Let us be true with ourselves ; as we must be true with Him whether we will or no. Let us make sure that He dwells in us, that He is sovereign of our soul, that there is nothing in our life which is in conflict with His blessed will.

> Only the rays of God can cure the heart,
> Purge it of evil ; there's no other way,
> Except to turn with the whole heart to God.

Unanswered Prayer

Lam. iii. 44.—' Thou hast covered thyself with a cloud, that our prayer should not pass through.'

' To a beginner in the high art of praying,' writes Dr Fosdick, ' the Bible is often a very disheartening book. Its characters appear at first sight to enjoy the uninterrupted experience of answered prayer. The refrain of the Psalmist seems typical : " Thou hast given him his heart's desire, thou hast not withholden the request of his lips." If the Bible, however, knew no other experience with prayer than the enjoyment of successful petition, it would be a Book utterly inadequate to meet our needs. One of the sorest trials of our faith is petition unanswered. It is worth our notice, therefore, that the Bible itself records the experiences of ungranted prayer. Even in the Psalms one finds not alone jubilant gratitude over petitions won but despondent sorrow over petitions denied : " O my God, I cry in the day-time, but thou answerest not ; and in the night season, and am not silent." Indeed, upon examination, the Bible turns out to be full of unanswered prayers. Moses prays to enter the Promised Land, but dies on Nebo's top, his request refused. In the midst of national calamity the patriot lifts his lamentation, " Thou hast covered thyself with a cloud, that our prayer should not pass through." '

When thus we are afflicted with perplexity, questionings arise in the mind as to whether we have any right to expect that our prayers should be heard. There are those who assure us that to pray with the hope of any objective result is a mistake, for the entire universe is bound together by laws which cannot be broken. Prayer may benefit the inner life of those who pray, but how are we to expect the course of outward events to be changed to suit our pleasure or convenience? God is the Almighty Ruler of the universe, the author of those laws by which the world is sustained; but so great a God cannot stoop to consult our petty and capricious desires. We must accept our lot and bear it. But from this view our soul revolts. We feel that prayer, even in the sense of petition, is an instinct. Certainly it is wonderful that God should interest Himself in our affairs, but were He unable or even unwilling to do this, He could not be our God. Moreover, we have evidence in the recorded lives of others and in our own unrecorded experience that God does answer prayer, and this only makes it the more difficult to understand why some of our requests have been denied.[1]

1. In some cases the difficulty will yield to a little reflection. Often the answer does not come, *because we fail to do our part.* We pray earnestly for an object, and we wait in expectation that the object will fall into our hands. But we must never forget to use the means which God has provided.

(1) Only when we are exercising the *intelligence* God has given us can we ask for Divine aid. Is it not clear that if, as in fairy-tales, we had the power of omnipotent wishing conferred upon us, we never would use our intelligence at all? If life is to mean development and discipline, some things must be impossible until men think, no matter how hard men pray. If a boy asks his father to work out his arithmetic lesson because he wishes to play, will the father do it? The father loves the boy; he could work out the lesson, but he must not. The boy's prayer must never be made a substitute for his intellectual discipline. The father, in answer to the boy's request, may encourage him, assist him, stand by him and see him through; but the father must not do for the boy anything that the boy can possibly do for himself. Harsh though at times it may seem, God surely must require us as individuals and as a race to endure the discipline of painful enterprise and struggle, rather than find an easy relief by asking.[2]

[1] J. Colville, *The Christian Optimist*, 103.
[2] H. E. Fosdick, *The Meaning of Prayer*, 127.

(2) Again, it is only when we are using all our *strength* that we can claim the help of omnipotence. God's help is an aid to earnest effort, not a substitute for it. Even the old Greek wrestler understood this truth when he prayed before the contest: 'If all things, O Jupiter, are rightly prepared on my part, and if I have done all that I could do, then do me justice and give me the victory.'

¶ A young student, on learning that one of his professors began work every morning at six o'clock, said he had often wished to do the same, and had sometimes thought of asking God's help in prayer. He questioned the professor as to whether he ever made it a matter of prayer. 'No,' replied the professor, 'I just get up.'

2. Again, some of our petitions are refused *because they are unwise.* We do not always know what is best. We are like children, short-sighted, foolish, and ignorant, not knowing what we ask. Our Heavenly Father, because He loves us, must refuse our prayer. James and John in an excess of emotion asked Christ if He would grant that they might sit the one on His right hand and the other on His left hand in His Kingdom, and Christ told them plainly that they did not know the meaning of their words. We have all offered these foolish prayers, and have lived to thank God that they were never answered. We asked for a gift that was denied, and we see now that we have been far better without it. We prayed to be delivered from what we thought would be a great calamity, but God did not heed our cry, and we found that the dark cloud was big with blessing. At the time our faith almost failed, but now we have learned patience. We can understand the confession of an aged saint: 'With one exception I have lived to know that every time God denied my supplication He was right and I was wrong, and some day I expect that the mystery of this one exception will be cleared up as well.' We are now prepared to say:

O God, what things are good alway,
  Sought or unsought, supply;
But when for what is ill we pray,
  These things always deny.

3. Once more, God sometimes denies us our request *in order that He may bestow upon us a*

richer blessing. He is able to do exceeding abundantly above all that we ask or think. A man prays for an appointment which he greatly desires, and when his petition is not granted, and another steps in before him, his faith falters, his feet well-nigh slip. But with the afterlook of years he can see that to have received that appointment would have meant exclusion for ever from the far happier course his life has pursued. He sees that God has provided some better thing for him, and he is glad that his short-sighted prayer remained unanswered. There is in the life of Christ an illustration of this truth. Lazarus, the friend of Jesus, was sick, and Mary, feeling certain that if Christ knew He would come, sent a message : ' Lord, he whom thou lovest is sick.' Doubtless she expected that Christ would at once come to the bedside of His friend. But when Christ received the message He abode two days in the place where He was. Were they tempted to think Christ callous and indifferent ? Would this temptation not be deepened when Lazarus died ? What were the feelings that surged into their hearts when they beheld the lifeless form of their brother ? Did they for the moment lose their faith in the absent Christ and doubt His friendship ? When He came, Mary said, ' Lord, if thou hadst been here my brother had not died.' And then Christ answered the meaning of their prayer far more wonderfully than they could ever have expected. They had hoped that He would come at once and cure their brother. But when He came He raised him from the dead. In this way does Christ sometimes come into all our lives, more wondrously than we had ever dared to hope ; and, withholding the gift for which we prayed, He loads us with His benefits. ' So find we profit by losing of our prayers.'

And yet there are cases of unanswered prayer which these explanations will not meet. A man makes his prayer to God, and so far as he can see at the time his prayer is not unwise. The passing of the years does not convince him of its folly. He does his very best, and he feels that there is no greater blessing he can desire. But God remains silent. The man, baffled and dismayed, goes out into the lonely wilderness of unbelief, where the sky is grey and the wind is chill and piercing, and where he misses the light and comfort which the presence of the great Companion brings. Because that prayer remains unanswered, and perhaps must for ever remain unanswered in this present mortal life, he cuts himself off from so much that is beautiful and helpful and true. Would it not be wiser to have patience with God ? He has so often in the past been right. May it not be that here also He is doing all things well ? We are still in the valley, and much is dim to our eyes, but everything will be clearer when we reach the crest of the hill, and see shining before us the gates of the city of God. As we look back over the strange and perplexing path of life along which we have been led, we shall be able to see what now is often hidden from our eyes—that all that happened to us was for the best. Meanwhile we must learn to give God time, we must wait patiently for Him, and when clouds and darkness are round about us, we must offer this prayer :—

Teach me to feel that Thou art always nigh,
  Teach me the struggles of the soul to bear,
To check the rising doubt, the rebel sigh,
  Teach me the patience of unanswered prayer.[1]

De Profundis

Lam. iii. 57.—' Thou drewest near in the **day that I** called upon thee : thou saidst, Fear not.'

1. THE writer is recalling a time of great distress in his life. What his precise experience was we do not know. As it shapes itself to his memory, he says that he was in ' the lowest dungeon.' The phrase suggests the thought of the Hebrew *Sheol.* So dark was his experience that it seemed to him as if he had indeed been plunged into the very abode of the dead. Yet here he found utterance for prayer. While in this most wretched state he cried to God for help, and, as he now recollects for his present encouragement, he received a distinct and unmistakable answer. There was a Divine voice in response to this cry to God. It consisted of but two words, but these two words were clear and definite, and quite sufficient to satisfy the listener. The voice said, ' Fear not.' That was enough.

Does God answer prayer ? Who is to decide ? Why should this man say so if He hadn't ? Who is the best judge of whether a man's prayer is answered—the sceptical psychologist

[1] J. Colville, *The Christian Optimist*, 103.

or the man himself ? What does it matter whether a man's theory of how a thing happens be right or wrong, as long as it happens ? ' Thou heardest my voice ; thou drewest near in the day that I called upon thee : thou saidst, Fear not.'

¶ Some time ago the Abbé Brémond, one of the most spiritual minds in France, said in *The Spectator,* ' I remember well the stupefaction with which we in France realized by the publication at the beginning of the twentieth century of William James's *Varieties of Religious Experience,* that prayer had now become an object of science.' But the fact of prayer is ten times as important as the theory of it. Theories don't alter facts : though facts often alter theories. Therefore pray : for ' more things are wrought by prayer than this world dreams of.' [1]

¶ ' A Fleet Street friend has been turning up the file of *The Morning Post* for 1899–1900, and has discovered Mr Churchill's description of his experience after his capture by the Boers and his escape from Pretoria. He says that in the chilling reaction of the day after his escape, faced with hunger and the likelihood of recapture, he found no comfort in philosophical ideas, which seemed only fair-weather friends. " I realized with awful force that no exercise of my own feeble wit and strength could save me from my enemies, and that, without the assistance of that High Power which interferes more often than we are always prone to admit in the eternal sequence of causes and effects, I could never succeed. I prayed long and earnestly for help and guidance. My prayer, as it seems to me, was swiftly and wonderfully answered. . . ." ' [2]

2. Most frequently, no doubt, the answer to prayer is not vocal, and yet the reality of it may not be any the less certain to the seeking soul. It may be most definite, although it comes in a deed rather than in a word. Then the grateful recipient can say with the psalmist :

This poor man cried, and the Lord heard him, And saved him out of all his troubles.

But the more important truth to be considered is that in some way, if only by spiritual impression, God does most really speak to His children, and that He speaks now as surely as He spoke in the days of Israel. We have no new prophets and apostles who can give us fresh revelations in the form of additions to our Bible. But that is not what is meant. The poet did not receive a statement of doctrine in answer to his prayer. The voice to which he here alludes was of quite a different character.

This was in bygone days ; but if then, why not also now ? Evidently this writer regarded it as a rare and special occurrence—a single experience to which he looked back in after years with the interest one feels in a vivid recollection which rises like a mountain, clear cut against the sky, above the mists that so quickly gather on the low plains of the un-eventful past. Perhaps it is only in one of the crises of life that such an indubitable message is sent—when the soul is in the lowest dungeon, *in extremis,* crying out of the darkness, over-whelmed, almost extinguished. But if we listened for it, who can tell but that the voice might not be so rare ? We do not believe in it ; therefore we do not hear it. Or the noisy clamour of the world and the busy thoughts of our own hearts drown the music that still floats down from heaven to ears that are tuned to catch its notes ; for it does not come in thunder, and we must ourselves be still if we would hear the still small voice, inwardly still, still in soul, closing our ears to the din of the world. There are those to-day who tell us with calm assurance, not at all in the visionary's falsetto notes, that they have known just what is here described by the poet—in the silence of the hills, in the quiet of a sick room, even in the noisy crowd at a railway station.

3. The message which this man received was wholly reassuring—' Fear not.' That was said to Abraham ; it was said to Joshua, and to David, and to the prophets. Our Lord Himself said it. It was whispered to St Paul through the Holy Spirit. It runs like a golden thread of courage and hope through the whole of the Scriptures. This is the word that God is continually speaking to His faint-hearted children. When ' the burthen of the mystery,' and

the heavy and the weary weight Of all this unintelligible world

oppress, when the greater sorrows threaten to

[1] H. E. Brierley.
[2] A. G. Sleep in *The Christian World,* May 22, 1941.

crush outright, listening for the voice of God, we may hear the message of love from a Father's heart as though spoken afresh to each of us; for we have but to acquaint ourselves with Him to be at peace.

Our troubles are never overwhelming if we believe that God hears our cry. Many of our prayers are like voices thrown out in the dark. We are not sure that they reach the ears of the all-pitiful One. We are never in doubt about the answer if we are only sure about the hearing. We are afraid that the prayer may be lost on its way in the multitude of prayers that go up to Him. If it reaches Him we can leave the rest. For the love which condescends to hear will never refuse to help. There was one who said long time ago : ' I know that thou hearest me always.' And in that word He told the secret of His peace. He had troubles manifold, heartbreaking ; but He rose above them. He had a thousand things to bring Him fear and darken His path with clouds and shadows. Yet never, except perhaps once, in the Garden, did He know what fear meant. His fears looked into the Father's face and were lightened and dispersed. ' I know that thou hearest me always.' That was where He found strength, deliverance and joy.

¶ ' There is no justice,' Olive Schreiner asserts ; ' all things are driven about by blind chance.' Mr John Davidson rings out the same hopeless strain—' The years went slowly by ; but still to me the universe was dumb.' But their dismal creed is not true. God lives. God hears. God answers me.

The poet does not recall this scene from his past life merely in order to indulge in the pleasures of memory. His object is to find encouragement for renewed hope in the efficacy of prayer. He who was so gracious to the cry of His servant on that ever-memorable occasion will surely attend again to the appeal of distress. This is always the greatest encouragement for seeking help from God. It is difficult to find much satisfaction in what is called ' the philosophy of prayer.' The great justification for prayer is the experience of prayer. It is only the prayerless man who is wholly sceptical on this subject. The man of prayer cannot but believe in prayer ; and the more he prays and the oftener he turns to this refuge in all times of need the fuller is his assurance that God hears and answers him.

The Book of Lamentations

Lam. iv. 9.—' They that be slain with the sword are better than they that be slain with hunger.'

THERE is a Book in the Bible which, I am afraid, we very seldom open. I mean the Book of Lamentations. It may be that the title ' Lamentations ' rather keeps us off the book. We don't want to read a book of Lamentations, just as we call Jeremiah ' a Jeremiah,' and are apt to take not very much more interest in what he may say. And yet, it is a great loss to us. First of all the sheer beauty of the book is a thing to wonder at. It may very well be that in the piping times of peace it offended us to read a book so full of grief and the memory of unutterable cruelties ; but it is a Book to be read in these days. Again and again you will be impressed by its contemporary value, because, to put it in a word, the book of Lamentations celebrates the most staggering events in the history of God's people. We simply cannot imagine what the Captivity meant to the people of Israel. There are verses in it that give us an idea of the kind of horror of that time : ' They that be slain with the sword are better than they that be slain with hunger : for these pine away, stricken through for want of the fruits of the field. The hands of the pitiful women have sodden their own children : they were their meat in the destruction of the daughter of my people.'

1. We cannot realize—although we can better realize than we could have done a few years ago —what this meant to God's own people. Like every people of the earth they believed, of course, in their own security, and they had more reason than others to believe in their own security, because they had been most marvellously cared for throughout their history. And it did seem from a political point of view, that they were safe. So long as they kept clear of Egypt, Assyria would let them alone, and so long as they kept clear of Assyria, Egypt would let them alone ; and so by remaining neutral they defended their own security. But a day came when they went against the guidance of the earlier Isaiah.

First the ten tribes were carried into captivity, and later on, about 600 B.C., Judah and Benjamin followed.

You have only to read some of the deeper Psalms to see how the iron had entered into the soul of the people of God ; how every promise of God seemed to have been contradicted. It was a time that shook the faith of Israel to its very centre and basis. May it never return. I have no doubt at all that had our latest enemies triumphed, it would have shaken and destroyed the faith of thousands or millions of people up and down the earth. It would be wrong, but it would be the fact. The Captivity would have that effect upon unnumbered souls in the day in which it happened. They either said, ' There is no God,' or ' We cannot understand God's ways at all.' ' Here are we,' they said, ' this little country. We have a higher ethic than any country round about us. We have our sins —of course we have our sins, but they are not the sins of Babylon and Egypt. And here are we, under the supervision of God, wiped away as by a mighty wave, literally wiped out.' Because that was the method those great empires took. They found that, instead of sending expedition after expedition into a country which they had once conquered, the easier way was to carry the population into their own country and make them slaves, and to send some of their own people to colonize the vanquished territory. By this means a double consequence was secured. First of all, an element, which might have proved troublesome away at the frontier, was brought close at hand and made to work, and secondly, a new people was sent to the far-off place, a people which was bound by all the ties of affection and sentiment to the empire itself.

2. Before the Exile, the religion of Israel was very much a natural religion. After the Exile, it is a spiritual religion which reached its perfect expression in the Christ of history. And that is how we learn anything ; we learn by a process of contradiction and disillusionment. You find allusions to the consequences of that great event up and down the Book.

There is the consequence of sheer unbelief. When a dark thing comes our way the first danger is a danger of sheer unbelief, and that happened. You find it in the wisdom books of the Bible, Ecclesiastes, and many of the Proverbs ; a kind of feeling that in this world the fewer swelling words we use the better. A day at a time. Live at peace with all men. Don't entertain any very extravagant hopes. Don't commit yourself very much beyond where you can step back again. Go cautiously. As it happeneth to the wise man so it happeneth to the fool.

And secondly, the terrific pressure of that time raised in finer minds the great problem of the nature of the government of this world. Is there a loving God at the back of things ? That, of course, is the great controversy of the Book of Job. The element of over-throw is an element that remains in life.

There was another result which you find in the later Isaiah—a material consequence. These other two are rather in the region of theology, but in the region of natural life there were other consequences. After they were carried away captive into Babylon, most people quite frankly abandoned their religion. They were tempted as people are tempted who come from a strict little village and emigrate to another country that has a different religion, and live in its great godless cities. Many of them never dreamed of going back. They did not want to go back. We have no hesitation at all in saying that the Exile ruined them morally and religiously. What is our little God in Jerusalem, they asked, compared with the god of the Babylonians ? What is our little country church compared with the inconceivable monuments of Babylon ? (Alexander the Great was so fascinated by Babylon that he could not leave it, and was ruined there.)

The ten tribes, so to speak, were lost. They do not appear in history again. Where they are we don't know. There are those who think that we are they. But my own impression is that the great masses of them were absorbed, that is to say, they married and intermarried amongst the old empires and were lost ; and thus you can trace the Jewish cast of countenance in all the Oriental peoples.

3. These, then, were some of the consequences of that shaking event in history, and these, undoubtedly, are the dangers which beset us in this time in which we are living. These are the voices which will speak to us—the tendency to unbelief, the tendency to secularism, the tendency to a kind of cosmopolitanism. These are the very dangers which are going to beset us. Along what line is our true duty ?

Well, again and again the final truth dawns

upon a prophet, notably upon Jonah—making that little book perhaps the most precious in the whole Word of God, the most near to the Cross of Christ. In the Book of Jonah we have what I seem to see as God's guidance to us after a time of world-shaking disaster. What is it ? *Foreign Missions !* It dawns upon one or two men : What if God scatter us in order that He might perpetuate us ? What if God has lifted us out of our little securities ? What if He broke all our little traditions of which we are so proud ? *That* dawned upon Jonah, He saw that not only is there no respect of persons with God, but there is no respect of *places* with God. That the God of Jerusalem is not the God of Jerusalem unless He is the God of the whole earth. No nation has the monopoly of God. A nation belongs to God ; God does not belong to a nation. *That* you will find most perfectly in Jonah. ' The word of the Lord came to Jonah.

. . . Go, preach in Nineveh.' ' Preach in Nineveh ! ' said Jonah, ' Nineveh, that trampled us under foot, that outraged and violated us all. Preach in Nineveh ! Never ! ' and he set off in the opposite direction. But he had to preach in Nineveh !

That seems to be the Word of God to people like ourselves standing in the midst of the shaking events which we have witnessed and have borne. We, also, shall be tempted to think that God doesn't care. All manner of temptations will beset us. The line of our duty and the line of our deeper insight is this : that the God we were worshipping all the time belongs not to us. We belong to Him. We are here not to make our religion a luxury. We are here to make our religion a passion, a crusade.[1]

JOHN A. HUTTON.

[1] *The British Weekly*, Nov. 8, 1945.

THE BOOK OF JEREMIAH

COMMENTARIES FOR REFERENCE

BALL, C. J., *The Prophecies of Jeremiah* [The Expositor's Bible] (1890).

BENNETT, W. H., *The Book of Jeremiah*, xxi.-lii. [The Expositor's Bible] (1895).

BINNS, L. E., *The Book of the Prophet Jeremiah* [Westminster Commentaries] (1919).

CHEYNE, T. K., *Jeremiah: his Life and Times* (1888).

DRIVER, S. R., *The Book of the Prophet Jeremiah: A Revised Translation* (1906).

GREEN, E. T., *The Book of Jeremiah and Lamentations* [The Temple Bible].

LEWIS, H. E., *The Book of the Prophet Jeremiah: a Devotional Commentary* (1924).

LOFTHOUSE, W. F., *Jeremiah* (1925).

PEAKE, A. S., *Jeremiah and Lamentations* [The Century Bible] (1910).

ROBINSON, H. W., *The Cross of Jeremiah* (1926).

—— in *Peake's Commentary on the Bible* (1919).

SKINNER, J., *Prophecy and Religion* (1922).

SMITH, G. A., *Jeremiah* (1929).

STREANE, A. W., *The Book of the Prophet Jeremiah together with the Lamentations* [Cambridge Bible] (1913).

THOMSON, W. R., *The Burden of the Lord* (1919).

WELCH, A. C., *Jeremiah: a Study*.

INDEX TO SERMONS

I. 11.

Newton, J. F., *The Sword of the Spirit*, 160.
Christian Commonwealth, xxxviii. (1918) 205 (J. F. Newton).
Christian World Pulpit, lxxvii. 250 (F. Birch); xciv. 169 (J. E. Rattenbury); cxiii. 225 (W. H. Condy); cxxiv. 239 (G. H. Wright).
Commonwealth, xv. (1910) 31 (G. A. Purton).
Examiner, July 26, 1906 (J. H. Jowett).

I. 11, 12.

Bowen, W. E., *In the Beginning*, 11.
Jowett, J. H., *The Eagle Life*, 112.
Sykes, T., *The Price of Providence*, 26.
Christian World Pulpit, lxxxvi. 78 (J. H. Bodgener).
Life and Work, 1912, p. 193 (R. S. Calderwood).

I. 18.

Jowett, J. H., *The Eagle Life*, 116.
Christian World Pulpit, cxliv. 180 (W. L. Wooding).

II. 2, 3.

Black, H., *Christ's Service of Love*, 316.

II. 12, 13.

Christian World Pulpit, cxxvi. 241 (C. Brown).

II. 13.

Boreham, F. W., *A Faggot of Torches*, 203.
Jeffrey, G. J., *Christian Resources*, 75.
Meyer, F. B., *Jeremiah*, 24.
Christian World, Sept. 3, 1914 (J. H. Jowett).
Examiner, Oct. 19, 1905 (J. H. Jowett).
Guardian, lxxiv. (1919) 157 (A. V. Baillie); lxxxv. (1930) 742 (H. A. Wilson).

II. 26.

Black, H., *University S.*, 153.

II. 28.

Fosdick H. E., *Living under Tension*, 134.
Christian World, Nov. 23, 1939 (H. E. Fosdick).

II. 33.

Young, D. T., *The Travels of the Heart*, 237.

II. 36.

Rutherford, W. G., *The Key of Knowledge*, 30.

III.–VI.

Meyer, F. B., *Jeremiah*, 32.

III. 19.

Drummond, R. J., *Faith's Certainties*, 149.
Iverach, J., *The Other Side of Greatness*, 68.
Christian World Pulpit, lxiii. 257 (J. T. Forbes).

IV. 1, 2.

Christian World Pulpit, cxxiii. 124 (A. J. Russell).

IV. 2.

Christian World Pulpit, cxi. 235 (P. C. Simpson).

IV. 11.

Selby, T. G., *The Imperfect Angel*, 397.

IV. 19.

Christian World Pulpit, liii. 356 (J. M. Lang).

IV. 30.

Christian World Pulpit, xcii. 17 (E. Beal).

V.

Christian World Pulpit, xli. 12 (R. F. Horton).

V. 1.

Thomson T. B. S., *The Quest of Youth*, 138.
Warr, C. L., *Scottish S. and Addresses*, 142.
Christian World Pulpit, xxviii. 276 (W. M. Arthur); xxxvii. 117 (J. R. M. Mitchell); cxiv. 35 (G. B. Dibden); cxvi. 98 (E. R. Squire).

V. 1, 2.

Almond, H. H., *Christ the Protestant*, 118.

V. 1–5.

Christian World Pulpit, cxl. 36 (J. Pickthall).

V. 10.

Brooks, P., *The Law of Growth*, 80.
Hutton, J. A., *Discerning the Times*, 238.
Morrison, G. H., *The Wind on the Heath*, 30.

V. 22.

Mills, B. R. V., *The Marks of the Church*, 129.

V. 23–25.

Christian World Pulpit, lxxi. 113 (H. H. Henson).

V. 24.
Davies, T., *Sermons*, ii. 162.
Christian World Pulpit, lxxviii. 156 (P. White-hurst) ; cxl. 119 (A. W. Poulson).

V. 30, 31.
Christian World Pulpit, lxx. 161 (H. H. Henson).

V. 31.
Black, H., *According to My Gospel*, 102.
Figgis, J. N., *Some Defects in English Religion*, 29.
Horton, R. F., " *This Do*," 35.
Christian World Pulpit, cxxvii. 114 (F. H. Ballard).
Church Times, Aug. 25, 1916 (J. N. Figgis).

VI. 14.
Fosdick, H. E., *The Hope of the World*, 165.
British Weekly, Aug. 28, 1930 (H. E. Kirk).
Christian World, Jan. 27, 1944 (L. E. Cooke).
Christian World Pulpit, xxxviii. 45 (C. S. Horne); liii. 99 (R. Leggat) ; xcii. 185 (D. Robertson).
Expositor, xxviii. (1927) 473 (W. G. Kennedy).
Jewish Chronicle, Aug. 27, 1915.

VI. 16.
Fosdick, H. E., *The Power to See It Through*, 237.
Gray, W. H., *Old Creeds and New Beliefs*, 1.
Greenhough, J. G., *Half-Hours in God's Older Picture Gallery*, 202.
Horne, C. S., in *S. and Addresses*, 24.
Shelford, L. E., *By Way of Remembrance*, 143.
Christian World Pulpit, lxxvii. 7 (R. Borland) ; lxxx. 409 (H. W. Slader) ; lxxxii. 164 (R. Key) ; cxxxiv. 99 (W. S. Scott) ; cxl. 182 (W. E. B. Taylor) ; cxli. 57 (R. Griffiths).
Church Times, May 21, 1909 (E. Talbot).
Guardian, lxxvii. (1922) 997 (J. H. Bernard).

VI. 19.
Black, H., *University S.*, 304.
British Congregationalist, Sept. 29, 1910 (H. W. Clark).
Christian World Pulpit, cxxv. 303 (B. R. H. Spaull).

VI. 29, 30.
Aitken, W. H. M. H., *Temptation and Toil*, 275.
Christian World Pulpit, liv. 170 (P. R. Frothing-ham).

VII. 2.
Christian World Pulpit, cxliii. 85 (G. M. Wylie).

VII. 3–7.
Christian World Pulpit, cxliv. 134 (A. L. Thomas).

VII. 24.
Robinson, J. W., *Sunlit Hopes*, 239.

VII.–X.
Meyer, F. B., *Jeremiah*, 39.

VIII. 4.
Watkinson, W. L., *The Ashes of Roses*, 63.

VIII. 7.
Dale, W., *Short Studies on Bible Subjects*, 1.
Kerr, H. T., *Old Things New*, 124.
Christian World Pulpit, cxxx. 80 (H. G. Jones) ; cxxxii. 244 (A. E. Phillips).

VIII. 8.
Christian World Pulpit, lxxxii. 401 (H. E. Lewis).

VIII. 11.
Figgis, J. N., *Some Defects in English Religion*, 40.
Fosdick, H. E., *The Hope of the World*, 164.
British Weekly, Aug. 28, 1930 (H. E. Kirk).
Church Times, Sept. 1, 1916 (J. N. Figgis).

VIII. 18.
Horne, C. S., *The Rock of Ages*, 221.

VIII. 20.
Roberts, W. Page, *True Religion*, 106.
Tipple, S. A., *Sunday Mornings at Norwood*, 39.
Christian World Pulpit, lxviii. 177 (J. Parker) ; lxxviii. 155 (W. B. Moss) ; xcviii. 249 (N. C. Raad) ; cii. 188 (F. R. Swan) ; cxvi. 260 (W. A. Headey).

VIII. 21, 22.
Christian World Pulpit, xxxvi. 328 (W. M. Sinclair).

VIII. 22.

Heron, J., *A Large Place*, 232.
Jeffrey, G. J., *Christian Resources*, 52.
Whitelaw, T., *Jehovah-Jesus*, 49.
Christian World Pulpit, xlvi. 301 (A. A. Toms).
Experience, viii. (1916) 161 (A. J. French).

IX. 1.

Christian World Pulpit, cxxxii. 265 (E. B. Storr).

IX. 2.

Moffatt, J., *Reasons and Reasons*, 45.
Morrison, G. H., *The Unlighted Lustre*, 102.
Christian World Pulpit, xxxvi. 273 (G. A. Smith) ; lxxxi. 301 (J. L. Munro) ; civ. 78 (C. F. Aked).

IX. 3.

Jowett, J. H., *The Eagle Life*, 138.

IX. 23, 24.

Addis, W. E., in *The Verities of Religion*, 103.
Christian World Pulpit, xxxvi. 300 (A. Le Marchant) ; xxxvii. 150 (J. P. Gledstone) ; xliv. 122 (A. E. Tonkin) ; lxxxii. 167 (W. D. Crane) ; lxxxix. 21 (J. Jones) ; cii. 259 (F. C. Spurr).

IX. 24.

Christian World Pulpit, cxix. 49.

X. 2.

Christian World Pulpit, cxxxvi. 135 (W. C. Timmons).

X. 10.

Figgis, J. N., *Antichrist*, 119.
Experience, xiii. (1921) 98 (W. J. May).

X. 11.

Farmer, H. H., *The Healing Cross*, 1.

X. 15.

Macgregor, W. M., in *The Professor as Preacher*, 161.

X. 19.

Ainsworth, P. C., *A Thornless World*, 18.
Christian World Pulpit, xci. 117 (W. H. Hamilton).

X. 19, 20.

Watkinson, W. L., *Themes for Hours of Meditation*, 44.
Weatherhead, L., *The Eternal Voice*, 180.
Homiletic Review, lvi. 211 (W. L. Watkinson).

XI. 5.

Meyer, F. B., *Jeremiah*, 48.

XII. 5.

Black, H., *Edinburgh S.*, 267.
Gossip, A. J., *The Hero in Thy Soul*, 106.
Jerdan, C., *The Wells of Salvation*, 83.
Macmillan, E., *Finding and Following*, 133.
Meyer, F. B., *Jeremiah*, 58.
Ranken, W. H., *Faith and Duty*, 150.
Watkinson, W. L., *Themes for Hours of Meditation*, 107.
Whyte, A., *With Mercy and with Judgment*, 263.
Christian Commonwealth, xxxiv. (1913) 57 (R. J. Campbell).
Christian World Pulpit, cxxiii. 86 (J. Colville) ; cxxxviii. 138 (R. E. McIntyre).
Experience, viii. (1915) 44 (A. Barraclough).
Methodist Times, June 18, 1925 (F. W. Boreham).

XII. 9.

Watkinson, W. L., *The Ashes of Roses*, 12.

XIII. 16.

Macbeath, J., *The Hills of God*, 149.

XIII. 20.

Christian World Pulpit, cv. 266 (D. T. Young) ; cvi. 18 (R. F. Horton).

XIII. 23.

Banks, L. A., *The Sinner and his Friends*, 240.
Burns, J., *Laws of the Upward Life*, 162.
Lennard, V. R., *Our Ideals*, 100.
Mackay, D. S., *The Religion of the Threshold*, 105.
Mackay, W. M., *Problems in Living*, 53.
Speirs, E. B., *A Present Advent*, 51.
Stephen, R., *Divine and Human Influence*, i. 219.
Expositor, xlv. (1943) 286 (J. S. Rhine).
Christian World Pulpit, xlix. 198 (J. Stalker) ; lii. 205 (A. Brooke) ; lxix. 88 (L. T. Dodd).

XIV.
Meyer, F. B., *Jeremiah*, 66.

XIV. 8.
Moody, C. N., *Love's Long Campaign*, 12.
British Weekly, July 16, 1931 (A. B. Scott).
Christian World Pulpit, cvii. 54 (J. T. Inskip) ;
  cx. 193 (G. S. Russell) ; cxvi. 126 (H. Cook).

XIV. 8, 9.
Christian World Pulpit, xxxvi. 273 (G. A. Smith).

XIV. 9.
King, G. H., in *The Keswick Convention*, 1932, p. 99.

XIV. 10.
Christian World Pulpit, cxiv. 255 (T. R. Williams).

XIV. 21.
Jack, J., *A Great National Question*, 101.

XV.
Meyer, F. B., *Jeremiah*, 66.

XV. 17.
Hislop, D. H., in *United Free Church S.*, 80.

XV. 18.
Fosdick, H. E., *Successful Christian Living*, 55.

XV. 19.
Mackay, W. M., *Words of This Life*, 211.

XV. 19, 20.
Snell, B. J., *Gain or Loss ?*, 93.

XVI. 14, 15.
Christian World Pulpit, xci. 34 (A. C. Hill) ;
  cxx. 244 (D. D. Smith).

XVI. 20.
Fosdick, H. E., *Living Under Tension*, 134.

XVII. 1.
Stanton, A. H., *Faithful Stewardship*, 103.

XVII. 1, 7.
Christian World Pulpit, cxix. 106 (W. T. Burkitt).

XVII. 5.
Hutton, R. E., *The Crown of Christ*, i. 217.

XVII. 5–8.
Aitken, W. H. M. H., *God's Everlasting Yea*, 45.

XVII. 6, 8.
Maclaren, A., *Triumphant Certainties*, 241.

XVII. 7.
Pearse, M. G., *The Gospel for the Day*, 75.
Expository Times, xlviii. 325 (W. Macdonald).

XVII. 7, 8.
Christian World Pulpit, cxxxvi. 243 (R. Griffiths).
Experience, xii. (1920) 71 (A. J. French).

XVII. 9.
Christian Commonwealth, xxxiv. (1914) 649 (R. J. Campbell).

XVII. 9, 10.
Ryle, J. C., *The Christian Race*, 1.

XVII. 12.
Banks, L. A., *Sermons which have won Souls*, 381.

XVII. 15.
Christian World Pulpit, cxvii. 97 (G. Shillito).

XVIII. 1, 2.
Mitchell, D. C., *The Nonsense of Neutrality*, 50.
Christian World Pulpit, lxxviii. 380 (J. M. Munro) ; cxxxviii. 70 (H. Derbyshire).

XVIII. 1–4.
Thomas, J., S. (*Myrtle Street Pulpit*), iv. 337.
Christian World Pulpit, cxxxiii. 265 (W. K. Burford).
Church Family Newspaper, Oct. 1, 1909 (Canon Barnes-Lawrence).

XVIII. 1–6.
Banks, L. A., *Sermons which have won Souls*, 59.
Holden, J. S., *Supposition and Certainty*, 29.
Record of Christian Work, 1917, p. 280 (J. Gardner).

XVIII. 1–10.
Expositor, iv. 469 (E. H. Plumptre).

XVIII. 2.

Black, J., in *The Scottish Pulpit*, 11.

XVIII. 2–4.

Carroll, J. S., *The Motherhood of God*, 138.
Ingram, A. F. W., *The Potter and the Clay*, 3.
Christian World Pulpit, lxxxix. 97 (A. F. W. Ingram).

XVIII. 2–6.

Christian World Pulpit, lxxxi. 214 (W. Harvey-Jellie).

XVIII. 3.

Duke, J. A., *The Untroubled Heart*, 76.
Macaulay, A. B., *The Word of the Cross*, 13.
Mackay, W. M., *The Goodly Fellowship of the Prophets*, 121.
Townsend, W. J., in *Great Texts of the O.T.*, 171.

XVIII. 3, 4.

Taylor, W. M., *Contrary Winds*, 150.
Welldon, J. E. C., *Youth and Duty*, 181.
Christian World Pulpit, cxxviii. 123 (H. S. Shergold).

XVIII. 4.

Alexander, A., *The Glory in the Grey*, 11.
Holden, J. S., *Some O.T. Parables*, 32.
James, F., *A National Pentecost*, 24.
Kerr, H. T., *Old Things New*, 62.
Knox, D. B., *The Haunted Heart*, 68.
Meyer, F. B., *The Soul's Ascent*, 19.
—— *Jeremiah*, 75.
Morrison, G. H., *The Gateways of the Stars*, 99.
British Weekly, Oct. 14, 1926 (G. H. Morrison).
Christian Commonwealth, xxxii. (1912) 777 (R. J. Campbell).
Christian World Pulpit, lxviii. 315 (H. Kenward); lxxviii. 1 (R. F. Horton); xc. 100 (J. S. Richards); xciv. 254 (R. Ballard); cxiii. 199 (J. Reid).

XVIII. 6.

Cash, W. W., in *The Keswick Convention*, 1934, p. 122.
Morgan, G. C., *The True Estimate of Life*, 111.
Sclater, J. R. P., *The Enterprise of Life*, 335.
Christian World Pulpit, cvi. 199 (J. W. G. Ward); cxxvi. 42 (W. Cash).

XVIII. 13–15.

Christian World Pulpit, xciii. 162 (J. R. Legge).

XVIII. 14.

Macmillan, E., *Finding and Following*, 119.

XVIII. 17.

Christian World Pulpit, cxxx. 239 (N. Popplewell).

XIX. 10.

Mackay, W. M., *The Goodly Fellowship of the Prophets*, 121.

XX. 3.

Oman, J., *The Paradox of the World*, 210.

XX. 7.

Morrison, G. H., *The Wings of the Morning*, 298.
Christian Commonwealth, xxxiii. (1912) 41 (R. J. Campbell).

XX. 7–9.

Williams, T. R., *Belief and Life*, 47.

XX. 7, 14.

Christian World Pulpit, lxxxiv. 387 (N. H. Marshall).

XX. 9.

Meyer, F. B., *Jeremiah*, 84.
Welldon, J. E. C., *Youth and Duty*, 219.
Record of Christian Work, 1918, p. 16 (H. E. Kirk).

XX. 10.

Horne, C. S., *The Rock of Ages*, 161.

XXII. 10.

Paget, E. C., *Silence*, 82.
Wilson, J. M., *Truths New and Old*, 190.
Christian World Pulpit, lxxxii. 165 (H. W. Merchant).

XXII. 15.

Skrine, J. H., *Saints and Worthies*, 107.

XXII. 16.

Dawson, W. J., *The Comrade-Christ*, 135.
Mackay, D. S., *The Religion of the Threshold*, 323.
Homiletic Review, lxii. 489 (W. L. Watkinson).
Methodist Recorder, Sept. 22, 1910 (W. L. Watkinson).

XXII. 29.

Wilberforce, B., *Power with God*, 129.

XXIII. 5, 6.
Wickham, E. C., *Words of Light and Life*, 24.

XXIII. 6.
Collins, W., *Hours of Insight*, 141.
Driver, S. R., *S. on the Old Testament*, 204.
Macbeath, J., *What is His Name?*, 113.
Purves, P. C., *The Jehovah Titles*, 58.
Webb-Peploe, H. W., *The Titles of Jehovah*, 152.
Whitelaw, T., *Jehovah-Jesus*, 87.
Christian World Pulpit, xxiv. 390 (S. Leathes).
Record, Nov. 29, 1923 (H. C. de Candole).

XXIII. 7, 8.
Christian World Pulpit, lxv. 1 (H. S. Holland).

XXIII. 16, 17.
Christian World Pulpit, cxxxviii. 74 (S. Myers).

XXIII. 23, 24.
Christian World, Jan. 18, 1940 (H. H. Farmer).

XXIII. 24.
Whyte, A., *With Mercy and with Judgment*, 3.
Christian World Pulpit, lxxii. 97 (R. F. Horton).
Church Family Newspaper, Jan. 26, 1917 (J. A. MacCulloch).

XXIII. 28.
Taylor, W. M., *Contrary Winds*, 21.
Christian World Pulpit, xliv. 392 (J. G. Rogers) ; lix. 253 (G. Lorimer), 267 (J. T. Parr) ; cxiv. 30 (E. W. Shepheard-Walwyn).

XXIII. 28, 29.
Whittuck, C., *Learning and Working*, 104.

XXIII. 34, 35.
Brooks, P., *New Starts in Life*, 303.

XXIII. 36.
Duke, J. A., *The Untroubled Heart*, 86.

XXIV. 1.
Watkinson, W. L., *The Education of the Heart*, 120.

XXV. 8, 9.
Christian World Pulpit, lxxii. 33 (N. H. Marshall).

XXV. 9.
Christian World Pulpit, xciv. 302 (G. K. Grice).

XXIX. 5, 6.
Christian World Pulpit, cxv. 13 (J. Black).

XXIX. 10, 11.
Jones, J. S., *Saved by Hope*, 9.

XXIX. 10–14.
Taylor, W. M., *Contrary Winds*, 51.

XXIX. 11.
Jeffrey, G. J., *Christian Resources*, 60.
Kirk, H. E., *The Glory of Common Things*, 9.
Reid, J., *Making Friends with Life*, 220.
Smith, D., *Man's Need of God*, 269.

XXIX. 13.
Barnsley, J., in *A Book of Lay S.*, 207.
Chavasse, C. M., *Christ and Fairies*, 36.
Maclean, A., *High Country*, 164.
Morison, E. F., *The Lord's Prayer*, 1.
Sangster, W. E., *God Does Guide Us*, 37.
Thomson, J. K., *I Have Kept the Faith*, 175.
Whyte, A., *Lord, Teach Us to Pray*, 194.

XXX. 2.
Fosdick, H. E., *Successful Christian Living*, 248.

XXX. 17.
Horne, C. S., *The Life That is Easy*, 95.
Christian World Pulpit, cxx. 260 (G. C. Britton).

XXXI. 1.
Brown, C., *God and Man*, 95.

XXXI. 2.
Church Family Newspaper, June 25, 1915 (W. Williams).

XXXI. 3.
Armitage, W. J., *The Fruit of the Spirit*, 11.
Boreham, F. W., *A Faggot of Torches*, 45.
Davies, T., *Sermons*, ii. 53.
McLean, A., *Where the Book Speaks*, 200.
Macrae, K. A., in *The Free Church Pulpit*, 192.
Christian Commonwealth, xxxiv. (1914) 285 (R. J. Campbell).

Christian World Pulpit, xcii. 117 (E. D. Shaw) ;
cxx. 98 (W. A. Painter).
Guardian, lxxii. (1917) 648 (E. D. Shaw).
Homiletic Review, lxi. 147 (H. W. Battle).

XXXI. 10, 11.
Christian World Pulpit, lv. 161 (J. Clifford).

XXXI. 12.
Little, W. J. K., *Labour and Sorrow*, 131.
British Weekly, Aug. 20, 1931 (A. B. Scott).

XXXI. 15, 16.
Christian World Pulpit, lxxxvii. 5 (A. D. Belden).

XXXI. 16.
Watkinson, W. L., *The Shepherd of the Sea*, 200.
Homiletic Review, lxxxii. 318 (W. L. Watkinson).
Methodist Recorder, Oct. 23, 1913 (W. L. Watkinson).

XXXI. 18.
Watkinson, W. L., *The Fairness of Trial*, 237.

XXXI. 18-20.
Aitken, W. H. M. H., *God's Everlasting Yea*, 188.

XXXI. 19.
Wilberforce, B., *The Power that Worketh in Us*, 16.

XXXI. 21.
Ainsworth, P. C., *A Thornless World*, 45.
Lockyer, T. F., *Seeking a Country*, 16.
Christian World Pulpit, cxxi. 22 (J. O. Ritchie).
Expositor, xlii. (1940) 290 (J. O. Ritchie).

XXXI. 28.
Butcher, C. H., *S. preached in the East*, 14.

XXXI. 29.
Record, Oct. 6, 1921 (H. H. Matthew).

XXXI. 29, 30.
Christian World Pulpit, lxxxi. 161 (G. C. Morgan).

XXXI. 31.
Masterman, H. B., *The Challenge of Christ*, 52.

XXXI. 31-33.
Christian World Pulpit, lxxx. 269 (E. J. Barson).

XXXI. 31-34.
Macgregor, W. M., *Jesus Christ the Son of God*, 27.

XXXI. 33.
Driver, S. R., *The Ideals of the Prophets*, 44.
Robinson, J. W., *Hearts Aflame*, 45.
Christian Commonwealth, xxxiv. (1914) 741 (R. J. Campbell) ; xxxvi. (1915) 45 (R. J. Campbell).

XXXI. 33, 34.
Christian World Pulpit, lxxxiv. 387 (N. H. Marshall) ; xcv. 61 (W. R. Inge) ; xcix. 97 (F. W. Norwood).

XXXI. 34.
Adeney, W. F., in *Men of the O.T. :* Solomon to Jonah, 197.
Barber, W. T. A., *The Morning of Life*, 54.
Ingram, A. F. W., *Rays of Dawn*, 90.
Jones, E. Griffith, *The Unspeakable Gift*, 193.
Christian Commonwealth, xxx. (1910) 549 (R. J. Campbell).
Christian World Pulpit, lxxii. 282 (E. Griffith Jones).
Guardian, lxxi. (1916) 271 (A. F. W. Ingram).

XXXI. 35.
Sanderson, T., *The Illimitable Domain*, 51.

XXXII.
Moule, H. C. G., *Prayers and Promises*, 55.

XXXII. 8, 9.
Christian World Pulpit, xcii. 213 (J. C. Harris) ; cxxxiii. 222 (L. E. Cooke).

XXXII. 9.
Macmillan, H., *The Touch of God*, 175.
Simpson, H. L., *The Intention of His Soul*, 171.
Christian World Pulpit, xcvii. 93 (C. Brown) ; cxxxviii. 126 (W. D. Jackson).

XXXII. 9, 15.
Christian World Pulpit, cxliv. 59 (A. L. Trudgeon).
Record of Christian Work, 1921, p. 790 (H. E. Kirk).

XXXII. 15.
Expositor, xliv. (1942) 22 (S. C. Tiller).

XXXII. 17.
Berry, S. M., *The Crucible of Experience*, 155.

XXXII. 25.
Christian World Pulpit, cxxi. 89 (J. Wilson).

XXXII. 25–27.
Christian World Pulpit, cxix. 2 (H. C. Carter).

XXXII. 27.
Christian World Pulpit, cxxvi. 232 (W. Kiek).

XXXII. 41.
Young, D. T., *The Enthusiasm of God*, 1.

XXXIII. 3.
Christian World Pulpit, cxix. 205 (G. Laws).

XXXIII. 6.
Christian World Pulpit, cxi. 198 (F. S. G. Warman).

XXXIII. 8.
Maclaren, A., *After the Resurrection*, 156.

XXXIII. 16.
Macbeath, J., *What is His Name?*, 113.
Purves, P. C., *The Jehovah Titles*, 58.

XXXIV. 17.
Banks, L. A., *The King's Stewards*, 123.
Watkinson, W. L., *The Blind Spot*, 213.

XXXV. 2.
Young, D. T., *Neglected People of the Bible*, 147.

XXXV. 6.
Waller, C. H., *The Names on the Gates of Pearl*, 365.

XXXV. 15.
Thompson, J. R., *Burden Bearing*, 91.

XXXV. 18, 19.
Wickham, E. C., *Words of Light and Life*, 190.

XXXV. 19.
Almond, H. H., *Christ the Protestant*, 1.
Tuckwell, W., *Nuggets from the Bible Mine*, 105.

XXXVI. 3.
Heron, J., *A Large Place*, 270.
Kingsley, C., *National S.*, 316.
Wickham, E. C., *Words of Light and Life*, 16.

XXXVI. 21–23.
Hadden, R. H., *S. and Memoir*, 181.

XXXVI. 22, 23.
Butler, W. H., *The Reality of Things Unseen*, 41.

XXXVI. 22–25.
Kellogg, S. H., *The Past a Prophecy of the Future*, 219.

XXXVI. 23.
Burrell, D. J., *The Morning Cometh*, 198.
Davidson, J. T., *The City Youth*, 225.
Greenhough, J. G., *Half-Hours in God's Older Picture Gallery*, 210.
Christian World Pulpit, cxx. 200 (W. W. Johnson).
Expositor, xxiii. (1922) 1007 (H. E. Wilkinson); xxxi. (1930) 1397 (C. H. Nabers).

XXXVI. 23, 28.
Mackay, W. M., *The Goodly Fellowship of the Prophets*, 134.

XXXVI. 23, 32.
Christian World Pulpit, xxxiv. 238 (H. Jones).

XXXVI. 24.
Christian World Pulpit, lxxxii. 393 (W. R. Inge); civ. 223 (W. R. Inge).
Guardian, lxxxvii. (1932) 893 (W. R. Inge).
Record of Christian Work, 1913, p. 495 (W. R. Inge).

XXXVI. 32.
Aitken, W. H. M. H., *What is Your Life?*, 209.
Skrine, J. H., *The Heart's Counsel*, 139.
Christian World Pulpit, lxxviii. 218 (J. G. Tetley).

XXXVII. 17.
Jeffrey, G. J., *Christian Intimacies*, 55.
Struthers, J. P., *The Word and the Road*, 99.

XXXVIII.
Champness, T., *New Coins from Old Gold*, 206.

XXXVIII. 1–20.
Morrison, G. H., *The Footsteps of the Flock*, 336.

XXXVIII. 3, 4.
Christian World Pulpit, lvi. 324 (F. W. Aveling).

XXXVIII. 7.
Young, D. T., *Neglected People of the Bible*, 165.

XXXVIII. 7–13.
Christian World Pulpit, lxxxv. 29 (H. Jeffs).

XXXVIII. 12.
Christian World Pulpit, xcviii. 244 (W. P. Williams).

XXXIX. 1–18.
Morrison, G. H., *The Footsteps of the Flock*, 344.

XL. 4–6.
Morrison, G. H., *The Unlighted Lustre*, 102.

XL. 6.
Alexander, A., *A Day at a Time*, 83.
Christian World Pulpit, civ. 78 (C. F. Aked).

XLIV. 2–4.
Church Family Newspaper, Sept. 8, 1916 (S. Elliott).

XLIV. 4.
Christian World Pulpit, lxx. 3 (W. Mincher); cxxxi. 93 (W. Harvey-Jellie).

XLIV. 4, 5.
Black, H., *University S.*, 9.
Christian World Pulpit, cxxxvi. 73 (H. E. Kirk).
Record of Christian Work, 1917, p. 634 (H. E. Kirk).

XLV. 1–5.
Brooke, S. A., *The O.T. and Modern Life*, 319.

XLV. 5.
Archibald, M. G., *Sundays at the Royal Military College*, 18.
Campbell, R. J., *S. to Young Men*, 95.
Lennard, V. R., *Our Ideals*, 197.
Morrison, G. H., *Flood-Tide*, 241.
Skrine, J. H., *Saints and Worthies*, 114.

Watkinson, W. L., *The Education of the Heart*, 15.
Christian World Pulpit, cxxxiii. 203 (A. H. M. Sime).
Experience, xi. (1918) 32 (H. Smith).
Sunday Strand, vii. 61 (W. L. Watkinson).

XLVI. 18.
Guardian, lxvii. (1912) 404 (Canon Horsley).

XLVII. 6, 7.
Christian World Pulpit, xcii. 141 (E. S. Kiek).

XLVIII. 11.
Taylor, W. M., *The Limitations of Life*, 358.
Christian World Pulpit, lxxxii. 312 (C. S. Horne); cxxxvi. 164 (E. G. Manby).

XLIX. 8.
Christian World Pulpit, xci. 38 (T. Phillips).

XLIX. 23.
Morrison, G. H., *The Afterglow of God*, 190.

XLIX. 30, 31.
Swanson, W. S., *Gethsemane*, 53.

L. 4, 5.
Christian World Pulpit, lvi. 168 (H. S. Holland).

L. 5.
Banks, L. A., *Hidden Wells of Comfort*, 12.
Jeffrey, G. J., *Christian Intimacies*, 145.
Jowett, J. H., *The Eagle Life*, 109.
Reid, J., *The Springs of Life*, 250.
British Weekly, Feb. 2, 1932 (J. Reid).

L. 34.
Christian World Pulpit, lxxix. 70 (C. Brown).

LI. 7.
Morrison, G. H., *Sun-rise*, 240.

LI. 29.
Christian World Pulpit, cxli. 77 (J. W. Newby).

LI. 50.
Brooks, P., *Christ the Life and Light*, 57.

LAMENTATIONS

COMMENTARIES FOR REFERENCE

See page 165

INDEX TO SERMONS

I. 9.

Watkinson, W. L., *The Blind Spot*, 255.

I. 12.

Brooks P., *Christ the Life*, 163.
Driver, S. R., *The Ideals of the Prophets*, 50.
Fosdick, H. E., *Successful Christian Living*, 213.
Foxell, W. J., *A Mirror of Divine Comfort*, 101.
Hanks, W. P., *The Eternal Witness*, 44.
Hird, A., *The Test of Discipleship*, 133.
Houghton, C. A., *Problems of Life*, 125.
Hunter, J., *God and Life*, 277.
Jerdan, C., *For the Lord's Table*, 163.
Jowett, J. H., *The Eagle Life*, 154.
Rutherford, J., *The Seer's House*, 85.
Sanderson, T., *Unfulfilled Designs*, 72.
White, J., in *The Scottish Pulpit*, 237.
Yates, T., *A Happy Warrior*, 135.
Christian World Pulpit, lix. 159 (G. Body); lxviii. 273 (J. Hunter); lxx. 360 (C. S. Horne); ciii. 23 (J. C. Mantripp); cxv. 119 (H. Jeffs); cxxxv. 185 (C. H. S. Willson).

II. 19.

Stephenson, T. B., *The Words of a Year*, 68.

III. 7.

Morrison, G. H., *Life's Nobler Penalties*, 19.

III. 22.

Nicoll, W. R., *Ten-Minute S.*, 159.
Record, Oct. 14, 1938.

III. 22, 23.

Spurgeon, C. H., *Grace Triumphant*, 9.
Christian World Pulpit, xcix. 41 (J. L. Corkey); ci. 102 (J. G. McKenzie); cxxvii. 4 (F. J. Miles); cxxxix. 57 (A. A. Reid); cxl. 61 (R. H. Turner).

III. 22–26.

Gibson, J. M., in *Looking Backward and Looking Forward*, 43.

III. 23.

Brooks, P., *Christ the Life*, 102, 108.
Selby, T. G., *The Imperfect Angel*, 94.

III. 24.

Pearce, J., *The Upper Gate*, 17.

III. 25, 26.

Selby, T. G., *The Lesson of a Dilemma*, 220.

III. 26.

Holden, J. S., *Unlikely Ministries of God*, 41.
Moss, R. W., *The Discipline of the Soul*, 73.
Simpson, Mrs. A. R., *These Three*, 25.
Christian World Pulpit, lvi. 200 (J. G. Greenhough).

III. 27.

Dods, M., *Why be a Christian?*, 1.
Mackenzie, R., *The Loom of Providence*, 216.
Expositor, xxxvii. (1935) 319 (C. H. Nabers).

III. 28.

Christian World Pulpit, lvi. 133 (F. Hastings).

III. 33.

Gillie, R. C., *The Gospel for the Modern Mind*, 66.

III. 35, 36.

Christian World Pulpit, lxii. 22 (J. Stalker).

III. 37.

Christian Commonwealth, xxxv. (1914) 145 (R. J. Campbell).

III. 39.

Young, D. T., *The Travels of the Heart*, 207.
British Congregationalist, Feb. 5, 1914 (A. R. Henderson).
Christian World Pulpit, cxv. 170 (F. B. Meyer).

III. 39, 40.

Watkinson, W. L., *The Ashes of Roses*, 149.

III. 40.

Robertson, J. A., *Concerning the Soul*, 26.
Christian World Pulpit, xli. 169 (H. Jones).
Expositor, xxxvii. (1935) 440 (W. T. McElroy).

III. 51.

Burns, D., *The Song of the Well*, 109.
Waterston, R., *Thoughts on the Lord's Supper*, 28.
Young, D. T., *The Travels of the Heart*, 149.

III. 57.

Christian World Pulpit, xc. 39 (E. F. H. Capey).

III. 58.

Christian World Pulpit, cxxvi. 292 (D. T. Young).

IV. 1, 2.

Pearson, A., *The Claims of the Faith*, 1.

IV. 3.

Christian World Pulpit, xcix. 120 (H. A. Jump).

IV. 7.

McCook, H. C., *The Gospel in Nature*, 132.

IV. 9.

Commonwealth, xxix. (1924) 157 (M. Donovan).

V. 16.

Christian World Pulpit, lxxx. 132 (J. F. Sanders) ; civ. 7 (G. Lawrence).

V. 19.

Methodist Times, Sept. 22, 1910 (F. R. Smith).

V. 21.

Gibbon, J. M., *The Vision and the Call*, 177.
Churchman, xxvii. (1913) 782 (J. E. Gibberd).